The Civil Wars in Britain and Ireland

1638–1651

MARTYN BENNETT

BLACKWELL
Publishers

The right of Martyn Bennett to be identified as author of this work has been asserted in accordance with the Copyright, Designs and Patents Act 1988.

First published 1997

2 4 6 8 10 9 7 5 3 1

Blackwell Publishers Ltd
108 Cowley Road
Oxford OX4 1JF
UK

Blackwell Publishers Inc.
238 Main Street
Cambridge, Massachusetts 02142
USA

British Library Cataloging in Publication Data

A CIP catalogue record for this book is available from the British Library.

Library of Congress Cataloging-in-Publication Data

Bennett, Martyn.
      The civil wars in Britain and Ireland, 1638–1651 / Martyn Bennett.
          p.   cm.
      Includes bibliographical references and index.
      ISBN 0–631–19154–2. — ISBN 0–631–19155–0 (pbk.)
          1. Great Britain—History—Civil War, 1642–1649.   2. Great
      Britain—History—Commonwealth and Protectorate, 1649–1660.
      3. Ireland—History—1625–1649.   4. Ireland– History—1649–1660.
      I. Title.
      DA415.B35   1996
      941.06′2—dc20   95–38662
                                                                            CIP

Typeset in 10¹/₂ on 12 pt Plantin
by Graphicraft Typesetters Ltd, Hong Kong
Printed in Great Britain by TJ Press Limited, Padstow, Cornwall

This book is printed on acid-free paper

Contents

List of Plates

List of Maps

Acknowledgements

Many people have helped with the work towards this volume. Acts of scholarship are only occasionally solitary; for the most part they are the product of discussion and debate on many levels and to many ends.

The Record Offices that are listed in the bibliography have all provided me with a great deal of assistance, and whilst I have singled out a few of the archivists for mention, it by no means denigrates the work of the others. I would like to thank, in particular, Anthony Hopkins of Gwent County Record Office, Geoffery Veysey of Clwyd County Record Office, Kate Thompson of Hertfordshire County Record Office and Adrian Henstock of Nottinghamshire County Archive Office.

I must also thank the Chief Lord and the other Lords Feoffees of Bridlington for their permission to use the contents of the Bridlington Town Chest held at the Bayle, Bridlington. I am also grateful to Mrs Elizabeth Staunton of Staunton Hall, Nottinghamshire, for allowing me access to the Staunton family papers. I should also like to thank the historians who have helped me with advice whilst I worked on this volume: Dr Ronald Hutton of Bristol University, Professor Nicholas Canny and Mr Padraig Lenihan of University College Galway, Professor Raymond Gillespie of St Patrick's College, Maynooth, Professor Jane Ohlmeyer of Yale University and Professor Geraint Jenkins of The National Library of Wales.

I should also like to thank the British Academy for assistance provided for the early stages of some of this work. Many thanks are due to the Faculty of Humanities at Nottingham Trent University, which has made the research for this book possible by the provision of funds to undertake research around the British Isles during 1993–5. They also provided other material assistance and the staff in the faculty, in particular the Department of International Studies, provided the encouragement which was, at times, most necessary. It is also a pleasure to thank Linda Dawes, the International Studies cartographer, for her patience and for the excellent maps in this volume.

I must also record my gratitude to my late father, Warwick Bennett, who, in May 1992, ferried me around parts of Yorkshire to record offices. It was he who accompanied me to Bridlington, and I am sure that it was his record as a Head Choirboy at the Priory Church that eased my access to the papers of the Lords Feoffees. In the same vein, I should like to thank my sister, Julie Garstin, for also taking me to other record offices in Yorkshire during the same period. Thanks are once again due to my partner, Dr Deborah Tyler-Bennett, whose ceaseless encouragement has kept me going whilst I worked on this book.

Introduction

They being dead yet speaketh
The banner of Haswell Lodge, Durham Miners' Association

This book has several purposes. The first is to serve as an introduction, not only to the period itself and to the dramatic events throughout the British Isles, but also to the arguments and debates amongst historians about the origins, natures and outcomes of those events. A second objective is to examine the effects of the wars in England, Ireland, Scotland and Wales, using material that is culled from a wide range of secondary material by historians who have painstakingly examined local and regional communities, as well as from papers held in local and central record repositories throughout the three kingdoms and the principality that made up the British Isles in the seventeenth century. The third principal aim, which relates to the second, is to encourage further study by both the academic student and the student outside academia. Our understanding of the past and our views of it are altered and developed through the work of people inside and outside academia. Their work is complementary, and neither should reject the other in a search for some 'truth' about the past. As this work is so wide-ranging, some of the conclusions and assertions made about the effects of the war have to be tentative. I have had to accept that no matter how attractive I may find my own conclusions, they cannot and should not please or satisfy everyone. Although I am able to draw some general assumptions from this study, I fully expect, indeed I encourage, students to take them apart, to contextualize them in a way in which I have been unable to do, to test them, challenge them, support them or overturn them. Only if I fail to persuade people to examine my conclusions will I consider this work to have failed in its intent.

To return to the issue of the geographical scope of this work, several historians within the last ten years have called for studies of the civil war to examine the conflicts from pan-British and Irish stand-points. From this has come the use of a new name for the series of conflicts, the 'war of the three kingdoms'. It is easy to see why this name has come about. The traditional appellation, 'the English civil war', does an extreme disservice to the reality of a conflict that occur-red throughout the British Isles and Ireland. Moreover, it reduces the emphasis on the wars outside England and presupposes the centrality of the Anglo-Saxon nation, turning the wars in Wales, Ireland and Scotland into a series of side-shows which, if you like, merely distracted attention away from the 'main' issues happening in England. The 'war of the three kingdoms' is certainly a start, but it either subverts Wales by accepting that it was turned into a region of England by the Acts of Union of the 1530s, or misses it out altogether. And to add 'and the principality' is both clumsy and pro-blematic; for before Wales became a principality of the English crown after the defeat and death of Llywellyn in 1285, it had been a king-dom itself, or rather a series of kingdoms under a high king. Hence the use of the term 'war of the four kingdoms' by several Welsh scholars. This may provide a useful starting point, for as Jane Ohlmeyer has pointed out, the fact that France, Spain and the papacy were also embroiled in the conflicts at certain times offers scope for incorporating further kingdoms into the title or range of titles. However, to evade the problems inherent in using the term 'three kingdoms', I have elected within this text to borrow from Professor Hugh Kearney and to refer to the 'four nations'.[1]

The problem of title is not the only one encountered when exam-ining the range of involvement. There has been much discussion of the nature of a history that covers the archipelago that encompasses Britain and Ireland. A starting point has been Conrad Russell's assertion that we can understand the causes of the wars only if we examine the political interrelation between England and Scotland and England and Ireland, but there have also been assertions that we need to understand the relationship between Scotland and Ireland too. There have also been calls to include social and cultural aspects of these relationships, something generally not tackled by Professor Russell. John Morrill has argued that there is a need for an all-embracing history of the period, taking in what he has described as the Britannic Isles in his attempt to avoid unintentionally excluding Ireland by the use of the term 'Britain'. Such a view is not particu-larly new. In the seventeenth century, Edward Hyde, Earl of Claren-don, also included Ireland in the subtitle of his book on the rebellion, and his contemporary, Lucy Hutchinson, sought to explain the outbreak of the civil war within the context of relations between England, Scotland and Ireland. Two centuries later, Samuel Rawson Gardiner's study encompassed Scotland, Wales and Ireland. More recently, the eminent narrative historian C.V. Wedgwood embraced all four nations in her work in the 1950s.[2]

This book attempts to continue such work and to examine the part the peoples of the four nations played in the war. It also seeks to explore the way in which the war burned itself on their memory, and the way in which they constructed narratives of their own when reckoning the financial and other costs that the war had imposed upon them. We have narratives written by principal participants in the military and political events of the period, and several diaries of other participants too survive.[3] But many other people kept no such record, and not every village kept an account of what had been required of it either; the constables of Edwinstowe, Nottinghamshire, simply passed over the period with this note: 'many mighty accounts in the years 1642, 1643, 1644 between the town of Edwinstowe and Miles Ouldham Constable that because of the war could not be then or now counted'.[4] Yet the war provided some opportunities to keep an account of the war as it affected ordinary people in the four nations, in the form of claims for redress. Part of this work uses such English, Welsh and Scottish information to seek to explain how people's experiences of war changed their perception of the society around them, and how this in turn affected the histories of the four nations. The civil wars of Britain and Ireland did impinge upon what Linda Colley has termed the 'thought world' of the people of the four nations, and it brought them into direct contact with the political and religious upheavals.[5] For me this book is only the beginning of such work, and the materials dipped into here form the beginnings of a much longer period of study, on which I will embark even before the last key is pressed in the writing of this book.

The text begins with a brief examination of some of the social and political features of the four nations that became central to the way in which the wars were fought. Following a discussion of inherent conflicts in chapter 1, it moves on to the immediate religious and political issues that resulted in two wars between Scotland and England and Wales. This war embroiled the Irish people in a mixture of fears and hopes, and gave the Scottish and English political nations the opportunity to change fundamental principles of their government. The second part of the book examines the consequences of these changes, first as the king attempted to overturn them, and subsequently as the people of all four nations became drawn into the ensuing wars. This widening involvement had major consequences. War pushed the political world into everyone's domain, and the conflicts throughout the four nations became the people's wars. This stake in the war, together with the way in which the people, once aroused, forced their will into the political arena, forms the background to the third section's exploration of the revolutionary and counter-revolutionary impulses of the period 1646–1651.

Martyn Bennett
History Section
Nottingham Trent University

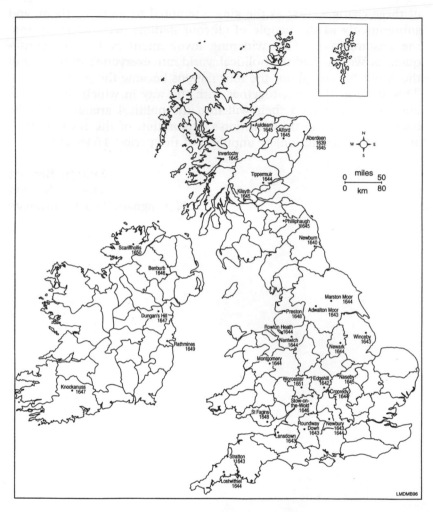

Map 1 Main battles, 1639–51

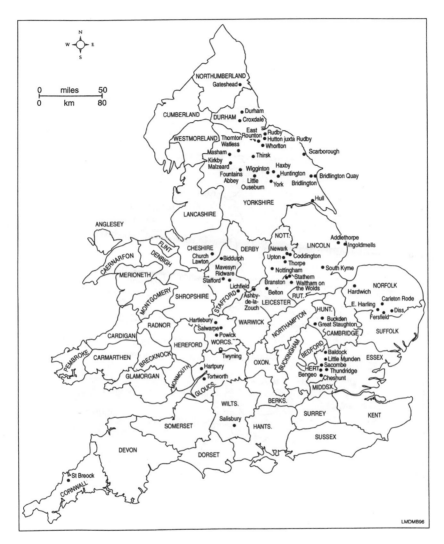

Map 2 English communities referred to in the text

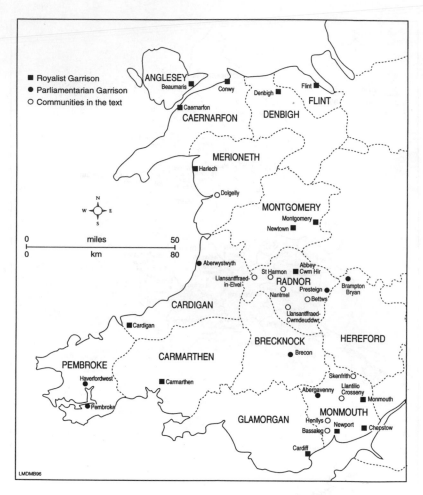

Map 3 Welsh communities referred to in the text

Map 4 Scottish communities referred to in the text

Map 5 Ireland: Confederation of Kilkenny, army winter quarters
1644 and 1646 (Leinster army only – shaded counties)

Map 6 Ireland: Confederation of Kilkenny, excise and sequestration receipts, April 1646 to January 1647 (shaded counties)

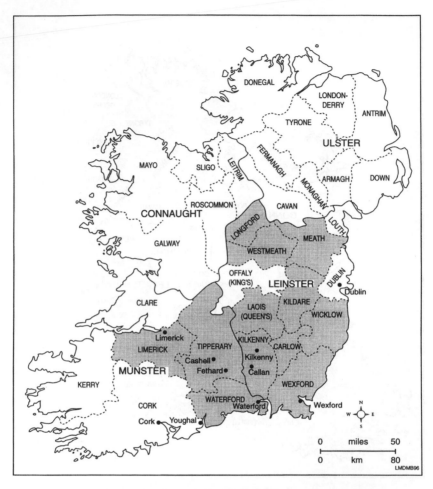

Map 7 Ireland: Confederation of Kilkenny, grand applotment allocation, March 1646 to January 1647 (shaded counties)

PART I

Rebellion

1

Britain and Ireland in 1638

Projects of all kinds, many ridiculous, many scandalous, all very griev-
ous, were set on foot[1]

On 23 July 1637, a 'blak doolful' Sunday, Edinburgh's St Giles
Cathedral was packed to the doors and crowds stood outside. Many
of King Charles I's Scottish Council were there, but a few members,
ominously, were absent. As the Dean began to read from the new
Scottish Book of Common Prayer, he was confronted by what must
have appeared to be a vision from hell. The people of Edinburgh
assembled there, mainly led by women, one of whom was allegedly
called Jenny Geddes, rose up and began to disrupt the service, hurling
both abuse and stools at the prelate. Added to the chorus of their
shouts, was a furious banging on the cathedral doors, accompanied
by the chanting of the crowds outside. As shocking as this attack
on the archbishop and on the authority of the king may have been,
it was neither unexpected nor entirely unwelcome. One observer, a
lawyer called Archibald Johnston of Wariston, was well satisfied. He
had spent years being fearful of God's dire anger and punishment
for the direction in which the church in Scotland was moving. Now
it began to appear to Johnston that the changes were all God's own
plan designed to lead in a mysterious way to the fall of Babylon and
the prospect of Sion being raised in Edinburgh.[2] Four years later an
English minister in Lincolnshire may have had the Edinburgh events
as well as recent local incidents in the back of his mind when he
cited Revelation 19:6: 'And I heard as it were the voice of a great
multitude, and as the voice of many waters, and as the voice of
many thunderings, saying, Alleluia for the Lord God omnipotent
reigneth'.[3]
A great deal of myth surrounds the events of the 'blak doolful'
day; and the identity of Jenny Geddes is by no means certain. Yet
a visit to St Giles today adds form and shape to the rebellion in the

The Arch-Prelate of S.t Andrewes in Scotland reading the new Service-booke in his pontificalibus assaulted by men & women, with Crickets stooles Stickes and Stones.

Plate 1   The throwing of chairs at the reading of the prayerbook at St Giles, reproduced by courtesy of The Bodleian Library, Oxford.

church. The spot from where Jenny hurled her stool is marked, and close to it stands a sculpture of such a three-legged stool presented to the cathedral by women's groups in Scotland. Although her existence in 1638 is shadowy, Jenny's reality today as a heroine of Scotland is not in doubt. She is certainly a useful and versatile figure. Whereas in the seventeenth century she personified Scottish religious fervour and anger, now she represents at once Scottish nationalism and Scottish feminism. As Raphael Samuel and Paul Thompson wrote in the introduction to *The Myths We Live By*, it is the habit of us 'Anglo-saxon historians' to puncture myths, denying ourselves in particular the power to understand popular movements. Such an approach, however, would hamper our examination of what happened in Edinburgh that day.[4] There was a real Jenny Geddes alive in Edinburgh at that time; she was later to be found running a luckenbooth (lockable shop) hard by the cathedral. It may not have been she who hurled the first stool; but she was probably there, somebody believed that she did, and she may well have done so. In a sense it does not matter whether she did or not. Women did throw stools, and one of them at least looked like Jenny, and it did not seem improbable to onlookers that she would be amongst them.

To begin to understand why men and women in Edinburgh were so incensed, it is necessary to examine some of the features of the societies within England, Scotland, Ireland and Wales at the time. This chapter concentrates upon the recurrent stresses and strains that turned rebelliousness into war and revolution, and on the administrative organization that explains how the war efforts of the four countries were established.

On the face of it the disturbance at St Giles Cathedral could appear localized, a popular rejection of the service or even of the archbishop himself, but it was far more than that. The very nature of the prayerbook that the archbishop had opened was being challenged. Moreover, the existence of the book in Scotland had prompted the reaction. The reasons behind this comprehensive public rejection are contentious. That the prayerbook was unpopular is unarguable, but who opposed it, and what were their reasons for doing so? On the first point one historian has argued that the Scots may simply have rejected the prayerbook, which was an adapted version of the English Book of Common Prayer then being used in England, as an unwarranted English intrusion, a feature of the arrogance of the English nation.[5] Alternatively, they may have rejected it because, as Archibald Johnston believed, it reintroduced popish liturgy. Popery and popish superstition made Johnston at once both so angry and fearful that he reached for the most depraved analogy he could think of when writing in his diary. A return by the Scottish church to the polish faith, he recorded, would be like a dog returning to its own vomit – a revolting attraction for that which had earlier been expelled for the good of the body. But exactly which Scots were refusing to accept the liturgy? Were the people of Edinburgh themselves rejecting the prayerbook, or were they merely providing the muscle power of other interested groups, especially, as one historian claims, the aristocracy and/or the clergy?[6] These questions are of the utmost importance, impinging not only on the issue of whether what followed was a revolution but also on the relationships between the peoples of the four nations of the British Isles. One thing is abundantly clear: these relationships are at the heart of the issues which brought about the massive conflicts and revolutions that preceded and followed the stool hurling at Edinburgh.

Recently some historians have argued forcibly that England was at peace with itself in the 1630s. These scholars have sought to discredit the notion that there was any long-term reason for the conflict that followed, suggesting that there was no 'highway' to civil war. An archipelagic view of the period may reveal that such internal peace, even if it really existed, was fragile and subject to stresses imposed by England's position as part of a more complex series of relationships. To begin to explore these issues and problems, then, it is necessary to examine the state of the four nations. This book will refer throughout to certain towns and villages around the four nations, which constitute the variety of types of settlement that characterized Britain at that time. For example, the varied experiences of the citizens of such urban areas as York, Worcester, Aberdeen, Glasgow, Haverfordwest, Caernarfon, Dublin and Youghal will be called on at certain times to illustrate the effects of the war on these communities. Several rural areas, reflecting different agricultural systems, pastoral/ woodland and arable farming, will be examined across three of the four nations.

It has long been acknowledged that there were regional differ- ence. David Underdown has even begun to divine allegiances in the war based on such differences.[7] From the Highland fringes of Aberdeenshire, the settlement of Crathie provides evidence of the damage done to it during the wars in Scotland, while from the Low- lands Dolphinton demonstrates the horrors and costs of political allegiance in the later years of the conflict. In England, where the material evidence of communities is more forthcoming, a variety of regions are covered, from the Leicestershire Wold villages of Branston and Waltham on the Wolds to the edges of the North Yorkshire Moor settlements of Whorlton and East Rudby. From St Breock in Corn- wall to Croxdale and Hullam in the Palatinate County of Durham, people experienced the varied effects of war. Not all of them were to be the unwilling spectators of sieges like the inhabitants of Hartlebury in Worcestershire, or observers of battles like the people of Powick in the same county, or even the victims of racially motiv- ated 'cleansing' of towns like the Gaels of Youghal in Munster or the Catholic wives and children of absentee men in Dublin. No citizens in England or Wales were forbidden to wear their traditional clothes, as were the Highland Scots in Edinburgh during 1649. On the other hand, people from Dublin in Leinster to Great Staughton in Huntingdonshire had soldiers billeted upon them. From Church Lawton in Cheshire to Bridlington on the east coast, taxpayers had to lay out great and increasing sums of money to pay for the wars across the four nations. War united the people of all these nations as culture, race and language did not, but this bond proved not as strong as these other factors. Cultural issues tended to influence the ways in which wars affected the people. For people in Worcestershire to be descended on by a force of Parliamentarians in 1644 was very different than it was for people in an Irish county to be descended on by such a force. The inhabitants of Church Lawton in 1645 resented the Scots army that arrived in their community, but the people of Crathie, Aberdeenshire, had a very different experience when the same army visited them a couple of years later. Unity of experience thus could not overcome the fundamental disunity of the four nations. This text takes as its context the work of historians of all of the four nations and aims to direct the student towards further study of the effects of the war and the experiences of a wide range of people.[8]

One other general aspect of society should be touched on before this chapter turns to the four nations separately. Women's history is a growing field of historical study, and this development is reflected in this book to some degree. Perceptions of the role of women in seventeenth-century society were subject to contemporary challenge, and the wars threw some of these questions into sharp focus. Widely regarded as the 'weaker vessels' in society, and enjoined by law to be perpetual adjuncts to their fathers or husbands, women were perceived to have stepped out of role, at least temporarily, during the civil war period. Women like Brillianna Harley at Brampton Bryan or Lady Offaly at Geashill Castle, County Offaly, became garrison commanders, and many more women, often unnamed, took part in the defence of their homes in urban areas – building defences, loading weapons and fighting in the streets.[9] Still more, as will be shown in chapter 7, paid for the war effort alongside men as taxpayers and producers across the four nations – in their own right, not as deputy husbands or stand-ins for absent men.[10] Other women took up writing in response to the contemporary challenges and changes in society. Some of them drafted petitions to Parliament for recompense or to gain access to sequestered assets. Others, like Katherine Chidley, drafted public petitions that were then subscribed by thousands of names. Still others wrote histories or memoirs of the conflict, like Lucy Hutchinson or Margaret Cavendish, while yet more joined in the religious debate as authors and preachers or even as visionaries.[11] Like their male counterparts, these women were exceptional people; those who put their names to petitions or who listened to the visionaries and preachers were more ordinary. With the exception of fighting, for many women the war may have made little difference to their physical role, but perhaps the very weight and level of their contribution had two consequences for women: first, in the eyes of contemporary observers it increased the need for women to contribute to taxes or levies in kind; food, livestock and durable goods such as linens were collected as part of general taxes or separately. Second, the burden may well have increased women's perceptions of themselves as important members of the economic community with vested interests in the political scene, which directed taxation. This awareness may well in turn have inspired women's political participation in the mid-seventeenth-century wars and revolutions.

SCOTLAND

Scotland in the 1630s was a modernizing nation of somewhat under a million people. The country was not culturally homogeneous. Since the fourteenth century there had emerged a distinct cultural divide, and a series of monarchs, including James VI, saw Highland (as opposed to the Lowlands) culture increasingly as 'backward'. The Highlands were Gaelic-speaking areas, in which the form of English introduced into Britain by the Angles (known by the fifteenth century as Scots) was at best a second language.

One factor which united all of Scotland was that it was, like its immediate neighbours, principally an agricultural economy. Over 90 per cent of Scotland's population lived on, and derived an income from, the management of the land's resources. Large areas, principally the Highlands and Islands, were suited only to pastoral farming. The goats, small horses, sheep and cattle found on these lands made up an integral and essential part of the local economies. Marginal lands skirting the high ground, along the borders and in pockets such as that along the Great Glen, allowed for mixed farming with a higher proportion of cereal production. Surviving contemporary sources from Crathie in Aberdeenshire suggest this sort of community. True arable farming was largely concentrated in parts of the east coast and in small areas in the west, where wheat and legumes were produced and exported to inland areas and shipped by sea to the islands; contemporary documents from Dolphinton demonstrate that it was also this type of community. Some historians have described Scotland's economy as underdeveloped, since its international trade depended too much on exporting raw materials and buying in finished products from abroad.[12] All Scotland's agricultural systems were inefficient and failed to provide the resources needed to sustain the development of towns. Both the methods employed and the tenure arrangements, therefore, were beginning to be challenged.[13]

Agricultural improvement in Scotland was closely linked to the contemporary perception of the cultural divide. The Highland pastoral areas were considered agriculturally backward and inhabited by Gaelic speakers who wore distinctive dress: both the people and the country were regarded as lawless and uncivilized. In an attempt to bolster Scotland's economic and political development, various 'improvements', forerunners of later 'clearance schemes', were being introduced across the country. In the sixteenth century large sheep granges with single owners had been developed in the less profitable Highland regions and on the borderlands. By the middle of the seventeenth century traditional communal or joint tenancies in the Lowland areas were being eradicated in favour of massive single-owner estates. One result of these experiments was to make it harder for the peasants to become small-scale landowners. Unlike many continental states, which sought to bolster the rights of the peasant against overweening landowners, the Scottish government strengthened the hand of the agricultural capitalist out of political motives.[14] Attempts to alleviate the poverty this caused failed in some areas because no fully unified system of government existed in the Scottish countryside.[15] This failure highlighted a structural problem in Scottish governance, which in some way had prompted the government to support larger estates and rich, powerful landlords. In the Highlands the monarch could exercise influence over clan chiefs but could not coerce them into obedience; and even in some Lowland areas, monarchical power was sometimes restricted by conflicting loyalties amongst subjects.

Recently it has been argued that the 'cultural and linguistic identity of Gaelic peoples were under attack'.[16] Given this view, which is undoubtedly right, the cultural war in the Highlands can be seen as a large-scale conflict involving economics and agricultural systems as well as issues of governance and royal power. James VI's struggle to modernize the state went hand-in-hand with the cultural war. It must be remembered that at this stage in Scottish history, the clan system was not seen as something which distinguished the Highlands from the Lowlands but rather, especially to James VI, as something which united the two areas in 'incivility' or lawlessness. The

existence of powerful chieftains, united by blood to the majority of
the clan and by hereditary service or conquest-derived clientship to
other lesser clans, limited royal power throughout Scotland.

   Gaelic agriculture was also perceived as backward and in need of
'modernization' in the same way as language and law and order.
The attempts at the plantation of Lowlanders on Kintyre, Lochaber
and Lewis were designed not only to drive a wedge between the
Gaelic people of Ireland and Scotland, but also to bring agricultural
advancement to the region itself. Such methods failed, however, to
bring about fully the pacification of the western Highlands. More successful was the policy of winning over the Highland chiefs like the
leading Campbells, giving them government positions and opportunities to slaughter their enemies on the king's behalf. The Earl of Argyll
and his Clan Campbell were allowed to displace the Macleans, defeat
the MacDonalds of Islay and 'extirpate' the MacGregors to the
extent of forbidding the very use of their name. While at first these
extreme policies did not bring peace, once one clan reigned supreme, peace of a sort could exist. The situation in effect amounted
to internal colonization; the subjection of a periphery to the hegemony of the centre, represented, in this case, by the monarch in
Edinburgh and exhibited through attacks on language, social structure and economy.[17] Such a policy also confirmed that regional
power and peaceful, large-scale property holding depended on loyalty to the monarch. The subject's greater interests were firmly bound
up with the monarch's own desire for peace, stability and compliant
local administration. By the end of the sixteenth century, Scotland
was being brought to order by James VI, and his transformation to
British monarch in 1603 strengthened his hand still further, removing him from the still present danger of coercion by powerful Scottish nobles. It also created a new class of Anglo-Scottish lords who
participated to some extent in British government and married into
the English aristocracy. The distinct Highland culture was subsequently isolated, the traditional language of Scotland disowned –
being called Erse or Irish to mark it out as foreign – and dominance
over the country given to those of its pre-eminent subjects who had
an economic and political interest in extending royal control.

   From the mid-sixteenth century on, the cultural struggle also
involved religion; accusations of agricultural backwardness combined
neatly with Protestant fears about the continuation of the 'old religion' in the 'dark corners' of the realm. Roman Catholic lords and
people in the Highlands and Islands maintained close links with

their co-religionists on Ireland. On the other hand, Protestant co-religionists in Scotland as well as England readily saw the spiritual and temporal benefits of eradicating the culturally diverse parts of the four nations. Protestant Lowland Scots were enthusiastic colonists in the plantation regions of Ulster, just as they were in 'settling' the Scottish Highlands. As in America, colonies in those places could act as 'cities on the hill' or 'candles in the night', bringing civilization and godliness to the backward regions. Ironically, as the Episcopalian church began to press inwards on the Presbyterian Scots in the Ulster plantation, the religious bonds forged earlier by the Roman Catholic Gaels were mirrored by the oppressed Protestant Scottish settlers and their homeland.

The uniformity of interest within the Scottish religious sphere was not solid. Compared to the Reformation bloodbath in England, Scotland's Reformation was a quiet affair conducted with little rancour.[18] Apart from religious proscriptions, the Catholic clergy were treated leniently and allowed to retain two-thirds of their income for life; the monasteries were not dissolved but turned into business corporations. Under Queen Mary the church trod carefully, aware that its legal foundations were somewhat insubstantial because she did not ratify what Parliament had done in the year before her return from France, although she tacitly accepted the Protestant church as a *fait accompli*. After Mary had been deposed in favour of her infant son in 1567, the Protestant church in Scotland was established more firmly. The parish became the centre of its framework, with clerical and lay involvement in local affairs. Superintendents watched over the work of the ministers, and the General Assembly, which was created only because the Catholic Mary could not be head of the church, continued to oversee the national framework. In 1572 the church took an Episcopalian turn when the Concordat of Leith established the practice of filling the vacant bishoprics.

So far the church was united in its undoctrinal and pragmatic development, but just before John Knox's death a more rigid and academic theological approach to Protestant reformation appeared.[19] Andrew Melville became principal of the University College at Glasgow in 1576. Imbued with Theodore Boza's teachings at Geneva, he decried the drift to episcopacy and proposed a new system of elective leadership within a framework of church courts, presbyteries, synods and a re-framed General Assembly. The status of the church was to be raised in some cases – generally moral and spiritual issues – to establish its superiority over the state, from which it was to be quite separate. In 1578 the General Assembly accepted Melville's reform programme, which included taking over the estates of the old church. This radicalized approach was accepted neither by Parliament, which refused to ratify the actions of the General Assembly, nor by the young King James VI, who in 1584 reasserted the power of the episcopacy with the so-called Black Acts. His action was partly overturned in 1592 when in the Golden Act Parliament recognized the structure of the Presbyterian church while suspending some of the ecclesiastical power of the bishops. James VI continued to press for the reinforcement of the episcopacy, and in 1610 and 1612 the bishops regained some of their influence as a compromise of sorts was reached. The bishops became permanent members of the presbyteries and a more secure financial basis for parishes was established. James continued his attempts to strengthen the episcopacy. In 1618 the General Assembly at Perth passed five articles concerning liturgy that Parliament confirmed in 1621. The articles of Perth established practices rejected by the Kirk, among them kneeling at communion, administration of sacraments and feast days. Even though James was careful not to insist too much on conformity with the articles, they remained unpopular and not widely accepted. James had finally eased his pressure for conformity before his death in 1625.

IRELAND

Ireland, like Scotland, had an underdeveloped yet growing economy. Within it there were underlying trends in landownership which, even without the ensuing war, would have changed the social structure of the nation. People caught up in the 1641 rebellion later claimed that Ireland's economy was successful and prosperous on the eve of the revolt. This was not quite the case; a downturn in the economy in the 1630s caused hardship to thousands, adding to the grievances of the Catholic population, which surfaced in the violence of 1641–2. Ireland had ceased to be a lordship of the English monarch and had become instead an imperial kingdom in 1541. An older piece of legislation, Poyning's Act, had established the rights of the Parliaments held at Dublin. Of principal importance in this act was the proviso that all bills had to have royal approval before being presented to the Irish Parliament. In 1541 Ireland was not entirely under English control; and it was not until the 'flight of the earls' in 1607, when principal Gaelic lords Tyrone and Tyrconnell left the country, that England's rule went unchallenged. In the aftermath of the flight, but more particularly after the ruthless suppression of O'Docherty's rebellion in 1608, a major plantation policy was introduced. Concentrated principally in Ulster, the northernmost of Ireland's four provinces, it later spread into other provinces. As a result of this policy, the native Catholic Irish in the province were allocated perhaps less than one quarter of the land, effectively one barony in each of six out of the nine counties; the rest was parcelled out for plantation, by people from England and Scotland. Although the process of the plantation stalled significantly at times, by 1637 the British population of Ulster seems to have been 40,000–45,000. The province of Munster may have had a further 22,000 settlers, and about 25,000 more may have been scattered in urban areas and in other counties in the province of Leinster. To put these figures in context, the Marquis of Ormond estimated that there were fifteen times as many native Catholics as settlers in 1641, in a total population of between 1.2 and 2 million. Most of these people lived in rural areas and the urban sector remained small, especially in Ulster. Most of the larger towns – such as Cork, Youghal and Limerick in Munster – were on the coast and had derived their growth from international trade. By the 1630s the capital, Dublin, was much larger; indeed, its population of some 20,000 inhabitants was larger than that of any English town bar London.

The political world of Ireland was a complex web. A four-way division derived from the cultural divisions present in the country. First came the native Catholic Irish, making up the vast majority of the population, and their leaders, from whom power was ebbing away. Next were the Old English, or as the Kilkenny Confederation referred to them during the war, the New Irish, who also saw power passing away from them. These Catholic English were descended from the colonists who had settled in Ireland from the twelfth century onwards and had been the principal political force in the pale and the outlying areas of the lordship of Ireland. However, from the time of the Elizabethan Parliaments onwards and, more crucially, from the Parliaments of Charles I, political power was increasingly being concentrated in the hands of a third group, the New English. Beginning with the reign of James VI and I, to a lesser extent power was also given to the last faction, the New Scots, who had been imported to create the plantations of Ulster. Settlement had a wide range of aims, and the destruction of Gaelic culture was central. In Ireland, religion was at the heart of this attack. The Church of

Ireland had become Protestant along with the Welsh and English churches at the Reformation. However, although it had won control of the properties of the Roman Catholic church, it had not won over the hearts and minds of the people. The Roman church remained in existence, maintaining a structure and an episcopacy, and more important, a flock. Tithes went to the established church, causing further resentment amongst the Catholic population as well as financial problems for the Roman Catholic church. The official aim of English policy in Ireland was the conversion of the Catholic population and the extirpation of the Catholic religion. In general this aim was not fulfilled, and the Elizabethan church never managed to dominate Ireland completely. Although the policy of plantation gave Protestantism new vigour – along with the general expectation that civilization, in the form of agricultural improvement, English language and dress, would be brought into Ireland – the attempt to make Ireland Protestant failed. By the 1630s the Catholic presence in Ireland in fact amounted to that of an established church, in structure and form if not money and real estate.[20]

Even the Protestants' broad cultural aims remained unfulfilled by the 1630s. As several Lord Deputies discovered, some form of coalescence with the native Gaelic Catholics was necessary in order to maintain any stability of governance. At the other end of society, some planters compromised and took up native agricultural methods when they found them more appropriate. Nevertheless, English rulers attempted to keep the various groups apart and in Ulster the religious differences helped. Physical segregation was less rigid. To facilitate plantation, confiscated estates were divided up into parcels of about one thousand acres and sold to an undertaker, who further subdivided the land and brought a party of settlers onto the estate. Settlement also entailed the construction of towns and villages for the settlers. Forts were also constructed to provide defence in case the undertakers rebelled within three years of taking possession of the land.

Few of these arrangements proved practical. Even the larger undertakings such as the Derry plantation assigned to London turned out to be underfunded, while parts of the confiscated lands were soon in danger of becoming underpopulated. Injunctions against the letting of land to Catholics proved worthless, and even in supposedly entirely Protestant areas pockets of native Irish people worked alongside those who were supposed to have marginalized them. Only in some parts of Ulster did the proportion of Catholic landowners fall below 50 per cent. In some areas the establishment of plantations met with concerted and successful opposition. For example, Ulricke Burke, Earl of Clanricarde, rejected Lord Deputy Sir Thomas Wentworth's plans for the plantation of parts of Connaught.[21]

Historians have regarded the effects of plantation as mixed. It has been suggested that the policy had the economic advantage of spreading agricultural innovation, particularly in Munster. Other historians have proved somewhat less enthusiastic about plantation, arguing that the relationship was more of a two-way one in which natives and settlers learned from one another.[22]

Colonization turned out not to be a one-way process. As did the Welsh before them, some elements of the Irish elite saw the benefit of absorbing something of the alien culture forced upon their country. Moreover, loyalty to the English monarch was not universally viewed as necessarily anti-Irish. Gaelic poetry written in celebration of Irish chiefs did not condemn them for turning their backs on their co-religionists or their erstwhile allies. Marriage into foreign British elites was praised because it established a dynastic connection to a distinguished ancestry. Recently one historian has demonstrated that a combination of apparently contradictory loyalties could be accommodated in the educated elite's view of itself and its lords, except perhaps when it originated with the sophisticated polemic of Catholic cleric-poets.[23] The Irish elites had never been isolated from their counterparts in Scotland and England; both Old English and Gaelic lords had married their British social equals. English lands, titles and marriages drew the Irish elite closer to the English aristocracy and gentry, and for those who eschewed the Catholic church the rewards could be great. The branch of the Butler family led by the Earl of Ormond and Ossory is a case in point. The young earl was brought up in England and the English church as a ward of the crown and an associate of the Duke of Buckingham. When Wentworth became Lord Deputy of Ireland, Ormond so impressed him that he was placed on the Dublin Privy Council, from which base he steadily built up his standing and influence. Notwithstanding his links with prominent families on both sides of the religious divide, and later with leading Confederates, Ormond remained principally associated with the crown.[24] Yet loyalty was not to be automatically associated with religion, nor with Wentworth's favour: Ulricke Burke, Earl of Clanricarde, remained true to the old church and in opposition to Wentworth, yet loyal to the king and the Ormondists.

As with Wales, the colonization of Ireland involved the shiring of the area controlled by England. Much of this was undertaken while Ireland was a lordship, particularly in Munster and Leinster. The process continued under Queen Mary I when West Leinster was incorporated into two counties and plantations settled. The counties were named in honour of Mary and her husband Philip II of Spain as Queen's and King's County. Under Elizabeth, Ulster and Connaught were also shired between 1560 and 1585. The counties were subdivided into baronies which served the role of English hundreds and bore some relation to the Welsh cantrefs or commotes.[25] However, the Irish counties were not administered in quite the same manner as their English and Welsh counterparts. Quarter sessions were not introduced, nor were lords lieutenant. Although some sheriffs were drawn from the Old English elites, there was concern in Carlow and Kildare that New English were taking over local offices. The issue was important, because sheriffs were the principal loci of power within the counties, as they had once been in England. They still held tourns and represented the principal judicial figure.[26] In the case of the later shires the sheriffs held important military powers, and their ability to summon a posse comitatus was more significant than in England, where military powers had largely passed to the lords lieutenant.

ENGLAND

England in 1637 was well on the road to modernization. It was also at peace and, in Scottish eyes at least, complacent to the point of slavery. Enjoying a highly developed trade with Europe and colonies in the New World, England was already on the verge of becoming a great trading empire. Even so, England was not a country completely at peace with itself, although certain historians have argued that there was nothing at this time that 'bode some strange eruption' to the state. At home, the processes of government were being modernized, that is, power and the transmission of governance were being standardized. To some degree it was also being centralized in the hands of the monarch; as in Scotland, there were fears of a royal attack on property rights. Traditional features of government by consent or, rather, with the co-operation of the nobility and gentry in the shires were being eroded by the use of 'governments by commission', minor governmental activities sold to undertakers. This system was not popular with the traditional rulers, who resented this intrusion on their power and, occasionally, their property by members of the lower classes. After 1629 their resentment combined with fear that they had little chance of recourse to the traditional means of protest, Parliament.

The centre of the English polity was the family, in microcosm the state, with the *pater patriae* at the head, in the manner of the monarch, and the wife and children in the role of subjects.[27] It was the very model of the notion that power flowed downwards from the monarch through all the functions of the state to the lowliest citizen. In the family as in life, there was the ruler (the man), who was assisted by the petty rulers (the wife) with duties of instruction in moral and religious matters, and those who were ruled (the children). It was an imperfect model, for even theorists acknowledged that the father was not exactly like the monarch. He had no right of life or death over the family, as the king had over his subjects, and the exact nature of the relationship between man and wife was not always straightforward. Women did participate in household and estate management and had an interest which the husband was expected to incorporate into his own. Moreover, women were sometimes heads of families, too. And if such a woman's position was not temporary (in which case she could be deemed a deputy husband), the patriarchal role model could not explain it. In wealthier families, the head of the principal branch of the family was also the central figure in the network of the nuclear family, at the head of a chain of economic and social relationships, which again reflected society at large. If the family was of a certain status, the head, and perhaps some of the lesser luminaries, would cross the seamless boundary of the private and public spheres and shoulder the duties of local government, moving on to play the father of a larger family.[28]

In England county government was conducted through a principle of mutual interest. There was no centrally paid or structured civil service within the shires, which were governed by crown appointees who received no remuneration, only the kudos of advanced social status, for their work. They did it on the understanding that the preservation of peace and harmony was in their own interest as well as the king's. The strands of local government in England, some of which were transferred to two of the other three nations by conquest and to Scotland by absorption, were manifold and their relationships to one another complex.[29] Principal amongst them were the forces of order, which consisted of the shrievalty and the commission of the peace. The latter had absorbed some of the powers of the former and was part of a judicial framework including the assizes, or courts of Oyer and Terminer, which heard and determined (hence the name) cases forwarded by the quarter sessions courts. The assizes met twice every year, except for the northern circuit – covering Yorkshire, Northumberland, Westmoreland, Cumberland and Lancashire – which was held only once a year. The circuit judges, sent out from London, were dispatched not only to hear the cases of murder, grand larceny, treason and witchcraft passed on by the justices of the peace, they were also expected – particularly by the Stuart monarchs – to oversee the work of the justices and to ensure some form of parity of law enforcement. This supervision was to some extent resented, for the justices did not consider themselves to be amateurs.

The justices of the peace (JPs) were appointed centrally by the monarch, but largely from names supplied by the county. They were generally drawn from the titled gentry and prominent members of the squirearchy. Each commission was headed by a selection of honorific appointments from the court and the Privy Council, but the work was done by a core of local men, if possible well spaced around the county for which they were responsible. They conducted business privately at special sessions in their own homes, and publicly at the quarterly general sessions of the peace. The Book of Orders, which in the 1630s became a standing set of orders rather than, as it had previously been, a temporary expedient in times of trouble, also inveighed upon the magistrates to assemble monthly and then to draw up a report on the state of their counties and forward it to the Privy Council. Even though only the quorum had to have legal training, the others were still local experts, versed in the structures and strictures of provincial society. Their knowledge of how the county 'felt' was reflected in their concern for keeping the peace. After all, as major property holders peace in the county was largely to their benefit. Parity of action across the country was not therefore considered necessary, local conditions, tradition and custom being required instead. In the years before the civil war justices had other grounds for resentment, too. Many of their functions were being taken over by commissioners deputed by the king to license various functions, such as alehouses, which were previously controlled by local magistrates. Their knowledge of the community was thus being superseded by strangers whose motives were purely financial, as indeed had been the king's when selling them their commissions.

These commissioners made a profit on selling licences over and above the money they paid the crown for their commissions.

The sheriff's office was filled annually except in Westmoreland, where the post was hereditary in the Clifford family.[30] At one time most of the responsibility for administering justice had fallen to the sheriff, but by the seventeenth century the post consisted of ceremonial duties at sessions of the peace and assizes and maintenance of lists of potential jurors as required by the law courts and the coroners' courts. Nevertheless, the work was still onerous and there were generally two sheriffs: the High Sheriff, upon whom ultimate responsibility fell, and an under-sheriff, whose duties probably ranged from administrative responsibilities to acting permanently in place of the sheriff of Westmoreland when the post was held by Lady Anne Clifford. Sheriffs were responsible for administering the collection of taxes, which in the 1630s included ship money. They had to be men of high social standing (titled gentry and established members of the squirearchy) and of some wealth, for they bore the costs of entertaining the judges of assizes. This expense included more than bed and board. As recorded by Lady Anne Clifford in her diaries for the period when she was the hereditary sheriff of Westmoreland, it also included public banquets in the town or city where assizes were held.[31] During the civil war period, both sides tried to capitalize on the tradition and office of the shrievalty by employing the sheriff on the wartime administration. Consequently, there were sometimes two rival holders of the office in some counties.

A third strand of administration in the county, newer than the law bodies and the shrievalty, was the lieutenancy.[32] At the abandonment of privately assembled levies, county-based forces raised as required by commissions of array formed the main body of armed forces in the country. In the sixteenth century these had come under the military leadership of the monarch's lieutenants in the shire. These were court appointments and were usually filled by members of the nobility, many of whom were absent for at least part of the time and ran the office through deputies drawn from the nobility and upper titled gentry. In addition professional soldiers were appointed as mustermasters to drill and train the soldiers on a regular basis. By the 1580s the lords lieutenant had become permanent fixtures, although until the Militia Act of 1608, funding for them remained in the hands of the justices of the peace. The lords lieutenant were also interfering with traditional functions of the justices. Not only did they completely control the militia after 1608, they also began to take charge of disarming recusants and collecting fines from them too. These conflicts were caused by a lack of sensitivity to, and, it could be argued, knowledge on the part of the monarch, which, moreover, ultimately did Charles I a disservice. Conflicts in the shire government resulted in weaknesses within the system which affected the efficacy of county government at a time when, because there were no Parliaments to intercede and endorse the king's actions before the community of the kingdom, he could only work through the very bodies between which he had introduced conflict. These then were the principal bodies that became embroiled in the civil war. All were in themselves battlegrounds for political control, or provided countywide meeting places for political factions to try to cultivate support for petitions. The lieutenancy and the county forces, the trained bands, became integral to the attempt to create military forces, but the justices too became embroiled in the administrative duties of the war efforts of the two sides.

As two historians have recently indicated:

> The system of local government did not merely allow participation: it was dependent for its smooth running on the active involvement of men of all ranks.[33]

This statement is important for several reasons. First, it warns us that government lay not simply in the hands of those outlined above, but was also involved through the composition of juries and the service of petty officials in the local communities. Second, it affirms that government was generally the work of men. Margaret Cavendish wrote:

> Like birds in cages, to hop up and down in our houses, not suffered to fly abroad to see the several changes of fortune ... Thus by an opinion, which I hope is but an erroneous one, in men, we are shut out of all power and authority; by reason we are never employed either in civil or martial affairs, our councels are despised and laughed at.[34]

With the exception of Anne Clifford at the upper end of the scale, women's influence on government took place behind the scenes when there was not a reigning queen. Henrietta Maria in particular was important in Charles's government, and current research may well demonstrate that she was crucial to the running of government in the 1630s as well as important in the war period. In local government women were active as prosecutors in cases in secular and ecclesiastical courts, but in terms of the machinery of the law their only involvement was in juries of matrons, which were called in specific cases of alleged rape or to determine the veracity of a convicted woman's 'pleading the belly' (claiming pregnancy to escape capital punishment, at least temporarily).

The active involvement of men to which Fletcher and Stevenson refer was principally at the level of minor offices, such as constable, the principal secular official in parish government. Other offices included churchwardens, who administered the finances of the church and ensured church attendance, and overseers of the poor who administered the poor rate in England and Wales. Most often these were men, but women often served in the office, sometimes on a regular basis, and recently we have been shown that women were not debarred from overseers' posts. Women did serve as constables but may well have been subject to substitution by men. One woman holding this office appears in the present work: Jane Kitchen of Upton in Nottinghamshire was in office in 1644, during a particularly crucial period in the first civil war, and she thus became embroiled in the campaigns that preceded and influenced the outcome of the war in the north in that year, which saw the Royalists lose control of the north of England. Much of the information about the effects of the war in different localities comes from the papers of these minor government officials, particularly the constables, who served alone or in teams within both urban and rural communities. Constables were drawn from the social elites within their communities. Thus they could range from husbandmen, if there were few substantial yeomen, to minor gentry, if they had a significant presence in the community. In many cases they were drawn from the same social groups as their fellow administrators, the overseers and the churchwardens, although in communities of Norfolk recently researched, the churchwardens were of a markedly higher standing.[35] Constables were essentially the servants of all the government officials – JPs, judges, lieutenants and high sheriffs – and as such quite often at the brunt of the conflict of the 1630s. They had an additional burden, too, for they were expected to represent their community and its views of social order, which did not always correspond to views held by its principal officials.

In addition to these principal groups of officials, there were others. The church was represented throughout society via the diocesan structure, which ran all the way from the bishops down to church-wardens. There were also ecclesiastical courts, whose status had fallen after the Reformation but was being revived under the regime of William Laud. In the archbishop's search for order and conformity in religion, whether or not it was based firmly in doctrinal Arminianism, the church courts were a means of establishing conformity for both the laity and the clergy. With regard to the latter, the courts could not only stamp out licentiousness and laxity amongst the clergy, they could also enforce conformity to the canons of Laud's church, and remove Puritan practices that tended towards preaching rather than adherence to the liturgy of the Book of Common Prayer. For the laity the church courts could act as an instrument to enforce moral codes, claiming jurisdiction over bastardy cases or even swearing if blasphemy was involved. Of course, they could also eradicate non-conformist practices such as the seeking out of alternative ministers who eschewed Laud's church. The ecclesiastical courts could thus provoke hostility from the committedly religious, whom we may perhaps call Puritans, as well as from the secular courts, which also claimed jurisdiction over bastardy and swearing as potential attacks on the social order. Recent revisionist historians have tended to play down the importance of such conflicts in England, suggesting that the country, including Wales, was at peace and that it had few of the social stresses inherent in Ireland and Scotland. Chapter 2 takes up this issue, arguing that stresses in English society were important and manifest, and contributed to the problems caused by Charles's actions towards Scotland and Ireland.

WALES

Wales in 1637 could be considered by some to have been part of a greater England for one hundred years. The whole of Wales – the royal estates (shired areas) of Anglesey, Caernarfon, Merioneth and Flint in the north and Cardigan and Carmarthen in the south, and roughly the old kingdoms of Gwynedd and Deheubarth[36] – were brought together with the Lordships of the March, which consisted of a series of self-governing units based on traditional divisions inherited from the kingdoms of Northern Powys, Southern Powys, Rhwng Gwy a Hafren, Brycheiniog and Gwent and the gwald of Morgannwg. The new principality had been thoroughly reorganized after the 'acts of union', resulting in a certain degree of anglification.

Both Welsh historians and historians of Wales disagree about the effects and the merits of this process. Some point to the positive effects for peace and social order that the abolition of the cantrefi (the provinces of the old kingdoms) had brought;[37] others are less convinced. Certainly for some sections of Wales the changes were dramatic and were conducted with an imperialist or colonial zeal, and some background detail is necessary in order to be able to pursue the taxation systems followed by both sides during the war and by Parliament afterwards. In the older shired areas the county system in effect perpetuated the older territorial divisions of the cantref and the commote (cymwd), the latter becoming equivalent to English hundreds. In the new shires the traditional boundaries were largely ignored, and new hundreds were carved out by commissioners. Each county gained a commission of the peace along English lines, consisting of eight justices, and twelve Welsh counties were grouped into four circuits for the great sessions that had been originally created in the old shires after the defeat of Prince Llywellyn. These served as an equivalent of the English assizes, but Monmouth was added instead to the English Oxford assize circuit. These units, which formed the basis of the wartime administrations, proved to be the same mixture of convenience and dilemma for the agents of administration. Through such arrangements were the leaders of Welsh society drawn into supporting the English hegemony, by being given offices and titles which conveyed power to them. And thus did their interest and the state's coincide as it did in England, and as it was increasingly doing in Highland and Lowland Scotland too. Along with these changes, linguistic and cultural attacks were launched against the Welsh people in an attempt to civilize them as if they too were an internal colony. Religious impositions were also made at the Reformation, although attempts to reform the parishes there stumbled as they encountered poverty, language difficulties and the unwillingness of graduate ministers to venture into the Welsh highlands.

Wales was administered by the Council of Wales and the Marches. It was not an easy relationship. The power of this prerogative court was challenged in the sixteenth century by the quarter sessions and great sessions in Wales and by some borough courts, quarter sessions and the assizes of the English border counties, some of which had achieved independence from the Council in the sixteenth century.[38] Moreover, the growing confidence of the gentry in Wales and their representatives in Parliament was also proving to be a challenge. In the early seventeenth century it had been the English shires

– Hereford, Shropshire and Worcestershire – that attempted to break free, only to see James VI and I restore the Council to full power and safeguard its existence. The king did this precisely because, to him, its powers over the other courts in English and Welsh counties represented a part of his prerogative powers. This enhanced and public expression of monarchical power in turn led to further criticism in the 1630s when such power was identified with Charles I's fiscal policy.[39]

IMMEDIATE STEPS TOWARDS REBELLION

The reign of Charles I heightened many of the underlying tensions in the four nations. It has been claimed that James VI and I died at a difficult time. Harvests had been bad for three years, there were serious floods and a murrain affected livestock. Moreover, a war with Spain was being fought in the aftermath of Prince Charles's disastrous Spanish-match adventure. The success of James's reign lay partly in his diplomatic ability and partly in his patience where opposition to his will was concerned. His son, however, uninterested in his home country, undid in ten years all that his father had achieved.[40] There is much to substantiate this view, even if the belief that James brought the Kirk to heel is rejected in favour of the view that the end result of James's policy was some form of compromise between monarch and Kirk. And there is much to commend the idea that Charles began his rule of the northern kingdom badly. The new king took his cue from the ready vote of taxes by the Scottish Estates in October 1625, which he wrongly interpreted as a sign of compliance rather than a gesture of goodwill. He began to insist on the contentious policy of revocation. In Scotland a monarch traditionally had the right to revoke all grants of land made during his or her minority. In a country where several kings had been enthroned in their infancy, this policy was viewed as part of the monarch's rite of passage into majority, as it enabled him or her to shake off the effects of the malign influence of court factions. Charles stretched the precedent to claim the right to revoke all grants which he regarded as prejudicial to his rights, and this appeared as a direct challenge to property rights in general. Charles's principal goal was to revoke lands alienated from the Scottish church with the intention of using the income from the reclaimed lands to fund the Kirk more effectively. But his policy was ill received, chiefly because it provoked real fears for property, and also because it was not explained clearly. This public relations failure turned out to be a major problem and one which was to recur as Charles remained unconvinced of the need to clarify his motives. His view of the position of the monarch was an uncompromising evocation of the divine nature of the right to rule. Believing that his position was vested with godly sanction, Charles behaved as though he understood that his actions were, too. The practical outcome of this attitude was that he failed to grasp the need to explain his policies to those he had to work with, or those who would be affected by his policies. Furthermore, the new king did not feel obliged to accept advice; he would take it when and if he felt he needed it. Governance to Charles was not a product of consultation and agreement between the monarch and even the narrowest of political spectrums. This air of having 'made his mind up' was quickly noticed by Scots observers like the Earl of Marr, and contrasted sharply with the Scottish Privy Council's notion of consultative government as practised, however imperfectly, under James.[41] Consent therefore was not on his mind as he set about the revocation. As a result, Charles alienated a good number of the members of the political class with whom he would have to work in future.

Charles's religious policies shared many of the same aims as his father's, such as the continued empowerment of the bishops, but none of the finesse. The king recognized that the five articles had been decisive in the past, but he insisted on new ministers abiding by them, perhaps his only concession to the gradualism that marked his father's reign. To many Scots these policies were unacceptable, as they were perceived as not only innovative and intrusive but also foreign. It had become clear within three years of James VI becoming king of England that the English did not perceive the union of the crowns as anything but an alliance of two unequal states. Whereas James and other Scots talked of the creation of a British political union, the English did not, and in 1607 the English Parliament rejected the notion. In England, Scotland was viewed as politically and economically inferior, and most Scots suspected that, despite James's accession to the throne, the English regarded Scotland in the same light as Ireland, that is, as a conquered nation. This point is important, as it creates the light in which the changes in Scotland's economy, polity and Kirk, imposed by James, but more particularly by Charles, came to be viewed. Thus, the introduction of English-style vestments, suggesting that the English church was somehow superior, or at least a model for the Scottish Kirk to follow, appeared to be part of a process of anglification which some see as being as important as any of the liturgical issues.[42] Moreover, this appeared not to be the only example of such a tendency. An attempt to open up Scottish fishing grounds to English boats angered the coastal burghs, which depended largely on the fishing industry. Scottish money was required to finance wars in which England was involved, despite the opposition of a Convention of Estates. Additionally, Charles set about reconstructing Scottish government on the basis of both his misunderstandings and his continued failure to consult widely. And so he set about removing nobles from the principal law body, the Lords of Session, largely in the mistaken belief that the court dealt with criminal law and because he thought that the nobility should be concentrated in the Privy Council. Charles's visit to Scotland for his coronation in 1633 was a model of the king's attitude to the country.[43] He was crowned not at the traditional coronation site, but at the Abbey at Holyrood, with a specially built altar at the eastern end. As if this was not offensive enough, the service mirrored an English model and some of the Scottish bishops wore English vestments. It could hardly have been designed to be more repugnant to the Kirk. Nevertheless, it was not the limit. The service may have been a hitherto rare airing of English liturgy, but it was not to be the last.

2

The Scottish Rebellion

we ar driven in such straits as we must ather, by process of excommunication and horning suffer the ruin of our estates and fortunes, or els, by breach of our covenant with God and foresaking the way of true religion, fall under the wrath of God which unto us is more grevous than death[1]

From out of the stresses within the Anglo-Scottish relationship developed a major religious and then political crisis, which in turn fuelled the drive to war and revolution. The culmination of Charles's liturgical changes in Scotland was to be the introduction of a Book of Common Prayer. This was essentially an episcopal document, modelled upon the one in use in England and Wales, but adapted for the Scottish church. Nevertheless, the aim was to bind the Scottish, English and Welsh churches closer together, and to the Scots this goal was doubly unacceptable; the prayerbook was foreign, and it further undermined the Kirk. The well-publicized date for its introduction, set for 23 July 1637, gave opponents plenty of time to organize the protests discussed at the beginning of chapter 1. After the protests in the Edinburgh churches, opposition to the prayerbook grew. Charles I was clearly bewildered, and he looked in the wrong direction to find a source to blame. Unable to accept that the opposition to his religious policies was genuinely based on theological or sectarian grounds, he would not take the words of his Scots opponents at face value. Instead, he saw them as a cover for some other form of attack, one he even believed was provoked by outside agents, perhaps – somewhat improbably – the French. He was sustained in this notion by the Spanish minister Count Olivares, who provocatively and maliciously hinted at French collaboration in the Scottish challenge. Of course, in some ways this fiction was convenient for Charles, obviating the need to reconsider his policies or approach; rather, he could denounce his opponents as rebels and proceed accordingly. His actions were in keeping with his general attitude to Scotland, which was that it was there to be ruled, but not necessarily understood. As long as John Stewart, Earl of Traquair (Charles's treasurer from 1636) pursued the king's policies, there was little for his master to be concerned about. Traquair was a loyal governor, somewhat prone to dropping dramatic dark hints about the king's policies in order to alarm his enemies perhaps, but essentially a man who was working a 'thorough' policy. He increased the king's revenues and worked hard, but the king expected him simply to follow orders and not to use his own initiative. Part of the reason the king's reaction to the events in Scotland was so vehement is that he regarded himself as misunderstood, misrepresented and let down by those whom he expected to follow orders.[2]

Violent reaction was not the only response to the prayerbook. One different approach to the reaction of the lawyer Archibald Johnston that has been noted, for example, is the slower progress of the minister of Kilwinning, Robert Baillie, toward rejection of the book. Baillie then continued to have nagging doubts about his reasons for rejecting it. He suspected that he might have done so out of fear for his personal safety after other ministers had been stoned by women for reading the book. Baillie also retained an intellectual attitude to the issue and regretted that the opposite case could not be put, because in the atmosphere of violence 'no man may speak any thing in publick for the king's part except he would have himself marked for a sacrifice to be killed one day'.[3] Yet he still opposed the prayerbook himself, and it has been pointed out that every time Baillie was provoked into questioning the virtue of opposition to the prayerbook, Charles's own reactions to that opposition quelled his doubts.

The Scottish Council itself also had doubts of its own over the prayerbook; some members maintained a diplomatic absence from church services on 23 July. After the 'blak doolful' day, the councillors began to frame their doubts into a policy of opposition using the usual channels open to them. They offered advice to the king and petitioned him for change. At the same time they were trying to influence the prominent Anglo-Scots around the king – the Marquis of Hamilton, the Earl of Morton and the Duke of Lennox. In turn the Council itself was being importuned by various groups of people who were angered by the religious situation. The communication was a two-way process, and it seems that there was close co-operation between elements of the Council and the protesters. One thing is clear; the protesters and the Council, although not united on specifics, pressed the king both directly and indirectly to withdraw the prayerbook completely. But the king was not really listening, partly because he was convinced that there were other motives behind the opposition and partly because he heard only what he wanted to hear. Russell explains how the message sent by the Earl of Traquair, hitherto Charles's loyal lieutenant, to the effect that the prayerbook must be withdrawn to 'free ye subjects of y feares they have conceaved of innovance of religion' became transmuted. The king decided to interpret the statement to mean that the prayerbook would be accepted once the Scottish people were convinced that it was not an innovation leading down the road to popery, rather than to understand that Traquair was insisting that it really was an innovation which had to be withdrawn.[4] This failure to accept anyone else's view was not wholly the king's fault. When Charles declared in November 1637 that he would not introduce any religious innovations into Scotland, some of his opponents believed that he was effectively apologizing and promising to remove the offending book. Of course, this was not what Charles meant; instead he was demonstrating his belief that the policy was sound (and thereby unalterable), but that the message just was not getting across clearly.

During the seven months after the initial riots, Charles and the Scottish Council communicated with each other to little effect over the prayerbook. The Council was pressing, often in coded fashion, for its withdrawal, whereas the king, through his representative, Lord Lennox, insisted from September onwards that the Council should enforce it and explain its true purpose to the people. Progress was therefore not really possible. In the meantime, opponents outside the Council continued to demand the complete withdrawal of the offending text. On 18 October they presented a Supplication and Complaint to the Privy Council, in which they placed the blame for the prayerbook firmly on the Scottish bishops, claiming:

> All of which canons were nevir seen nor allowed in anie General Assembly, bot ar imposed contrair to order of law appointed in this realme for establishing of maters ecclesiastick.[5]

The presentation of the Supplication was accompanied by enthusiastic and violent public protest. Charles responded by insisting that the Council try the ringleaders of the group, which became known as the Supplicants. To prevent the undue influence of the Edinburgh 'mob', he further ordered the Council to move to Linlithgow and Dundee.[6] Instead the Supplicants petitioned for the prayerbook to be subject to legal consideration and again blamed its inception on the bishops. Traquair was at a loss and eventually gained permission to attend Charles in London, hoping that he could impress on the king personally the seriousness of the problem. The king himself refused to answer any petitions or supplications. Worse, when Traquair arrived in the winter of 1637–8, his enemies at court had already spread stories of his willingness to make deals with the Supplicants. The king therefore ignored Traquair's advice and instead turned to Robert Maxwell, the Earl of Nithsdale. Nithsdale advised the king to try to win a period of calm, during which some Supplicants would be punished to demonstrate regal power. At the same time there would be less pressure to enforce the prayerbook. Nithsdale's plan essentially involved no change in policy; the Court of High Commission and the prayerbook were to be retained. On a more sinister note, however, Nithsdale also suggested that all castles should be prepared for war so that Scotland could be secured militarily. Charles ignored Nithsdale's more pacific suggestions and sent royal proclamations to Scotland threatening petitioners with imprisonment.

In mid-February 1638 Traquair was sent home from Westminster with orders to press on with the king's original policy. He went to the Council, now based at Stirling, carrying with him a proclamation. Although he did not announce the contents, Johnston and others knew what they were through their contacts with the English court. Traquair intended to have the proclamation published in Stirling, away from the heady political atmosphere of Edinburgh. Forewarned, the Supplicants made their way to Stirling to confront Traquair, but on 19 February, Traquair and the Earl of Roxburgh left Stirling in the dead of night for Edinburgh, apparently to outwit them. Traquair had carefully leaked this secret to the Supplicants through one of his servants. Two leading Supplicants, Lord Lindsay and Lord Home, rushed to the Council at Stirling and lodged protests against the proclamation. The published proclamation had two main features: first, it 'forgave' the Supplicants if they now stopped objecting to the prayerbook and went quietly home. Those in Stirling were given six hours to leave. Second, it declared the king solely responsible for the prayerbook, in an effort to wrongfoot his enemies by confronting them directly. The Supplicants had up to now avoided attacking the king personally by blaming the bishops; Charles now challenged them to attack him directly. Naturally he expected them to climb down. It was a great mistake, one Charles had made before and one he was to commit repeatedly. By placing himself at the centre of the matter, he made the monarchy and the particular political issue indivisible. If the policy itself was attacked, then so was his position as monarch. In short, Charles relied on the Supplicants simply to give up in the face of his sovereign status, which he believed they would regard as unassailable.[7]

Instead of accepting Charles's royal authority, however, the Supplicants responded with the National Covenant. In the wake of Charles's proclamation, a committee was established in Edinburgh consisting of four lairds, four burgesses and four ministers together with the noble Supplicants. Its members created a bond or union in the face of the royal attack. They discussed 'renewing the old Covenant for religion' as the basis for their bond and their stand against Charles's religious policy.[8] They were referring to the 1581 Confession of Faith, also known as the Negative Confession, which had been sworn by James VI, his court and 'people of all ranks'. At its core the new Covenant reaffirmed the Confession and condemned all religious changes undertaken thereafter. Although it was based on the Confession and thus a religious statement, it went much further and was a harbinger of future events. By binding its adherents to a defence of a Presbyterian Kirk in the manner of a traditional band or bond, the Covenant was cast in a familiar form. But the National Covenant, drafted in the last days of February 1638 by Johnston and Alexander Henderson, minister of Leuchars in Fife, went beyond traditional bounds. On the one hand it bound the Scottish people together in defence of the church in the same manner as the 1581 oath, but it also referred to the need for a free General Assembly to take stock of affairs, thereby hinting that some previous general assemblies may not have been free and that the acts passed in unfree assemblies were unenforceable.[9] As such the Covenant was levelled at most of the religious policies of James and Charles.

It may be presumptuous to claim that the Covenant served as a radical political manifesto, but its role in political change was substantial.[10] It has been argued that it was a conservative revolutionary document, revolutionary in the way it marshalled support for the defence of the Kirk but conservative in that it looked to the past for its political and religious initiatives. On the other hand, many historians feel that the protagonists themselves recognized the novelty of their mode of expression[11] and that the revolutionary nature of

the Covenant remains unquestioned. The Covenant was undoubtedly a radical enterprise for the whole Scottish nation, almost a
declaration of independence.[12] A significant section of the Covenanters, including Johnston, wanted something more than just a restoration of the church to its position before James and Charles began
the march back to episcopacy. They also wanted a church free from
government control and future royal meddling, with its loyalty to
king and state conditional upon the compatibility of political and
religious aims. Since the Covenant gave legitimacy to all of these
demands by its references to the Negative Confession and the acts of
the free assemblies, it attracted the widest possible support. Although
to some it was a radical manifesto, in order to win over moderates
and monarchists it was worded in such a way as to allow a wide
range of meaning to be inferred. This strategy worked; support soon
extended beyond the nobility and other social elites to attract the
signatures and marks of a wide cross-section of Scottish society.
Moreover, the Covenant gained support across the political spectrum, from monarchists like the Earl of Montrose to political and
religious radicals who thought like Henderson and Johnston.

On Wednesday, 28 February 1638, in an atmosphere charged
with emotion, the Covenant was signed by the nobles and lairds
assembled at St Giles Cathedral, Edinburgh in a ceremony that
lasted four hours. On the next day, the Covenant was taken to the
Tailors' Hall on Cowgate, where it was signed by ministers in the
morning and by representatives of most of the royal burghs in
the afternoon. A day later the people of Edinburgh set their hands
to it at the College of Trinity Kirk.[13] Copies were then circulated
around the country to be signed by as many Scots as possible, often
under the exhortation of their ministers. Signatories were principally
male, but women too set their hands to it. Women's participation,
in addition to their predominant role in the riots, demonstrates that
political and religious issues were by no means a male preserve at
this time, despite the social injunctions that would in some areas
have dictated that only men sign the Covenant.

There were outright refusals. Most of the people of Aberdeen,
under the influence of their college academics, refused to sign, on
the grounds that the commissioners bearing the Covenant 'ar not
com authorezed nor clad with commission from his maiestie nor
Lords of previe counsell to exact any such subscription', even though
they 'culd not disallow of the said confession of faith in sofar as the
same is consonant and agreable with Gods word'.[14] But despite

Aberdeen's hostile reaction, the Covenant fulfilled its purpose and bound a great part of the Scottish people into a united front against Charles I's policies. It also wonderfully concentrated the mind of the king, who recognized at last that he was facing an organized opposition.

As the Covenant was being signed, the organization at the heart of the opposition was being reformed. There was now a series of executive bodies known as the Tables (the English equivalent would be a board). They had originally been established in November 1637, growing out of the power vacuum created when Charles had sent the Privy Council out of the capital. The Tables first appeared out of the mass meetings as a large consultative committee of Supplicants, consisting of four groups, one for each Estate. A single negotiating committee was elected from among these bodies to deal with Traquair. On 6 December the structure was consolidated: four Tables were established from representatives of the country as a whole. A fifth Table – consisting of gentry, burgesses and ministers – acted as the executive.[15] Finely honed as this was, involvement with the cause was so great that there were thousands of commissioners and associates assembled at Edinburgh during 1638. The king's cousin, James, Marquis of Hamilton, now assumed Traquair's position as the king's commissioner. He was sent north in May, only to find that the Privy Council had been 'shorn of bishops' and was in broad sympathy with the Covenant.[16] Although the king was now alive to the Scottish problem, he and Hamilton were several steps behind their opponents in their grasp of the political situation. The Tables would not compromise on the Covenant as Hamilton hoped and as Charles still seems to have expected. The Tables now wanted a General Assembly of the Kirk to ratify, and thus sanction, their opposition. Hamilton was under instructions to try to deny this ambition, but because he had been given little leeway, he had to return to London in both July and August to receive fresh instructions. In the end the king had to concede to the Tables and a General Assembly was summoned for 21 November to meet in Glasgow.

This was not the end of the trial of strength. Aberdeen's opposition to the Covenant was being worked on, both by the academics themselves and by a growing Royalist faction. A Covenanter delegation, which included the Earl of Montrose and Alexander Henderson, visited the city to try to persuade the town council and the academics to accept the Covenant. The doctors were not won over, asserting that although the Covenant was not contrary to God's law, neither was episcopacy. They went further and declared that the people could not oppose their prince for religious or any other reasons. Hamilton seized upon this fairly moderate stance and claimed that it constituted support for the king's position. Some historians have also claimed that Aberdeen refused to send delegates to the Tables, and that the Tables in turn ignored Aberdeen, primarily because of the city's stance but also because the Tables were unable to do anything about it. This view would appear to justify Hamilton's interpretation of what Aberdeen was doing. However, it is not accurate. Aberdeen's omission from the deliberations at Stirling in the spring and early summer of 1638 was apparently accidental rather than deliberate.[17] Hamilton had misread the situation. The Aberdeen doctors and the town council did not have the political inclination, will or power to mount a thoroughly oppositionist stance. Even so, much more was made of Aberdeen's position than the doctors had intended. The Royalists hijacked their rejection of both the Covenant and opposition to the monarch as a political justification of their position. Furthermore, Hamilton was inspired as a result to propose a new Covenant – the King's Covenant. This combined the Negative Confession with a bond of 1589 enjoining people to support their monarch against internal enemies. That bond had been specifically aimed at Catholic plots in the wake of Queen Mary's execution by Queen Elizabeth of England. Hamilton now aimed to use it to split the covenanting movement, and for a while it caused consternation. Moderate Covenanters felt able to sign it without contravening their bond with the National Covenant. Before the Assembly met, some 28,000 people had subscribed to the King's Covenant, but these signatures represented particularist support and came from areas where there was active opposition to the National Covenant, such as in the territory of the Gordons in Aberdeenshire, where Lord Huntly pressed its acceptance, and in the areas around the seats of the king's councillors.[18] In general Hamilton failed; and the effectiveness of his device was entirely swept away when he attempted to get the Council to endorse episcopacy. This pressure induced Lord Advocate Hope, who had been examining the legality of episcopacy, into publishing his judgement that it was illegal and contravened the 1581 Negative Confession. Covenanter leaders were thus able to claim that the King's Covenant and the National Covenant were compatible because both abjured episcopacy.

In the wake of Hope's judgement, the General Assembly completed the rout of Hamilton's policy. Hamilton had hoped to capitalize on the welcome Glasgow had shown for the King's Covenant and upon his own patronage, as his estates were in the vicinity. However, the city showed that it was not in the thrall of any noble faction, and Hamilton's mother, the dowager Countess Anne Cunningham, negated any influence her son had in the region. She also threatened to shoot her son if need be. A formidable Covenanter, it was she, moreover, who controlled the Hamilton estates, and she manipulated the political support from their dependants, not her son.

The General Assembly proved beyond Hamilton's control. It was composed of representatives from the whole country; according to the 1597 Act each presbytery sent three ministers and one baron or gentleman, and each of the royal burghs sent a commissioner. Arguments developed over who constituted an 'elder' and whether he should be a minister or a lay representative. In the end each presbytery sent two ministers and an elder, who was generally a lay Covenanter. These elders numbered seventeen peers, nine knights and twenty-five lairds, to which were added forty-seven burgh representatives and 142 ministers.[19] The Covenanters controlled the elections, non-Covenanter ministers having been effectively debarred and sympathetic elders chosen from their presbyteries, while the bishops dared not enter the assembly. Hamilton was at sea, and even though there was an opposition group present which suggested imposing some form of limitations on the bishops rather than abolishing the episcopacy outright, it had little influence. The group had some justification for its position. A whole generation had matured in a church system in which James VI's revamped episcopacy had played a part; and the notion of a complete church revolution had not yet been widely instilled.[20] This debate was soon ended when Johnston of Wariston produced the old registers of the assembly which contained the act condemning bishops. Hamilton, realizing that the episcopacy was doomed, tried to close the assembly, but the moderator refused to end the session. Hamilton made for the door, hoping perhaps that the departure of the king's representative would be recognized as symbolizing the end of the session. Unfortunately for him, a combination of high drama and farce ensued. Fearing just such a ploy, someone had had the foresight to lock the door and hide the key. Hamilton thus blundered into the fastened door and had to wait, humiliated and frustrated, while the key was produced. His eventual exit did not produce any of its hoped-for effect: the five articles, the prayerbook liturgy, the Court of High Commission, the canons and the bishops themselves were swept away.

Still, Hamilton was not yet finished, and he was playing a double game, for his master the king was beginning to exhibit the duplicity which was to dog his diplomatic and political behaviour over the next eleven years. As Hamilton talked to the Covenanters, he was also assessing the potential support in Scotland for a war against them. Along with Hamilton and Nithsdale, a small coterie of English councillors was involved in this project, which at its grandest planned attacks on Scotland from Ireland, England and the sea. Charles himself was in favour of a limited offensive war, believing that the Covenanters would not invade England, as they could not then claim to be acting to defend their church. His principal aim was to capture Edinburgh and, by so doing, to deal a body blow to the Covenanters. Accordingly, Sir Jacob Astley spent much of the summer in Holland buying arms.[21] However, the Covenanters too realized that war was likely, and by the time the Glasgow assembly met, they were already planning their own response.

IRELAND AND THE COVENANT

As the conflict in Scotland sharpened, the repercussions were beginning to be felt throughout the four nations. In Ireland, Lord Deputy Wentworth began to limit possibilities of a political or religious consciousness amongst Presbyterian colonists by force. The cultural and physical links between the Presbyterians of Ulster and Scotland were well known. The Kirk acted as a sort of mother church, and Scotland had provided a refuge for those fleeing Wentworth's enforcement of Anglicanism or Arminianism on the Church of Ireland referred to in Chapter 1. Wentworth's principal strategy was to impose oaths abjuring the Covenant. This approach could be seen as a logical extension of his religious policy; and indeed its effect was to drive Scots back to Scotland of their own volition or by force if they refused the oath. Although this outcome served Wentworth's purpose, landlords in Ulster were unhappy at having deserted tenancies on the eve of harvest. Moreover, rents were late and the refugees took their cattle and other livestock with them. Desertions, which some landlords described as involving 'great numbers', contributed further to the dramatic economic consequences of the war as land values fell, in some places by 50 per cent.[22] The continuing effects of this exodus were seen in the following years; the harsh conditions in spring which followed the abandonment of crops the previous harvest were compounded by the stationing of yet more troops, this time in readiness for Wentworth's planned invasion of Scotland as part of the more complex attempt to exact revenge on the Covenanters.

The oath imposed by Wentworth, known to its opponents as the Black Oath, was first introduced in early 1639 and prompted riots in Ulster – one at a graveside in Killinchy in County Down when the rector was pushed away by an armed crowd of men and women.[23] Almost immediately, enforcement became much more difficult after the Pacification of Berwick in June removed the impetus for dividing the Scots. The consequences of not swearing the oath were dramatic, and prerogative court proceedings were brought against refusers from the summer of 1639. Among them were Henry and Mary Stewart, who were brought before the Court of Castle Chamber in September 1639. Henry Stewart declared that the Covenant was a loyal instrument, which suggests that he was aware of its origins in the 1581 Negative Confession and even knew that the king had introduced his own version, which was now considered compatible with the National Covenant. Neither Henry nor Margaret had sworn the Covenant, but neither would they abjure it. Their argument was logical: if it was not disloyal, then there was no need to swear an oath to that effect. It is also probable that the couple rejected oath swearing in general, which may have influenced them with regard to the Covenant. To the Attorney General, their refusal was of more sinister origin, and he used their trial to make a statement attacking the ascendancy theory of power:

> The Court having observed that all recent rebellions have arisen from the fact that people thought that authority was derived from the people to the king, thought fit unanimously to declare that the authority of the king is not derived from the people, nor assumed by kings, but immediately given them by God.[24]

This judgement effectively converted the case from one of refusing an oath to one of rebellion, and the couple were sentenced accordingly. Henry and Margaret were each fined £3,000 and imprisoned for life.

Wentworth was also involved in the strategic planning for the war. Randall MacDonnell, Earl of Antrim, offered to raise an army composed of MacDonnells in Ulster and the MacDonalds of the Highlands. Charles accepted, partly because Antrim had suggested that he would call out his clan, which would serve him personally at no cost to the state; but Wentworth objected on the grounds that the MacDonnells were Catholics. Employing a Catholic army against Protestant Scotland would only incense Protestants in all four nations, and in any case Wentworth did not believe that Antrim could raise, or lead, an effective force. As historians have pointed out, Antrim's aims were at least as much related to the long-standing conflict between the Clan Campbell and the Clan Donald as they were to the rift between the king and the Covenanters.[25] The hope of many of the Clan Donnell appeared to be that they would regain lands lost to the Campbells during the previous forty years. Wentworth, recognizing this potential conflict of interest too, wished Irish involvement to be in the form of an army of Protestants assembled by himself. Apparently trusting the king only within defined limits, Wentworth arranged for the Irish army to be armed through independent arrangements with Dutch arms manufacturers, thus preventing the king from diverting funds from it. Moreover, much of the Deputy's advice on the coming war went unheeded, as he himself had feared. Dumbarton, which Wentworth had urged Charles to seize, fell to the Covenanters; and Lord Clifford, a local magnate sent to garrison Carlisle with troops from Ireland, was replaced by a complete stranger to the area, a son of the courtier Arundel.

THE REACTIONS IN ENGLAND

According to some historians, this was a period of peace. Fissel observes, for instance: 'The Personal Rule had not been popular, but it had worked: England was governed peacefully enough for a decade'.[26] At the end of his study of the personal rule, Kevin Sharpe argues that 'though there were financial complaints about, provincial discontent with, legal and constitutional doubts about, and religious objections to the personal rule', they did not form such an issue that they drove political events in England.[27] In fact England has been seen as being in 'working order' at this time, and a range of examples from the ruling elites reinforces this view. But the peace and quiet of the Earl of Salisbury cataloguing his pictures would be very different from the experiences of William Reeves, husbandman of Balderton, Nottinghamshire, or of Thomas Walker, constable of Elston in the same county – both hauled up before the justices of the county for not paying their ship money. And they were not alone.

At the Nottinghamshire quarter sessions of 1638, twenty-six people were taken to court over non-payment of taxes. Only five of these cases related to local lewns – taxes levied to support local government officers such as the constable. The following year no fewer than forty people appeared charged with default of taxation, and only two cases involved local levies. Most of the cases before the courts at this time would have related to ship money and, after 1639, coat and conduct money defaulters would be presented, too. Even though during 1640 there was a fall in the number of prosecutions, the following year saw a dramatic rise. In 1641, seventy-two people were charged with non-payment of levies. The backlog of pending cases ensured that sixty-four more appeared in 1642, after ship money and coat and conduct money had been swept away. This was an unusual occurrence; cases of default did not usually take up court time. In previous years the one or two cases in the county had been dealt with at privy sessions and had involved technical disputes over eligibility rather than principled objections. Even in years of harvest problems, defaults on taxes were at a much lower level than that experienced from 1638 to 1642. Yet there was a change after 1628, when the Forced Loan caused opposition throughout the Midlands. After that there were only two years, 1635 and 1636, when no defaulters were presented to the Nottinghamshire bench. If there was now a concerted effort to try these cases in court, perhaps it was the result of a recognition amongst the governing classes that these objectors were making principled objections.

Individuals were not the only sources of problems; the sheriffs had headaches in several counties where borough or other liberties claimed exemption. In Staffordshire problems arose in 1635. When the borough of Lichfield attempted to assess the cathedral close, the inhabitants objected, claiming that they were not part of the town. It was a dispute that dragged on until 1637, when the then High Sheriff asked the Privy Council to confirm his power to tax the borough and the close.[28] In Nottinghamshire there was a long-running dispute between the town of Newark and the county as represented by the sheriff. In 1637 the Council threatened the mayor of Newark with a summons if the borough did not pay £70 in arrears. In May 1639 the town used the device of a petition to claim that it could not afford to pay because of 'dullness of trade' and the absence of gentry and 'able men'. The Council refused to take much notice of their suggestions and reminded Sheriff Chaworth that the town still owed £11 from 1637.[29] Some historians have seized on such complaints about eligibility expressed by individuals and by boroughs in particular. Russell supports this charging that most attacks on the ship taxation were technical and dealt with eligibility rather than with the central issues, namely, taxation by consent and level of assessments. This argument is not without its strengths, although it ignores the possibility that complaints phrased in such a way may have been a strategy to cover other dissatisfactions and may also have been a more effective method of proceeding. Whatever the individual arguments expressed by each defaulter, their sheer numbers were to have repercussions; the increased opposition to the combined levies of ship money and coat and conduct money began to freeze local government. In May 1639, as the build-up for war reached its height, Lord Chaworth, the High Sheriff of Nottinghamshire, told the Council that Newark refused to pay its part of the levy and that the gentry were shutting their gates and taunting him to come and get distraint if he could. The High Sheriff of neighbouring Leicestershire had to use his own servants to collect the taxes during the same month, because the regular officials were not able to get refusers to pay. By September, the Privy Council was forced to recognize that the crisis in Staffordshire had caused the normal systems of government to break down. Co-operation between each of the elements of local government had failed. The Council instructed the sheriff to collect the money himself and not to rely on minor officials.[30] The problem of default of pay continued throughout the year; the constable at St Breock in Cornwall had to collect a warrant from his superiors against coat and conduct defaulters as late as October 1639.[31] The preparations for the war caused the sheriffs to pause in their tax gathering, and priorities were rearranged on the hoof. When constables in Denbighshire began to use ship money to pay coat and conduct levies, the sheriff was unable to stop them.[32]

A great debate has arisen over the situation in England in the years of the Scottish crisis and the bishops' wars. At the centre of the controversy is the nature, and indeed the very existence, of opposition in England. Of course, any notion of an organized political party in opposition is untenable, but this is not the only form which opposition can take, nor is such opposition necessarily a symptom of a genuine challenge to government. We must also be aware of the limitations of any notions about republicanism, although it is perhaps a little misleading to suggest that everyone was a monarchist in the seventeenth century. Alternative systems of government existed outside Britain and Ireland and no doubt had their admirers within. Nevertheless, the politics of opposition at various levels was carried out within the framework of a monarchy, in much the same way that it is now carried out within the framework of democracy. Political factions wanted to achieve change within the system rather than to overturn the system itself. They wanted to change personnel and policy at the court level of church and state, and to change secular and religious policies at lower levels as they affected people on a daily basis.

PREPARING FOR WAR

While there were initial problems for both sides as they mobilized for war, the Covenanters had the easier task. Behind their cause was a manifesto with the registered support of large swathes of the population, whereas in England and Wales there was no such thing. The king was trying to galvanize a population behind a largely unexplained policy, at a time when his government was becoming increasingly unpopular because of its fiscal policy. Moreover, popular hostility to the war was a distinct possibility. Impositions of further taxation, in the form of coat and conduct money to cover the initial costs of mobilization, came on top of higher ship money demands. Sections of the trained bands were also not likely to welcome the war openly – for a number of reasons. First, they were generally regarded as county defence forces not to be involved in an international war except in case of invasion, and second, the soldiers who belonged to them may well have been faced with the same financial burdens imposed on their fellow citizens, and would not be entirely well disposed to the king. The trained bands were composed of people drawn from groups who would pay taxes. The Suffolk pikemen whose occupations are known were clothiers, while the Gloucestershire trained bandsmen were overwhelmingly husbandmen or yeomen. They had trades, businesses and livelihoods to protect.[33] A high proportion of them were likely to be literate, and all would be capable of forming their own political and religious views. They were not simply an unthinking body to be used to enforce policies blindly. Moreover, the Covenanters had spent several months communicating with prominent figures in England such as Lord Saye and Sele and disseminating information about their cause. Some of this information undoubtedly filtered through to other ranks in society through trading networks and other forms of social intercourse, although there is little direct evidence to confirm this. At Mrs Cromwell's lodgings in Shire Lane, London, a discussion between Reverend Swadling, Mrs Grace Southcott, Dr Edward May and a Scottish Captain Nappier turned to the abolition of the Scottish episcopacy and the possibility of an intra-national religious and political purge.[34] Certainly, the preparations for war were being felt in England. And in some places they were clearly being resisted. In early January the Privy Council ordered muster defaulters from Leicestershire to be brought to London if they failed to satisfy the joint lords lieutenant (the Earl of Huntingdon and his son, Lord Hastings). The Staffordshire defaulters were brought before the Epiphany quarter sessions by the county's lieutenant, and their names were sent to the Council on 2 February 1639. In May the same men were ordered to appear in person. Besides the resistance of the soldiery, other problems beset the lords lieutenant. In neighbouring Nottinghamshire there were problems over the weaponry; the muskets, weighing in at 18 to 20 pounds each, were too heavy to be used. In Derbyshire the weather was too horrible to permit a muster, a situation that was to be repeated across the country that year.[35] The remaining sources emanating from the localities leave few indications of the burden as it was experienced first-hand, there being very few parish or constable accounts that survive with sufficient detail. However, some examples do give indications of the costs. Given that these sources display remarkable consistency in aspects discussed later, even this small sample may be seen as representative. In the county at the farthest point from the Scottish border, the constable of St Breock in Cornwall made the seven-mile journey to St Columb on 7 May to receive details of the 'conduit rate'. Musters were held there on 19 June.[36] The expenditure involved could be quite high. At Carleton Rode in south Norfolk, Constables John Nixon and Thomas Nuby oversaw the charges for the military preparations, which included conduct money, clothing for the four soldiers, knapsacks for three of them and shipping armour from Old Buckenham. The ensuing muster and training involved even more expense as the village paid for copies of the king's military oath, powder and match, and repairs to bandoliers and muskets. In all, out of a recorded annual expenditure of £23-4s-5d, no less than £9-3s-11d went on the military expenditure.[37] At Worcester it cost £71-3s-4d – collected in the form of four single levies rated at one-fifteenth of income – to equip fourteen soldiers for the war in May 1645. In the previous September the corporation had had to arm itself as a company of foot with the aldermen (the twenty-four) armed as pikemen and the common hall (the forty-eight) as musketeers in readiness for war.[38]

In Scotland, military preparations backed the propaganda effort and individual Scots, including Hamilton's mother, began to stockpile arms. The Tables began to construct an effective relationship with the localities. Committees of war were set up in the shires to raise forces and exact levies to obtain the resources necessary to equip and pay the soldiers. These committees, which were essentially secular, comprised four gentlemen representatives from each presbytery. The convener of each committee communicated directly with the Tables, and two members of each county committee – except for Sutherland, Caithness and Orkney, which elected a commissioner on a rotation basis instead – were in Edinburgh in three-month shifts. The presbytery committees carried the main burden. These were also secular, and although their geographical structure was the same, they were composed of prominent gentry from each constituent parish and were distinct from the presbytery church court or synod. Nevertheless, the religious functionaries were not excluded from decision making. Parish representatives or commissioners worked with the minister to assess taxation, levy soldiers and periodically examine the consciences of the parishioners. The burghs were run by their own councils as normal but sent a commissioner to the shire committee. Essentially, this system, devised by the assembly in November 1639 and put into effect by the Tables under the guidance of the Earl of Argyll (now a Covenanter and free of his father's opposition), was to serve Scotland for the next decade.[39] Forces were to be levied in each parish and rents assessed to provide estimates of funding, whilst a 200,000-merk loan (c.£11,000 sterling) was to provide immediate funding. Money to the value of £293,650 Scots (c.£21,970 sterling) was minted.[40] Small-scale loans filled coffers as parish valuations designed to force costs onto local communities were not completed that year. On the other hand, parish troop levies remained a parish charge during 1639, sparing pressure on the central treasury.

Even as Hamilton tried to manage the assembly, musters of the English trained bands were held. At the end of the year, Sir Jacob Astley had mustered the forces of Staffordshire, Derbyshire, Nottinghamshire, Leicestershire, Rutland, Lincolnshire, Northumberland and the West Riding of Yorkshire, as well as the towns of Hull and Newcastle.[41] By the new year the English nobility received orders to attend the king at York on 1 April. In England the machinery

of local government with responsibility for the militia, the lieutenancy, ground into action. As it began to stir, the lesser organs of
government – the constabulary still with the albatross of ship money
about its neck – received instruction for assembling the trained bands
and assessing and collecting coat and conduct money to provide
initial funding for the expeditionary force. Forces from the English
West Midlands and Wales were ordered to rendezvous during April
at Selby, from where they would move northwards to join the king
at York.[42] Hamilton himself raised a force in East Anglia for the
seaborne descent on the Scottish coast, only a minority of whom
were experienced soldiers. Jacob Astley surveyed the defences on the
borders and established himself at York, overseeing the restructuring
of local trained band regiments and the construction of armouries
at Newcastle upon Tyne and Hull.[43] The strategically important
towns of Berwick upon Tweed and Carlisle were only slowly supplied with men and materials, despite dire warnings from both
Hamilton and Wentworth, who planned to use Carlisle as a landing
point for his army. Leaving these towns relatively unprotected made
poor strategic sense, but Charles may have expected to seize bases
in Scotland, although no firm plans for such an operation were
made. Instead the Covenanter forces seized and occupied Dumbarton, Aberdeen and Edinburgh, thus denying the king either a
landing site or any other foothold in Scotland. By March 1639 the
Covenanters were rumoured to be about to capture Berwick, and
Astley moved north in response. Both Berwick and Carlisle were
occupied simultaneously with help from troops landed from Ireland.

WAR

The king's strategic options had received a blow, and new plans now
had to be made in more limited circumstances. A variety of options
still remained open to him. A strike northwards from Northumberland that could be co-ordinated with an attack launched from Hamilton's fleet was one. Another was a defensive war, which Charles
found more attractive because of the propaganda value of having the
Scots attack him. Wentworth, on the other hand, advised waiting for
adequate funds to arrive to support a greater effort, but the king was
impatient to restore his tarnished honour and preferred not to wait.
Accordingly, Charles left York and went north. During May the
army was on the move too, straddling the roads north from York and

arriving piecemeal at Newcastle and the borders. Already cracks were beginning to appear in the king's armed display. Prominent nobles began arguing with the king over the war. Lord Saye and Sele and Lord Brooke, who had both been in touch with the Covenanters, had already refused to supply arms as requested and at York publicly objected to their summons thither and to the war itself. They both refused to take the military oath drawn up in support of the king. This was a serious problem. Saye and Brooke pointed out that they could not be compelled to serve abroad and that if there really was a danger of invasion, Parliament should have been summoned to help the king defend the country. It was an attack not just on the immediate situation but on the whole previous decade. The two lords were only at the forefront of criticism that could be heard coming from a cross-section of English and Welsh society. In Ashby Magna, Leicestershire, the reading of the king's proclamation on the war prompted heated arguments about the nature of the war. John Oneby, a lawyer, argued that the wars were priests' wars caused because the Scots rejected the prayerbook and bishops and that they would lead to rebellion. Although he later denied it, some witnesses were convinced that he blamed the English bishops for the problem, claiming that they were meddling in matters of state in which they should have no part. William Sherrat of Newport, Shropshire, was alleged to have said much the same thing in an oral attack on the bishops and church government at about the same time.[44] Such arguments gave the Covenanters the proof they needed that England was not united behind its king and partly explain the failure of the English and Welsh nations to rally behind the king.

The king's troubles continued to grow, and in the royal army encamped west of Berwick at the end of May 1639 the generals began to debate the security of their position. They felt vulnerable being so close to the border, especially as their forces had been weakened when Hamilton was given the East Anglian forces. These valuable regiments could not be used for their original purpose because the coastal attack had been called off. In Scotland, however, the promise of such an attack had inspired local Royalists under the Earl of Huntly to oppose the Aberdeenshire war committee in May 1639. A rebellion broke out, and Royalists captured Aberdeen in June and opened it to a Royalist landing. This challenge came to an end when Huntly's son Lord Aboyne was defeated by the Earl of Montrose and a Covenanter army at the Bridge of Dee on 19 June.[45]

Depending on a poor intelligence network, the English generals
did not know much about the Covenanter army under veteran general Alexander Leslie, except that it was rumoured to be large and
moving closer to them. Many felt the king to be in imminent danger. In contrast to the reputation of the Covenanter force, the English and Welsh army of 15,000 was disparaged by its own side as
being ill fed, uncommitted to the cause and badly trained. It was
certainly armed with antiquated weapons, some of which – like the
outdated firearm, the caliver – had recently been withdrawn from
use in the trained bands. Owing to a lack of financial resources,
bows and arrows had been sent north too. Even though these were
no longer used by English forces, Scots troops in Europe had used
them and they were still used in Ireland. On top of these difficulties,
an outbreak of smallpox occurred and took a heavy toll in several
regiments gathered on the border.

In spite of a few minor border clashes, serious fighting did not
break out at this stage, largely because neither side was ready. The
Scots were unsure of their army's preparedness and of their legal
position, while the English, as we have seen, were experiencing
logistical difficulties. When military manoeuvres finally began, the
English were humiliated in the only situation that could have led to
a major engagement. This brief confrontation in turn served to propel
a move toward a peace settlement. On 4 June 1639 a force of about
four thousand English soldiers under the Earl of Holland moved
into Scotland in the vicinity of Kelso. Holland was reacting to a
rumour that Leslie was moving southwards in the king's direction
and drove on with the cavalry in the hot weather, leaving the weary
footsoldiers lagging miles behind. He ran into a small Covenanter
force at Kelso, but as he prepared to attack, the Scottish army
appeared to grow in size, cavalry appeared on its flanks and the
ranks of pikemen seemed to multiply as more and more colours
appeared on the field. Observers agreed that Holland was heavily
outnumbered; estimates of the Covenanters run as high as fifteen
thousand. There are a number of plausible reasons to suggest that
such numbers are probably an overestimate and that Leslie actually
had only about five to six thousand men, drawn up carefully in
narrow frontages and interspersed with herds of cattle to create the
impression of a much larger army. In any case Holland and the
English cavalry retreated, carrying with them in their hurried flight
wild and worrying estimates of the size of the Covenanter forces.[46]
The nerves of the English commanders were almost shattered as

estimates of the Covenanters' total forces reached as high as forty-five thousand. In fact, it is probable that the Scots' total force may only have been a third of that; one estimate is that Leslie commanded at most twenty thousand men.[47]

The Scots followed their bizarre 'victory' with proposals for discussions, partly because they realized the legal weaknesses of their position. By raising the army, they were in effect in rebellion against a legally constituted power, a position which they did not really want to be in. Hamilton had analysed the nature of the Covenanting movement fairly successfully over the past year. He had tried to get the king to relax his stance, warning him that by refusing to countenance the Covenant, he was forcing the Covenanters into an ever more radical stance. He had also suggested to Charles that a war against Scotland could open up divisions in the other three nations, and this was plainly happening.[48] However, the king still refused to accept such an analysis. The English forces were growing, and supplies were reaching them by June. Certain English commentators like Sir Edmund Verney, having earlier believed in the strength of the Scottish forces, now began to believe that the English army was superior to, and possibly even larger than, Leslie's army. This growing confidence was never put to the test in 1639, but it was to play an important role in the attitude of the king and some advisers into the following year, when a belief that 'one more push' would have won the war was adopted. During the summer of 1639 the problem of dissent continued to plague the English, and the Earl of Bristol suggested the calling of a Parliament. Although Charles refused to consider this, he did realize the general weakness of his position. Discussions between the two sides therefore began on 11 June, albeit in bad grace and with only temporary expedients in the king's mind. Charles was quick to prevent the Scots from exploiting differences between him and some of the English nobility. The Covenanter leaders, hoping that a major proportion of the English aristocracy accompanying the king would intercede on their behalf, sought face-to-face negotiations with representatives of the nobles with this end in mind. To their surprise, however, the king attended the discussions personally and accused the Covenanters of being wholly in the wrong, asserting his belief that he should be obeyed in all his commands. The Covenanters seem to have been taken off guard by the king's mien; and the more conciliatory ones were perhaps genuinely shocked when Archibald Johnston astutely countered by accusing the king of 'playing for time'. The king was certainly offended. Charles was touchy about such directness, especially when it was so accurately aimed. Other Covenanters may have been fooled, or else beguiled by their own fears for the legality of their stance into trusting the king's word and believing that the Covenant and Kirk were safe.[49]

The peace negotiated near Berwick was vaguely worded in order to secure a rapid cessation of hostilities, which both sides earnestly desired. The Covenanters were uncertain of their own strength and had displayed some weakness of purpose in their confrontation with the king. For his part, the king wanted an immediate end to the fighting so that he could develop a position of military strength from which to crush the Covenanters. On 19 June the Pacification of Berwick was concluded. The armies were to disband, and a Scottish Parliament was to meet in the autumn with Charles in attendance. But the facade soon crumbled. Charles made it abundantly clear that the acts of what he called the 'pretended Assembly' of Glasgow were to be annulled by a new assembly, in which the Scottish bishops were to sit. This action was flying in the face of political and religious possibility. There were now no bishops in Scotland. By way of example, the synod of Argyll was already referring to Neil Campbell as the 'sometime pretended Bishop of the Isles'; and Campbell himself readily and publicly acknowledged his fault in abandoning the true path of the Kirk.[50] The reaction in Scotland to Charles's demands was quite predictable. On 1 July there were riots in Edinburgh. Traquair, who had been given the task of announcing the calling of a new General Assembly, was saved from the anger of the mob only by the timely intervention of some Covenanter gentlemen. Shaken, he hurried back to the king with a new plan in mind. His suggestion was that by not summoning the bishops to the assembly or the Parliament, Charles could both quell the riots now and use the absence of the clergy later as an excuse for annulling the acts of what would be improperly constituted bodies.[51]

In this fractious spirit, the relationship between the two nations entered its next phase. In England, the peace signed at Berwick was a cover for the king's renewed preparation for war. He summoned Wentworth from Ireland to assist in these plans. In Scotland he displayed outward compliance with the Covenanters' requests at the peace treaty. The new General Assembly opened on 12 August and reinforced the acts of its predecessor. The former Bishop of Orkney, like the Bishop of the Isles, repented his part in the episcopacy and repudiated his former office. Traquair mounted a rearguard action, but he was overwhelmed and forced to accept the assembly's acts on behalf of the king. The Scottish Parliament, the Estates of nobility, clergy and burghers, met on 31 August. At that time, the Scottish Parliament, or more properly the Estates, was a very different assembly from its Westminster counterpart. One of its most important constituent parts was the steering committee known as the Lords of the Articles, which produced and directed the bills coming before the unicameral assembly. As the intermediary between the king and Council and the Estates, the Lords basically drew up the bills and presented them to Parliament, which then simply voted on them without debate. The Lords of the Articles also acted with the authority of the Estates as a whole during the long adjournments that marked the sessions of Parliaments. This committee, control of which was therefore crucial to the management of the House, was usually chosen by nobles and clergy. In the days of the resurrected episcopacy, the monarchs relied on the clergy to choose amenable men from each of the Estates. In 1639 selection fell to the nobles alone because of Traquair's now defeated plan. Archibald Campbell, Earl of Argyll, persuaded them to select Covenanters from each Estate as many of the committees of war in the shire had demanded. For the future, he arranged for each Estate to choose its own nominees, confident that even if the nobility split over the Covenant, the other Estates were more likely to be dominated by Covenanters.[52] With its executive structures effectively controlled in this manner by Covenanters, the Estates confirmed the acts of the recent assembly. For seven weeks of closed sessions, the Lords of the Articles marshalled the petitions and demands for religious security and political change. The committee also began to work towards strengthening the position of the Parliament in government, and increasing the participation of the whole body, by placing limits on its own actions. The demands for radical reform or political revolution were not unanimously supported, and Traquair continued to try to exploit divisions by making stands on issues which increased the democratic elements of the Parliament at the expense of the king. Nevertheless, by the end of the seven weeks of debate he had not managed to destroy the basic unity of the Covenanters.[53] Charles began to show his hand and refused to ratify the decisions of the Lords of the Articles while Traquair delayed the sitting of the Estates. On the king's orders, the session was prorogued on 14 November until 2 June 1640. This decision was given a hostile reception, and although the Parliament acceded, it did so angrily declaring the order to be illegal and appointed a committee to continue to sit at Parliament House while the Estates remonstrated with the king. Charles had taken the decision in London to prorogue the Estates with the assistance of a new Scottish Affairs committee of eight privy councillors instigated by Wentworth, who had arrived in September. Only one Scot, Hamilton, sat on the committee. Charles reasoned that by 2 June in the following year, military defeat would make the Scottish Estates far more tractable. It is time now to turn to the consequences of this fundamental misreading of the situation.

3

Parliaments in Opposition

the beginning of that unhappy and rebellious Parliament, which was
the cause of all the ruins and misfortunes that afterwards befell this
kingdom[1]

THE CALLING OF THE SHORT PARLIAMENT

In the English camp the belief that the war of 1639 could have been
won with just one more push grew. The king himself was intent on
continuing his campaign against the Covenanters, and war preparations continued throughout the winter of 1639–40 as the Scots
changed the fundamental relationships within government. One of
the problems Charles faced was lack of money. The preparations for
war in the previous year had exhausted the treasury, and there was
growing evidence that the English taxpayers were beginning to oppose continued levies. A possible solution to the problem was beginning to appear in an unexpected form. Several of the king's supporters
argued that an English Parliament could serve a dual purpose; it
could provide the necessary money and give legitimacy to the war
and the taxation policies of the king. The basis of the king's decision
to call an English Parliament in 1640 was the advice of Sir Thomas
Wentworth, Lord Deputy of Ireland, who had joined Charles in
September 1639 and had become part of an inner council consisting of Laud, Hamilton and the Earl of Northumberland. He was at
the apogee of his power. Before leaving Ireland Wentworth had attacked the opposition to his position as part of his drive to improve
the government of Ireland, perhaps best interpreted as an attempt
to make that kingdom profitable for the crown, rather than a drain
on it.

The Chancellor of Ireland, Viscount Loftus, represented the class
of politician that had dominated the government of Ireland before

Wentworth's arrival. By 1638 he had already fallen into disfavour, compounded by his treatment of a farmer during a legal case begun in 1637, in which Loftus behaved unjustly. After trying to suppress the farmer's petitions to Wentworth, Loftus was called upon to explain himself before the Council, where he shouted and blustered his defence. As a result he was sequestered from the Privy Council and forbidden to exercise his chancellorial powers.[2] By the time of Wentworth's visit to England, Loftus's case had been reviewed and Wentworth's actions against him vindicated. The Lord Deputy himself was elevated both in social and political status. His position in Ireland was consolidated when he was created Lord Lieutenant with the right to appoint a deputy of his own, and at new year 1640 he was created Earl of Strafford.

Strafford's desire for the calling of a Parliament in England was closely linked with his position in Ireland. The Dublin Parliament of 1634 had been a successful one for the Lord Lieutenant. Wentworth had also met with some success in managing the Irish elections, and he was supported by an Upper House that was now dominated by Protestant lords rather than the Catholic aristocracy as before. As a result of astute political management, the Parliament had approved Wentworth's proposed financial measures.[3] This was the example he set before the king in late 1639 when he and the other councillors persuaded Charles that the ordinary and ancient way of a Parliament should be tried. The plan was for Wentworth to hold a session of the Irish Parliament before Easter 1640, when the English Parliament was to meet. The Irish Parliament would set a series of precedents for the English body. In addition, precedents from the 1634 Parliament would be employed: financial matters would be dealt with first before grievances were attended to. Moreover, the Irish Parliament's expected compliance in voting subsidies to the king would be a model for the English Parliament. Nevertheless, there was a third, more subtle, precedent that the Lord Lieutenant may have overlooked. An examination of the 1634 Parliament has shown that there was a strong possibility that political alliances between Wentworth's opponents on both sides of the religious divide could have, in different circumstances, blocked Wentworth's actions. Moreover, it appears that Wentworth was not always capable of understanding the grounds of opposition to his policies.[4] Regardless of these difficulties, and the complete failure of attempts to manage the Scottish assemblies and Parliaments in 1639, the new earl proceeded to apply what he perceived to be the lessons of experience to orchestrate both the Parliaments.

This position clearly caused great problems. The king saw Parliament as necessary to serve a specific purpose: the funding of a war against rebellion in Britain. However, as James VI and I had failed to establish a greater union, it could be argued that there was no such political entity as Britain. If this was the case, the king's war with Scotland was a foreign war, not a domestic one. And English Parliaments had developed a long tradition of debating the conduct of a foreign war.[5] Given the precedents of the 1620s, when Parliament had questioned the efficacy of the Duke of Buckingham's war effort, any assumptions about the compliance of Parliament seem somewhat naive.

In terms of funding, too, there were risks inherent in Strafford's policy. As soon as the new Parliament was announced in England, ship money payments began to tail off. Deputy lieutenants began to see developing opposition to coat and conduct money, necessary for the armed forces. Moreover, members of the trained bands were refusing to leave the boundaries of their own counties, using the provisions of the Petition of Right as justification.[6] It was widely expected that Parliament would take up all of these issues as grievances. Others, including Edward Nicholas, Clerk of the Privy Council, saw Parliament and ship money as incompatible. In other words, ship money was an extraordinary tax, not to be collected when there was a Parliament to set ordinary levies. It was, to some, a matter of surprise that ship money was obviously being continued when the warrant for the Parliament was sent out.[7] This policy served to sharpen the edge of the divisions which the non-parliamentary government of the 1630s had created in England and, to a lesser extent, in Wales. The result of this was a shift in the nature of parliamentary selection. At this period in history Parliaments constituted events rather than permanent features of the political process. English Parliaments were more about status than service; the principal point of being chosen was the kudos that accompanied the position. Furthermore, most members of Parliament gained their seats as a result of selection rather than actual elections, which could be regarded as exceptional and representing a breakdown of cohesion at the county government level.[8] Thus, if we accept these views – and we need not – Parliament was really the public face of the counties at large, a face untroubled by inner turmoil. However, a wide selection of evidence demonstrates that this vision of the selection process cannot be all-embracing. In many county seats – and probably in borough seats too – the electorate were not simply faced with a *fait accompli*; they could interfere in the process and upset this superficial harmony.[9] It is also clear that the first 1640 election forced a change of pace on the process of election or selection. Voters were able to detect which candidates were associated with Charles's government. In Leicestershire the political ascendancy of the Hastings family was seriously dented. The head of the family, the Earl of Huntingdon, was traditionally able to impose his candidates on the county and borough electorates. But this time the family failed two major hurdles: religious policy and political affiliation. The Hastings family had a strong tradition of Puritanism, but in the fifth earl and his second son Henry Hastings, one of his candidates, this had lapsed. Second, Huntingdon was the Lord Lieutenant of Leicestershire and Rutland, responsible for a host of non-parliamentary levies, including the distraint of knighthood over ten years earlier. He was also associated with ship money through his client, Sir Henry Skipworth, a vigorous collector of the levy while High Sheriff some five years before and now Huntingdon's second candidate. Most recently Huntingdon had been embroiled in coat and conduct money collection. As a result of these associations, the Hastings family's Puritan opponents, the Greys of Stamford and the Hesilriges of Noseley, triumphed.[10] The Leicestershire elections were not the only contentious polls. Popular verses extolled the virtues of those considered suitable because of their opposition to the government. In some places elections were accompanied by politically charged violence, not in itself unusual but unique in its intensity. The Scots Covenanters entered the fray with their pamphlet *Information from the Estates of the Kingdome of Scotland to the Kingdome of England*, which argued their case for the war against the king. The king responded with his own justification of his position and had the Scots' work publicly destroyed, but the damage was done.

THE IRISH PARLIAMENT

Across the Irish Sea Strafford's plan seemed to be progressing well. The new Parliament met on 16 March 1640, after what seem to have been fairly uneventful elections managed in Strafford's absence by Sir George Radcliffe.[11] There was later to be a series of allegations about the interference of the executive in the elections, but the consequences of this were as yet unseen. Certainly, ten boroughs which had previously returned Catholic members were deprived of their representation. However, the attempt to return a Protestant majority may have been low key and achieved by compromise and muddle. Even so, the number of Catholic members fell from over one hundred in 1634 to only seventy-six in 1640. When Strafford returned to Ireland after a gout-ridden journey across England, Wales and the Irish Sea, the parliamentary session was two days old. The speaker compared him to Solomon and extolled the success and wisdom of his administration. This seeming apotheosis continued. Within a week the Parliament approved of four subsidies of £45,000 each for Charles I. The first would be collected from 1 June. Further, the willingness to conform led some to suggest that the king should continue to collect money through Parliament. A declaration drawn up by the MPs and sent as a preface to the financial acts did not go quite this far, but it did promise to raise more money to fight the Covenanters if necessary.

THE SHORT PARLIAMENT

So pleased and confident was Strafford that his stay in Ireland was brief. He returned to England in time for the meeting of the English Parliament, having prorogued the Dublin assembly to 1 June. He was not alone in his hopes of a compliant and awed English and Welsh assembly. 'God grant us grace here to follow this good example', wrote the Earl of Northumberland to the Earl of Leicester.[12] But England was a different place – and the contentious elections offered a different scenario. On 13 April, as the Parliament went into session, Charles addressed the House briefly and then left it to the Lord Keeper, John Lord Finch, to explain his purpose. In many ways Finch was not the man for this job. His previous Commons role, as Speaker during the 1629 session, had ended in him being held in his chair by Sir John Eliot and others while an angry Commons declared itself opposed to the king's religious innovations. Many of those listening to him on 13 April intended this new Parliament shortly to discuss those very events and their consequences. Finch stated that the king was faced by a 'tumult of disloyalty' and that Scotland was a 'distempered body'. He made comparisons with Ireland and described that state, formerly in a 'distemper', as now 'ordered' and having given acceptable 'testimonies', a reference to the subsidies and their accompanying declaration.[13] The king, Finch continued, wanted Parliament to 'lay aside all other business and hasten the payment' of subsidies to support his war effort. Finch then dropped what he hoped would be a political bombshell. He had possession of a secret letter, which he claimed contained evidence that the Scots wished to throw off Charles's rule and submit themselves to the French monarch. The letter was from the Earls of Marr and Montrose and Lords Rothes, Forrester, Montgomery and Loudoun and General Alexander Leslie to Louis XIII, asking if he would mediate between them and Charles I. The king tried to use it as evidence of Scottish treachery, suggesting that the letter's form of address, *Au Roy*, was used only by subjects to their king. Russell suggests that the letter, which was undated, was probably written before the Pacification of Berwick.[14] In any case it was flimsy evidence; and the Lords only came to discuss it belatedly because Charles gave it to Lord Cottington, who had not yet had his patent of nobility read in the House. In the Lower House, too, it was coldly received. On the first day of full business, the Secretary of State, Francis Windebank, first reminded the Commons of their primary task, the voting of supply, and then referred to the letter to Louis XIII, reading it aloud in French and English. However, the Commons paid little heed to it after Harbottle Grimston rose to his feet and pointed out that the trouble was that Scotland 'standeth at a distance', although he wished that it 'were further off yet'. There were, he argued, pressing issues nearer at hand, such as the attack on property and liberty as witnessed in England and Wales during recent years. Sir Benjamin Rudyard spoke to the effect that Parliament should be restored to its 'ancient lustre', while Sir Francis Seymour argued that grievances should be discussed first before subsidies were voted upon.[15] This set the tone of the House.

The following day, John Pym gave frame to these discussions and set what might be seen as an agenda for the House to follow. In his first major speech of the session, Pym defined three areas of problems: first, the liberties of Parliament; second, religion; and third, property. In effect these summed up what others had said before, but Pym put them succinctly and in a manner which could guide future business. The first issue concerned what had happened in 1629 and how this affected the future position of Parliament. He argued that the courts which dealt with the members involved in holding down Speaker Finch in 1629 had had no right to do so because Parliament was the supreme court in the land. Moreover, the dissolution of 1629 was a punishment inflicted on the House akin to putting to death a good subject. On the issue of religion Pym identified a series of points. People of the 'popish religion' were being encouraged and laws against them were being suspended or not put into effect. Significantly, all of this was apparently leading towards 'a conversion to Rome'. This was being effected by various means; the numerous popish books in print, the 'discouragement' of the best 'professors of our religion', the (re)innovations in church such as genuflecting at Jesus's name, and the increasing power of the bishops. On the third issue, property, the collection of illegal or unusual levies such as tunnage and poundage without consultation, together with the use of courts such as the Star Chamber, was interfering with the liberties of the people of England and Wales. The following day these grievances were discussed. This was far from the House that the king required; instead it had set its own agenda and was now working on it.

By 24 April the king was so angry at the Commons' proceeding that he intervened personally in the Lords. There he briefly answered Pym's three points but went on to suggest that the Commons were on a 'preposterous course' and urged the Lords to pull them off it. At a joint conference the next day representatives of the Lords put this idea to the Commons. All they accomplished was to inflame the sensibilities of the Commons, who suspended their discussions on grievances to turn to this new breach of privilege, the interference of the Lords in their business.[16] By 2 May the king's patience was wearing thin, and he again demanded that the Commons turn to supply issues. Instead they requested time to bring their discussions to an end. Two days later Charles made an offer. If the Commons voted four subsidies immediately, as the Irish Parliament had, he would stop ship money collections. As the Commons considered this proposal, two strands of thought developed in the ensuing debate. One was that coat and conduct was a heavier burden than ship money and that it should be abolished too; the other was that as ship money was probably illegal, and certainly not to be regarded as an ordinary tax, offering to abolish it when it should not be there at all was a poor bargain. On 5 May Charles, angry at the further delays, dissolved the House. Some MPs were thrown into despondency. Sir Edward Hyde later recalled that he was made miserable by the apparent loss of the chance to negotiate with the king on the major grievances that affected the country. Others, including Oliver St John, saw it as a golden opportunity: the issues at stake would not go away and the pressure for changing the state of affairs, both amongst the political classes and in the country as a whole, would only increase.[17]

DISORDER IN ENGLAND ON THE EVE OF WAR

The dissolution of Parliament excited rather than depressed opposition to taxation and the preparations for a new war. The sheriff of Derbyshire, John Agard, wrote to the Council on 11 May, only six days after the dissolution. He informed the members that there was a 'great disaffectedness' because of the closing of Parliament and that as a result, people were challenging his right to 'distrain at [his] peril'. In neighbouring Staffordshire constables were being attacked, and goods they had taken as distraint were being liberated. Since the beginning of Parliament, wrote John Bellot just before the session ended, none would pay. Once Parliament had gone, the situation deteriorated further; no one in Staffordshire could be persuaded to purchase the distrained goods.[18] In Nottinghamshire the quarter sessions were still dealing with excessive numbers before the courts for non-payment of levies. The session always met on the first day at Nottingham, adjourning for a second day at Newark and then again for a third day at East Retford. During the April and July sessions, all three days saw time taken up with such cases. In 1640 a total of over thirty people appeared before the courts.[19] In the same year thirty people in Leicester were distrained for non-payment of the levies imposed on the town.[20]

Opposition to taxation was only one form of disorder witnessed in the aftermath of Parliament. Religious dissatisfaction, too, began to manifest itself strongly. While Parliament met, a Convocation of Bishops had also been in session. Despite Parliament's open disapproval of the innovations which Charles seemed intent on imposing, expressed as early as 1629, and despite Parliament's attempts to slow the progress of the meeting by not allowing the bishops in the House of Lords leave to attend, by the time its business was over the Convocation had confirmed the religious changes that had taken place. This deepened hostility. The planned mobilization for the new war had to go on even without Parliament's blessing and funding. Money borrowed from a variety of sources over the winter was used to support this effort. Nevertheless, the lack of funds delayed the preparations and the mobilization for a summer offensive originally planned to take place after the strategic points of Carlisle and Berwick had been fortified and reinforced.[21] It was during this period of delay that trouble began in England. Soldiers passing through certain areas launched a 'reformation' of their own. They entered churches, demolished the altars and their rails and smashed the

Plate 2 The plundering English Irish Soldier woodcut from
The Thomason Tracts, 669 fg, reproduced by courtesy of
The British Library, London.

stained-glass windows. They also attacked clergymen whom they believed to be Arminians or Laudians, ripping their vestments into shreds. In July 1640 at Bocking, Essex, footsoldiers emboldened by drink launched into a discussion of religion. As a result of their debates they set off for the church, removed the rails and burned them on their captain's doorstep. They then proceeded to another church and repeated the process. In Hertfordshire the new window in the church at Haddham was smashed; so was the one at Rickmansworth. Such acts were repeated throughout the regions during the summer months. Soldiers seemed to be demolishing what they perceived to be elements of popish superstition. The altar tables and their rails sanctified the place where, according to Catholic theology, the eucharist (the bread and wine) underwent transubstantiation and became the physical presence of God. The Arminian church did not accept this doctrine but nevertheless sought to keep the place where Christ was commemorated free of abuse and thus removed the communion table from the body of the church where it might be leaned on, sat on or used as a convenient repository for hats, clothing and the like. Accordingly, it was often set up at the eastern end of the church and railed off, roughly in the manner of an altar. Insistence that the congregation kneel to receive communion made it look very much as if Catholic transubstantiation was being enacted. This outward show simply incensed many. Whether or not they could appreciate fully the theological aspects of the debate, the appearance of an altar-like structure and subservient kneeling had the feel of Catholicism. The soldiers and civilians who had begun such work in isolated incidents before 1640 now encouraged others in their work of 'reformation'.[22]

The attacks on church fabric were only one form of defying the state. Officers were murdered by their men, often in a most brutal and public manner. At Faringdon, Berkshire, Lieutenant William Mohun of a Dorset regiment was the target of a vicious attack in which he was clubbed and left for dead. When the soldiers found out he was still alive and receiving medical help, they dragged him through the streets, beat his brains out and put his mangled corpse into the stocks. The county authorities succeeded in putting down the ensuing two-day mutiny, but their task was made much harder because the rest of the army officers had fled. Indeed, the sheriff was successful in restoring order largely because the rebellious soldiers had vanished into the countryside. In another incident at Wellington, Somerset, Lieutenant Evers of a Devonshire regiment was set upon by soldiers who thought him a Catholic. In public view he was cudgelled, slashed and beaten to death, after which his corpse was robbed. The local authorities made no move to help or to try to find his murderers.[23] Rampaging soldiers attacked gaols up and down the country. At Marlborough, Wiltshire, soldiers released trained bandsmen from the gaol where they had been held because they refused to pay coat and conduct money. In Yorkshire the Wakefield house of correction was wrecked, and at Selby the prison was broken into. In Gloucestershire, the Cirencester prison was attacked, prisoners released and a lawyer held there on a contempt charge taken out against his will to act as legal adviser to the troops. A rampaging force, nominally under the command of Sir John Beaumont, attacked the Earl of Huntingdon's park around his castle at Ashby-de-la-Zouch in north-west Leicestershire and killed his tame white deer. The soldiers were then led to Derby, where they entered the prison and enquired of each prisoner his or her crime before releasing those whom they considered to be political prisoners. In the rest of the county they attacked other estates, including those of Sir John Coke at Melbourne and Sir John Harpur at Calke Abbey.[24]

The riots amongst soldiers and willing helpers from the local populace had a variety of causes, some related to longer-term problems than the rule of Charles I. Enclosures, the cause of the massive Midlands revolt of 1607 and of hundreds of localized riots before and afterwards, excited anger. It was Sir John Coke's enclosures at Melbourne that the rioting soldiers in Derbyshire had attacked. In the neighbouring moorland area around Uttoxeter in Staffordshire a large-scale enclosure riot took place on 1 July 1640. Soldiers raised in two of the county's five hundreds, Seisdon and Cuttlestone, were to rendezvous at Uttoxeter on that day. The two constables of Uttoxeter were instructed to arm some men themselves to keep order at the muster. At about 9 p.m. one of the constables heard that there was to be an attack on a nearby enclosure in Uttoxeter Wood. By the time the deputy lieutenant and the constables arrived along with their armed men, ten roods (between 60 and 80 yards) of fence had been removed and burned. As most of the rioters ignored the deputies' call to stop, attempts were made to arrest them. Those few who were apprehended by the armed townsmen were promptly rescued by the other soldiers. By 11 p.m. the deputies decided that they had failed and that they could not arrest anyone or record the names of the ringleaders because the men were unknown to them. The following day, with the help of the High

Constable, Mr Warner, some rioters were arrested, but by 9 p.m.
they had been rescued and returned to the woods to burn the rest
of the fences. All the deputies could do that night was to set guards
around Uttoxeter to prevent more soldiers encamped in the county
from joining the riot. By 3 July the rioters were quelled by an
assembly of justices of the peace, Uttoxetermen and armed men
from all towns within a five-mile radius. When the soldiers were
placed under military rule, the High Sheriff empanelled a jury for
a special or private session of the peace to be held on 14 July.[25] This
was not the first time that these enclosures had been attacked. A
year earlier, with the possible connivance of Constable John Gregory,
local rioters and some soldiers had demolished the fences at Uttoxeter
Wood and the Forest of Needwood. The rioters were then summoned to appear before the Star Chamber.[26] The riots seem clearly
to have been related, yet the soldiers who rioted were not local; they
had come from the two hundreds in the south-west of the county
whereas Uttoxeter was in the north-eastern hundred of Totmansloe.
The Privy Council stated that the enclosures had been made legally
between 1635 and 1637 and with the consent of the local common-
ers. It is possible that in 1640 the soldiers were taking a broader
view of enclosures, attacking not just a local arrangement where
they had an interest in the land enclosed but attacking the principle
of enclosure itself. Perhaps they were attacking more than that.
Since the woods belonged to the king, and he had initiated the
enclosure, it might have been an attack on the head of state. Given
that other acts of disorder involved attacks on men who held the
king's commission, on the law and its prisons, and on church structures personally associated with the king's religious preferences, this
interpretation may not be far off the mark. Historians do not agree
on the nature of these problems. Some believe that these acts of violence are subject to misinterpretation. Altar rails could be smashed for
fuel, or by miscreants drafted into the 1640 army; and the destruction need not be taken as evidence of political or religious sympathies.
On the other hand, it can be argued that for some people there was
already a war in England, a war of good – Protestantism – against
evil – Catholicism – and that the riots of 1640 were a part of this.[27]

Were the years of the bishops' wars more violent than normal
years? They may not have been; but it is perhaps important that
contemporaries perceived them to be so.[28] In the turmoil of summer
1640 can be seen the common people's adoption of Pym's platform
of grievances outlined in his speech of 17 April. At the same time,

non-violent sections of the community were putting his plan at the heart of their petitions to government.[29] The two major issues of the period, frustration over taxation and rioting, can be viewed as separate, but there is an argument for tying them together closely. Research on Nottinghamshire in the early 1640s suggests that there was only a small increase in rioting in these years and that the county was quieter then than in the early 1630s and the early 1620s. Nevertheless, the justices of the peace seem to have been far readier to hold special sessions of the peace between 1640 and 1642 than they were in previous years. No special sessions at all had been held between 1633 and 1640. In 1632 they had been held against the backdrop of a food crisis, at a time when the JPs were trying to regulate the markets to prevent disorder inspired by shortages. It would seem that the JPs in 1640 perceived the situation to be just as dangerous. The riot in the Newark area which provoked the session was a very minor affair, probably no more serious than many since 1633 which had been dealt with at ordinary general sessions. However, the riot in 1640 took place against a background of the increased volume of work at general sessions caused by ship money default. Thus, ship money and rioting can be linked as closely as some assert that iconoclasm and agrarian disorders were.[30] But these riotous actions should not be seen as being revolutionary in themselves. What is important is the belief among the social and political elite, like the Nottinghamshire JPs, that they threatened impending social disruption and heralded revolt. It might be argued that this interpretation is splitting hairs. If the actions of the soldiers and civilians were directed at the functionaries of the king's government, at the facets of religious change and at his and other landowners' enclosures, can they not be classed as political acts? May it not at least be argued that they were aimed at changing the state of affairs? Clearly a wide range of people were aware of what was going on outside England. Scotland's propaganda was quite effective in reaching people and, consequently, inspiring debate. The soldiers who smashed up the church at Bocking in Essex had related their discussions about religion to what was happening in Scotland. Further, by June some people were aware of what was happening in Ireland. In Wales fears that a popish army was about to descend were prevalent, and prominent Welsh Catholics were held in suspicion.[31] In England John Bosworth of Welford, Leicestershire, had heard that the Irish Parliament was already reconsidering its vote of subsidies as early as 26 May 1640.[32]

RENEWED PREPARATIONS FOR WAR IN SCOTLAND

Even if what was happening in England did not constitute revolutionary behaviour, the actions of the Scots certainly did. The summoning of the English Parliament for April was expressly aimed at financing a war with Scotland, and as such it gave the Covenanters their cue for making firm military plans. The Tables were replaced by a permanent Committee of Estates, with twelve members drawn from each estate. Behind this executive, the Estates, which Charles had tried to dissolve, continued to meet. Together, these two bodies validated the previous actions of the Covenanters and elected their own King's Commissioner to replace Traquair. The Estates ratified the Presbyterian reformation enacted at the General Assembly of 1638 and abolished the clerical estate. As a replacement they doubled the voting powers of the shires, allowing one vote to each shire commissioner rather than having one vote per shire. They altered the very structure of the Estates, by downgrading the committee of the Lords of the Articles and making it responsible to the Estates. In other words, legislation, once framed by the executive before being put to an undebated vote, was now to emanate from the floor of the unicameral Estates. From there, proposals would go before preparatory committees before returning to the House for debate and voting. A triennial act, making a Parliament mandatory every three years with or without the monarch's authority, was also passed.[33] Changes in central government were matched by a reorganization of local government structure, aimed initially at gearing the shires for war. A national levy of one-tenth of land or commercial rented values was enacted, based on the assessments begun a year earlier. All of this preparation was well in hand before the English Parliament met. The Earl of Nithsdale astutely summed up its nature in a letter to Hamilton warning of the penalties for failing to comply: 'though it is termed a voluntarie contribution yet they must look to themselfis, which refuse'. In a later letter to Charles, Nithsdale expressed the thought that the bond for the levy might anger many 'of the meaner sort of your subjects' because it was apparently an unlimited right to exact taxation.[34] A further levy of one-twentieth was imposed as a loan to cover the shortfall in income from the assessments of the previous year. This new administration was also geared toward the spread of moral and religious values, propaganda and government information, which were disseminated through the presbytery structure. The Scottish armed forces drilled during the spring. Weapon showings, or wapinschaws, which were the equivalent of an English or Welsh muster, were held in the burghs. At Edinburgh the weapon showings of the fencibles (men of military age) were to muster on 16 April; a further 500 men were to be levied in Leith. All of this had to be funded by a loan of £50,000 Scots (about £4,166 sterling).[35] The principal source for evidence about the collection of monies at a local level remains the minute book of the Kirkcudbright War Committee. This book demonstrates the way in which orders for troops, horses and money were put into effect. Money to pay for the soldiers was raised in proportion to rental values as arranged; for example, a levy of 50 merks and 15 merks for horse and foot respectively was raised on each 1,000 merks of rent in July 1640. The money was to be raised in each parish by a commissioner and brought with newly raised soldiers to a general rendezvous at Milnetoun.[36] The commissioners had wide powers. They were not only able to select soldiers and choose replacements if nominated soldiers absented themselves from the 'uplifting'; they could also 'plunder' or distrain those who did not pay their contributions. Unlike the English constables charged with similar duties, the commissioners were drawn from the Scottish gentry, the lairds. In addition, the committee compiled lists of men suitable to lend money for the war effort and organized the collection of silver, for which the owner was offered security at £3 Scots per ounce of Scottish silver and £3-2s Scots per ounce of English silver. Each presbytery was to have an office, and just after the battle of Newburn the committee established an office at the Tollbooth in Kirkcudbright under the direction of a three-man commission to receive silverware between 10 a.m. and 2 p.m. The demand for silverware was great, and the commission was harsh in its treatment of petitions asking to keep silver. Grissell Gordoun was refused permission to keep six spoons belonging to her and two pieces of silverware belonging to the church at Urr. Marione McClellane had to hand over her 'bairne's silver worke . . . notwithstanding of the reassones preponit in the contrair'.[37]

The new administration turned on its opponents at home first. 'Anti-Covenanters' were not to be allowed on any of the administrative committees, even if they were short of commissioners, and the Royalists in the north-east were suppressed. Aberdeen's doubts about paying the tenth part were dealt with forcibly. In a letter to the burgh council dated 20 March, Covenanter leaders pointed out that non-payment would be seen as an 'ill example'. Just to hammer home the inadvisable nature of such a course, Colonel Monrois's regiment was to be stationed in the town 'as wele to kepe off forrane invasion as to redress intestane jarrs'.[38] The Earl of Nithsdale's castles, which he had once promised the king in a letter ('I still preserve two houses for your service till the cannon blas them about our years'), were besieged as he expected, and the king's castles in the south were closely watched and deprived of supplies.[39] The small loyal garrison in Edinburgh Castle was beleaguered, and many of its members scaled the walls from the inside to get away.

THE SECOND ANGLO-SCOTTISH WAR

The Scottish army this time planned an offensive campaign, with a larger, better trained and more disciplined army than that of 1639. A detailed strategy was agreed at Edinburgh on 6 May 1640.[40] Aware that the king was contemplating a direct attack on Edinburgh, the Covenanters decided instead to wreck his preparations by invading the north of England.[41] This was not a difficult option to take, as constant delays through lack of funding and discipline problems had already weakened the English strategy. The planned use of the new Irish army of 8,000 men was deferred because of the failure to co-ordinate with the English and Welsh forces straggling northwards in the summer of 1640. Wales was more directly involved in the second war than in the first. Some 2,000 men were drafted out of the Welsh shires for Charles's army, a process which proved logistically complicated and expensive for the principality. Moreover, in Montgomeryshire large numbers of the soldiers deserted, and it has been estimated that mobilization doubled the level of taxation on the counties.[42] Assembling the army was difficult; while parts of it were on the borders by July, a good proportion was still at York or en route north. Still more sections had not even arrived at the Selby rendezvous point by July. The nine men levied on Baldock in Hertfordshire were still in the village on 27 June, even though their weapons had been repaired as far back as April.[43] A large part of the army was unarmed when it assembled because the supplies of weapons had reached the collection points only after the troops had passed by.[44] On 20 August the Scots crossed the Tweed.

Invasion gave Charles a strong legal position *vis-à-vis* the Scottish rebellion, but by then it was too late for legal debate. The garrison at Newcastle soon came under threat as the Berwick forces were swiftly bypassed. This was to be a war of movement, and both fortified strongholds and legal niceties were immediately swept into irrelevance. Newcastle, which supplied coal to London, had to be held to prevent the Scots from gaining leverage over the English capital. A large part of the English army had massed in an effort to hold on to the Tyne as a line of defence. Leslie made straight for the crossing at Newburn, which was defended by English forces. From the higher positions on the north bank, which the English failed to hold, he was able to direct accurate and devastating fire on the English. It was a brief battle, and as a result of their defeat the English withdrew first from the Tyne and then from Newcastle, where they had neglected to build defences around Gateshead to the south of the river. In their wake the Scots, with no military force to impede them, passed through northern England with impunity and occupied Durham. With no defensible positions on which to fall back, the English forces retreated in disgrace all the way to York. There Charles regrouped the army, which still stood at 16,000 foot and 2,000 horse, and summoned the remaining trained bands to join him. The significance of Newburn was slow to sink in. In military terms it had been a minor action, and one which the strong military position at York and the enforced consolidation of the English army suggested might be overcome. Certainly the king felt so, since he regarded the major problem as financial. However, the political impact of Newburn was ultimately massive.[45]

Within England the impetus for reaching an accommodation with the Scots was growing. On the very day that Newburn was won and lost, a group of oppositionist politicians met in Bedford House in London to frame and sign a petition calling for a new Parliament. The men present included the Earls of Essex, Bedford and Warwick; Lords Saye and Sele and Brooke, the two men who had opposed the king at York the previous year; and Russell. Also present were Oliver St John; his most famous client, John Hampden; and John Pym. It was Pym and Oliver St John who drafted the document, but only the twelve peers signed it.[46] The petition began by rehearsing the peers' concern that England was in imminent danger and that the king's person was at risk. It then turned to the now familiar refrain: the country was overburdened with military charges and suffering from dangerous riots. There were 'sundry innovations in matters of religion' and an attendant increase in 'popery'. It was rumoured that an Irish army was about cross the sea and was likely to cause 'mischiefs'. Moreover, there was still the burden of ship money. The desired solution, according to the petitioners, was a recourse to a Parliament.[47]

IRELAND: BREAKING STRAFFORD'S GRIP

In Ireland, which only a few months earlier had provided an example to the short-lived English Parliament, events were already shifting the balance of power out of Strafford's favour.[48] The English blockade of Scotland was affecting Ireland's trade, and this in turn affected the organization of supplies for the new army, now under the charge of the Earl of Ormond during Strafford's absence. More problematic for both Strafford and the king was Parliament's flexing of its muscles during the second session, which opened in June. The seven boroughs disenfranchised by the earl were restored and his bill for establishing plantations in Connaught was effectively shelved, but the major issue was the discussion over the subsidies. Just as John Bosworth of Welford, Leicestershire, had heard back in May, there were now second thoughts about them. At first these were tackled indirectly. While the first collection went ahead, the Commons imposed its own methodology on the other three instalments, substantially reducing their worth. The second instalment was now worth only £9,922-10s-8d – compared with the £45,000 for the first.[49] The attack on the Lord Lieutenant's government continued, and the Master of the Rolls, Sir Christopher Wandesford, whom Strafford left in charge, could not control the Commons and was forced to prorogue Parliament on 17 June until 1 October. This action, of course, had its effects on events in England. First, Charles received only a fraction of the money he had expected, which contributed to the general lack of resources available for the war with Scotland. Second, the session of the Irish Commons reopened in the aftermath of the king's defeat at Newburn and just as he began negotiations with the Scots. The Dublin government was quickly attacked over its handling of the elections in the seven restored boroughs, which it had tried to delay, and the Commons moved further down the road to constitutional change by establishing a committee 'for drawing up acts'. As in Scotland, bills traditionally originated in the executive, although Poyning's law did not make this mandatory. The Commons' innovative action, coupled with an investigation into the action of the Council in sending bills to England, presented a threat to the established form of government. To compound these difficulties, the whole issue of the subsidies was brought into question. To further the attack on Strafford's administration, a remonstrance of grievances against the Lord Lieutenant's government was prepared in the Commons. Wandesford began to prepare to prorogue the Parliament but was hindered by the absent Strafford who, ill prepared for the attack on his position and ill informed about its nature, insisted that the Connaught bill be passed first before the House was dispersed. This gave his opponents the time they needed to get the remonstrance through the Commons and to take further defiant steps. Aware that prorogation was imminent, the Commons established a committee of representatives from every province to meet with the king. Wandesford, in desperation, responded by proroguing the House and forbade the committee members to leave the country. Not completely coincidentally, denial of access to the king was one of the complaints highlighted in the remonstrance, which consisted of sixteen clauses of economic, legal and constitutional issues. The economic clauses complained of a deadness of trade, the adverse effects on the economy of monopolies established by the government and the failure to secure land tenures. The legal clauses complained of the Council's increasing role in the assumption of tasks normally undertaken by the courts. The constitutional attacks complained of the overweening power of some officials at the expense of Parliament's authority. Despite Wandesford's attempt to stop them, the committee members took the remonstrance to England, arriving just as a new English Parliament had got under way.

THE NEW PARLIAMENT IN ENGLAND

During the summer, Charles had sought to head off calls for a new English Parliament. In two of the four nations Parliaments had tampered with constitutional matters, and in the third, members had insisted on airing grievances. A session of the Edinburgh Estates had gone much further when, as the troublesome second Irish session got under way, it had sanctioned the war against the king. At the end of the war, with a third Irish session opening, the king met with the Scots commissioners to find that part of their peace terms was a demand that an English Parliament be summoned. The king had attempted to work with a smaller and more controllable body by summoning a Council of Peers to York in the aftermath of Newburn.

The Privy Council had probably supported this move in the hope that a larger Council might be able to influence the king into calling a Parliament.[50] Already, the twelve peers' petition had been prepared and, once presented, had found widespread support; it appeared likely that the Council of Peers would simply back it too, despite the king's hopes. There was already evidence of support going beyond this government core. On the eve of the war, the grand jury of Berkshire had called for a new Parliament in a petition incorporating much of Pym's projected agenda of 17 April. The City of London had also petitioned for a new Parliament at the beginning of September. By 16 September the Privy Council had come to the same conclusion, thus isolating the king. To avoid the appearance of having capitulated to his opponents when he met the Council of Peers, on 24 September the king announced the calling of a new Parliament. It was clear that he had little choice, for as well as the mounting pressure in England, the Scottish army was clearly acting as the military muscle behind the demands of the Scots negotiators and the English petitioners.

In the meantime, at York the king and the peers discussed possibilities for negotiations with Scotland. The king and a group of the peers led by the Earl of Bedford represented the opposing facets of English policy towards Scotland. Charles was still determined to inflict a military defeat upon the Scots with the help of Parliament, whereas Bedford and his associates realized both the necessities and opportunities created by the present situation. The earl was forced to point out to the king that he had in fact lost the war, and that he could no longer speak of 'reducing' the 'rebels'. The commissioners for the negotiations who were appointed by the Council included seven signatories of the peers' petition. The first meeting between the commissioners and the Scots took place in Ripon at the end of September. Charles hoped to have the treaty completed before Parliament met, but he was frustrated by the Scots' demand for financial compensation as a precondition of negotiations. By 6 October they settled for a reduced figure of £50,000, to be paid at the rate of £850 a day for two months. Yet Charles was not downhearted by this reverse; on the contrary, he still saw advantages to be gained. The demand for money, together with the Scottish presence on English soil, might, he believed, galvanize Parliament and the people into backing him.[51] In reality he was adrift in the political sea. By 23 October it was agreed that the treaty should be negotiated in London and submitted to Parliament; a Scottish commission would therefore be present in the capital when Parliament sat.

The king would have to have acted quickly and effectively to head off the consequences of his powerlessness in September 1640, but he did not. Apart from giving only the minimum statutory notice of forty days to limit the opposition's ability to organize, he took little effective action to surmount this crisis. The king's friends were simply not elected. As in April, actual royal supporters, those perceived to be supporters, and government officers were all rejected in large numbers, while those of a godly mind – by which was meant those opposed to Charles's religious and political policies – were returned. The effect on the composition of the new House of Commons was enormous; by mid-1641, after six months of radical readjustment in the frame and form of government, only some 12 per cent of the 501-strong chamber were prepared to support Charles publicly.[52] Moreover, behind his elected opponents who assembled on 3 November 1640 were the petitioners of England and Wales. There had been a series of petitions awaiting the earlier Short Parliament, complaining of military and financial burdens, but in November those that arrived often bore the imprint of Pym's April speech. However, they were never free of the localism that was inherent in such petitions. National grievances about the collection of ship and coat and conduct money, about religious impositions and parliamentary freedom, mingled with complaints about weirs on rivers and localized deadness of trade.[53] Nevertheless, this does not diminish the impact of their collective requests for what the Cheshire bench called, 'redresse and reformacion'. Indeed, the fact that traditional grievance petitions were subverted by the inclusion of common national complaints indicates how much, to many with access to a means of petition, the times demanded action. Strengthened by this support, the members in the new Parliament defined their own agenda. Pym's speech on 7 November embellished only slightly what he had said some seven months earlier. The king had also entered the new session with a reframed but similar agenda; he still wanted Parliament to support his stance against the Scots. Whereas in April he had presented the letter to Louis XIII as his evidence that the Scots were in rebellion, in November he pointed out their occupation of the northern counties and demand for money as proof of their insurrection. His plan for the session was essentially the same too: first drive out the rebels and then discuss grievances. Parliament took no real notice, and the king was obliged to return to

Parliament on 5 November to explain his opening speech and to
retract his depiction of the Scots as rebels. Nevertheless, Charles was
surprised when Parliament agreed to the Scottish demands for rep-
arations and made it apparent that it considered the Scots' cause
just.[54] Charles was now bereft of either an initiatory role or a policy.
The initiative was clearly in the hands of the Parliaments in Edinburgh, London and to some extent Dublin, although in the latter,
Strafford's dead hand of government still had some part to play. The
result was the dismantling of the king's prerogative government across
the four nations. Deprived of policy and initiative, the king's agents
were left isolated, and both they and the machinery of personal
government were to be swept away. In Scotland the process had, of
course, already begun, and the restructuring of the constitution
lacked only symbolic royal approval. The Irish Parliament may in
practice have been to some extent stifled, but the demands for change
existed there too; and it was also involved in helping the English
Parliament with its work. The Irish Remonstrance committee had
arrived in England and probably initiated Pym's attack on the Earl
of Strafford. On 11 November, the Lords acquiesced to the Commons' request and committed the Lord Lieutenant of Ireland to the
Tower. Ten days later, after Archbishop William Laud had been
committed to the custody of the Gentleman Usher, preparations
were made for trying Strafford. At the same time attention turned
to other of the king's men. John Finch was under suspicion, for one.
He had been the Commons' speaker held in his chair in 1629, and
had been in favour in the 1630s, seemingly as a reward for having
suffered in the king's service. He had been made Lord Chief Justice
of the Common Pleas and had decided in the king's favour in the
Hampden case. When on 7 December Oliver St John, Hampden's
former counsel, presented the report of his committee on ship money,
Finch's fate was sealed, and impeachment proceedings commenced.
Secretary of State Francis Windebank was another victim of the
purge. Believed to be sympathetic towards Catholics, he was accused of involvement in seventy-four instances of the use of royal
power to suspend the laws against the prosecutions of priests. In the
climate of anti-popery stirred up by Pym's denunciation of the popish
plot undermining the state, Windebank was shown to have an unacceptable penchant. During a discussion of the queen's religion
and other aspects of Roman Catholicism in England, it was decided
to impeach him. He himself did not wait, fleeing instead across the
channel to await vindication from the king.[55]

At the same time, a concerted attack was mounted on the machinery of government. The alleged abuses of secular power, such as ship money, as well as church bodies such as the Court of High Commission, were facets of misgovernance which had to be swept away as effectively as were the supposed 'evil councillors', Strafford, Laud, Finch and Windebank. Furthermore, effective safeguards had to be erected to prevent future misgovernment.[56] This effort involved stronger measures than the Petition of Right, which the king had simply ignored. St John's committee on ship money had followed a line of reasoning similar to his arguments in Hampden's defence, claiming that the 1628 Petition of Right had clearly delineated the respective roles of king and Parliament regarding taxation and that the king had breached them from 1629 onwards. Naturally, such an accusation could be stretched to included all of the king's financial excesses during the past eleven years, including his illegal collection of tunnage and poundage, and resurrected medieval levies and impositions such as forest fines and distraint of knighthood. Since it was constitutionally difficult to criticize the monarch, Parliament focused on attacking the principal figures of government, but the covert attack on Charles himself occasionally came close to open confrontation.

Pym believed that he had identified the root of the problem. There was, he claimed, a popish plot afoot in England designed to lead England and Wales back in to the Roman fold. Religious change was only one component of this plot, because popery was associated with tyranny and arbitrary government such as were practised in England and Wales in the 1630s. Therefore, military charges, ship money and the other grievances could all be identified as symptoms of a popish conspiracy against the state. The plot was undoubtedly part of the Catholic Counter-Reformation on the continent, as indeed was the attack on the Scottish Kirk.

Other opponents of the king's personal rule – the period of his reign since the expulsion of Parliament in 1629 – were not so convinced. Edward Hyde, a moderate opponent of the king, declared on 7 December that ship money was the origin or pattern for 'all our sufferings', contradicting St John's assertion that the illegal taxes were aimed at joint religious and political subversion and running counter to Pym's claims too. For Hyde ship money was not part of a wider-ranging plot, but nevertheless represented a dangerous attack on the rule of law and principles of taxation established by Parliament.[57]

The Scots commissioners in London had adopted the tenor of

Charles I's argument for a uniformity of churches in the three mainland nations. However, whereas Charles had intended a parallel episcopate, the Scots wanted a Presbyterian system. They had some English support for this, as there were those in England who favoured a similar system in England and Wales. To this end the Scots commissioners received hospitality from a collection of MPs, Lords and ministers in London. The Scots were well aware that the king was duplicitous and could not be trusted to adhere to any settlement not somehow bound up with changes in the English and Welsh political and religious systems. Moreover, if they negotiated a peace based simply on Scottish affairs and took their army home, the English reformists would then be left without support and impetus for their programme of changes. Thus, it was in the Scottish interest to foment the constitutional changes which lay at the heart of the English reformers' plans. In turn, the English MPs drew much of the inspiration for their programme from the Scottish example. There were two areas in which the Scots and the English co-operated closely during the late days of 1640: the development of a religious policy and the formulation of the case against Strafford.

PRESSURE FOR RELIGIOUS CHANGE

The first of the co-operative efforts was not an untarnished success. Support for religious change was coming into Parliament in the form of petitions late in 1640. More than a dozen of them demanded massive structural changes and contrasted with those that required only the suppression of the Laudian developments of the past fifteen years. On 11 November a petition from the City of London signed by 15,000 people was presented, providing a model for sweeping changes. Few of the Puritans in England were opposed to the episcopate form of church government as a general principle. The problem here is that defining a Puritan is very much like looking into a kaleidoscope; one slight movement of the mirrors or of the eyeline changes the image entirely, one twist of the end creates a completely new picture to study. There was never a time when all Puritans were alike. Although all of them wished to continue the reformation of the church, few of them were separatists. Rather, they saw reform as something to be generated from within. Although James VI and I had demonstrated an almost allergic reaction to the Presbyterian form of the new church, the tradition of reformism

remained strong in England and Wales. Reactions had changed by
the 1630s, after James had put pressure on the reformists in the
church by encouraging conformity and after Charles had continued
this policy with sledgehammer subtlety, seeking not only conformity
but shifting the focus of that conformity in the direction of a new
church. In response to Charles's pressure, not only had more reformists begun to see separatism as a viable alternative to the restricted opportunities for change from within, but some had left the
country for the colonies. In England small, independent groups met
in London and the provinces and alternative churches were established in Wales like that at Llanfaches. By 1639 this 'alternative
church' had adopted a form of Calvinist covenant binding its members to the older form of service while sanctioning outward conformity to lessen the chances of persecution. In the heady days of 1640,
similar groups were established at Swansea, Cardiff and Haverfordwest.[58] Although Geraint Jenkins argues that to some reformers
Wales was as unknown and as hostile as the American colonies, to
others there was no substitute for the pilgrimage across the Atlantic
to found the new church or the New Jerusalem, a City on a Hill or
a 'candle in the night' beckoning the faithful. Some of the godly
who considered emigration turned away from the prospect. Oliver
Cromwell, a fenland justice of the peace and MP, was one who
thought it over, only to reject the idea of leaving England. Others
who remained in England, John Pym amongst them, facilitated the
exodus of others through the company formed by the oppositionists
Lord Saye and Sele and Lord Brooke. The Saye–Brooke company
or Providence Island Company established settlements in America,
but it also kept together politically aligned reformers during the
1630s. The exodus to America was not a universal panacea. Some
colonists found the hostility of the land and the indigenous peoples
too exhausting; others found that while God's work itself was exciting, it did not ease their consciences. As the situation in England
developed, there was growing fear that rather than the emigrants
having been the vanguard of God's plan, they had actually deserted
his true ideal. This fear resulted in a reverse migration in the early
1640s as the godly returned to fight for God at home.[59]

While the pressure for religious change was undoubtedly great,
the nature of change proved problematic. The London petition called
for the complete abolition of the episcopacy, a hitherto extreme
demand in England, which had now become more widely accepted
as the only way to ensure that there was no return to a 'Romish'

form of worship. Naturally this pleased the Scots too, as it would offer them protection against any Episcopal religious imperialism. However, there was little widespread approval in England yet. It has been calculated that there were about 130 men in the Commons who supported the Scottish position on the need for reform, but in the Lords there were barely fifteen.[60] The Lords, on the other hand, could be persuaded if such reform became essential to the peace with Scotland, or if Charles behaved so provocatively as to oblige the peers to take religious power out of his hands. The London petition came to be described as the 'Root and Branch' petition, from the phrase in which it demanded that the episcopate form – the arch-bishops, bishops, deans and archdeacons – 'with all its dependencies, roots and branches may be abolished'. The petition attacked the tenets of Laud's church, comparing them with those of the church of Rome and contrasting them with Calvinist theology. There was, it declared, an increase in those 'idle, lewd and dissolute ignorant and erroneous men' who, among other things, genuflected and were 'zealous of superstitious ceremonies'. Ministers, it went on, were so in fear of the bishops that they failed to preach the word of God relating to the doctrine of predestination.[61] There were some twenty-eight complaints in the petition, and although some referred to mono-polies and to ship money, the majority were concerned with the church and its many abuses. When it was presented and debated, the petition encountered problems. The reception was not hostile, but it was not universally positive. Some MPs considered the issue to be too weighty to debate and decided quickly. Others who did not like it at all agreed with this assessment to prevent its immediate acceptance. Realizing that there was considerable resistance, its supporters quietly let it drop. Plans to capitalize on the demands for an end to the bishops therefore lay dormant into the next year.

The pall cast over the London petition was really a great blow to the Scots, although they may not have realized it at the time, as in other matters the two kingdoms began to move hand in hand to-ward reform. The current Estates in Scotland was not to be dis-solved by the king, and Parliaments in both kingdoms were to meet every two to three years, whether the monarch desired it or not. The progenitors of the bishops' wars in both countries were to be pros-ecuted by their respective Parliaments. Neither kingdom could go to war without the consent of both Parliaments, and the heir's prospec-tive marriages were to be vetted in both assemblies. On a religious note, papists were to be forbidden court positions, and there was to be a joint confession of faith in both kingdoms. Only some of the points at issue embraced Ireland. The Act of Oblivion, which was to protect the actions of those involved in the war against legal challenges, except for the progenitors, was extended to cover Ireland. Reparation for those Scots Strafford had persecuted in Ulster was also approved.

THE TRIAL OF THE EARL OF STRAFFORD

It was the punishment of the perceived progenitors of the war – the 'evil councillors' – which was the most successful area of Anglo-Scottish policy and which united the opposition, at least for a time. Although Strafford was only one of the people at the centre of the attack on the king's men, he was the most prominent. Traquair, Laud, Finch, Windebank and George Radcliffe (Strafford's agent in Ireland) had all been attacked, but it was the earl to whom the attentions of Charles's critics in Ireland, Scotland, England and Wales turned. The charges against Strafford were truly international, prepared by men from all of the four kingdoms. Chief among them was the accusation that he had hoped to use the new Irish army on the mainland. Ostensibly, this army was for use in Scotland, which angered the Covenanters enough, but it was also charged that he had suggested using the Irish army in England to suppress the king's opponents.[62] The Irish Remonstrance provided a major part of the material for the charges which in sum accused Strafford of maintaining a tyrannical and ruinous government in Ireland, of seeking to subvert the government of England and Wales and of making war on the kingdom of Scotland.[63] Yet while the spirit of persecution was strong, the body of evidence was weak. The case was prepared during winter and brought to trial in April. The charges were insufficient to prove treason if taken one by one, so the Commons tried to insist that they be taken together.[64] The forceful way in which the Commons pressed their case made it clear that they were set upon Strafford's death regardless of its probity. The first two of the twenty-eight particulars were demolished by the defence with ease; on the first the prosecution had invented dates for instructions and commissions involving the government of the north, to fit their case; the second, the charge that Strafford had declared the king to be more powerful than the law, depended upon hearsay and the evidence of a witness who turned out to be deaf.[65] Many of the other charges hinged on similarly weak evidence and lies and were easily exposed. Regarding the charge that he had threatened to use the Irish army in England, Sir Harry Vane reiterated what he believed Strafford to have said about using the army to 'reduce this kingdom'. Vane swore that he interpreted the words as Strafford meant them, as referring to England. It was a weak argument and no other witness from the Privy Council even remembered the words being uttered.[66] The final day of the proceedings in Westminster Hall was a farce. Strafford outwitted the prosecution again, but did neither the king nor himself a service in the end, for the Commons group had already drawn up a Bill of Attainder. This was a medieval instrument which simply took suspicion of guilt as proof. The twenty-eight charges were redrafted to form the grounds of this suspicion. Vane's notes were produced to add weight to article twenty-three and to persuade the Commons to vote in favour of the bill. They did, but its passage drove a group of fifty-nine men who opposed it into publicizing their opposition. The Lords wavered on the bill for some time before passing it, and perhaps did so only in the hope that the king would reject it anyway. The king's speech to them on the issue may have convinced some of them, even though it did not really help Strafford's case in any other way. The earl's fate was effectively sealed.

In the meantime the work of reforming government machinery proceeded. A bill calling for annual Parliaments was presented by Oliver Cromwell and William Strode, but after some debate, the proposal was watered down somewhat to become an English version of the Scots' Triennial Act. This act provided the mechanisms to ensure that Parliament met automatically every three years; Charles assented to it on 15 February 1641. A further bill which complemented the Triennial Act was passed three months later. The *Act to prevent inconveniences which may happen by the untimely adjourning, proroguing, or dissolving this present Parliament* took away Charles's prerogative powers over Parliament more or less completely. From now on he would have to win over a significant party or subvert the parliamentary process entirely to overturn the political situation. It is a mark of Charles's duplicity that he tried both.[67]

There were attempts during the winter of 1640–1 to bring together the two opposing groups. The king hinted at official appointments for his enemies, whilst they considered moderating some facets of the programme. The Earl of Bedford, the recognized leader of the main grouping of oppositionists – which included Pym and St John – toyed with some form of religious solution which did not involve the destruction of the episcopacy.[68] Instead, bishops would be reduced in status and their decisions approved of by the clergy at large. In effect this was a form of the compromise that had once existed under James VI in Scotland, whereby the bishops had been regarded as elders of the church.[69] Other similarities with the Kirk were the establishment of regional synods as in Scotland and of a national synod similar to the General Assembly. At the same time further, if less far-reaching, attempts were made to alter the church. A bill barring the bishops from sitting in the Lords was passed through the Commons, but the Lords resented this as an intrusion on their powers and it was shelved. Instead a Protestation was drafted committing signatories to defend the church against popery as well as to defend the monarch and Parliament, the rights of the subject and to preserve peace between the three kingdoms. Although not entirely uncontentious – the Lords secured the exemption of bishops and Catholic peers – the Protestation was passed. Initially aimed at MPs and officeholders, it was soon to be passed throughout the kingdom, almost as a form of covenant. In the country as a whole in the spring of 1641 there arose a sudden sense of danger, against which such a bond was felt necessary.

The king's hand of friendship, or at least conciliation, was extended in February 1641 when he appointed Bedford and five more of the twelve peers who had signed the petition of August 1640 to the Privy Council. Oliver St John was appointed Solicitor General, and further appointments for the erstwhile opponents were supposedly imminent. Some saw this as a promising sign that conciliation was possible. On the other hand, some of the Scots, who described the appointees as 'our old friends, the new Councillors', feared that their friends might lose their commitment to the cause. Indeed, it is probable that there was a growing division amongst the new councillors, and that the Scots had discerned lack of enthusiasm on the part of some for thorough reform of the church. Bedford, for example, was probably never a 'Root and Brancher'. In any case, other events had shaped the backdrop to the passage of the Bill of Attainder. During the latter days of the trial, rumours of a plot began to infiltrate the capital. Earlier in April, a group of officers in the English army had drafted a petition calling for the retention of episcopacy and adequate funding for the king's government. The officers were particularly angry at the diversion of £25,000 destined for the English army. The money had been granted by Parliament after the Covenanter army had threatened to advance southwards.[70]

They also asked that the new Irish army be kept in readiness to defend the English church if necessary. The petition was addressed to the commander in chief, the Earl of Northumberland, but the senior officers refused to accept it. Nevertheless, the junior officers who drafted it went on to suggest further that the army might be led from its northern quarters and marched to London to rescue Strafford if possible. The plan found some support in London, and in the City a group of one hundred men was recruited to rescue Strafford. By 3 May these desperadoes were ready and the king sent them to the Tower of London. The Lieutenant refused access, however, and Parliament was informed. The Lords took charge, dispatched the Earl of Newport to take over the Tower and told the king what they had done, forcing him to back down. At the same time, the queen had planned to go to Portsmouth, where the port had been fortified in readiness; but the Lords discovered this part of the plan too and forbade her servants to go. Just how far the king intended the plan to go is unclear. He did prohibit the army from proceeding with the planned march south, and it is possible that he leaked information on this part of the plot to Bedford. Since he and the queen were perceived to be deeply involved, she was threatened with impeachment. Meanwhile, the discovery of the plot certainly helped the case against the doomed Strafford and eased the passage of the Protestation.

One other piece of ill luck was yet to befall the earl. Although some government posts fell open in late April, when Lord Cottington retired through ill health, plans to fill them with oppositionists failed. The posts of Lord Treasurer and Chancellor may have been offered to Bedford and Pym, and the Mastership of the Court of Wards was to be offered to Saye and Sele. This appointment had advantages for the king, for the Court of Wards was one of Bedford's targeted sources of royal income, and Charles probably thus hoped to excite divisions amongst his opponents. But on 9 May Bedford suddenly fell seriously ill and died within days, and the prospect of conciliation faded quickly. So did any last hopes of saving Strafford. Angry crowds were massing in London around the Tower and at Westminster demanding the earl's execution. Moreover, they were also stirred up by the rumours of the plot and the queen's part in it. The king was apparently genuinely afraid that she might be impeached too. On 10 May Charles assented to the Bill of Attainder, and the earl was executed two days later.

The execution of the earl left the king in a very weak position. His most effective minister was dead, and he felt morally responsible for his death. His ability, and perhaps briefly his will, to stand his ground was severely sapped. Bills designed to remove more of the king's prerogative government were passed through Parliament, and the powerless king assented to them. The Courts of Star Chamber and the High Commission were abolished on 5 July. On 7 August ship money was finally declared illegal, and the royal forests were limited to the sizes known in James VI and I's day rather than the medieval dimensions resurrected by Charles. On 9 August distraint of knighthood was abolished too. As the king prepared to go to Edinburgh to complete the peace negotiations with the Scots, many people felt that it might be time to aim for stability and an end to political conflict, as the worst excesses of the personal rule in England and Wales appeared to have been eradicated.

4

Rebellion in Ireland

That this whole and studied plot was, and is, not only to extinguish religion (by which we altogether live happy;) but likewise to supplant us and raze the name of Catholicke and Irish out of the whole kingdom[1]

The events of recent months had embroiled the Irish political world in conflict and had increased both political hopes and religious fears. In Ireland events had moved quickly after the Lord Lieutenant had left for England. Political questions raised at Dublin dominated not only the relationships between the king and Ireland, but also that between Ireland and the Westminster Parliament. However, the fact that this bi-party discussion largely ignored the interests of the Ulster Irish was to have important consequences within months of Strafford's execution. The third session of the Dublin Parliament had seen the opposition to the government become strident. Objections to Strafford's rule formed the basis of the Remonstrance sent to England which arrived just after the Westminster Parliament had met and went on to form an important part of the case against him. Political factions developed within the Dublin Council, and an oppositionist group sought to perpetuate the changes wrought by Strafford's fall. His formerly quiescent enemies, including the Earl of Cork, began to wheedle Straffordians out of office, instead insinuating their own supporters into positions of importance. This was only one of the power struggles in Irish politics. The executive itself was being challenged over its control of affairs by an alliance of Old English and New English MPs, and behind them a broader set of issues was also surfacing. The Commons sent a set of twenty-one 'Queries' on the liberties of the subject to be answered by the judges in the Lords.[2] They enquired whether the judges could lawfully stay suits on government orders and queried the relationship between Irish subjects and English common law. The principal targets of these questions were the office of the Lord Lieutenant and the powers of the executive. It was clear to the judges that the Queries went beyond questioning Strafford's rule. Calling the very basis of government into question, they ranged from general issues, such as the power of the 'Chief Governor' to try cases and the powers of the Court of the Castle Chamber, to specific points, such as the legality of monopolies. The Queries also challenged the power of the Chief Governor and the executive to deny Irish subjects access to the king and freedom to travel to England. The Lords, too, added a twenty-second question about the judges' role in exacting composition on defective titles. These 'humble enquiries' were no less than an attempt to determine the powers of the government by an alliance of Old English members of the Lords and Commons, in line with similar challenges to royal authority in England. The judges managed to put off a reply until after the session had ended, but a parallel attempt to eradicate all traces of the government of Strafford was afoot. A Commons committee informed the Lords that it intended to impeach several of Strafford's supporters.[3] Impeachment was an innovation in Ireland, but this did not prevent the arrest of the Lord Chancellor, Richard Bolton, and the Lord Chief Justice of the Court of the Common Pleas, Gerard Lowther. A third target, Sir George Radcliffe, had already been imprisoned in England. The remaining members of the executive managed to retain some grip on affairs and in early March 1641 succeeded in adjourning Parliament until May.

Adjournment could only delay matters, for when the Commons reassembled, the Queries and the impeachment were again the main issues of discussion. These important political issues united groups of both Old and New English members, and their determination to proceed was a serious threat to the administration, which may have hoped that the issues would go away once Strafford had been executed. Instead, the reopened Parliament continued with its attack. In July, the Commons voted on each of its own twenty-one Queries and established a committee to investigate all government business conducted since 1633. Other issues loomed: financial matters were particularly pressing, and the final two subsidies remained to be collected. Despite Strafford having paid off government debts during his governorship of Ireland, the state debt had mounted as soon as he departed, and by summer 1641 it was even higher than it had been when Strafford took office. Moreover, because of the Commons' actions in adjusting the rates the previous year, the third and fourth subsidies were of little value. Dislocation in overseas trade during the bishops' wars had also depressed the customs revenues, and other income was already much reduced by the economic decline which had begun in the late 1630s.[4]

There was also the issue of the Irish army to consider. Naturally, it was expensive and, at this time of financial crisis, an unaffordable luxury. The main pressure for its disbandment came from England and the Westminster Parliament, which erroneously associated it with Catholicism and held it up as a threat to ensure support for the continued demands for reform. Indeed, much of the attack on Strafford in England had played on this fear of a popish plot involving the Irish army. The earl, Pym's supporters claimed, had allowed the Catholics of Ireland great freedom. This was far from the truth. The Graces, which would have granted secure rights to Catholic Irish subjects, remained unratified during Strafford's rule; and there was more pressure for them to be implemented after he had been swept from office. Part of the very Remonstrance used to damn Strafford related to his failure to ratify the Graces, although naturally these clauses cut no ice across the Irish Sea. During the lieutenancy of Strafford, Catholics had gained no security for their estates; and his plan to establish plantations in Connaught, although successfully fought off by the Earl of Clanricarde in the 1630s, still posed a threat. In April 1641, Charles had made some offers to secure the estates of the Old English, but the English Parliament set about ending their religious 'freedom'. Furthermore, the Scots were pressing for some unity of church not just in three nations but in four; they wanted to draw Ireland into a Presbyterian system too. This concerned not only Irish MPs; fear spread across Irish society, adding another dimension to the eventual disbandment of the army in May 1641.

Leading Catholic Irishmen were convinced that the Scots meant to impose their religion by force. Owen Roe O'Neill, one of the Irish exiles, foresaw a 'great tempest' about to descend upon the Catholics which would 'deprive them of their property, and reduce the survivors to perpetual slavery'; and in the Dublin Commons some Catholics began to call for the retention of the soldiers.[5] Their calls were answered in an indirect manner. Preparations had already been made for some of the disbanded soldiers to be recruited by the Spanish for service in Europe, but a change in English foreign policy towards Spain halted the embarkation, and only one regiment set off.[6] There were some encouraging signs for the Catholic Irish. The new Lord Lieutenant, the Earl of Leicester, despite his worrying connections with the radical Protestant factions, appeared willing to listen to the Old English Catholic representatives in London. By July, members of the Dublin parliamentary deputation in London were able to assure their colleagues at home of Leicester's good intent. Further, the earl himself seems to have concluded during the summer that the Dublin assembly should be independent of Westminster.[7] This position was more radical than the king had been prepared to countenance, but the king had now moved some way towards the demands of the Old English and their newcomer allies, if not towards the Catholic Irish. The powers of the prerogative courts would be relaxed, the Court of High Commission would be suspended as in England and Wales, and monopolies would also be abolished. On Poyning's Law, however, he would allow no change of policy; it was to remain in force. In other words, Ireland would continue to be governed at the 'King's pleasure'.[8]

In one significant area of the country, there was more concern than elsewhere. Ulster Catholics were separated by only a few miles of sea from where their Presbyterian enemies were colonizing the Highlands, whose culture and religion they shared. They were suffering physical displacement on a level not experienced elsewhere in the country, and yet the Ulster Irish were largely ignored in the discussions of 1641. The Gaelic gentry of the province were prevented by law from expanding their estates, whilst the English and Scots settlers could continue to buy up the land of Catholic landowners. The threat of encirclement was thus very real to Ulster Catholics, even though the plan to exclude Catholic tenants from English- or Scots-owned estates had failed and the planter population was growing only slowly. Such concerns were largely ignored when the Old English talked to Leicester; there was only a vague promise that the new Lord Lieutenant would look into this discrimination. In their isolation, groups of influential Gaelic landowners began to discuss possibilities for self-defence by means of gaining a position of strength from which to fend off attacks by radical Scottish Presbyterians.

THE 'INCIDENT'

In the meantime, Charles I had journeyed to Scotland, ostensibly to finalize the treaty of London but in fact with another mission in mind. He wanted to gain support in Scotland for his struggle with the Westminster Parliament. The king was largely powerless; Parliament had the political momentum, and in the summer of 1641 it had embraced a series of revolutionary policies, some borrowed from the Covenanters. As a result, the constitutional balance of the English policy had fundamentally shifted. No longer would Parliament be called only at the whim of the monarch, because by virtue of the Triennial Act and the Act [against] the Dissolution, it had been transformed from an 'event' into a constant feature of English and Welsh government.[9] Charles had had to back down in the face of its demands to limit his power, to give up his trusted officials and to disband his army. The king had commanded only a small group in the Commons and had an uneasy relationship with the Lords. His army's loyalty had proved dubious, despite the attempts of some officers to use it as a political weapon; and the potential for militant Royalists was decidedly limited. For his opponents, on the other hand, things were very different. Behind them stood the Scottish army in the north, which acted as the muscle of the Presbyterian reformists, and beside them was a groundswell of popular support. Presbyterian ministers and employers could effectively marshall a mob in London to support political attacks either on the queen and her supposed papist plotters or against the Anglican bishops. The mob had played its part most effectively in wrecking the king's resolution to save the Earl of Strafford.

By the summer all of this co-operation appeared to be vanishing as the Scots and English drifted apart. It was clear to the Scots that the English and Welsh Parliament was proving a weak instrument for God's work. After all, plans for the abolition of the episcopacy had stalled several times since 1640. It was also clear that support in the Commons for godly reform did not always go hand in hand with a liking for the Scots. One group in the House had no liking for a Presbyterian system at all. Indeed, Strafford's death appeared to put a cap on the expectations of many. It was hoped that stability would follow his execution; peace with Scotland could seal it. As Edward Nicholas wrote in a letter to Vane, it could make a 'happy and good conclusion of all differences here'. Russell has argued that because the king saw events in personal and not political terms, the opposition had not really succeeded in its attempt to show the king that he could not use men such as Strafford, while at the same time they had made such a central figure of 'Strafford the evil councillor' that they had created false expectations of peace after his death. This was not what Pym wanted when pressure for reform lapsed into something of a doldrum in the wake of the death of the Earl of Bedford. The Ten Propositions of June 1641 were designed to revive the impetus for reform. Amongst other things, they called for the army to be reduced in size, and thereby cost, and for the Scots to be enjoined to begin a withdrawal. They wanted the king to delay his journey to Scotland to allow time for the passage of a series of bills, including church reform and the abolition of the Courts of Star Chamber and High Commission and ship money, which had not yet received assent. Demands to control appointments to government and to deprive the queen of her co-religionists and cosset her with hand-picked nobles were included, papists were also to be kept from court as much as possible and no ambassador from the pope was to be received in the country.[10] These measures addressed both concerns about the possibility of a popish plot at home and a fear that this plot was all-embracing and international. The pope was accused of encouraging a clique around the queen, which in turn affected the composition of the court, the education of the king's children and the stability and safety of the state. It was either an example of paranoia or, more likely, a means of pressing for further radical political changes to protect England and Wales under a populist anti-Catholic banner. It remained true that as the king had appointed oppositionists like Pym, Oliver St John and latterly Saye and Sele to government office, he could just as easily remove them. As matters stood there was no way for Parliament to intervene in the king's choice of ministers, except by way of impeachment. Such attempts to galvanize support for radicalism continued over the summer months, with no reference to a very real Catholic plot which was happening just across the Irish Sea.

The king had also devised an agenda of his own. The Covenanter army was growing weaker during its stay in England, lack of pay was affecting morale and discipline was suffering. In full knowledge of this, Charles pursued a dual policy aimed at neutralizing the Scottish influence in English and Welsh affairs. One strand of his policy aimed to get the Scots army to go home by offering significant concessions on government structure to the Covenanters as an enticement to leave England alone. Second, the king opened discussions with disaffected Scots in the hope of creating a Royalist Scots party. This action is the source of some controversy. Some historians have claimed that the king was attempting to gain the support of Scotland against the Westminster Parliament and that his negotiations convinced him this was possible. Others dismiss this claim as lacking foundation, arguing that the king was rather aiming to provoke a challenge to the Covenanter government from within which would result in its overthrow.[11] In any case the end might have been the same, for surely a Royalist government in Scotland might have begun to dismantle the revolution, and the next logical step would have been to turn the force of this counter-revolution onto the southern kingdom.

Whatever the case, Charles prised himself away from his Westminster Parliament after signing a series of bills and after dismissing the Ten Propositions with statements to the effect that he knew of no more 'ill councillors' after the purge of Strafford, Laud, Finch and Windebank. In early August he headed north, through the rapidly demilitarizing north of England; and in his wake Parliament passed a piece of innovative legislation, the full consequences of which were to become apparent the following year. In order to continue the legislative process while the king was away without having to accept the distrusted queen as regent, on 20 August, Parliament passed an ordinance, which was to have the full effect of an act without the king's signature. As it stood, this was a temporary expedient; the ordinance would be signed on the king's return and become an act in the normal manner. It was only a means of enacting urgent business in the monarch's absence. However, as a precedent it was of lasting importance, for it provided Parliament with a legal means of assuming executive powers.

In Scotland the king continued his dual policy of negotiation and plotting. One of the principal Covenanter generals, James Graham, Earl of Montrose, along with others, was becoming somewhat uneasy with the progress of affairs. He had been a principal actor in the Covenanters' victory and had supported the abolition of the episcopacy and limitations on the king's power. Moreover, he had been responsible for suppressing opposition in the north-east in 1639 when his army had occupied Aberdeen in the campaign against Lord Huntly. Although perfectly happy to back a threat to invade England to abolish episcopacy there if the king did not agree to abolish it in Scotland, the earl was concerned that Scottish government was now as firmly in the hands of an unaccountable few as it had once been in the hands of an unaccountable king. He opposed the second war and began to organize a group of men with similar doubts. Chief amongst his suspect 'few' was the Marquis of Argyll, with whom he in any case had a familial and clan rivalry. There was more to it than this, however. Montrose also suspected that Argyll was setting himself up as a dictator or was prepared to do a personal deal with the king. Montrose responded by signing the Cumbernauld Band in August 1640, along with Lord Namier and sixteen other nobles and lairds. The purpose of the band was vague, but its general aim was probably as 'a pledge to promote the "public ends" of the Covenant in opposition to the "particular and indirect practising of a few"'.[12] Montrose was thus probably trying to get the king to accept what had happened in Scotland quickly before his power was entirely swept away. In other words, it was similar to Hamilton's policy of 'damage limitation' in 1638, although the political landscape had changed dramatically since then. A speedy end to the conflict would head off Argyll's attempts to assume power, either as a direct dictator or by association with a potential rival claimant to the throne. The Marquis of Hamilton had a well-recognized claim to the throne, and Argyll's daughter had married him in 1640. In Covenanter eyes Montrose's objections to the second war and his correspondence with the king seemed dangerous. He was imprisoned in May 1641; and proceedings against him began the month before the king arrived in Edinburgh.[13]

So when Charles arrived in Edinburgh on 14 August 1641, there was already a division within the Scottish leadership, which he aimed to exploit. He concentrated his efforts on Lords Rothes and Loudoun. Hamilton himself no longer played any part in the king's plans at this point; he had not only married Argyll's daughter but had signed the Covenant and become active at Argyll's side. The plan to win over Loudoun came to nothing, and after Rothes's death at the end of the month, the plot failed. Charles was forced to recognize his political weakness and to approve the religious and political legislation constituting the Scottish revolution. He clearly regarded this as acceptance of a *fait accompli* only, however, not as a true mark of approval. Even so, the changes were established and in force.[14]

Charles did not consider this humiliation the final act. In July a plan had been hatched to seize prominent Covenanters in Edinburgh if other plans went wrong. Since by October things clearly had gone wrong, the plan was resurrected while discussions on the control of the Scottish treasury were in progress. Montrose offered to accuse Hamilton and Argyll of treason, just as the king's temper appears to have been inflamed by the Westminster and Edinburgh Parliaments' joint approval of foreign policy. The plan was to lure Hamilton, Argyll and perhaps Lanark (Hamilton's brother and Scottish Secretary) to the king's withdrawing room and then have them seized.[15] The army was disbanding right across the country, and the radicals would have no means to challenge the coup. The Cumbernauld Banders could then form the basis of a new, more moderate government with no plans for interfering with English affairs.

The plot, which became known as the Incident, was betrayed by one of the middle rank of actors, Lieutenant Colonel John Hurry (or Urry). After he reported it to Alexander Leslie, it was communicated to Hamilton, Argyll and Lanark, who all went into hiding. The king proclaimed his complete innocence, although no one really believed him, and a parliamentary committee began to investigate the plot. Yet because it had failed, it was in no one's interest to rake it up and destroy the facade of co-operation, and Lord Loudoun set about calming things down. The committee duly produced its report on 1 November, but by then another issue was holding the attention of the Scottish Parliament.

REBELLION IN IRELAND

In Ireland the central government's ignorance of the fears which were endemic in Ulster was matched by a lack of apprehension on the part of the colonists themselves. There was a veneer of co-habitation on the face of Ulster society.[16] Gaelic families and Old English families like the Bellews of County Louth were involved in local government throughout the province.[17] This seeming harmony existed at all levels, and intermarriages took place among the offspring of small farmers as well as among the gentry. Further, daily social and economic relationships, on the land and in the market-place, gave the appearance of bonds between the Protestant newcomers and the indigenous Catholic Gael. But the issues were not purely social and political; there was the important confessional difference, which would not remain dormant. Even if the more grotesque stories of the supposed failings of Gaelic culture were meant for an audience that would never visit Ireland or come across its inhabitants, they had created expectations abroad of the nature of Ireland. This expectation would always be related to the religious issue and provide a backdrop for those in England, Wales and Scotland with a vested political interest in having people give credence to a popish plot. In Ulster itself, the newcomers in authority saw little prospect of trouble. Ireland had been quiet since 1615, and at the local and central levels, the need to be armed in case of trouble was perceived as less urgent and less necessary in the 1630s than at any time that century.[18] Pretended fears in Britain about the Irish propensity for rebellion bore little relation either to the views of the Dublin government and local governors in the counties and provinces or to the reality of the situation in Ulster. Yet underlying the Ulster veneer was fear. The Scots settlers were believed to be bringing the Bible in one hand and the sword in the other to extirpate the Catholic faith. Naturally, for the Gaels this meant that these settlers already constituted an enemy within. In the end no amount of social intercourse, trade or intermarriage could overcome their mistrust.[19]

In a sense it can be argued that there were two Irish rebellions, one generated by the political failures of the Dublin Parliament's unwillingness to answer Gaelic grievances and the other springing from the fears of the ordinary Catholic Irish man and woman. The two shared related causes and a related impetus, but while one had a distinct leadership, the other often had none at all. The first rebellion was devised during the summer of 1641 by a group of Catholic Irish gentry. Many historians have assumed that this plot had the backing of the king and originally involved an attempt to keep the new Irish army together. Some see the hand of the king as sustaining the plot and rely on the evidence of the Marquis of Antrim given in 1650 to officials of the Commonwealth, suggesting royal involvement.[20] Histories based on Antrim's evidence suggest that at some time during the May session of the Irish Parliament, Charles made contact with a group of Catholics and Old English in order to create pressure for keeping part of the Irish army together. This plan came to nothing in itself but began to foment the eventual plot. More recently, other historians have attacked the idea of Charles's complicity, basing their rebuttal on inconsistencies within Antrim's evidence and the fact that at a later date he claimed not to know of the king's involvement at all.[21] Instead, it is asserted, there were two or three plots. The first was an Old English plot with support from Gaelic Irish such as Rory O'More, Lord Maguire and the Armagh O'Neills. The second plot 'was assisted by some elements of the Catholic church'; and there may have been a third plot involving Owen Roe O'Neill, the exiled claimant to the earldom of Tyrone.[22] This third plot involved the capture of Dublin Castle, because O'Neill insisted that seizure of the centre of government was crucial to the success of the rebellion. According to one argument, the first and last of these plots became intertwined during the summer, whereas another view is that they were one and the same plan, namely, the Colonels' plot, which in turn had its genesis in the king's attempt to hold the Irish army together.[23] Indeed, the argument that there was an Old English plot is not easy to sustain, as this faction's aims were not compatible with those of the O'Neills and the other Gaels. This division was later to account for a wide range of attitudes, ranging through the alliance at Kilkenny between Old English and Catholic Gaels to those who stayed loyal to Charles or to Parliament. Indeed, the evidence for this 'Palesmen's Plot's is weak, based as it is principally on Ormond's impression of what was happening and some remarks by Sir Phelim O'Neill suggesting that the Old English were as deeply involved as the Catholic Irish. It is possible that these are all different shades of the same process of the development of a plot. No one at the time had a clear perspective on what was happening, and we are at the mercy of the viewpoints of a limited range of people involved. In a sense by trying to make them all fit together, we are in danger of distorting the picture further. It is certainly reasonable to believe that Charles had no need of the Irish army in June and July 1641, because he hoped to get a grant of tunnage and poundage in England. If Antrim's vague evidence has any validity at all, then it is in his inference that Charles made the approach to the Catholic Irish during the session of Parliament beginning in May, in the aftermath of the Bill of Attainder passed on Strafford. Any subsequent switching of Charles's hopes first from the English sphere and then to the Scottish scene would account for his abandoning the plan, because consistency was not his forte. In the end, when the Colonels' plot went into abeyance, another stage came into play, involving an association between the prominent Catholic plotters at home and in Europe, perhaps in association with some of the old English. Their immediate objective was to gain control of strategic and important sites in order to strengthen the bargaining position of the native Irish. From this position of strength they sought to secure the political, social and economic ends represented by the Graces and by demands to change the constitutional relationships within government.

The plot did not achieve all of its military ends, perhaps because of its loose nature and the diverse range of interests involved. The one part of the plot that Owen Roe O'Neill had insisted on, the seizure of Dublin Castle, failed. However, on Friday 22 October military targets across Ulster were secured, often without a fight. That night Sir Phelim O'Neill took over Dungannon and Charlemont

Castle, and by the following day, a string of garrisons had been established across central Ulster, dividing the province in half to prevent the Dublin government from mounting concerted opposition with its forces in Antrim, Down and Tyrone. On 24 October Sir Phelim O'Neill announced that the rising was not against the king, nor against the English or Scots settlers, but was aimed only at securing the safety of the native Irish. He was to develop this stance considerably eleven days later. On 4 November, in a move which was to have immense repercussions, O'Neill announced that he held the king's commission for the rising. Although it has long been acknowledged as a forgery, the validity of the commission was widely believed at the time and thus seriously affected the situation in England, Wales and Scotland.[24] Yet militarily, the rebels' impetus was already beginning to wane in some places, and resistance to the rising was growing in strength. Rebel incursions in Down were halted, and government forces moved into the county in some numbers, enabling the preservation of Carrickfergus and Belfast. In the meantime, spontaneous risings had occurred across Ulster, with Rory Maguire taking over most of the county of Fermanagh before the end of the first weekend. The Irish in that county succeeded in dividing the Scots settlers from their English counterparts. Owen Roe O'Neill had suggested that the rising should not be aimed at the Scots in Ulster, and letters had been sent to at least one leading planter assuring him that no harm towards the Scots was intended. Some Scots sided with Irish, including the Fermanagh mustermaster.[25] This co-operation soon appears to have become an exception, however, and the Scots in other counties were attacked and robbed with a ferocity at least equal to that meted out to the English. In south Ulster, the momentum remained with the rebels, and the small armed forces of the government were driven onto the defensive. Lord Moore was besieged at Drogheda in early November by forces led by the Cavan O'Reillies and by Colonel MacMahon's Monaghan forces. A relief force sent to Moore's aid was defeated at Julianstown on 29 November by a detachment of O'Reillies.

The large-scale military attacks characterized only one of the rebellions. Alongside them a second, popular, rebellion consisting of smaller, spontaneous risings may have sprung from similar immediate causes but had a less direct link to the tripartite negotiations between Dublin, the king and Westminster. The fears of a Scottish invasion and the decades of deprivation and displacement created an accumulated anger for which the central plot allowed a release.

The risings began as a rural phenomenon and spread quickly to urban areas. We know a considerable amount about the events of this period from the statements of thousands of people who made depositions before representatives of the Dublin government in 1641, 1642 and again from 1650 onwards. The depositions were collected with the intent of examining losses incurred and gathering evidence about those involved with a view to prosecutions. They still provide fertile ground for studying the events of the rebellion, particularly the nature of this second rebellion.[26] This popular rebellion caused government to stop functioning and provoked fears that the Old English, who had retained their position in society despite the influx and influence of the newcomers, would side with the Gaelic rebels. By mid-November, within three weeks of the rebellion in Ulster, the government of Leinster had collapsed. The victory at Julianstown gave a substantial boost to the morale of the rebels and acted as an impetus for the attempts to unite the Catholic Irish with the Catholic Old English. Colonel Monaghan initiated meetings with the Louth Old English as he approached Drogheda, and prominent members of the gentry joined him. One such case was John Bellew of Willestone, in County Louth in Leinster, who in 1641 was appointed sheriff of the county. He was also a collector of the fourth of the subsidies promised to Charles I by Parliament.[27] By December 1641 all of this had changed. In a letter to Mr Christopher Barnewell of Rathesbey, also a subsidy collector, Lord Moore, under siege at Drogheda, referred to Bellew, who was negotiating with the rebels for the release of prisoners. He expressed the hope that the matter would be 'dealt with to the satisfaction of all'. However, despite the fact that Moore had secured a pass for Bellew and James Butt of Athcanne to travel between Drogheda and Dublin, there is an air of unease about his letter. It seems that Moore may have already been suspicious about the nature of Bellew's relationship with the rebels.[28] A week earlier, Moore had written to the Council informing them that Bellew had been with the rebels but that it was not clear to him what Bellew was up to. Another of the subsidy collectors, John Stanley, a Drogheda alderman, was also consorting with the rebel faction, and he told Moore that the county gentry had sided with them. Moore referred in his letter to Barnewell to the poor state of communications which was impeding his understanding of affairs, and it was this which prompted his unease. His uncertainty was well founded, and his lack of knowledge was worse than he suspected, for Bellew maintained stronger links with the rebels than Moore guessed. Moreover, Barnewell was also a rebel.

Within weeks Bellew's intentions were known and he, Stanley and Barnewell were named as rebels in the proclamation issued by the Council and Lord Justices on 8 February 1642. Another subsidy collector from Louth, Oliver Cashell, was also named as a rebel at the same time.[29] No less than a third of the men appointed as minor officials of the state in Louth on the eve of the rebellion proved to be what the Council declared 'ungrateful, detestable, vile, and unnatural traytors'. Probably the deep personal sense of betrayal as well as the general rebellion affected the Council's reaction. After all, Sir William Parsons and John Borlasse had issued Bellew's shrievalty warrant as Lord Justices, and it cannot have been pleasant for them to find out that a man they had trusted had other loyalties. The proclamation was vicious and punitive; the loyal subjects of the king were empowered to

> pursue and plague with fire and sword, apprehend, destroy and kill, by all ways and means they may all the said persons, their partakers, aiders, maintainers, comforters, confederates, complices, and associats.[30]

At the same time it was an expression of powerlessness. Bellew, whether or not he was pursued with fire and sword, was not caught. He raised a unit of soldiers, and by 1646 he was the commander of the guard to the train of artillery in the Confederates' Leinster army.[31] Later, he raised a company of footsoldiers for Ormond's army in 1648, which again acted as a guard to the train of artillery.[32]

The Council's vicious attitude toward Bellew was not universally shared. Several Protestant English colonists owed him gratitude. In a testament supporting Bellew's attempt to escape transportation to Connaught in 1654, Cecily Jones wrote:

> at the beginning of the rebellion, John Edens, Richard Lason and myself came accidently to Mr Bellew of Willestone in the county of Louth, house where our lives were preserved by him, and ourselves civilly entertained and safely conveyed by him to Tredath and I did then observe that the said Mr Bellew and all his family were as much for the preservation of the English as any could be.[33]

However, not every Catholic in Ireland felt as Bellew did. Pent-up anger at their displacement, their financial indebtedness to the newcomers and their exclusion from the processes of government resulted in mass murder. Small leaderless risings got out of hand, and Catholic rebels killed individual Protestants in robberies attempting to take over settler estates. In Fermanagh, the mayor was threatened with murder by one of his employees, who said he would have his house and estate. By early November isolated attacks on the homes of settlers had developed from robbery and assault into the murder of large numbers of Scots and English. Although the effects of this violence may have been less serious in areas where there were stronger contacts between the settlers and the native Irish, in others, where contacts principally centred on the indebtedness of the Irish, their fury was greater. Many attacks involved large numbers of women, and some commentators also mention the participation of children. Some of the women involved acted as leaders of the attacks on Protestants; Jane Hamskin reputedly led an assault on a cottage in Armagh. Mary O'Dowd has shown that as the rebellion spread throughout Ireland, women did not simply appear at the head of mobs but took on administrative offices usually reserved for men, claiming to act as sheriffs and as jurors.[34] It would seem that they were either mimicking English government form in a kind of charivari or, perhaps more likely, reinforcing the Gaelic Irish anger at being excluded from governing their own lives as a result of the English conquest.

There was considerable speculation on the role of the Catholic clergy in the rebellion, particularly the popular rebellion and its attendant murders. In several areas the attacks on settlers were allegedly led or urged on by priests, and historians have used deposition evidence to affirm the role played by the English government. It seems certain that the clergy was a very important factor in the outbreak of rebellion in County Mayo in Connaught.[35] Indeed, the Catholic Archbishop of Tuam, Dr Malachy O'Queely, was accused of provoking the rebellion during the summer of 1641 by suggesting that Catholics had the right to expel Protestants because they were Puritans and were acting contrary to the wishes of the king.[36] Dr O'Queely further began to bind together the disparate raiding parties which hitherto characterized the rebellion in Mayo and give them a common political purpose based on shared religious grievances and the economic depression. By December the military governor of the county, Viscount Mayo, was swamped by the number of disturbances in the shire and unable to do more than try to buy off one party or another in the face of instructions to maintain order which he could not carry out. The county also saw bloodshed on the same scale as was witnessed to the east. At Shrule a convoy of settlers and Protestant ministers being escorted by Viscount Mayo's

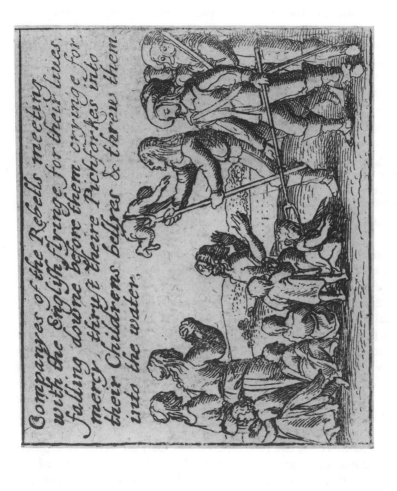

Plate 3 Barbarous and Inhumane Proceedings against the professors of the reformed religion, London, 1665, courtesy of The British Library, London.

forces towards Galway was massacred by some of its own guards, led by, amongst others, the high sheriff. This event forced Mayo to align himself first with the Catholic faith, perhaps for his own safety, and then with the rebellion, as it widened to include support from the Old English.

The murders of many Scots and English settlers guilty only by association with plantation and displacement rapidly became, in a Protestant myth, a massacre of appalling proportions. Historians have debated the scale of the killings. Without using the term massacre, some still suggest that about 4,000 people died as a direct result of violence, with a further 8,000 dying of starvation and exposure after being driven naked from their homes into the autumn and winter of 1641–2. Moreover, the Protestants, out of fear and anger, responded in kind and a cycle of violence began. Whether we choose to use the term massacre or not is really beside the point. For those involved it was a frightening and horrific period of indiscriminate violence. At Portadown there certainly was a massacre. The settlers were driven into the river and drowned by assailants under the command of Toole MacCann. When such things as this actually happened, it is little surprise that other myths developed, nor is it surprising that these were believed and that there were retaliations on Catholics later. In 1641 censorship in England had come to an end with the abolition of the Court of the High Commission. As a result, the English press burgeoned. The accounts of massacres, accompanied by gruesome woodcuts, made ideal gutter-press material, containing as they did salacious material and dire religious portents. This lurid information was supplemented by the large numbers of displaced colonists who fled across the Irish Sea and travelled the roads of England and Wales in search of new homes. Such refugees were provided with passes entitling them to help in each of the parishes through which they passed. No doubt in each village that received the refugees, the massacre would be a major topic of conversation.

By the end of 1641, the rebels had developed the series of defined aims which had been announced initially in the declarations of Sir Phelim O'Neill. It was these aims which had won over men like Viscount Mayo, who had been initially loyal to Dublin. In December, a Remonstrance was passed to Dublin through a prisoner held by the rebels, George Wentworth. This set out the issues over which the rebellion had broken out, and included the statement that the rebellion, as O'Neill had said, was aimed not at the king but, as

Dr O'Queely had urged in County Mayo, at Puritans who were subverting his majesty's government. Further, the Dublin government had been composed of unworthy men who, being of little estate themselves, had lined their pockets at the expense of Ireland. To prevent the king from hearing their pleas, the Irish had been banned from leaving the country to present their case. The Remonstrance attempted to embrace even Episcopalian Protestants into the cause, speaking of the deposed Protestant bishops as victims of the Puritan faction.

The rebels asked the king for his support and promised to undertake whatever he required for the defence of the Irish and their religion against the Puritans.[37] The demands were further honed in the document O'Neill sent into England on 10 February 1642 on behalf of the army in Ulster and Leinster. Here the demands were stiffer, involving the return of the Catholic church in Ireland to its position in the reign of Queen Mary, which was in effect a complete re-establishment of the old faith. The abbeys, priories and monasteries were to be reconstructed and their old lands and incomes restored to them. There was also to be a papal nuncio resident in Ireland, and contacts with the papacy were to be reopened. In government, only Catholics were to be allowed to deal with Catholic religious issues and only Protestants with Protestant concerns. Secular government was to be shared by both religions, not subject to English interference. Any governor was to require Irish approval.[38] Discussions on the development of these aims suggest that in effect the executive would be Catholic and Parliament would be dominated by Catholics. These propositions were also to be put to Charles, although they were quite unacceptable to him; even in his days of most extreme need over the next six years, the king sought to avoid committing himself to them. In one way they were no more extreme than the Covenant in Scotland, which had committed the nation to Presbyterianism. However, because of the post-Reformation development of the Protestant church in the other three nations, Ireland's attempt to be a Catholic state across the Irish Sea was not to be accepted. This partly explained the toning down of the one-church theme in the proposition sent to the Westminster Parliament, but this subtlety had little or no effect on the attitudes of the Welsh and English MPs, nor did it appease the Scots.

The often vicious reaction of the Dublin government only exacerbated the affair. Faced with such draconian measures, many who had avoided commitment began to believe that since the government had already decided their guilt, they had little to lose by associating with rebels, and so rebellion spread. The spring hiatus allowed for the effective intervention in Ulster of forces from Scotland, but it was also important for the Dublin government to finance its own military needs. Its sources of income were dramatically reduced; the subsidy money was soon gone; and when the rebellion began, access to the main legitimate funding, the customs and excise duties, collapsed. The treasury books of the Lord Justices which survive for part of 1642–3 detail much of the expenditure, but little of the income which had to be subsidized. Credit and loans from Britain began to arrive by the end of 1641, although not in the amounts promised. Of £50,000 promised, only £16,500 arrived before the new year. The accounts reveal that the Dublin government had to rely very much on international trade for basic needs. Well-tried and trusted trade routes and patterns already existed to supply the government in Dublin. Wine routes included not only European ports but also substantial use of western British ports such as Chester and Beaumaris. These ports were used by Dublin during the early years of the Irish war for a variety of goods.[39] We can get some idea of these by looking at the claim for expenses submitted by Thomas Lawton to the Lord Justices of Ireland in September 1642.[40] In July 1642 Sir William Anderson had commissioned Lawton to import shoes from Britain for the army.[41] Lawton's difficulties arose when he attempted to obtain the promised fee for his services, as opposed to payment for the shoes themselves. His bill for £14-10s-02d in wages and his claim for expenses, submitted in September, tell us precisely how he undertook the business and from where he purchased the materials. Initially he crossed from Dublin to Anglesey and then journeyed to England.[42] The exact pattern of his journey is unclear, but it seems to have involved travelling to Kirkham in central Lancashire and then back to Manchester. At some point the shoes and shirts were put aboard gabards, inland waterway craft, possibly at Chester. They were then transshipped onto barques for Ireland at Chester's outlying anchorages at Neston or Caldy on the Dee estuary. It appears that at Ness or Neston the goods may have been disembarked for some reason and moved along the coast on the sands of the estuary before eventually departing from Caldy. By 13 September, Lawton had been paid only £5 of the £14-10s-02d which the journey had cost him and he petitioned the Lord Justices for recompense. The petition was sent to Anderson for confirmation and payment allowed.

In Britain the reaction to the rebellion had major consequences. The king received the news while in Scotland, and the Edinburgh Parliament, soon absorbed in discussing the issue, immediately lost interest in the 'Incident'. Charles sent arms from Scotland to the Dublin government at his own expense and began to raise volunteers for an army to go over to Ireland.[43] He quickly left Edinburgh and returned to an apparently tumultuous welcome in London on 25 November 1641.[44] Once again the king was more or less powerless in the face of Parliament, and his attempt to speed up the creation of an army was seen as dangerous interference. In January 1642 Charles published a proclamation against those in arms, followed by a publicity drive of sermons on fast days containing information about the war. By then Charles's role in affairs was being subjected to greater public and political scrutiny because of his attempted coup d'état on 4 January.

PARLIAMENT AND THE REBELLION

Parliament had reassembled on 20 October. During the king's absence, Pym had attempted vainly to maintain momentum for the continued attack on prerogative government. However, he had been thwarted largely by the period of relief which had followed the successful passage of the remaining legislation of the first session just prior to the king's departure for Scotland. As peace appeared to be breaking out, the potential fear for the 'popish plot' diminished, remaining again out of step with events in Ireland. Oppositionist policy was to try to keep up pressure on the queen, who was identified with the 'popish plot', and to draft a Remonstrance to the king which would serve three purposes. First, it would rehearse the grievances of the 1630s; second, it would sum up what had been done so far to remedy them; and third, it would lay out demands for further changes. In effect the Remonstrance would bind the oppositionists together by declaring the platform from which they would launch their new agenda for the second session. The document was being drafted when news of the rebellion arrived in Westminster. Consequently, discussion turned on the means to put down the rebellion and the means by which an army could be raised. It soon became clear that despite the rapid dissemination of horror stories and public expressions of dismay at what was happening in Ireland, there was little enthusiasm for a volunteer army.[45] Of an army which was designated to be 10,000 strong on 11 November, only 1,400 men had arrived at the end of December in Ireland – with no pay and too few arms.[46] Problems with funding had to be seriously debated. Parliament realized that a sum of £400,000 was necessary and began to acquire it in the form of a loan from the City of London. How to raise the sum to pay back the loan was an even greater problem.

The draft Remonstrance, presented to the Commons in November, was ill received. The backdrop of a real Catholic rebellion turned out to be less of a spur than the fictional one had been. The spirit of conciliation was not be eradicated. Rather, there was a belief that there was a need to shelve differences to tackle the rebellion effectively. The Remonstrance was perceived to be out of step with this mood, opening up old wounds at a time when people were thankful that they had healed, and proposing that the revolution be carried further at a time when many saw the Irish problem as more pressing. The document also referred to the planned alterations in the constitutional structure. Parliament was to be given more control over foreign policy, and it included a call for an immediate Protestant alliance in Europe. Control over the upbringing of the king's children was extended to control over the lives of their guardians, their education and their marriages. This measure was a direct extension of the Ten Propositions and Pym's policy of trying to implicate the queen in plots to control the heir to the throne. Another extension of earlier policy was the furthering of attempts to control executive appointments. The appointments in the early summer, the so-called bridge appointments aimed at building connections between the executive and the opposition, were clearly not enough. They were made at the king's will and could just as easily be reversed. What Pym and others required was some way of making the choice themselves, or at least obtaining the right of veto over such appointments. The Scottish experience had suggested that it was perfectly possible to achieve this aim, and that the king himself could be brought to agreement.[47]

The Remonstrance was not entirely welcome; in Clarendon's words, 'The House seemed generally to dislike it'.[48] On the other hand some did feel it was necessary. The king had been welcomed home by the London populace, and there did appear to be a spirit of conciliation, but the deep doubts in many people's minds were not eased either by the 'Incident' or by Sir Phelim O'Neill's claim to have the king's commission. The fictional popish plot and the real rebellion in Ireland had now blended into one in the City, and the judgements from God – smallpox and the plague – visited on the

City during the summer sharpened perceptions that something was still amiss, even before the Irish rebellion. Once the rebellion had broken out, these perceptions were further underscored. The London woodturner Nehemiah Wallington was able to link the rebellion directly to Strafford's supposed disarming of the Protestants and his creation of the new Irish army, probably at the king's behest.[49] Moreover, an immediate cause for concern was a group of discontented indigenous former officers. These had been disbanded along with the English army after the army plot had exposed their loyalties. Their presence stimulated the fears of the Londoners. In the end-of-year elections this expressed itself in the return of radical candidates to the City government.

Since the purpose of the Grand Remonstrance was also to reaffirm the support of the London crowds for radicalism, it had to be published. It may have been evident in the upper echelons of the political world that some of their supporters' optimism had disappeared. Nehemiah Wallington was probably looking at the tattered remains of a stalled revolution when he recorded the events of December 1641. The Root and Branch had come to nothing, and even the hearings concerned with scandalous ministers in August had likewise failed to prompt action.[50] The debate over the Remonstrance itself extended over a whole day, commencing at 9 a.m. on 22 November until 2 a.m. the following day. It was a long and often angry debate, and the measure was carried in the much-reduced House by only eleven votes. The debate over the publication was even more fierce, as it was realized that there was no intention to send it to the Lords first. Many of the moderate members of the House of Commons, who had supported the reforms of the past year, were stirring uneasily, believing rightly that the Remonstrance was intended for broadcasting to the general public and not simply as a petition to the king, who expressly forbade publication when he received it on 1 December.[51] Despite Clarendon's later fulminations and declarations of trickery, the majority in favour of printing the document was much greater than that in favour of its passage through the House. The king could muster only eighty-three votes on this contentious issue, with 135 against.[52]

THE JANUARY COUP

The king began his new double game. He responded to the accompanying petition rather than to the Remonstrance itself, and did so politely but firmly. He pointed out that he had co-operated with the reforms of the past year and that he had driven from his side those to which Parliament had objected most violently, claiming to be confused by references to 'wicked and malignant party' because he had already done as Parliament had asked. This response set the tone throughout, as Charles claimed that all had been done as required.[53] At the same time Charles began his plans for a military coup involving the disbanded officers in London, seeking to capitalize on their sympathies, use them to create an armed body in the City and seize control of the Tower.[54] On the same day that he replied to the Remonstrance he appointed Sir Thomas Lunsford as governor of the Tower, in an apparent repetition of the April plot. Reaction was swift and two-pronged. The Commons loudly debated the issues and claimed to see in it a desperate design against the House. The Lords as a whole did not concur, but the Commons appealed to a minority of peers who were clearly in sympathy to join a petition to the king. The second element in this counterattack was launched through the London pulpits on the following Sunday, when Londoners were regaled with stories of an impending Royalist crackdown. The result was predictable; the London mob gathered in the City that day and throughout the week. In response the king quickly dismissed Lunsford, but the Londoners now wanted more and turned their ire to the bishops, whom the crowd held responsible for the Lords' refusal to support the Commons in the petition against Lunsford. The streets from Westminster to the City were soon blocked by massive crowds of men and women who, on 27 December, imprisoned the Lords and bishops in their House. Those nobles who moved to and fro in their coaches had to put up with Londoners glaring in through the windows looking for secreted prelates. At Westminster, fighting broke out as soldiers, Lunsford amongst them, idiotically threatened the crowds in Palace Yard. Whilst some demonstrators near Charing Cross were apparently armed, those at Westminster were not. Lunsford and Nicholas Hyde's actions there caused panic, driving some Londoners into the Palace itself to take refuge in meeting rooms and courtrooms, sometimes interrupting proceedings. Lunsford's attack only increased the anger of the Londoners, who began to arrive in even greater numbers. Looking back on this day, some commentators claimed to have heard the apprentices in the crowd being referred to as 'roundheads' – an appellation somewhat equivalent to the late-twentieth-century term 'skinhead' in its description of the savagely short haircuts of the apprentice boys. The term quickly became applied to the whole crowd and beyond to all of the king's opponents. In turn the swaggering courtiers defending the bishops were soon likened to the armed defenders of the Spanish Catholic king, the *caballeros*, changed in the English tongue to 'cavaliers'.[55]

Despite a royal proclamation against the disturbances and threats to call out the trained bands, the crowds stayed out until dark, and the bishops had to be sneaked out of Parliament.[56] On the following day only two prelates made it to the House. What Pym had failed to achieve constitutionally was now being achieved by the people of London. The bishops had been deprived of their political voice, and a separation of church and state was being effected by popular acclaim. Further fighting broke out that day as the crowds surged around Westminster Abbey trying to find some apprentices who had been arrested the previous day. Prominent amongst the rescuers was John Lilburne, who already had a reputation as a radical. He had been imprisoned for distributing works by the Protestant radicals Prynne, Bastwicke and Burton and had been released in the early days of the Long Parliament at the instigation of the MP Oliver Cromwell. As the crowd approached the abbey, many people were assailed by men employed by the Archbishop of York, who was also the Dean of Westminster. This gang hurled stones at the apprentices from the roof of the building, injuring several people. Fighting broke out, and the disturbances continued over the next few days. In Parliament it proved a difficult Christmastide. The 'mob' was clearly not under the complete control of the oppositionists, even if their aims were in sympathy. However, the bishops effectively put the gun to their own heads when twelve of them protested on 29 December that the decisions of the Lords over the past two days were null and void because of their absence. The previous day the Lords had passed a resolution recognizing themselves still to be a free assembly, and the bishops were trying to invalidate this vote. The king received the prelates' petition and passed it to the Lords, who passed it to the Commons. In the Lower House it may have been seized on with some relief as it provided an escape hatch from the difficult situation of the tumults. The bishops were impeached for being a part of a plot to dissolve the Parliament illegally, and on 30 December they were imprisoned. The crowds had won a victory largely due to the bishops' naivety, and the tired citizens did not gather on that day.[57]

The king was still continuing his game by other means. He had decided that the time was ripe for his own coup, and as was becoming usual, he planned it as a double play. As he drafted his violent plans, the king elevated to government office two of his moderate opponents: Lucius Carey, Viscount Falkland – a beautiful young intellectual opposed to conformity and absolutism – and Sir John Culpepper – a shrewd and gifted MP. Culpepper stepped into the Treasury after, it was alleged, Pym had refused it; and Falkland became a secretary of state. Edward Hyde, later Earl of Clarendon, was also in favour, and these three were known to be drafting the king's moderate responses to the Commons' attacks on his position.[58] A small demonstration outside Whitehall Palace gates on 31 December seems to have been used as a poor pretext for the king's next move. On 1 January, as Ireland was being discussed in the Commons, Charles planned the arrest of prominent members of Parliament. In the belief that opposition to him was largely a personal affair led by a cabal rather than a phenomenon with widespread support, Charles tried to remove the prominent figures as he had in Edinburgh. He singled out Edward Montague, Lord Kimbolton, son of the Earl of Manchester in the Lords, who had long signalled his opposition to the king (as Lord Mandeville he had signed the petition asking for a new Parliament). From the Commons, Charles picked Pym and a series of his longest-serving opponents. One was Sir Arthur Hesilrige from Leicestershire, who had interfered with ship money collection in his own county and whose father had been one of the Five Knights prosecuted over the forced loan in the 1620s. The others were John Hampden – the best-known opponent of ship money – William Strode and Denzil Holles, both of whom had held Speaker Finch in his chair back in March 1629. It was an honourable collection of men, each with his own badge of courage in the face of the overweening government of Charles I. All were charged with subverting the laws of the kingdom and setting up what was in effect a democratic government, although the king called it tyranny. Charles further claimed to believe that they had incited the Scots to invade and that they had stirred up riots and had tried to turn the people away from their affections towards the king. The charges were passed to the Lords where the king wanted a committee to examine each individual charge and issued instructions debarring certain Lords, including Essex and Brooke, from being part of such a committee. Instead the Lords debated the charge as a whole to test its legality. On 4 January the Commons requested help from the London City government, and after lunch waited for events to unfold. Charles behaved foolishly, deciding to go in person to the Commons to ask the five MPs to surrender. With an armed guard he processed slowly across from Whitehall to Westminster, giving enough time for the five men to slip away down river to the safety of the City. Charles went into the Commons with the Elector Palatine and the Earl of Roxburgh, leaving the armed men outside. Realizing quickly that the five men were nowhere to be seen, the king asked the Speaker, William Lenthall, if they were there. Lenthall echoed words that one of the five members, Denzil Holles, had bellowed at Finch in 1629:

> I have neither eyes to see nor tongue to speak in this place but as the house is pleased to direct me, whose servant I am here; and humbly beg your majesty's pardon that I cannot now give any other answer than this to what your majesty is pleased to demand of me.[59]

The coup had failed. The king accepted that the five men had indeed left, declared that the 'birds had flown', gathered his scattered dignity and stormed out. Once he had left the House, Parliament decided that it was not safe to stay in Westminster and adjourned to the Guildhall in London. Any trust which had resided in Charles evaporated. Crowds had milled about Charles as he left Parliament shouting 'Privilege! Privilege!' In reality it was the king for whom Westminster was unsafe, and the queen was soon in particular danger.

In the City the trained bands were put under the command of Phillip Skippon, a veteran of the continental wars, without consulting the king. A joint committee of Parliamentarians and councillors was formed to ensure public safety, and the people of London prepared to fight the king's soldiers. But they never came. Charles had dismayed his moderate politicians; they had been duped by fair words into leaving their erstwhile colleagues in the Commons, and moderation, their stock-in-trade, was in an instant swept aside. As London prepared for war, with thousands of mariners and apprentices promising to live and die for Parliament, the court went into a period of inertia brought on by unexpected defeat.[60] On 10 January the royal family fled to Hampton Court, with the queen in fear of impeachment. Many believed that she had inspired the coup; Whitelock had written,

> Divers excuses were made for this action [the king's attempt to arrest the five members]: some said, it was the women's council and irritation

of the king (telling him if he were king of England he would not suffer
himself to be baffled about these persons) provoked him to go to the
house himself.[61]

That night the king, queen and their three children slept together
in one bed in a cold, unprepared palace, while in London triumphalism seized the people. On the following day, the members of
Parliament, Lords and Commons, processed from London to Westminster, accompanied by the trained bands of the City, to be rein-
stalled in the Palace. Elsewhere in the country, this instability at the
centre was greeted with less triumphalism, and rumours of Catholic
invasions from Ireland began to spread. Both king and Parliament
toyed with war preparations, but not yet in earnest. The king's mind
turned to evacuating the queen, and preparations were accordingly
made to send her abroad with enough money and crown jewels to
facilitate arms buying. By mid-February Henrietta Maria was ready
and the court went to Dover. On 23 February she left.

During the ensuing weeks, Parliament and the king were still in
communication on some issues. Charles had little option. Parliament was demanding that he cede control of the ports and forts of
the kingdom, and little help could be expected from elsewhere. The
Scots were in contact with Parliament, and the Catholic rebels in
Ireland had launched a fresh initiative. The policy of moderation
was resurrected, but it was mistrusted by the king's opponents.
When the king apologized and withdrew the treason charges against
the five Commonsmen and Kimbolton, Parliament responded by
arresting the Attorney-General for drawing up the charge. Stephen
Marshall, described by Wedgwood as a 'warm and lively preacher',
preached on the theme of 'Curse ye Meroz', the text of Judges 5:23,
about the duty to participate in the Lord's struggles and not to
stand aside. It was a text that was to have deep resonance amongst
the Puritans of the American colonies, who came to believe that
they had fled from the struggle for the soul of England.

The last joint acts of the king and Parliament concerned Ireland.
On 15 February an Impressment Act was passed empowering the
justices of the peace to conscript men for service in Ireland. A
second act dealt with the financial matters of funding this force and
the forces being raised in Scotland, which England and Wales were
to pay for. A loans scheme had been initiated in late January, but
this failed to bring in a great sum. The second plan was to raise one
million pounds by the sale to speculators of 2,500,000 acres of Irish

land, to be confiscated from the rebels when the rebellion was over. A third set of funds, totalling £400,000, was to be raised through a nationwide tax. Papers from the loans and gift scheme launched on 31 January 1642 survive in great quantities and provide ripe ground for study. A few, like those of Buckinghamshire or Surrey, have been printed or transcribed, but most are in manuscript form at the Public Record Office and provide the first major source for the war funding in England and Wales.[62] The collection contains groups by county but also several miscellaneous collections. Their values are manifold and demonstrate the operation of the levy at a local level in a way that will be examined fully in later chapters. John Morrill has commented upon the Buckinghamshire examples and demonstrates that this form of funding, like ship money, stretched well beyond the social confines of normal taxation levies. In each county a commission was established to oversee the collection of the tax; this was then devolved through the office of sheriff to the high or chief constables to the petty constables and thence into the parishes themselves. This form of material provides some idea of the social and gender composition of the taxpayers in local communities. Its benefits for studies beyond the scope of this work are immense. For our purpose here they demonstrate that a significant number of people around the country were at least concerned to help the refugees and other victims of the war in Ireland, even if they were less keen to support fully the military effort being prepared. The later levy, the collection of the £400,000, was to employ the same general mechanisms of the loan and gift; however, the later portions were to be employed in a different war to the one envisaged. The Irish rebellion was only just beginning to shake Britain's political, social and economic worlds, whereas the estrangement of king and Parliament was at the centre of a morass of ructions about to reverberate throughout England and Wales. The problem of the militia brought all of this to a head, and it is to the consequences of this issue that we now turn.

PART II

Wars and Civil Wars

5

The Agony of Choosing Sides

I finde all heere full of feares and voyd of hopes. Parents and children, brothers, kindred, I and deere friends have the seed of difference and division abundently sawed in them[1]

Fear played a major part in determining the next stages of the civil war period, fear that spread from the top of the political tree downwards. Although Londoners may have been triumphant in Westminster, Pym and his allies were not entirely jubilant over having been proved right about the king's plots and his untrustworthiness. Indeed, they may have been in fear for their lives. They had escaped the January coup, but the stakes had been raised. When Parliament returned to Westminster after five days in the City, Pym and his supporters went into the House only during daylight hours and remained hidden at night, and until March Westminster was guarded by the trained bands. The separation of the two principal branches of government, monarchy and Parliament, had also forced a serious crisis on England and Wales that reached from the top to the bottom of society in these two nations. During the ensuing year the crisis was going to force many people into making an uncomfortable decision about their loyalty and commitment.

Many individuals and corporate bodies like towns and cities delayed such decisions as long as possible, in the hope that the crisis would pass before a choice had to be made, although an unwelcome atmosphere of urgency hovered in the background. Already the issue was developing cosmic importance. Writers like the Lincolnshire minister Hansard Knollys had, like Samuel Rutherford in Scotland before him, identified the crisis with a great work of reformation – the preparation for the millennium. Knollys had claimed in 1641 in *A Glimpse of Syon's Glory* that the millennium would be hailed by 'the multitude but in a confused manner, as the noise of many waters but then God moves the hearts of the great ones, of noble, of learned ones; and they come into the work'.[2] Ministers like Stephen Marshall were urging people not to stand by and watch but to join in what was evidently God's work. Nevertheless, many motives provided a strong impetus to remain aloof. Uncertainty about the justice of the respective causes was a major issue, and the farther from the centre people were, the more clouded was their perception of these causes. Certainly, MPs at the centre were more 'acutely aware of the interplay of personality and politics, and had lived through and corporately experienced the great debates and traumas of 1640–1'.[3] They reacted in different ways. Some, like Pym, saw the need for cohesion and solidarity; others left Westminster for home as winter turned to spring, and at times it was difficult to keep the Commons quorate. It is also important to realize that the provinces viewed things differently. Some historians see the social order problem as central to some provincial perceptions, and it may be that the financial issues were also important. In both cases it was the involvement of the four nations which had a tremendous impact on people. The international aspect of events had already drawn people into the mesh of funding and taxation in a way that was already set to equal ship money for its penetration through the social hierarchy.

The fears of Irish invasions were another aspect of the international crisis. In Milford Haven and Anglesey there was panic, at least for a while, because of the fear of an Irish invasion. On Anglesey people were afraid that the local Catholics would seek common cause with the Irish rebels and that the island, a staging post in the trade with Dublin, would become the site of an invasion. Across the Menai Strait in Caernarfonshire similar anxiety abounded. The inhabitants of Anglesey petitioned Parliament in March 1642 on the issue of their defencelessness, even though the Impressment Act had made the Caernarfonshire trained band jointly responsible for the defence of Anglesey.[4] Similar fears were probably spread throughout the country by the increasing numbers of Irish refugees who were passing through the towns and villages of England and Wales in 1642.

Throughout England and Wales, rioting broke out in response to the crisis. In some cases it was inspired by the Irish threat, in others the rioters were airing long-standing grievances. The riots of 1626–8 at Gillingham Forest in Dorset were resurrected in September 1642 during the first weeks of the war. Fenland riots in north Nottinghamshire and neighbouring Lincolnshire, which had also begun in the 1620s, were periodically sparked off again in 1641 and in the spring of 1642.[5] It has not yet been fully determined whether or not there was a significant rise in the number of riotous incidents in 1640–2, and there is much scope for research in this field. In Nottinghamshire and Staffordshire there appear to have been no great increases in social instability, although this assessment does not tally with the perceptions of observers in the counties. Nottinghamshire quarter sessions dealt with about seventeen riots between 1639 and 1642. This number is not very different from the previous five years; it certainly does not equal the number of riots in the county during the years of food-supply problems from 1619 to 1623 (forty-three) or from 1629 to 1633 (twenty-nine). However, there were signs that JPs were not quite at peace. Special sessions of the peace were convened to deal with riots in 1640, 1641 and 1642. None had been held in the previous eight years, and they had not been held in comparable numbers for about twenty years. In 1642, however, the perceptions of the justices began to be matched by their actions. Quarter sessions were held in the county right up until October, dealing with eleven riots. They were generally confined to the south and east of the county, and a special session was convened in May at Ellkesley to deal with fourteen men accused of riot, affray and insult.[6] Even though perceptions and reality readily became intertwined, it is probable that we are looking at the actions of a worried and oversensitive administration. The Ellkesley sessions were not really dealing with anything constituting a major riot, and resolution could have waited until the July sessions. Yet perceptions are important. It is clear that many in the Commons in late 1641 were aghast at the involvement of the London rioters in the political debate, and their relatives and fellow governors from the shire were no doubt keen to prevent the same from happening in their areas too. If some MPs were driven to support Charles's apparently moderate tones because of the disorder at Westminster, many people in the counties of England and Wales would back the king for the same reason. Parliamentary rule seemed to some to imply the participation of the rude multitude, which left the king to stand for order and stability. What we do not really know is how many took this view and how many of society's governors saw the crisis as the spark, rather than blaming one side or the other.

As has been pointed out with much justification, 'Fear drove some men into royalism; it drove far more into neutralism'. This position must not be seen as negative, for people withdrew to their shires, where they constructed defences built upon tradition and upon the maintenance of social peace through the rule of law and custom. This was their attempt to prevent the country from being torn apart by anarchy and war.[7] We can see from county hierarchies such as Nottinghamshire's that some men believed in attempts to preserve order not through taking sides but by operating through the structures of government already in place. The tenacity of some of society's traditional rulers to carry on in this way is remarkable. It has already been mentioned that the Nottinghamshire quarter sessions continued until war had begun. The Staffordshire JPs tried to deal with the problem of open conflict by holding a special session in November, and Cornwall sessions continued for much of the war.

For some people the first crystallizing issue was that of the militia. There was widespread concern in some political circles that the king would misuse any forces commanded by him to put down the Irish rebellion. There were several grounds for this belief. An Irish army had loomed as a fearsome bogey in 1641; an English army had also produced sabre-rattlers in the north that year, and the swaggering cavaliers at Westminster in December had been its leaders. This precedent, coupled with the panic after 5 January, created the demand for the armed forces to be taken out of the king's hands, at least temporarily. Parliament's aim to control royal appointments was now extended to include the nomination of the lords lieutenant. Parliament was not enamoured of the lieutenancies and had recently investigated their role in government, following apprehensions that they were interfering in the functions of other county officers. Nevertheless, in early 1642 Parliament requested that the king allow it to nominate the lieutenants. It was, of course, a lot to ask the king to agree to the effective emasculation of the monarch's local power. Charles could not accede without surrendering a valuable prop to the might and power of the monarchy. The diminution of his power was mirrored by the smallness of Charles's court in the days after his flight from the capital. Hardly any of his Council had accompanied him, although his new allies, Culpepper and Falkland, were with him at Windsor. Hyde was also with Charles at the end of February, drafting the king's responses to Parliament's militia proposals.[8] The first of the king's rejections came at the end of January when he dismissed a parliamentary petition regarding the control of the militia, castles and fortifications. However, Parliament had proceeded, unhindered, to establish a committee in mid-January to oversee military matters. It devised a militia ordinance which would give Parliament power over the militia. Following the king's rejection of this second proposal in February, the committee chair, William Pierrepoint, urged more radical action. On 2 March negotiations with the king ended, and three days later the militia ordinance passed both Houses. The principle of government by ordinance had been established in the summer of 1641, and according to Anthony Fletcher, in 1642 there was 'no question of proceeding by bill; in other words, normal procedures were now inadequate. In themselves, ordinances were comforting in their traditional nature and could appear as temporary expedients while at the same time initiating ground-breaking legislation.[9] This measure did not end discussions over the issue entirely, and Charles continued to adopt a conciliatory tone. In April he suggested that Parliament's nominees for the lieutenancy remain in office for a year and that while he was in Ireland at the head of his army there, Parliament should have full control of the army in England and Wales. By now this was unacceptable to Parliament, and it is difficult to be certain how genuine the king's offer was. He left the south of England to journey north during March, passing through Theobalds, Newmarket and the suppressed Arminian colony at Little Gidding before going on to York. He certainly discussed other options en route. At Doncaster he thought about besieging Hull, where the majority of the national armoury was still languishing after being sent there during the bishops' wars. The town was now held for Parliament by Sir John Hotham. In early April the king returned to his 'Irish plan': he would raise an army in and around Cheshire (Yorkshire had already proved to be unsympathetic to his idea) and lead it to Ireland in person. Speculating on the king's covert aims during this period, Fletcher has suggested: 'He needed an army to crush the traitors at Westminster and the queen's projects of raising financial support for such a force from the Netherlands and Denmark at this stage looked promising.'[10] In these circumstances it would be impossible for Parliament to work with him, led as it was by a group of men likely to be at the sharp end of the king's wrath if their resolution failed then or in the future.

The context of the pronouncements emanating from both sides in the conflict was not readily appreciated by the recipients of their propaganda. Both sides bombarded England and Wales with pamphlets and papers expressing their desire to maintain the laws of the kingdom and promising to defend the Protestant church. Their means of going about it, however, were different but unstated, except in coded references to the rights of king and Parliament. The effect was to create an unfounded belief in the compatibility of both parties, which was contrary to the real state of affairs.

In Ireland a full-scale war developed during the spring of 1642. The English forces in Leinster were led by the Earl of Ormond, who because of his Old English background now faced an enemy with many of his relatives in its ranks. During the latter months of 1641 he had created an army, which on paper was composed of about three thousand men. With this he had counterattacked the Irish incursions on the pale, with some success. He defeated the Irish forces besieging Lord Moore at Drogheda but had been unable to move far into Leinster because of supply problems. No money from the king or Parliament was reaching him, and the promised £400,000 to be raised in England and Wales brought no benefit to him. Desertions followed his inability to pay the troops, and only the anger of the dispossessed Protestant Ulstermen stopped some units from fading away entirely.[11] Nevertheless, Ormond defeated Lord Mountgarret at the battle of Kilrush, but this ended only one thrust of the Irish attack on the colonists. By the summer, the Irish war effort was becoming more organized, and the forces in the four provinces were being consolidated into armies under four commanders, all veterans of the European wars. Owen Roe O'Neill returned to Ulster in the summer and began to forge an army out of what he initially saw as an unorganized mob. An Old English Catholic, Thomas Preston, commanded in Leinster, John Burke in Connaught and Garret Barry in Munster. Although the Irish were still fighting on several fronts during 1642, it was against often unco-ordinated enemy forces. In Ulster they faced a Scottish army, paid for by the English Parliament and led for a time by Alexander Leslie, Lord Leven (ennobled by Charles I in 1641).[12] For much of the time the Irish faced Robert Monro, who had landed in Ulster in April just as Ormond defeated Mountgarret and quickly made his mark on the war. Monro was very much influenced by the massacre stories that had come out of Ireland, and he acted accordingly. In May he marched on Newry, captured the town and murdered sixty citizens and two priests. Apparently, only the intervention of Colonel James Turner saved Newry's women from being murdered too. In July Lord Forbes led a mercenary force to Ireland paid for by the Merchant Adventurers Company, after the act carving up rebel estates amongst investors had given them the impetus. The force attacked the Munster coastline, burned the village and abbey of Timoleague, and rampaged through Kinsale without 'regard for friend or foe'.

This violence continued through Galway and especially angered the Protestant commander, Lord Inchiquin, because it provoked neutral Irish citizens into siding with the rebellion but provided no material help at all for his own forces.[13]

Steps towards unifying the Irish struggle were taken as early as April. In this aspect of the war, the clergy were of great importance. Clergy in County Armagh, Ulster, had met at Kells and drawn up a plan to finance the armies operating in the province. They had declared that the rebellion was directed against Puritans and re-affirmed that all risings in Ireland were part of one rebellion. They also began to investigate Catholics who supported the Dublin government or tried to remain aloof, with a view to imposing penalties on them, and they announced that all those who held church property confiscated since the Reformation would be left in quiet possession if they joined the rebellion.[14] The first post-Reformation synod of the Catholic church in Ireland in May confirmed these political and logistical decisions. In early June Leinster clergy began to build on this organization, which had hitherto been effective only in Ulster. On 7 June, following a series of meetings, clergy, drawn principally from Munster and Leinster, drew up an Oath of Association. It has been noted that it was the strength of the church structure developed during the decades before the war that made the administration of the oath possible. The oath, which emphasized the unity of the rebellion, brotherhood and obedience, was to be administered by the clergy after the oathtaker had undergone confession and communion. Anyone guilty of breaking the oath would be excommunicated.[15] Out of these discussions was forged a government structure, which was to be operative from 24 October with the convening of a General Assembly, elected on the same basis as the Dublin Parliament, at Kilkenny. Below this central tier each province was to have a council, and below that each county would have an elected council. The county councils would act as courts of law, assuming powers of Oyer and Terminer and gaol delivery. The new Irish state also appointed officers modelled on the English government of Ireland, ranging from sheriffs in the counties and coroners and petty officials down to the level of constables in the parishes.[16] The Catholic religion was to be re-established according to statutes of Henry III. Principles originally declared at the Kells meeting were adopted, and the four generals were to be co-ordinated from the centre. Poyning's Law was rejected, but in recognition of its Catholic-only membership, the unicameral General Assembly also rejected the name Parliament. With English rule in Ireland now challenged by a rival political and administrative power as well as by military attacks, Irish affairs had become more involved. However, events in England were now driving the process towards an all-embracing war throughout the four nations.

In Scotland a Royalist faction attempted to pressure the Edinburgh government into supporting the king. In the absence of a significant part of the Scottish army which had been sent to Ireland, the Royalists had grown more confident and had drawn up petitions in support of Charles. The king overtly distanced himself from direct contact with Scottish Royalists and refused Montrose and Lord Airlie access to court. Instead he received the Covenanter Lord Loudoun and hoped to persuade Leven and the army to side with him, but to little avail. In Scotland the chief Royalist petition was rumoured to be a cover for a plot to murder Argyll, and in any case it was rejected in Edinburgh. The Scottish leaders instead stressed that they would try to bring the two sides together. The king sent Hamilton, fresh from the councils at York, to try to change their minds.[17]

Meanwhile, in England and Wales the militia ordinance lay quietly on the books. Some of the old lords lieutenant began to surrender their warrants, and some new appointees began to take up their posts and appoint deputies, but little else was done. Not until 2 April did the Commons urge the Lords to act on the ordinance effectively.[18] Preparations on land progressed slowly and in an ad hoc manner compared to the maritime preparations. The suitability of each of the captains of the fleet being assembled was discussed in the Commons, and Parliament gave its chosen admiral, the Earl of Warwick, full control in opposition to the king's own appointee, Sir John Pennington. On the coasts, Parliament's activity was largely confined to keeping a watch on the Welsh coast near Ireland, ensuring trained band co-operation there, and fortifying Hull and Portsmouth. Even here there were flaws. Portsmouth was still in the hands of Sir George Goring, who had effectively betrayed the queen's plan to retire there during the army plot. His loyalty to Parliament was as yet untested, but it was soon to prove lacking. Hull's garrison was strengthened to 1,000 men, but the irresolute governor, Sir John Hotham, MP for Beverley, had not as yet been put to any test. Pay for these forces was also arranged through a series of temporary expedients; for example, Lewes used coat and conduct money left in the hands of council.

Hotham could not wrestle with his conscience much longer in isolation. The king's residence at York placed him on the front line, and the king's duplicity placed him at the very centre of the conflict. Even as Charles negotiated with Parliament, he also made plans for military action. Accordingly, on 22 April 1642, the king's second son, Prince James, newly arrived in York, was sent on a royal visit to Hull, still technically held in the king's name by Hotham. The governor could hardly refuse the prince access to the city, although he suspected a trap. Sure enough, on the following day the king was reported to be heading to the town with a troop of cavalry to rejoin his son. Hotham was in a quandary, but supported by the town MP, Peregrine Pelham, he refused the king access. Hotham knew full well that because it was known that part of the town supported the monarch and resented the enlarged garrison, the king's troop of horse would try to gain control of the magazine. So the gates of Hull remained shut in Charles's face; his second military coup had failed. Parliament congratulated Hotham and rejected the king's demand that they treat Hotham as a traitor for breach of privilege.[19]

The king's attitude to the militia ordinance now began to harden. Faced with military humiliation and the loss of the prize of Hull's magazine, he had to get hold of arms and men. In May he struck, declaring the militia ordinance to be illegal and an attempt to 'engage our good subjects in a war against us, as our town of Hull is already by the treason of Sir John Hotham'.[20] This was one part of a two-pronged strategy. The more direct part followed shortly, when a commission of array was directed to a group of Lancashire gentry. Within a fortnight others were being directed to nobles and gentry around the country. The commissions of array were committees of men set up in a manner similar to the commissions of the peace, and often of the same people. Charged with raising the trained bands, they had their origin in the thirteenth century and had been used until the fifteenth before falling into abeyance and finally being replaced by the lieutenancies. Issued in their original Latin form, the commissions were disliked and their legality questioned, although debates on this point were never fully resolved. Some historians regard the use of the commissions as a 'dreadful blunder', in view of Clarendon's comment that 'some men of very good affections to the crown, and adverse enough to the extravagant pretences and proceedings of the Parliament, did not conceal their prejudice to the commission of array, as not warranted by law'.[21] But others have argued that the king had little choice, and research on the commissions' temporary resurrection in 1640 indicates that they did have several advantages. For example, the commission of array did not carry with it the same burden regarding military service that had hampered the lieutenancy in the bishop's wars, to wit, the obligation placed upon the trained bands to defend their own counties. This duty had been perpetuated under the militia ordinance, and the arrangements made for the Anglesey and Caernarfon trained bands to assist each other were singular and particular. The commission system did not so limit the actions of the local militia, which could be raised and led to wherever the king commanded.[22] Moreover, the commissions freed the king from the need for coat and conduct money, which was supposed to be repaid at the end of hostilities. Instead the king could fund them by new means. The instructions issued to the Leicestershire commissioners allowed them to levy money on those unable to bear arms to fund those who could.[23] Another advantage, surely not lost on the king, was that the commissions were accompanied by reassuring notices to the effect that the trained bands were neither to be kept under arms nor augmented – both of which instructions were designed to calm fears about expense.[24]

Perhaps the blunders lay not in the use of the commissions per se but in their execution. The king's court at York had grown over the past months, but although he could consult with lawyers on the development of the commissions, he could not have been surrounded by many representatives of the counties.[25] It was even less likely that he could call on the expertise of many townsmen. In effect, government in the shires worked not through a professional civil service but through knowledgeable, experienced amateurs. Without a vast pool of local knowledge, the king would not have the ability to create effective commissions. That he was almost entirely dependent upon the men around him can be seen in the appointments he made to the commissions of array. He wanted nobles to lead the commissions, so he appointed those about him, for example Henry Pierrepoint, Lord Newark, a displaced Lord Lieutenant. Newark got his old county command, Nottinghamshire. Only seven of the thirty-six lords whom Clarendon lists as having signed the 13 June declaration that they and the king would abide only by the known laws of the country did not receive appointments to commissions of array that summer. Some nobles at York – the Earl of Monmouth and Lord Mowbray and Maltravers – were to serve on more than one commission; others, like the Earl of Cambridge – better known as the

Marquis of Hamilton but listed by his new English title – were omitted for the obvious reason that they had no part in English local government. The Earl of Clare, recently appointed by Parliament as the Lord Lieutenant of Nottinghamshire, was once again supplanted by Lord Newark. A longer list of the lords present in York on 13 and 16 June, compiled by William Dugdale, contains forty-six names, of whom only about ten did not become commissioners that summer.[26]

The creation of the commissions was not an overwhelming success. The Nottinghamshire commission, for one, included no representatives of the county town in the initial draft and thereby could command little support there. It underwent two redrafts by 18 August to ensure that the town was represented, in the end to little effect.[27] Analysis of the nature of support for the commissions across the country has shown that the commission was put into effect in only ten English counties and Monmouthshire in Wales. In a further eleven English counties, attempts to enact the commissions were thwarted. In the rest of England and Wales the commission seems to have continued to lie in abeyance.[28] But these numbers are not an indication of the distribution of Royalism as a whole. Some of the counties that held array musters had developing Royalist parties. Herefordshire had an active and politically dominant Royalist group, which had manifested itself in a petition supporting the episcopacy after the twelve bishops, including the Bishop of Hereford, were impeached in late December 1641. This petition was generalist in its support for the church, approving of episcopacy and the Book of Common Prayer (but not of Laudian reform). It had been followed by a letter to the county MPs from the Herefordshire JPs, who objected to Parliament's functioning without the king's presence. This Royalism, which was reflected in a series of petitions during the spring and summer, was constitutionalist and moderate. The JPs were not objecting to changes in church or government undertaken before December 1641, and they cited the king's confession of maladministration and his willingness to govern according to law in the future as a gesture of conciliation. Only the apparent crisis at the year's end had turned them into proto-Royalists. Their power to have their voice heard, however, was limited as Herefordshire's MPs, Sir Robert Harley and Humphrey Coningsby, were firm supporters of Parliament's position. The petition and the views expressed in the letters were thus not passed on to Parliament.[29] Denied any form of representation in this body, the JPs doubtless accepted Royalist militarism owing to the very real lack of an alternative.

At the beginning of July the commission was enacted, and Lady
Brillianna Harley wrote to her husband that 'I account myself [to
be] amongst my enemies'. The enemies she referred to included
family, friends and gentry with whom the Harleys of Brampton
Bryan had long maintained economic and social relationships.[30] The
principal nominees in some counties simply did not participate.
In the strategically important north Midlands, the leading figures
appointed to front the Derbyshire and Leicestershire commissions,
the Earls of Devonshire and Huntingdon, simply abrogated all responsibility. Indeed, across that region the initial action was left to
heirs and younger sons and the gentry.[31]

Parliament was not universally successful either. Although the
militia ordinance was put into effect in some twenty-three English
counties between May and October 1642, there were no musters
at all in Wales. Again, this does not really reflect the true state of
support for Parliament; in seven of the counties that did not hold
musters, volunteer forces were raised in towns and boroughs during
the summer. Parliament's problems may have been exacerbated by its
early start. When the new lieutenants were appointed, loyalties were
very much in a state of flux. Appointees were reluctant to show themselves, and some had not made up their own minds about their stance.
Thus, the Earl of Clare, appointed Lord Lieutenant of Nottinghamshire, later went to York. The Earl of Exeter, similarly appointed
in Rutland, seems to have lain low. The Earl of Essex, forced through
heavy military commitments to appoint a vice-lieutenant in Staffordshire, appointed a future Royalist.[32]

Parliament set forward its political position in June with the Nineteen Propositions.[33] These terms for a settlement demanded Charles's
renunciation of those men gathered around him at York, and further
pressed for parliamentary 'approbation' of the principal offices of
state, extending this principle downwards through lower state and
legal offices. The usual religious demands – for prosecution of the
laws against 'papists', for the continued reformation of the church
and for the exclusion of Catholic lords from voting in Parliament –
were joined by a demand that Parliament appoint a suitable guardian
and educator of the king's children. Furthermore, the royal children
were not to marry without the assent of Parliament. Three Propositions dealt with military matters – the militia, the forts and ports,
and the 'extraordinary guards and military forces now attending your
majesty'. Charles was asked to approve Parliament's action regarding
the first, endorse its possession of the second and agree to dismiss

the third. Parliament also sought to direct foreign policy by demanding that a new alliance with the United Provinces be entered into with the aim of restoring Charles's sister Elizabeth and her children to their Palatine state. Taking it for granted that Charles would reject the Propositions, Parliament at the same time declared itself to be sovereign in the king's incapacity.[34]

At this point it is worth asking what exactly Parliament was aiming to do. The declaration that Charles was incapable of government effectively meant that it was treating him as if he were a minor or suffering from a mental illness. It has been claimed that the inclusion of the Lord High Steward of England and the Lord High Constable in clause 2 of the Nineteen Propositions is significant. These medieval offices were claimed by leading peers amongst the oppositionists at Westminster; indeed, Essex claimed the office of Constable before setting off for Northampton to command the army. At least some members of the Parliamentarian faction believed that the government should be run by the aristocracy; the struggle that developed in the shires during the summer, for example Lord Brooke's fights with the Earl of Northampton over the ammunition in Warwickshire, is evidence of this.[35] Yet this was only part of the picture: a wider range of social groups was involved in these early struggles. As already pointed out, in the counties immediately to the north of Warwickshire very few of the nobility were actually involved in the early stages, even if it is true that in some ways these opening moves were redolent of older baronial conflicts. It may have been natural for the aristocracy to think in this way, but this was not the only mode of thought in the wake of the governmental revolution, as confirmed and set out with terms for the king's political surrender in the Nineteen Propositions.

The creation of a militant Royalist party also needs to be examined at this point. This was not to be a religious contest, as some historians have contended. Whereas some Parliamentarians did see themselves as participating in a religious war, it is clear that others did not. A recent survey of Royalist colonels shows that the motivation for the Royalists was to defend the monarch's position in government over and above religious considerations, thus enabling Catholics and Protestants to fight on the same side. Parliamentarians could not understand this and sometimes wilfully misunderstood this collaboration as evidence of the king's participation in the universal Catholic plot. It also led them to accuse prominent Royalist commanders, such as Newcastle or Henry Hastings, of having

papist sympathies or of being atheists.[36] Rebellion to the Royalists
was a most 'horrid' thing, since they regarded the security of the individual and the state as bound up in the monarchy. But the religious
issues may not have been uppermost in the colonels' minds, and a
study of the Royalist officer corps in the north Midlands army has
also failed to identify religion as a major cause.[37]

If this level of confusion reigned in the governing classes at the
forefront, then it can be no surprise that it was mirrored across society. Many people were thrown into a quandary by the appearance
of two rival sets of militia warrants. John Morrill's excellent collection
of documents in *The Revolt of the Provinces* gives several examples.
Sir Thomas Knyvett from Norfolk was right at the forefront.

> Oh sweete hart, i am nowe in a greate strayght what to doe. Waulkeing
> this other morning at Westminster, Sir John Potts, with commissary
> Muttford saluted me with a commission from the Lord of Warwicke,
> to take upon me (by vertue of an Ordinance of Parliament) my com-
> panye & command againe. I was surprised what to doe, whether to
> take or refuse. Twas no place to dispute, so I tooke it and desierd some-
> time to Advise upon it. I had not received this many howers, but I
> met with a declaration point Blanck against it by the King.

His attempted solution to this crisis of conscience was to 'staye out
of the way of my newe masters till those first musterings be over'.
Others were motivated by fear rather than conflicting loyalty. Mistress Eure, a correspondent of the Verney family, wrote that she
wished 'that the swete parliment woold come – with the olive branch
in its mouth' because 'wee are soe maney frighted peopell; for my
part if I here but a dore crake I take it to be A drom, and am redey
to run out of that little valer I have'.[38]

Not everyone reacted in such a manner. Brillianna Harley,
Nehemiah Wallington and Lucy Hutchinson, amongst others, were
convinced that the cause of Parliament was a godly one. Lady Brillianna wrote to her son Edward:

> I thank God i am not afraid, It is the lord's cause that we have stood
> for, and I trust though our iniquities testify against us, yet the Lord
> will work for His own name sake, and that He will now show the men
> of this world that it is hard fighting against heaven.

Wallington had a similarly apocalyptic vision. He saw the summer
of 1642 as a time when the 'spirit of Antichrist is now lifted up and

marcheth furiously' while 'at this very time the delivery of his Church and the ruin of his enemies is in working'. On the other hand, Lucy Hutchinson testified that although religion was a major issue for her and her husband, liberty was more important:

> though he was satisfied of the endeavours to reduce popery and subvert the true Protestant religion which, indeed, was apparent to everyone that impartially considered it, he did not think it so clear a ground of the war as the defence of the just English liberties.[39]

But even though John Hutchinson had made his mind up about the cause, he still sought to avoid participation at this point and to content himself with prayers for peace. However, the time for doing this was often brief, depending on one's location. About twenty years later Lucy Hutchinson reflected on the incident at Nottingham when her husband and Lord Newark scuffled verbally at the Shire Hall, as Newark attempted to remove the county magazine:

> Before the flame of war broke out in the top of the chimneys the smoke ascended in every county... Between these in many places contests and disputes, almost to blood, even at the first: for in the progress every county had the Civil War, more or less, within itself.[40]

The war in England and Wales has been said to have broken out untidily. In some ways it did. The conflict in loyalties and the competing impetuses to act or to pray for peace acted as a brake on the conflict. When it came, it did not do so in all counties equally or at the same time; for although Lucy Hutchinson is right in her analysis of the divisions within counties, not all felt impelled towards war as in Lancashire on 15 July, when Lord Strange all but launched an attack on Manchester in his attempt to gain control of the county magazine. Other places saw verbal battles such as those in Nottingham. In Leicestershire the attempt by the Earl of Huntingdon's second son, Henry Hastings, to muster the trained bands at Leicester fortunately ended in a farce when a sudden downpour extinguished the slow matches of Hastings's musketeers just as they were about to open fire on representatives of Parliament and the town's leaders. It can be argued that in some areas military considerations forced the pace onwards. The summer of 1642 can be seen as an exercise in brinkmanship, with both sides aiming to overwhelm the other with such military might that a full-scale war might never be fought. If this view is true, it demonstrates the naivety of such an approach. Armies are never satisfied standing still; they simply fall prey to disorder, as happened in 1640. They also become an expensive burden to the locale in which they are situated, and by July both sides appeared to have reached a position from which they each thought they could win. At his point, perhaps, the war became, if not inevitable, as close to inevitable as an historian can admit.[41]

Musters were being held across the country, and in a band of counties between the king and London in particular, and it appeared that the county munitions in the Midlands would fall into Parliament's hands unless the king acted. The king's response to this threat was the issue of commissions of array to the counties south of Yorkshire and orders to the commissioners to seize county magazines. On 1 July, the high sheriffs of Nottinghamshire and Derbyshire were ordered to assist the sheriff of Leicestershire in supporting the king's attempt to create a bulkhead against the Parliamentarian forces in Warwickshire. On that same day, Lord Brooke had seized the Warwickshire magazine from its store at Coventry and placed it in his castle at Warwick. The centre of action was now this county, as the Earl of Northampton tried to raise the commissions of array. So dependent were both sides on the trappings of traditional government that the Warwickshire Royalists' attempts were frustrated by the absence of the sheriff, just as those of the Leicestershire Royalists had been by the lack of co-operation from the sheriff there. As the Warwickshire Royalists tried to get their leading opponents indicted before the county grand jury, Parliament began to send artillery into the county to assist Brooke in garrisoning Warwick Castle.[42] The king then moved southwards, trying to use his presence as a weapon against the resistance of officials and as a prompt to generate support. This move was not an unqualified success. On 11 July he passed through Newark, where Lord Newark had mustered the trained bands to greet him, but two days later he felt it necessary to play down fears of war and express the hope that this was as far as the part-time soldiers would have to go.[43]

On 12 July, Charles moved on to Lincoln, the heart of early attempts to raise the trained bands for Parliament. The Parliamentarians, who were grouped around the new Lord Lieutenant, Lord Willoughby of Parham, had left the town, and the king was accorded a rapturous reception. A troop of horse was voted to be raised and financed by voluntary subscription. But it was not the same as having the trained bands, and the troop was smaller than the usual county contingent of horse.[44] Even so, this reception was an apparent volte-face, for Willoughby's musters had been greeted with equal enthusiasm earlier. However, a combination of factors may have created this seeming contradiction. First, the county's enthusiasms were not homogeneous. Boston, for example, remained steadfast in mustering its militia contingent for Parliament. There were certain areas in the east of the county where the king could not get support. Around the Isle of Axeholme, for example, the king had 'improved' the agriculture on crown lands and thereby disrupted an already functioning agricultural system to the disadvantage of large numbers of inhabitants.[45] There was also a powerful impetus to remain aloof and try to please both parties, which would entail cheering first Willoughby and then the king. The gentry must also have been concerned about the apparent collapse of order in the county occasioned by the fenpeople's seeming victory in regaining their traditional common land through their insurrection of 1641–2. Such men were society's natural rulers, concerned above all to stabilize government in the county, and the small forces voted at the king's visit reflected this. Not only were they not comparable in size to the trained bands, they were intended for county use only, to suppress disorder arising out of the dangerous times. In other words, these forces were neither for the king nor for Parliament – they were for the county.

If Charles's visit to Lincoln was a disappointment, his trips to Nottingham and Leicester were problematic. At Nottingham, Charles was greeted cordially, but with little promise of support. On his arrival at Leicester on 22 July, he was confronted by the seizure of the county magazine by a group of twenty-five gentlemen, one of whom was the munitions master, and some deputy lieutenants.[46] They barricaded themselves into the gatehouse where it was stored and challenged the king to get them out. He could not do so because he was not accompanied by a sufficient armed force. Instead, he was forced into accepting a humiliating climbdown and permitting the magazine to be divided up and dispersed around the county. With a good part already deposited at the Earl of Stamford's home, Charles had lost the prize.[47] He returned north via Nottingham and just after he left, Lord Newark and the sheriff, John Digby, tried to seize the magazine, only to be thwarted by a large crowd which stopped them getting out of the town hall and threatened to 'break my lord's neck and the sheriff's out of the window'. John Hutchinson and his brother George arrived and initiated a compromise: the magazine was fastened with two locks, one held by Alderman John James, whom Parliament had appointed to muster the militia in the town, and the other by Digby.[48] Moreover, the Lincolnshire magazine was returned to Parliamentarian hands within a month of Charles's visit. Yet all was not lost there; the county still provided fertile recruiting ground for the Earl of Lindsey and his son, Lord Willoughby d'Eresby, who raised two regiments of foot during August and September.[49]

The king was attempting to stop the development of a wall of Parliamentarian power between him and the capital, but he was not really successful. The magazines were denied him and retained by the counties or put into enemy hands. Yet the area was still volatile, and there was little cohesion on either side. Despite the early success of Lord Brooke, and undoubted urban support for him, the county of Warwickshire as a whole was not won over. In the wake of Charles's Midland venture, the commission of array was enacted at Southam, Stratford-upon-Avon and Coleshill. It was clear that a larger number of the county gentry had turned out to support the commission than Brooke could muster. It has been suggested that the king's claim to represent the rule of order may have drawn the county's greater gentry – those involved in local government, for example – to his side. In the face of this Brooke maintained a low profile, sending some of his garrison home from the castle. On 30 July, when the artillery Parliament had sent him arrived at Banbury, Brooke was confronted by the commissioners, led by the Earl of Northampton. Unable and unwilling to fight for the guns, Brooke agreed to their being deposited in Banbury Castle for the time being.[50] When Brooke returned to London, Northampton took possession of the guns on 8 August, led them to Warwick and bombarded the castle. The first of many sieges in the wars in England had begun. Northampton tried to get the trained bands behind him, but support was patchy. The siege was not really likely to succeed, but it nevertheless provided a central flashpoint for the war. There now followed a renewed, and eventually more deadly, arms race in the country.

All the evidence shows that the commissions of array and the militia ordinance failed to create the armies which eventually fought the war in England and Wales.[51] A whole range of problems prevented the trained bands from contributing greatly to the armies. First, the soldiers in them had been educated in their political and military responsibilities during the Anglo-Scottish wars. They were acutely aware that they need not be called upon to serve outside their county boundaries, and some crises in summer 1642 arose when trained bands, such as that of Leicestershire, refused to cross recognized county borders. Moreover, the political divisions in the country were reflected in the trained band soldiers, who were eligible for service only if they had a fixed interest in the kingdom. They belonged to a social class which made them perhaps literate, and certainly capable of practical, if not abstract, political action and thought. They and their social equals imbibed the propaganda directed at them. Therefore, the soldiers could hold political positions and act upon them, meaning that the trained bandsmen were divided into three groups: Royalists, Parliamentarians and neutrals. As the summer progressed and war became more likely, the willingness and ability of the third, and perhaps largest, group to turn up to both parties' musters declined. Despite the large crowds that greeted him and threw hats in the air as he passed, the king was failing to win the political war. His claim to be fighting against a Parliamentary conspiracy to overturn the state was novel, and less convincing than his opponents' assertion that the country was being threatened by a popish conspiracy. This claim was especially convincing because Catholic gentry were prominent amongst Charles's armed supporters in Yorkshire.[52] This was certainly why many bandsmen and others refrained from joining the king's army in Yorkshire and elsewhere.

Perhaps Charles's reaction was the only one possible; he began to disarm the trained bands and use their weapons for the volunteers who did turn up. Again, this provided Parliament with propaganda material. In the face of the supposed popish menace, the king was seen to be disarming the only defence forces the counties had. Instead, he began to create armed forces by issuing individual commissions to proven supporters. Often these men, like Lord Paget in Staffordshire, John Digby and Isham Parkyns in Nottinghamshire, and Henry Hastings and Sir John Pate of Leicestershire, were commissioners of array, but now they were working as individuals, not in their role as commissioners.[53] Hastings was to lead his forces, raised by warrant in early August, into Warwickshire to assist Northampton in his siege of Warwick and compensate for the tardiness of the trained bands.

Parliament had begun to shift its emphasis away from the militia ordinance as early as 6 June, when a new militia committee was established at Westminster. This committee drafted the Propositions, by means of which funds for an army for use in England and Wales were to be raised in each county. The plans went a little awry when some counties made it clear that they would use the money for self-defence, but by drawing on the resources of London and the home counties, Parliament began to construct an army. From out of the parades and recruiting drives in the City throughout July grew a body of horse and foot, which on 8 August set out for Warwickshire. Another group set out for Portsmouth where George Goring, the turncoat plotter, again switched sides and declared for the king. The forces were also intended to offset the recruitment drive in the West Country spearheaded by the Marquis of Hertford. The localist aspect of the military Propositions avoided the errors the king had made in disarming the counties; subsequently, there was less opposition to the existence of these unprecedented armed forces. In the face of it the king could proclaim Parliament to be in rebellion and the leader of its army, the Earl of Essex, a traitor. But he could not mount a sufficient force to challenge them.

When Charles issued his proclamations he called upon his loyal subjects to attend him at Nottingham on 25 August. He then left Yorkshire for a progress south to support the siege in Warwickshire. Yorkshire was glad to see him go, but not at any price; before he left he agreed to exempt his Yorkshire supporters from attendance at Nottingham. As a result, he took only about 800 horse and even fewer foot with him on 19 August. After passing through Lincolnshire and Northamptonshire, he made for Coventry. On 21 August he summoned the town to open its gates to him, whereupon it refused. Some shots were exchanged, but Charles was in no position to attack a defended town, and he withdrew. On the following day he went northwards to Nottingham. The royal standard was raised in a high wind within or just outside the north bailey of Nottingham Castle. The crowd assembled was small, and there were few troops present. This picture has been used as evidence of the king's military weakness, and given his inability to mount an attack on Parliament's growing army, the notion has some validity.[54] However, the pallid nature of Royalist support in Nottingham was caused by other problems, too. There was already a substantial body of horse being built up by the king's supporters by this time, and when Charles went on to Nottingham, his nephew, Prince Rupert, who had joined him from the continent at York, remained with it in Warwickshire. There were also important recruiting drives occurring in the west of the country, which could not yet be expected to send men on to

Nottingham. Moreover, warrants had been sent through the local channels at short notice, and assembling local trained bands was a slow process. At Upton, near Newark, Constable Humphrey Hallam had to hire three horses to get the village's soldiers to the Nottingham muster. It cost Upton 3s/3d on top of the soldiers' wages, Hallam's charges whilst in Nottingham with the soldiers and repairs to the town armour, which came to £1-10s-4d.[55] Speed was forced on him because of slow communications; normally the soldiers went to musters on foot. The numbers of soldiers at Nottingham thus grew over the next few days. Hallam's soldiers stayed in the town initially for four days, but he had to pay them over a month's wages too. Royalist forces were being raised across the country; the problem they faced in August was one of strategy, not of a major failure to muster support. The Parliamentarians created an army within a fairly limited geographical area and were able to feed it into the south Midlands, whereas the king's forces were raised over a large area and fed into the region from far greater distances. Even this situation is qualified by the presence of a large force of Royalist horse, which acted as a screen for the king's gathering foot forces at Nottingham and again as they moved towards Shrewsbury from 13 to 20 September 1642.

As the king shifted westwards, Parliament's army under the Earl of Essex was being reinforced by recruits sent from the south and London. Nineteen foot regiments, each supposed to comprise 1,200 men, were raised by individual warrant, and troops of horse consisting of sixty troopers each were mounted at the expense of Parliament to be assembled into regiments at a later date. When ready, they joined the army based in Northamptonshire. En route they engaged in the demolition of altars and church rails just as their predecessors in 1640 had done on the way to fight the Scots. The sergeant of the sixth company of Denzil Holles's Foot, Nehemiah Warton, a London apprentice, wrote to his master of his stay in Acton:

> the soldiers brought in the holy rails from Chiswick and burned them in our town. At Chiswick they also intended to pillage the Lord of Portland's house, and also Dr Duck's, but by our commanders they were prevented ... at Hillingdon, one mile from Uxbridge, the rails being gone, we got the surplice, to make us handercherers, and one of our soldiers wore it to Uxbridge. This day the rails of Uxbridge, formerly being removed, was, with the service book, burned.[56]

Essex had wished to move directly on Nottingham, but the king's march westwards forced a change of plan. Instead the Parliamentarian army moved on first to Coventry and then to Warwick as part of a general westward advance in late September. While in Warwick, Essex's forces commandeered a range of supplies and materials. Forty pounds' worth of wagons and horses were taken from William Webster of Gosford Street for the march towards Worcester.[57] As the army at Northampton had grown, so did that being assembled at Shrewsbury. Two days after the king's arrival there, the Royalist horse under Prince Rupert was reconnoitring south of Worcester. They were there because they were needed to guard a convoy of valuable plate being escorted from Oxford University to the king. The convoy was being trailed by a detachment from Essex's army, consisting of ten troops of horse under Colonel John Brown. Brown and his men approached Worcester from the direction of the village of Powick and crossed the bridge over the River Teme to face Rupert's men, who attacked and defeated them on the north bank.

Rupert withdrew in the face of Essex's advance towards Worcester, which was occupied on 24 September. The earl consolidated his forces around the city and dispatched a group to occupy Hereford. He tried to keep a close eye on the king's army and watched in case the king moved on London. On 12 October Charles did so, at the head of an army which was now around 24,000 strong and more than comparable with Essex's forces. The earl had weakened his army, which had started out with 21,000 men at Northampton, by leaving garrisons behind him in Warwickshire, Worcester and Hereford. In 1642 scouting systems were still in their infancy, and the king was able to slip between Essex and the Parliamentarian towns of Warwick and Coventry without being detected until he was between the earl and London. Essex belatedly followed, and on the night of 22–3 October the quartermasters of both armies tried to find billets in the same towns near Kineton.

On the following morning, the king drew up his army on the steep ridge of Edgehill. In the valley below, Essex's army faced him. The king waited much of the morning on the hill, even though it was very unlikely that anyone would have been foolish enough to attack him up there. A dispute broke out upon the hill as Field Marshal the Earl of Forth sought to impose a complex formation on the foot regiments drawn up in the centre of the army. Forth's role as Field Marshal was to position the troops on the field, and he wanted them to be in the complex Swedish pattern, whereby musketeers and pikemen would be interspersed with each other in smaller groups, rather than according to the Dutch practice favoured by others. To do so would mean overriding the wishes of the Lord General, the Earl of Lindsey, who may have believed that the simpler Dutch form was more appropriate to an army of untried mettle. The king and Rupert, who should have remained aloof, interfered and supported Forth. An underlying issue further complicated the discussions. As Lord General, Lindsey should have had overall command of the entire army, including Rupert, the Lieutenant General of Horse, but the king exempted the prince from taking Lindsey's orders. This dispute proved to be the last straw. Seeing his power of command effectively stripped from him, the earl flung down his baton and walked to the head of his own regiment to command it alone. This was the first major instance of the king's interference with the positions of those to whom he had delegated command; it was certainly not the last.[58]

When Essex failed to attack, the king marched down the hill and attacked him. Rupert's success at Powick was matched by the charges mounted by him on the right wing and by Lord Wilmot on the left. For the most part, the troops of horse facing them were driven off the field and back towards Kineton. It was probably during this disaster that the wagons and their teams supplied by William Webster of Gosford Street, Warwick, were destroyed. In the centre the fight that developed between the foot of both sides was less one-sided. The fall of the autumn night ended the late-starting battle in the centre, and as the Royalist horse began returning to the field, it was clear that it was too dark to fight further. A total of around three thousand men on both sides lay dead around the survivors, the majority of them ordinary footsoldiers lured or tempted by pay or political passion from their homes and workshops only to be caught up in the dreadful fight in the centre. Many other poor boys and wounded men lay on the field that night in the bitter cold of an early frost. For some the intense cold was a life-saver, as it slowed the flow of blood and helped stop bleeding wounds.

The two armies remained on the edge of the battlefield that night, and a mournful sight greeted those who woke the next day. The prone bodies of the living and dead had been stripped and robbed during the night, while those who could called out for succour. It was a far cry from the bravado cheering and heckling of the London mobs at the turn of the year. Some of these same people lay dead on the field, killed defending the cause for which they had frightened bishops and driven their king from London. Now all that had once seemed clear was confused. Essex consolidated his forces, separated the living from the dead on the field and, after facing the king for some hours, withdrew to Warwick. The king refused to rush on London as Rupert urged; instead, he progressed to Banbury as planned and thence to Oxford to begin the establishment of a head-quarters.[59] Although the route to the capital lay open, exposed by Essex's march north, Charles, perhaps shaken by the practical lesson in politics by another means, delayed going that way. By the time he did, Essex had force-marched his army to London and interposed it between the city and the king. Charles took Reading on 4 November and rejected overtures of peace. The Great West Road became the king's route to the city, but outlying forces in the shape of Denzil Holles's and Lord Brooke's regiments challenged his approach at Brentford on Saturday 12 November, giving the alarm to the rest of the army and the citizens of London. On the following day at Turnham Green, Essex and his army, along with a crowd of Londoners carrying makeshift weapons and food for the soldiers, awaited the king's approach. When it arrived, the king's army, now reduced to around 12,000 or so, was confronted by an opposing force of 24,000 or more. The two forces stood face to face throughout the day, but unlike the Sunday at Edgehill three weeks before, they did not move towards each other; in the evening the king, outfaced, withdrew and returned to Oxford. The war now spread throughout the country more rapidly than before. Any chance that a resolution to the political conflict and the war would be achieved by one great conflict had died on the field of Edgehill.[60]

Only some places in the four nations had as yet felt the brunt of war. Worcester had seen fighting, and soldiers had been stationed in places as far apart as Hereford, Derby, Shrewsbury, Oxford, York and Hull. But none had yet undergone prolonged attack, and only Newcastle upon Tyne had experienced occupation by an enemy force. In Ireland, by the time Edgehill was fought, the war had already been in progress for a year, several towns had been captured and the government radically altered, at least in terms of personnel. Moreover, some towns had been subject to brutal attack. Drogheda had been besieged for some time and Dublin was in a state of constant threat, with Catholic forces stationed close by many times. By October 1642, the town was effectively militarized, and the people subject to conscription for military tasks on the model to which English, Welsh and eventually Scottish burghs were to become

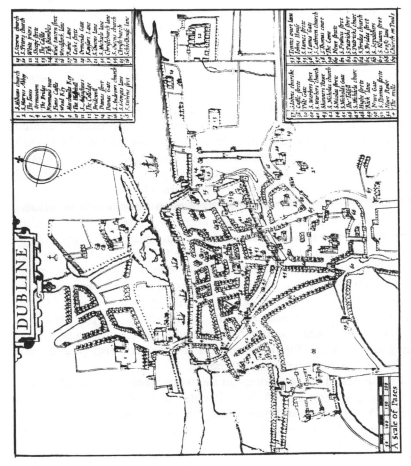

Plate 4   Speed, *Dublin City Map*, 1610, reproduced by courtesy of The National Library of Ireland.

accustomed. Large numbers of soldiers were permanently garrisoned in the town. The streets had been divided up to provide
zoned accommodation on a logical pattern for the regiments. A
document demonstrating this process survives for the following year,
showing that in October 1643 there were six foot regiments in the
town.[61] Four of the same regiments had been there a year earlier,
and the number of regiments in Dublin during late 1642 was probably about the same. The billeting list for 1643 used some forty or
so streets, most of them on Speed's map of 1610. The walled town
was thus heavily billeted and a great majority of the streets had a
military presence. In addition a substantial area north of the Liffey,
around St Mary's Abbey, was used. There were also units stationed
south of the walled town around St Kevin's Lane and the St Bride's
district. Other units were stationed a mile and a half away at Kilmain-
ham. Whilst these facts may suggest heavy overcrowding, the real
picture may be very different. Large numbers of people had left
Dublin, and some properties may have been unoccupied or under-
occupied already. War and plague exacerbated this trend, and within
ten years half the houses were empty.[62] The number of soldiers in
Dublin during late 1642 can be assessed from the Treasury Accounts. When on 26 and 27 September eleven regiments or parts
of regiments were given their wages, a total of 3,934 men was recorded.[63] As the population of the city had grown to about 20,000
by 1641, the military presence effectively added 20 per cent.[64] It
must have been a massive burden, especially as the money promised
by England was not forthcoming and the Justices also pointed out
that the excise revenue was decreasing.

Yet the costs of these soldiers in the town were not the only problem facing the people of Dublin. People could also lose their tools,
as well as room space and provisions. On 15 September 1642 Widow
Thombron in High Street handed over three spades, for which she
was paid 15d each. She was not alone; Mr Shele, Mr Nugent and
Widow Fitzwilliam of the Corn Market sold sixteen, ten and five
shovels respectively.[65] For smiths John Cassell, Phillip Goffe and
Robert Barksher the war offered travel; they and three carpenters,
two wheelwrights and two gunners were shipped to Dundalk 'to
work in their several trades'.[66] Captain John Russell was paid £2 to
ship them there in October. They were not the only people turning
their skills to military needs. An unknown number of workmen
employed by Matthew Tillet were paid £5 in wages for making
'wheel barrows and other necessaries' in October 1642. Matthew

Tillet was probably the man later named as Matthew Tilley, a carpenter, who teamed up with John Leen, a smith, for £10 apiece to produce tools for pioneers.[67] A group of coopers also worked for the council under the direction of Captain John Russell, who was given £2 to pay them. Other craftworkers made sixty-four beds for the two military hospitals, the wounded soldiers' hospital and the sick soldiers' hospital. These were set up just before 21 October at a cost of £200.[68]

Other residents of Dublin had a direct involvement in the military affairs of the city and garrison. In 1641 Trinity College, founded in 1592, was on the outskirts of town, not in the centre of the city as it is now. It lay on the south bank to the east of the walled town in an enclosure of its own, and the college was potentially useful in case of a siege. Funding for the Protestants-only college was a problem because of the war. It had been set up with an income derived from royal revenues and enfeoffed lands, but by March 1642 the lands were in Confederate hands. There being no money for the college lecturers' fees, they petitioned the council, suggesting that they would have to disperse if no money was forthcoming.[69] The council forwarded the letter to Leicester, hoping that he would be able to help. They had made something of an effort to help students and at the same time help themselves. Thirty-four students were paid sixpence a day from March for serving as soldiers to defend the college. Money was forwarded to the Vice-Provost for that purpose in November.[70] At Youghal, in Munster, the presence of military forces had been constant since the beginning of the rebellion. Viscount Dungarvan had been appointed governor in January 1642, and ships were directed there with troops in March, along with ten gavans of supplies. Additional local troops were sent to the town that same month, to be given 'competent lodging, fire, and candlelight'. There they remained, with the town meeting the burden of their charges and the further demands of the Lord President of Munster, first Sir William St Leger and then Lord Inchiquin, throughout the year. In November this entailed paying a levy of £200 in two weeks, which had to be especially rated on inhabitants and strangers – except for those already plundered by the Irish in rebellion. The garrison was further supplemented in the same month with a company of foot despatched from Cork.[71]

Throughout the latter part of 1642, towns were being militarized in England and their governments subjected to the demands of the military. Through published and unpublished borough records, these issues can be explored and still provide a fruitful area of study, as illustrated by recent work on the roles of town and country in the civil war.[72] Charles's occupation of Oxford was the second that the city had suffered. In September Lord Saye and Sele had occupied the city, but this occupation had been relatively quiet and lasted only a short time. As soon as Charles arrived in Oxford after Edge-hill, the town began to pay out for him. On 29 October, £250 was ordered to be raised for the king's expenses, and gloves were pro-vided for Princes Charles and James and Rupert.[73] The occupation of Worcester by the Earl of Essex had entailed increasing the num-bers of constables in the town because of 'extraordinarie providing of souldiers and other greate services concerning the great army now abiding in this cittie.' The maintenance of forces there cost money; the governor, Thomas Essex, was paid £40 on 3 December 1642. On 20 January a Parliamentarian captain was made a freeman of the city, and some six weeks later Essex ordered the council to exclude several aldermen and elect replacements.[74] In York, occu-pied by Royalist forces under the Earl of Newcastle by the end of the year, the army had done considerable damage. Soldiers were asked to forbear from felling trees and hedgerows about the city on 28 November.[75] Nottingham had housed the king's army in Septem-ber and as a result the meadows south of the town had been 'eaten upp', the Eastcrofte had also been used for feeding the guard's horses, and the aldermen were therefore deprived of their usual allotment of grazing. The respite caused by the king's departure came to a quick end with the seizure of the town by local Parliamen-tarians. The town raised £100 during early December, augmented by £200 from the surrounding area, just to pay the soldiers. Defen-sive measures had to be taken as well, and blocks of stones were laid across Broad Lane to block entry to the town.[76]

Nearby Leicester was not occupied at this time but was neverthe-less being surrounded by gathering Royalist and Parliamentarian forces and was thus facing a very difficult balancing act. In Septem-ber Prince Rupert, in the region with the Royalist horse, had de-manded £2,000 from the town. If they did not pay, he promised to 'appeare before your towne in such a posture with horse, foote, and cannon as shall make you knowe tis more safe to obey than to resist his majesties commands'. Charles himself quickly repudiated the demand, but the town's governors had already raised £500 and dispatched it to Rupert. They did not see it again. In January the town made its final attempts to remain aloof from the conflict and urged Henry Hastings, the local Royalist colonel, to understand that they would refuse to let his rival, Lord Grey, into the town with any forces. At the same time the mayor, Richard Ludlam, stressed that he did not know how his poorly walled town could stop Grey if he really wished to occupy it. Probably within a month, as part of an attack on local Royalists under Hastings at Ashby-de-la-Zouch, Leicester was occupied.[77] Coventry was in a state of 'corporate paralysis' from August to October, during which time there seem to have been no council meetings held at all. The town remained in Parliamentarian hands over the ensuing winter and had to put up with the expense and inconvenience of free quarter.[78] The strains and stresses of the war were beginning to make themselves felt across three of the four nations as the winter set in. We now move on to the development of the wars across the three other nations.

6

The War Develops

The enemy's cannon did play most against our Red regiment of trained bands; they did some execution amongst us at the first, and were somewhat dreadful when men's bowels and brains flew in our faces. But blessed be God that gave us courage, so that we kept our ground and after a while feared them not[1]

This chapter first begins to explore the way in which the war spread across England and Wales through the autumn and into the summer of 1643. While many parts of England and Wales were involved in the actual fighting, the war also spread in ways which did not involve violence. In most places the war made itself felt through its capacity to devour resources, and through the strong reactions that it caused throughout the political, administrative and social networks of the two nations. Following the battles of Brentford and Turnham Green, the principal forces of both sides went into winter quarters. However, the war was carried on in the shires of England and Wales by other, smaller forces raised during the autumn. In many areas fighting had already occurred while the field armies were dancing their deadly quadrille in the Midlands. In the south the principal Royalist stronghold of Portsmouth, garrisoned by George Goring, had been captured by Sir William Waller in September, and Royalist forces being raised in the south-west by Lord Hertford were forced out of Somerset. Hertford had attempted to publish the commission of array at Wells in August but succeeded only in provoking a popular armed opposition which forced him to take refuge at Sherborne Castle.

By the beginning of September his garrison was under siege from some admittedly fairly reluctant local forces, but after the fall of Portsmouth on 5 September, Hertford abandoned the castle and divided his army. The horse, under Sir Ralph Hopton, headed for Cornwall, and Hertford himself took the foot into Glamorganshire via the Bristol Channel.[2] In the wake of his successes Sir William Waller began to establish an heroic reputation for himself, ensured during the autumn when he secured control of several strongpoints in the south and west. After taking Portsmouth, he returned eastwards and seized Farnham in Surrey before going on to join Essex and fight at Edgehill. In December he set out again for the south, took Winchester and Arundel Castle and moved on Chichester by early January.[3]

Hertford made good use of his time in south Wales. He held musters in October and November, and converted to the Royalist cause two local magnates, Lord Herbert and Lord Carberry, who began to mobilize the resources of the area. In Pembrokeshire, which stood out against him, the county militia fortified itself in Tenby, Haverfordwest and Pembroke. Two distinct impulses for Parliamentarianism in the county can be identified. First, the three towns fortified by the county militia had substantial trading links with the industrially developed regions across the Bristol Channel, and the merchant classes in both areas shared a common Puritan culture. Second, gentry support was very closely linked to kinship ties, especially with the family of the Earl of Essex. Also, principal Parliamentarian soldiers had served with Essex in Germany, although many Royalists had, too.[4] Very early in the war, Charles's Welsh commissioners of array had come across the same problems as their English counterparts, finding that crowds who cheered for the king were not always prepared to fight for him. Yet as the war became more likely, the number of recruits increased, and many Welshmen served in the king's army at Edgehill. Moreover, Lord Hertford and his colleagues were able to put together an army of 7,000 at Cardiff by 4 November. Opposing them was the Earl of Stamford, who had been detailed by Essex to guard the approach to the Midlands and southern England by occupying Worcester and Hereford. Hertford's forces were involved in small-scale skirmishing with Stamford's men in the region for some time. However, by moving his main Royalist forces into Monmouthshire, Hertford rendered Worcester untenable for Stamford due to its exposure and proximity to the border. The earl withdrew to Gloucester and established a garrison there instead, and Hereford was soon abandoned to the Welsh.[5]

Funding the Royalist armies had become a major problem. Before the battle of Edgehill, Charles had dragged together funds from a motley combination of loans and collections of plate. He had even sold titles for cash; Richard Newport was ennobled for £6,000.

While he had repudiated Rupert's peremptory demands of Leicester back in September, the £500 he received from the town paid for only three days' bread for his tiny army. Charles himself had demanded arms and supplies from towns on the west Midlands during his stay there; he even fined the town of Nantwich £2,000 for attempting to remain aloof from the conflict, and Birmingham may have suffered a similar fate.[6] After Edgehill both sides began to create their own methods of funding (discussed in more detail in chapter 7), but as yet such structures were in their infancy. Herbert was faced with cash-flow problems which began to drain his personal resources. He obtained money from Wales by using the simple expedient of redirecting the assessment for the £400,000 being raised for Ireland. From Oxford he wrote to the High Sheriff of Flint in north Wales to take charge of the money in the hands of the collectors and pass it on to him. Charles claimed that the money was being used to further the rebellion against him and that it would be put to proper use in his hands, in other words used to fight the Parliamentarians.[7] The effects of this subvention are clear. Little or no money was arriving in Ireland from this tax, and collection of it collapsed completely. In most counties of England and Wales, the second instalment was never collected. In Wales it appeared that no money at all was received from either payment. The correlation is clear: there was less chance of any of the £400,000 levy reaching the Treasury from counties held or passed through by the king and his supporters, such as Derbyshire, Nottinghamshire and Yorkshire. Counties north of the king at York had also paid nothing on either instalment. Only Ely in Cambridgeshire, Essex, Hertfordshire, Norfolk, Somerset, Suffolk, Surrey and Wiltshire had paid anything on the second instalment. Some home counties, for example Buckinghamshire and Kent, had not paid their full amounts either. Here the problem was one of general dysfunction and disloyalty. The collector in Buckinghamshire wrote in his account of his appointee to receive the money for Ireland, Robert Serry: 'I finde hath dealt very ill with me in other things, and I doubt hath done the like in this'.[8] Much of the money that did find its way to the Royalist cause went into the hands of the king for the use of his field army rather than into the hands of local commanders like Hertford.

Hertford extended his control of the Worcestershire and Herefordshire corridor to Wales in early 1643 by occupying eastern Gloucestershire too. The Earl of Stamford now decided to tackle the Royalist presence before it became too much of a threat. In October,

Hopton had been arraigned before the quarter sessions by the Parliamentarians of Launceston. They charged him with disturbing the peace with the forces he had brought out of Dorset. On 13 October he appeared to answer the charges, bringing with him his royal warrant. He was cleared of wrongdoing and got the grand jury to declare that the Parliamentarians had assembled a riotous mob. The trained band was assembled to deal with the rioters and to capture strongholds, but they would not cross the Tamar. So Hopton and Sir Bevil Grenville marched into Devon with volunteer forces, occupied Tavistock and menaced Plymouth. By January, with Parliament's backing, Stamford was ready to take Hopton on with the forces gathered from the abandoned garrisons of Worcester and Hereford.[9] In the face of his advance, and short of supplies, Hopton pulled back from Devon and recrossed the Tamar, where the trained bands rejoined him. Stamford followed. Part of the Parliamentarian army pressed on and was caught and defeated by Grenville and Hopton at Braddock Down on 19 January. Confident, the Royalists marched eastwards, and this time Stamford retreated before them, allowing the Royalists to reopen a siege at Plymouth. Stamford had again failed to nip the growth of a Royalist force in the bud, and he compounded this failure by agreeing to a forty-day truce that allowed Hopton to build up his army even more.[10] His political masters were furious.

In the north of England the situation had undergone a series of dramatic changes. The incipient Parliamentarianism of a large number of the Yorkshire gentry, focused around the nucleus of the Fairfax family, became important in the months after Charles left the Earl of Cumberland and the Archbishop of York to organize support in the region following his departure in August. These two men proved to be unreliable. Cumberland was generally liked, affable and inoffensive. He possessed no military drive, however, and when he failed to steer the military effort, the archbishop was left to fortify his own palace at Cawood. When he was driven from there on 4 October by the young John Hotham, who sallied forth from his father's garrison at Hull, Cumberland found himself beleaguered at York as a result.[11] The local Royalists turned to William Cavendish, first Earl of Newcastle, a magnate whose estates and tentacles of power were entwined throughout the north and into the Midlands. During the autumn, he had seized control of the north-east, and once secure there, he marched south and replaced Cumberland. The earl succeeded in establishing control of the North Riding and driving a wedge between the Parliamentarians at Hull and those in the West Riding. When he linked up with the north Midland Royalists at the end of the month, Newcastle must have hoped that the enemy had been penned in.[12]

Penned in the Fairfaxes may have been, but they were not daunted; and Newcastle failed to defeat the Fairfaxes on their home turf in the West Riding. By the end of the year, Newcastle could be said to have been hemmed in himself. Hull and the port of Scarborough, under the command of Sir Hugh Cholmeley, were held against him, and the East Riding contained pockets of Parliamentarian sympathizers. Sir Thomas Fairfax held the west, and his father and the two Hothams were ranged to the south. The north Midland Royalists were themselves in no position to aid the Earl of Newcastle at present, as we shall see shortly. The queen now provided a distraction. It was already a year since she had gone abroad to arrange for military supplies and support. Her diplomatic efforts, waged in a Europe riven by war, had largely failed. Friendly states were in no position to offer aid, and others wanted to see the outcome of war within a rival state. The queen had bought supplies, however, and these had been sent over the North Sea the previous year. Charles had received a consignment at Chester in September while his forces lay around Shrewsbury. By the new year, Henrietta Maria was ready to bring a new consignment herself. She had hoped to make for the Royalist port of Newcastle, but storms first delayed her journey and then curtailed her plans altogether. On 23 February she landed at Bridlington Quay, a small port on the Gypsey Race, seaward of Bridlington Town. The town was sporadically occupied by Parliamentarians, but the queen met no opposition from the landward end. Parliamentarian ships chased her into Bridlington Bay, however, and began firing on her as she disembarked. The Dutch ships escorting her interposed themselves, and the Parliamentarians drew off, fearing an international incident. Having recovered from hiding in the Race valley as cannon balls rained around her, Henrietta Maria made her way inland, staying at Burton Agnes Hall en route for York and making contact with the governor of Scarborough on the way. The escapade was an undoubted success; enough arms were landed to help Newcastle's war effort, arm a new force under the queen's command and supply the king. All of this endowed the northern Royalists with a series of rosy prospects for the spring and summer.

In the north of Wales there was as yet little fighting, but Royalists

Cattermole.

R. Wallis.

The Queen at Burlington.

Plate 5 Queen Henrietta landing at Bridlington, 1643, The Mansell Collection, London.

and Parliamentarians were garrisoning the country's principal fortresses. In January 1643 Royalists seized Chirk Castle, the importance of which stretched far beyond Wales. It secured the Welsh border with Shropshire, and it was crucial for the Royalists to control the hinterland of the port of Chester if they were to hold on to the city and the region around it. Lord Capel led the war effort for the Royalists, with assistance from Wales and from the Midland Royalists. However, the slight Royalist edge in the region was under constant pressure from Sir William Brereton at Nantwich in Cheshire, and although Royalist north Wales may have appeared secure, the Royalists of the English marches were not. Attempts to dislodge Brereton failed.[13]

In the Midlands, the situation for the Parliamentarians had looked very optimistic during the first campaign.[14] The presence of the king had prevented wide-scale recruiting, and prominent local Parliamentarians had either taken their levies south to join Essex (like the Earl of Stamford), gone to Hull (like Sir John Gell of Hopton, Derbyshire), or gone to ground (like John Hutchinson). Conversely, when the king left, they began to return and made the region ripe for the picking. Charles had drawn with him the prominent, active men. Henry Hastings, the commissioner of array from Leicestershire, Sir John Digby, the Sheriff of Nottinghamshire, and others had been attached to the field army. In their wake and after the battle of Edgehill, Gell returned to Derbyshire with troops borrowed from Hull and the small garrison at Sheffield. The only organized Royalist forces to oppose him were a motley crew under the Earl of Chesterfield at his house at Bretby in south Derbyshire and a regiment of dragoons under Sir Francis Whortley who were roundly annoying people on both sides of the county's western border. With his borrowed troops and another two hundred raised from his own lead mines, Gell occupied Derby on 31 October and drove both Royalist groups out of the county and into Staffordshire. Following this success he helped John Hutchinson and Charles White establish a garrison at Nottingham.

In the meantime neutralism had paralysed Staffordshire. The expulsion of Whortley from Derbyshire into Staffordshire had prompted a special session of the peace in the county during November. Both Royalists and Parliamentarians attended the session and decided to raise armed forces to protect the county and keep both sides out of the shire. The events in the region prompted both sides into action. Parliament sent Sir William Brereton northwards to seize Cheshire and to try to dislodge Royalists from Chester. Stamford's young son Lord Grey seems to have been sent back to Leicestershire for the same reason. The king sent Hastings and Digby back too, and Sir Thomas Leveson fortified Wolverhampton and Dudley in south Staffordshire. The death blow to the county's attempted neutralism was dealt when Sheriff William Comberford fortified Stafford itself and Hastings garrisoned Tutbury Castle, turning the shire into a Royalist stronghold. Hastings also garrisoned his father's house at Ashby-de-la-Zouch, and Digby seized Newark with help from a Scottish professional soldier, Sir John Henderson, sent to him by Newcastle. Parliamentarian attempts to dislodge Hastings failed when an attack on his base at Ashby collapsed in January 1643. Midland Parliamentarians went on the offensive again in February, attacking Newark at the end of the month. Having secured Northamptonshire for Parliament, Lord Brooke marched into Staffordshire to join Gell in breaking the Royalist hold on the county. They attacked and captured Lichfield at the beginning of March, although Brooke died in the attempt. Brooke had been followed through Northampton-shire by his chief rival, the Earl of Northampton, who began regar-risoning the county for the king and then joined Hastings defending Stafford. At the battle of Hopton Heath on 19 March Northampton, the second of the great early protagonists, died. He was killed after falling from his horse as the Royalists defeated Gell and Brereton. Hastings, by now Colonel General of the region, went on to recapture Lichfield in April with help from Prince Rupert, thus re-establishing for a brief period his total control of Staffordshire.

In the south Midlands, Waller launched an offensive which pushed the Welsh forces out of Herefordshire. In fact they had never com-pletely dominated the county; in the north-west, Brillianna Harley had fortified her home at Brampton Bryan and had defied attempts by both Herbert's forces and the Radnorshire militia to prise her out.[15] Waller went on to break Lord Herbert's siege of Gloucester on 25 March 1643. He then evaded the attempt of Rupert's brother Maurice to corner him in south Wales and went on to capture Here-ford.[16] In May he attempted to capture Worcester the same way, but on this occasion he was driven off and soon left the region. During the summer he moved his army into the south-west to attempt to redress the situation there.

After the forty-day truce and its subsequent extensions ended in the west, the Royalists were defeated at Stouton Down. Stamford moved in to finish off Hopton by bringing him to battle at Stratton.

Stamford had encamped on a hill deemed easily defensible; however, the determined Royalists stormed up it and destroyed much of the earl's army on 16 May. This brought about the temporary collapse of Parliamentarian activity in the region and necessitated Waller's assistance. In the centre of England, the Parliamentarian field army had in April moved on Oxford, determined to press on the Royalist capital. Essex attacked and captured Reading on 26 April, and as a result of this pressure on Oxford, Maurice was recalled from the west and Rupert from Staffordshire. The campaign stalled, however, when Essex's army came down with fever in the vicinity of their new prize.[17]

Fighting was not the only way in which the war had made its presence felt. Fears of disorder, common in 1641–2, continued in the early months of the war. The Staffordshire special sessions had treated the incursions of Whortley as a problem of order. Their response was simply to extend the use of trained bands in times of civil disorder. They were not the only group of gentry to try to avoid or minimize the effects of the war in their county. As noted earlier, the Lincolnshire gentry tried to create a 'third force'; and the Yorkshire Royalists, partly in desperation and partly through a genuine desire not to see their county torn apart by war, had briefly engaged the Fairfaxes in treaty before the younger Hotham seized Cawood.[18] In the Midlands a similar chain of events took place in Derbyshire, where attempts to remain aloof were also crushed by outside interference, just as in Staffordshire. The efforts of the Derbyshire gentry to keep out of the conflict appeared to succeed until Gell made his dramatic entrance at the end of October 1642. Even at the end of the year, when Derbyshire gentry and communities wrote to the mayor of Derby in association with Henry Hastings criticizing Gell, they did so on the basis that trade was suffering rather than on ideological grounds.[19]

The Cheshire gentry attempted to present a militant neutral stance as early as June 1642, and by the end of the month, neutralists stood under arms at Nantwich determined to defend their loyalty to both king and Parliament. In August they proposed demilitarizing one of the county hundreds, as Royalists and Parliamentarians had almost come to blows. Right across the county the refusal to allow either side to disturb the peace was maintained throughout the summer. Only in September, when the Royalist army was in the region, did the neutralist movement fade away. Once the war began and the county became polarized between the Royalists in the city

and the Parliamentarians at Nantwich, attempts to resurrect neutralism were made, but the significant treaty of Bunbury should not
be seen as a genuine neutralist document. Although it did commit
both sides to disbanding their forces and reassembling them into a
joint force in case outsiders had to be driven out of the county, it
was more a stop-gap introduced by the Royalist commander Orlando
Bridgeman to prevent him from being forced out of the county. Thus,
for a while Chester had 'effectively contracted out of the war'. Charles,
knowing that he could only gain by the treaty, agreed to it. Parliament, on the other hand, was furious.[20] It was Westminster which
ended the treaty by sending Brereton home to tackle the Royalists.
It would appear that similar attempts at buying time or underhand
trickery occurred elsewhere. Hopton's truce with Stamford is one
instance of the former, and Hastings's attempt to keep Parliamentarians out of Leicester by appearing to offer to stay out himself is
an example of the latter. (He knew he was in no position to occupy
the town and that Lord Grey had more chance of doing so.) In
Nottinghamshire, attempts to hold bi-party talks were, probably
rightly, suspected by the Nottingham Parliamentarians as being a
Royalist trick aimed at capturing their negotiators.[21]

In the wake of the disappointment at Edgehill, the minds of the
political elite also turned towards peace. In December as Parliament
planned its early war taxes, the citizens of London signed a petition
calling on the Houses of Parliament to open negotiations to stop the
war, which was proving expensive in both lives and money. Crowds
besieged the Common Council and the Parliamentary Committee
for the Advance of Money, crying out for peace. In response to the
tumult, the Common Council, while rejecting the popular petition,
drafted two of its own, addressing one to Parliament and the other
to the king. The Lords debated the petition and drafted peace proposals to be sent to the king, which were then passed to the Commons. The Lords' proposals were moderate in tone, demanding
trials for prominent Royalists and the king's assent to taxes raised to
pay Parliament's war debts. They also included a new militia bill and
suggested a religious settlement based on debates to be conducted
by a council of divines. Despite some opposition in the Commons,
negotiations based on the Lords' suggestions were opened.[22] Before
they began, the representatives of the City arrived at Oxford with
their petition for the king. Charles, in imperious mood with the
tidings of selected good news from around the country in his ears,
received them rudely and dismissed them quickly. In London, beset

with less optimistic tidings, peace fever was filling the streets with apprentices and petition papers for signing; by 13 January crowds were awaiting the king's reply. Their hopes soon received a downward jolt; the king would renounce nothing, and furthermore he declared that all subjects should throw off the illegal arbitrary power of Parliament and arrest the mayor and four leading citizens on treason charges. The City's mood changed rapidly. Pym, who was present when the reply was read, was able to convince his audience that they could expect nothing from the king. Even so, the Lords proceeded to draw up offers of peace, and in February a delegation led by the Earl of Northumberland arrived with them in Oxford. At the heart of the proposals was Parliament's request for the abolition of the episcopacy, which had actually already been effected in law as well as in fact, and for the punishment of Royalist malefactors. There was also a renewed demand for prosecution of the laws aimed at papists, reinvigorated by the knowledge that there were several prominent Catholics about the king and by rumours that the Earl of Newcastle's army was full of them. Charles could not really have been expected to agree to the abolition of the episcopacy. He had continued to defend it while powerless, and since he now believed he could win the war, he was even less likely to consider it. In response to Parliament's suggestion that both sides should disband all of their armies, Charles demanded that the forts and ports should all be handed to him. It was not a proposal to be taken seriously, but it related to his demands in early 1642.

The third way in which the war had begun to intrude on English and Welsh society was through the logistical efforts of both sides. The effects of these at the local level in these two countries, as well as in Ireland and Scotland, will be discussed in more detail later. Here an overview of the county administration will suffice. Once Edgehill had been won and lost, the ad hoc nature of collecting money became entirely inappropriate. Funding bodies were needed to establish a firm basis of support, and both sides adopted similar methods but with different origins. In many places the Royalists revived the commissions of array, which had a limited taxation function explained in the covering letters sent out to the nominees. The commissioners were empowered to collect funds from those unable to bear arms to provide weapons for those who could. Small groups of commissioners met during the early months of the war in some counties and had already co-ordinated administrative matters. By the end of 1642 the areas under the control of Royalist commissions, embracing the sheriffs, were in place. Naturally, the membership was different to that established back in the summer. Research in the Midlands suggests that only about 40 per cent of the nominees actually played a part in the war effort.[23] As only a small amount of evidence related to the workings of the commissions has survived, there is some leeway in interpreting the figures, but even using the most generous estimate, it would appear that fewer than 50 per cent of those people appointed in 1643 actually served on the commissions. Some of the reasons for this are related to military or administrative service outside the county, others to personal incapacity. However, at least 11 per cent of the appointees to these commissions became active Parliamentarians, whereas almost a quarter took no recorded part in the war at all. The reasons for this shortfall are manifold. First, the king could not know enough about every nominee to judge his commitment, and many people were still undecided in their loyalty as the commissions were being drafted. Second, some future Parliamentarians may have been named as a way of trying to tempt them into joining the king. The active commissioners were quite experienced in government at the local level – most had been to university and there were fifteen former MPs amongst them. Yet Charles's attempt to place the militia in the hands of the aristocracy plainly failed at this level; only one serving commissioner in the north Midlands was heir to an aristocratic title.

It is clear that Charles continued to try to update the commissions in some regions, adding new names and cutting out dead wood. In the Welsh counties Charles was concerned to appear to maintain the peace on a level not seen in England. On 21 December he wrote to the High Sheriff of Monmouthshire, stressing that he was

> resolved allways to governe by the knowne lawes of the land, they may have a perfect enioynment of theyr liberty and propriety in the most happy condition that may be and be freed from such breaches of the same . . . [and that the sheriff should] require all our ministers and officers of justice of our said county to have a speciall care of the due execution of the lawes especially such as have beene made for the punishment of drunkards, prophaners of the Lords day, swearers and for the reliefe of the poore.[24]

In accordance with these aims Charles also kept reissuing commissions of the peace. In February 1643 Brecknock, Cardigan, Merioneth, Denbighshire and Flint all received adapted commissions of the peace; Merioneth received renewed array and peace commissions on the same day. These both pared Edward Merrick and placed Griffeth Namey, Robert Wynne and John Morgan on both, Humphrey Hughes on the array and John Wyne on the commission of the peace.[25] Within a month the benches of Brecknock and Denbighshire were further supplemented. April saw a further batch of alterations to the benches of Pembroke, which underwent a dramatic change, Carmarthen, Flint, Merioneth and Denbighshire, and in May there were a further three commissions of the peace and two of array. In June the first of the commissions of safeguard was created for Glamorganshire, Monmouthshire, Brecknock and Radnorshire. These essentially served the same function, as the commissioners were charged to defend the county and to establish the 'equall assessing and levying such sums as shall be thought fit', by appointing assessors and receivers throughout the county and distributing the money to the garrisons.[26]

The main functions of the English commissions were to raise funds for the forces based in their counties and to liaise with the garrison commanders. These were not destined to be easy tasks. In both countries the commanders were appointed not by the commissions but by the king or his regional generals, creating a conflict of authority which made working relationships in some counties problematic if the commanders were not on the commissions. Problems could arise over funding too, as taxation had to be agreed on by both the military and civilian governors. Taxation levels agreed on by the commissioners and the commanders were then passed through the county hierarchy to the local communities. Essentially, commissioners dealt with collecting a weekly contribution in both cash and provisions and sequestering enemy estates. Royalist administrators were also responsible for billeting troops in outlying areas and exacting necessary items such as beds and bedding. The English commissions should also have included several JPs, who fulfilled their normal functions of keeping the peace as well as regulating disputes over taxation.

Parliament too began to create committees in each county to administer its war effort. These were essentially to fulfil the same functions as the Royalist bodies and also included sheriffs and JPs. They were possibly based on the informal committees of deputy lieutenants which had administered the militia. In the Midlands they were clearly grouped around proven activists such as Sir John Gell and John Hutchinson and could thus be expected to have greater success than the commissions of array in attracting the energies of their appointees. As the months passed, numerous sub-committees developed to deal with a variety of affairs. There were committees of accounts, committees dealing with sequestration, committees to deal with the excise tax introduced in 1643, and committees to examine the clergy and remove 'scandalous ministers'. For the most part the membership of these sub-committees was drawn from the membership of the main, general or militia committee to avoid clashes of interest. What the committees failed to overcome, however, was the problematic relationships between civil and military leaders. For Parliament this situation was overlaid with a general structural problem centred on the power of the Earl of Essex. In the early days of the war, the deputy lieutenants, the precursors of the county committees, had charge of the militia, while all volunteer forces were under Essex's command. He retained the right to issue each commission, even after major generals had been appointed to command the county forces grouped into regional associations. The major generals, who were themselves theoretically appointed by Essex, were unable to nominate their own garrison commanders and officers. The relationship of the major generals to their associations and the counties that contained them was not fully worked through, either. Joint committees made up of representatives of each county committee have been referred to as 'toothless bodies'.[27] Even the most successful association, the Eastern Association, was unable to fulfil its commitments to the strategically important garrison at Newport Pagnell, and it was riven by dissent from the individual committees.[28] Other associations failed completely; for example, the one under Lord Grey in the Midlands was eventually broken up and divided amongst neighbouring associations.[29] The Northern Association was only really successful once the Royalist cause in its area was defeated and a heavy military presence, composed of its own forces and the Scottish army, established in the region.

In Ireland the situation had progressed dramatically since the creation in October 1642 of the Confederation of Kilkenny. The Confederation was not wholly united in its aims or even its logic. The Irish and the Old English were both Roman Catholics, and both groups were held responsible for the massacres of 1641–2 by the New English, the New Scots and their associates in Britain. Now they aimed at gaining a position of strength from which to secure their aims. Those aims, it should be remembered, were in themselves revolutionary, aiming as they did to readjust the balance of power in a way similar to the political revolutions of both Scotland

and England and Wales. However, what the Irish Catholics wanted was unacceptable to the Protestant states across the Irish Sea because the religious differences were insurmountable. The English and Scottish revolutions had been conducted within a Protestant framework; their religious elements did not touch the fundamental basis of the confessional structures of the three nations. The Catholics' demand for religious freedom and equality, which was unacceptable to Protestants, brought to the surface deep racial and cultural tensions associated with Protestant perceptions of the Gaelic areas of the archipelago.[30]

This forced the Confederates to address two issues at the time the Confederation was created. First, they had to come to terms with the likelihood that their demands would be unacceptable to the Protestants in the other three nations and their armies in Ireland. It was also unlikely that Protestants in the pale and its outposts, including Ormond himself, or even Catholics loyal to the king, such as the Earl of Clanricarde, would accept these terms. This process of realization was to take a long time, and it may have been achieved only after 1642, although it has been suggested that if the Confederates had thought harder about the Scottish revolution, they might have understood that even change *within* the protestant framework had necessitated armed rebellion. By 1643 it could be argued that they had attained a position of strength. The Confederation had created a unified war effort, with a chain of provisional and county government and related taxation efforts; it had also established provincial armies under experienced commanders. Although complete military victory had not been achieved, the English and Scots forces were largely penned in and, if not cut off from the mainland nations, after October 1642 they were not a priority for funding and supply. Yet even in those circumstances the king, who was most in need of Confederate help, would not concede to demands for a free church; for he could not do so and hope to retain his other two British crowns. Moreover, if he allowed a free Catholic church in Ireland, his spiritual power as head of the Church of Ireland would be diminished.

The second issue the rebels had to face was their need to achieve more than a position of strength from which to negotiate. There were Irishmen who saw that the policy of outright victory was not an option but a necessity. Amongst them was Owen Roe O'Neill who, in addition to having gained his military experience abroad, had returned to Ireland inspired by the Catholic Counter-Reformation.

With him came officers of a like mind, to whom complete military victory was important. At the same time clergymen returned to Ireland, determined that the achievements of the Irish Catholic church before the rebellion could be consolidated in its aftermath. These developments led to a further radicalization of the rebellion which took it beyond its initial aims; they were also unacceptable to the Old English, who had a traditional loyalty to the crown. The Old English demands were more moderate; for them toleration of Catholicism, even covert toleration, would suffice, if the king would agree to it. Theirs was a position built upon years of compromise. They had initially been thrown into a radical posture in 1641 out of fear for their own property tenure, and then into rebellion after the Westminster and Edinburgh Parliaments had compounded those fears by establishing the Adventurers to profit from confiscated land.[31] This division conspired to block the full advancement of the Confederation's cause and hampered O'Neill's attempts to achieve complete victory in Ulster. Resources he desperately needed were often diverted to Thomas Preston, the commander in Leinster, who had the confidence of the Old English at Kilkenny. Moreover, Owen was not given a free hand even in Ulster; in 1644 the inexperienced Lord Castlehaven was given command over an army raised for a campaign against the Ulster Scots.[32]

There was too a constant impetus for peace in Ireland, which diverted energy away from both the military campaigns and progress towards the full establishment of the Catholic church in areas controlled by the Confederation.[33] Both efforts, after all, were calculated to offend the king, and the Confederates were keen to demonstrate their declared loyalty. In the summer of 1642 they had made their desire for negotiations clear and had tried to discuss peace with Ormond, then the king's most successful general in the pale; but it was not until the following January that the discussions got under way in any serious manner. When Charles had been poised on the brink of war the previous summer, he had probably avoided serious negotiations to forestall the massive consequences of being seen to negotiate with Catholics while on the verge of open conflict with his Protestant subjects. For the rest of the year, the military campaigns no doubt occupied his mind. In the winter, as fighting lessened and Charles's hold on Chester and the Welsh ports was secured, the potential benefits of an end to the war in Ireland became clear. Troops sent over to support the pale would be recalled, and perhaps even an Irish army could be brought into England and

Wales. It was a dangerous policy, however. Any agreement with the Confederation would leave the king open to religious attack, and any Irish troops in England would anger many of his adherents. Discussions had to be secret, and the agreement could not extend to any overt religious freedom for the Catholic Irish. Charles therefore instructed Ormond to offer little: tacit toleration and no constitutional changes. At the same time, Ormond sought to divide the Old English from the Irish, leaving the latter to shoulder all of the blame for the rebellion. Any concessions at all would be made with this policy in mind.[34] But at the same time as representatives met at Trim on 17 March, the Council and Lord Justices sought in a letter to undermine the Catholic claim to be loyal to the king: 'a prisoner amongst the rebels . . . heard one of the rebels, a man of note amongst them, say that if he had your majesty where he then spoke he would flay you quick . . . others said they would have an Irish king'.[35] True peace, asserted the councillors, lay in the military defeat of the rebels, not in the discussions about to get under way at Trim. Neither this attitude nor Ormond's did much to convince the Confederates that they had anything much to gain from the king at this stage, and in the General Assembly some members rejected calls to take the discussions any further. Nevertheless, in June commissioners from the assembly met with Ormond, only to find the king intransigent again, although he had instructed Ormond to secure the support of an Irish army. The papal envoy Pietro Francisco Scarampi arrived in Ireland at the end of July and perceptively analysed the situation: in his view the Confederation appeared to be in no need to sue for peace; whereas it might well have had need a year ago, now it was neither defeated nor insolvent, especially as the king's terms were not generous. Scarampi's view, embarrassing to the Old English, was set aside and the negotiations continued. The Council in Dublin still objected to any cessation of hostilities and pressed for a continuation of the war. The members' objections were twofold. First, the king would not benefit materially in a way which would offset the damage to his honour as a result of the anger that a settlement would provoke in England, Wales and Scotland too. Second, they believed that peace would be no good for the Protestant people of Ireland, who would be placed in danger by being bound to keep the peace with their persecutors. As the Council had pointed out in March, if the Confederation allowed no government official to be drawn from the Protestant community, what sort of protection would it offer those who returned to their homes in Confederate hands?

The members appear to have been well aware that this level of consideration had probably never troubled the king at all. He saw Ireland essentially as a resource to be tapped in order to help him extricate himself from trouble in England and Wales. The cessation agreed to by the Confederation and Ormond effectively gave the king grounds for sustaining his attitude to Ireland. It obscured the differences between the Old English and the Irish, and in so doing hid the essential causes of the rebellion – the legal, religious and social deprivations forced on the Catholic people – instead playing up the loyalty to the crown which prefaced the declarations of the Confederation and perhaps, to the king's mind, turning the rebels into fellow sufferers at the hands of a Puritan faction. Owen Roe O'Neill's campaign in County Meath in Leinster posed a serious threat to the pale, and attempts to defeat him failed. Ormond told the Council that O'Neill's defeat of Lord Moore at Red Ralies Mill and the failure of Monro to reoccupy Portlester could lead to the province being overrun by O'Neill's army.[36] On 15 September 1643 the English agreed to a cessation of hostilities in the pale in the name of the king and the Confederation of Kilkenny. For some, like the Catholic Earl of Clanricarde, still loyal to Charles I, it came none too soon. He wrote to Charles nine days after the cessation about the affairs of Connaught:

> that the Irish forces were powerful there, and the number of English and those that continue firm and adhere to them so few and long neglected, that your majesty's castle of Athlone and all the garrisons and counties of Roscommon and Galway would have been lost: and in that number, if the cessation had not been timely concluded, must have fallen your majesty's poor most faithful servant . . .
>
> Most of the quality are well inclined and desirous of peace and inquisitive to find out those ways that may put them into a condition of being capable of your majesty's grace and mercy.[37]

It was not an all-embracing peace. For a start, it was to last only for a year; second, some of the English in pockets of territory outside the pale – Inchiquin in Munster and Sir Charles Coote in Ulster – bridled under its terms; and third, the Scots in Ulster were not bound by it at all.

The Dublin Council had been very perceptive; the consequences of the cessation of the rebellion were dramatic. The kingdom of Scotland reacted particularly strongly to the fact that the king had come to an agreement with Catholics. It must at all times be borne in mind, of course, that to many people, a state of war had existed long before the fighting began outside Kelso in 1639. A war between Catholics and Protestants was being fought in the hearts and minds of the people, and the gunfire from European conflict could be heard in the imaginations of the godly in the four nations. All of this background helps to explain the shock caused by the announcement of the peace in Britain. The Westminster Parliament had been attempting to draw the Scots into the war since the previous year. The Scots commissioners in London had clearly indicated during January 1642 that the Covenanters supported Westminster in the split between it and the king which occurred after the attempted coup, but the Scots had attempted to appear disinterested during the months when open warfare developed, despite receiving appeals from both sides. They were involved in Irish issues during that year, with an army based in Ulster which for a while was under the command of Leven. But the Covenanters were not the only Scots with an interest in the affairs of the four nations. The Earl of Antrim had been involved in the Irish rebellion before being captured. He had escaped in October 1642 and during the ensuing winter canvassed to extend the war in the four nations by tying them more closely together. He proposed that Royalists from all four countries unite with the Confederates and the Macdonnell/MacDonald clan in Ireland and the Highlands. The first aim would be to defeat the English Parliament and the next to turn on the king's opponents in the other two nations – Covenanters, Parliamentarian Protestants in Ireland and also extremist Catholic Irish. Antrim was thereby combining his clan ambitions and Royalism. At this point cultural conflict becomes a main part of the war in Britain as in Ireland. Over the past forty years, with royal approval, the MacDonalds in the Highlands had been dispossessed of their territory by the Campbells under the increasingly anglified Earls of Argyll. The current earl was of course the leading Covenanter, so dealing a blow to his territory would also strike at the heart of the Scottish government and win back lost MacDonald lands. Clearly, such a plan had problems. To get these different and often competing groups to form such an alliance would be difficult; it would also anger many of Charles's Protestant supporters in England, Wales and Scotland, if Confederate Irish and Highland Catholics were involved. In addition, it was likely to prompt the king's enemies into a similar alliance.[38]

The threat posed by this plot was exposed in May 1643 when Antrim was once again captured at Newcastle, County Down. He was on his way to open secret negotiations with the Confederates, who were already in negotiations with Ormond (there was rarely only one set of Royalists negotiating at once!). What turned his misfortune into a disaster was that he was carrying letters concerning his plans. Examinations of him and his servants filled in the details, and the plot was exposed. Impractical as most of it was, the grains of truth within it nevertheless opened up a frightening scenario, namely, a peace in Ireland freeing Irish and English soldiers for service in England. There was also the spectre of a Scottish Royalist rising with troops led by Huntly and his son Lord Aboyne, along with the Earls of Montrose, Airlie and Nithsdale. Although this undertaking was allegedly intended primarily to create a force to lead into England, there was at least one subsidiary plot in which Highlanders were to be armed to fight the Covenanter government. Although Antrim denied it, it was this dual plan which would destabilize the government in Edinburgh, win back the MacDonald lands and be 'decisive in precipitating [the Covenanters] into an alliance with the English Parliament'.[39]

Charles himself seems to have assumed that the Scots would simply stay out of the war, without much effort on his part. He consistently rejected the attempts of Scottish commissioners to mediate, partly because they wanted to tie the disciplines of the two churches closer together – in other words, to create a form of Presbyterian church in England. He was also listening to Hamilton, who suggested that a moderate line with the Scots on domestic policy might well bear fruit in the form of a political group capable of hindering Argyll from entering the war. Charles, too, was rarely to be found pursuing only one set of policies at a time, and another factor in the king's dealings with Scotland was the Earl of Montrose. While the king discussed political opposition at Oxford, Montrose was in York with the queen suggesting a pre-emptive military strike against an unready Argyll, until Charles sent Hamilton and Traquair to the queen to convince her of their arguments. For the time being Montrose was dismissed.[40] One analysis indicates that part of the international problem eluded Charles. While not interfering with the Kirk 'was as far as Scotland itself was concerned, wise and conciliatory', he did not take into account that Covenanters like Johnston of Wariston, and indeed Argyll, believed that security in Scotland would require some religious affinity with the English church. On this point Charles would not budge.[41] To compound the ill effects of this failing, Charles was deliberately rude to the Scots commissioners led by Loudoun; when they left Oxford he even tried to stop them from visiting London before returning to Scotland.

In May a convention of the Estates was summoned to Edinburgh. Although it was an informal meeting, to avoid the need to secure the king's permission, it was to be composed of newly elected members. The elections coincided with the discovery of Antrim's plot and the revelation that Montrose had been in Aberdeen talking with Lord Huntly. A frightening vista opened up before the assembly gathered at Edinburgh. Antrim's correspondence included letters from Huntly's son Aboyne, who had also been at York with the queen and Montrose. These was, it seemed, a plot involving the Gordons, who back in 1639, had fought the Covenanters in the north-east and the MacDonalds in the west with backing from Ireland. Nothing directly linked the king to all of this, but it was well known that he was negotiating with the rebels in Ireland through Ormond and that peace there was a prerequisite for the Gaelic rising across the sea. Flawed though this view may have been, there was enough truth in it to justify the horror with which it was greeted. In response the Edinburgh assembly sent copies of the Antrim papers to Westminster, where the members declared themselves a free assembly, throwing off the last of their chains to the king. An immediate demand for military co-operation with the English and Welsh Parliament was reciprocated in July, and plans for a close alliance moved forward. Even before the news of the Irish cessation arrived, the assemblies of three of the four nations were locked into a Solemn League and Covenant, promising mutual aid against their king. The English and Welsh assembly would provide the funding for military intervention and for the Scots forces still in Ulster; in return an army of 21,000 would enter England the following year.

While this Anglo-Scottish alliance has been described as the 'most important element in Pym's strategy for saving the Parliament', the policy was not universally popular with the supporters of Parliament.[42] It has been suggested that the possibility of a Presbyterian church being established in England was as great an apostasy to some as the cessation was to the Confederates.[43] Such people realized that the Scots wanted religious change in England for their own purposes and that they cared little about political affairs per se. As a result, they interpreted the words in the treaty referring to the founding of a new church 'according to the Word of God and the example of the best reformed churches' as referring specifically to a Presbyterian system, as indeed the Scots themselves did. It is

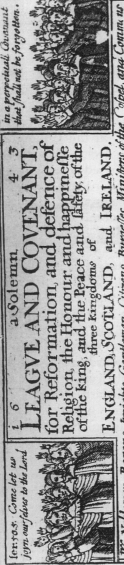

i 6   a Solemn   4 3

LEAGVE AND COVENANT,
for Reformation, and defence of
Religion, the Honour and happinesse
of the King, and the Peace and safety of the
three Kingdoms of

ENGLAND, SCOTLAND, and IRELAND.

We Noblemen, Barons, Knights, Gentlemen, Citizens, Burgesses, Ministers of the Gospel, and Commons of all sorts in the Kingdoms of England, Scotland, and Ireland, by the Providence of God living under one King, and being of one reformed Religion, having before our eyes the Glory of God, and the advancement of the Kingdome of our Lord and Saviour Iesus Christ, the Honour and happinesse of the Kings Maiesty and his posterity, and the true publique Liberty, Safety, and Peace of the Kingdoms, wherein every ones private Condition is included, and calling to minde the treacherous and bloody Plots, Conspiracies, Attempts, and Practices of the Enemies of God, against the true Religion, and professors thereof in all places, especially in these three Kingdoms ever since the Reformation of Religion, and how much their rage, power and presumption, are of late, and at this time increased and exercised; whereof the deplorable state of the Church and Kingdom of Ireland, the distressed estate of the Church and Kingdome of England, and the dangerous State of the Church and Kingdom of Scotland, are present and publique Testimonies; We have now at last, (after other means of Supplication, Remonstrance, Protestations, and Sufferings) for the preservation of our selves and our Religion, from utter Ruine and Destruction; according to the commendable practice of those Kingdoms in former times, and the Example of Gods People in other Nations; After mature deliberation, resolved and determined to enter into a mutuall and solemn Legue and Covenant; Wherein we all subscribe, and each one of us for himself, with our hands lifted up to the most high God, do swear;

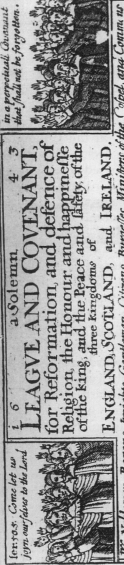

Plate 6 Detail from Hollar's engraving of the Solemn League and Covenant,
The Mansell Collection, London.

probable that they actually made such a vague statement because
the English treaty commissioners were hedging their bets or trying
to inveigle Independent support for it by being obscure. Those who
opposed any form of state or monolithic church and had cast down
the English and Welsh churches for that reason, rather than because
they regarded them as tarnished in themselves, could not accept the
creation of a Presbyterian church hierarchy any more than they
could accept episcopacy. This group became known as Independents
because they wanted congregations independent of an overarching
structure. It has been suggested that the term Congregationalist is
perhaps an easier way to describe their nature.[44] Even before the
Solemn League, they had been in a minority on the Council of
Divines, which had assembled at Westminster to decide what should
replace the episcopacy. The assembly was supposed to embrace a
wide spectrum of religious thought, but the Episcopalians who were
invited failed to attend, and the Congregationalists could muster
only five supporters. Instead the assembly was dominated by Presbyterians, egged on by the Scots and by preachers in the Presbyte-
rian-dominated capital city.

In Parliament there were possibly three groupings of political views.
They were not homogeneous parties, although the word *party* is contained in two of them, the War Party and the Peace Party. Indeed,
there have been challenges to the very notion of three groups, as
some historians have asserted that there may have been only two
large and loose groupings. In any event, there was a general consensus during the period before 1646, followed by adversary politics
afterwards. If there was a consensus of aims in Parliament before the
end of 1643, it was Pym's work. If there was a third group, it was
the Middle Group, which J.H. Hexter alleged often held the balance
of power with Pym at its centre, shrewdly manipulating members
of the two main groups into supporting him. The War Party was
determined to prosecute the war thoroughly and was prepared to
get rid of Essex in order to do so. The earl's summer campaigns
were seen to be ineffective, and his motives were suspect. The War
Party wanted to defeat the king and then open negotiations. The
Peace Party, conversely, wanted to open negotiations, perhaps at
any price, to secure an end to the war. This group also opposed the
entry of the Scots into the war. The Middle Group had a flexible
approach to victory and negotiations, supporting Essex in command,
although not over and above the other generals, Waller and Manchester. At the centre of this group, Pym was largely responsible for

steering through the negotiations with the Scots. Into these loose groupings the Presbyterians and Independents, or Congregationalists, fitted inexactly. The Independents did not approve of the Scots' entry into the war on religious grounds, but this did not make them Peace Party men. On war aims, prominent Independents like Oliver Cromwell were in favour of vigorously prosecuting the war and negotiating with the king only from a position of strength. Obviously, Cromwell could not agree with all parts of the War Party policy, particularly with regard to the Scots. The ability to balance the aims of these diverse groups, and to get some individuals to agree to policies proposed by groups from whom they were poles apart, marked Pym out as an exceptional Parliamentarian. When he died in great agony from bowel cancer on 8 December 1643, the Royalists lost no opportunity in lauding this event as the work of God, pointing to the nature of the disease as a reflection of what Pym had done to the nation.[45] It was foolish of them, for the path Pym trod would in the end probably have benefited them too; moreover, as Hampden, possibly the only person who could have matched Pym, had been killed at Chalgrove Field in June, Pym's death marked the end of effective moderate leadership.[46] The central group was held together after Pym's death by Oliver St John. Pym's swansong had been the alliance with the Scots, at which he laboured until his death. In so doing he assured that the war would enter a new phase in the coming months.

From Parliament's point of view, the new injection of military vigour which the Covenanter army could bring was much needed. Since the early summer its fortunes had been mixed, and only the failure of the Royalists to exploit their success in the summer had saved Parliament from defeat. Essex's campaign against Oxford had failed to achieve much after Reading had fallen. On 18 June the skirmish with Prince Rupert's forces at Chalgrove Field in which Hampden died of his wounds took place, and Essex was humiliated by a successful Royalist attack on High Wycombe to his rear.[47] Pym was prompted to remark that people were better protected by the king than they were by the earl.

In the west, Waller's career of conquest came to an end after a complex series of manoeuvres around Bath.[48] Waller achieved strategic success by occupying and then holding the high ground at Lansdown on 4 July against Hopton's attacks the following day. At the end of the fight, however, both sides withdrew exhausted. Victory on this occasion is difficult to apportion. It could be argued that Hopton achieved his objective by getting Waller off Lansdown Hill, which was strategically important because it dominated routes to Bristol. However, recent scholarship presents an alternative perspective. Waller can be regarded as the victor because his decision to withdraw left him in a stronger position than his enemies, and the 'Royalists admitted their defeated condition by withdrawing to Marshfield'.[49] The fact that Hopton was wounded in an explosion after the battle only added to the misery of the Royalist forces now cramped up in Devizes. Yet even with their commander on his sick bed, the Royalists planned audacious revenge as Waller advanced on them on 9 July. Maurice and Lord Hertford left Devizes with the horse and rode to Oxford for reinforcements, returning on 13 July with two more brigades of horse. They attacked Waller on Roundway Down, inflicting a massive defeat and destroying his army. The Severn Valley was now open to the Royalists. When Bristol fell to them in July, the king gained an important seaport for the first time since the war began. Although it had a merchant Puritan clique, Bristol was not overtly interested in national politics, and during the war it had attempted to remain aloof. However, when the combined Royalist forces attacked on 26 July, a group of 200 women led by Joan Batten and Dorothy Hazzard demonstrated that there was a faction in the town determined to keep the Royalists out. Hazzard and Batten built emergency defences and tried to encourage the soldiers with their own bravery in the face of the Royalists' attack on one of the city gates. Bristol's importance as a base for the small Royalist navy and its trading networks was immense, but so was its potential as a base from which soldiers from Ireland could be landed and sent off around the country.

In the north the Earl of Newcastle, with the help of the queen's ammunition supplies, had been able to go on the offensive and had secured the east coast ports of Yorkshire. At Scarborough the governor, Sir Hugh Cholmeley, had changed sides and had brought the garrison with him after negotiations with the queen. From the evidence of taxation returns, Bridlington Quay seems to have remained in Newcastle's sway even after the queen had left the vicinity. The possession of both ports enabled Newcastle to hold all of the trading network by diverting customs duties from Hull to Scarborough once Leeds and Bradford came into his hands in the summer.[50] There were setbacks for Newcastle. Goring, now back in England, was appointed to command part of the northern army. He was defeated at Wakefield, however, and captured by Sir Thomas Fairfax on

24 May. But in the same month Newcastle's forces defeated Oliver Cromwell at Sleaford and garrisoned parts of Lincolnshire. This both further encircled the Fairfaxes and threatened the Eastern Association counties, prompting a swift response from London: an Eastern Association army was created, with the Earl of Manchester in command and Oliver Cromwell to second him. The queen left York on 4 June and marched southwards, aiding Henry Hastings to capture Burton-on-Trent and assisting in an attack on Nottingham by the Newark forces. She joined the king on 13 July at Edgehill. In her wake Newcastle attacked the West Riding and defeated the Fairfaxes on 30 June at Adwalton Moor between Leeds and Bradford. The West Riding fell to Newcastle, and the Fairfax father and son team was quickly bottled up in Hull. They were lucky to find refuge there, for Hotham had been about to betray it when he was arrested on 29 June.

During the later summer and autumn, the Royalist forces failed to develop a major strategy, although some historians have long believed that a three-pronged attack on London was planned and thwarted by inherent localism.[51] In the north Newcastle turned his attention to Hull and launched what proved to be a disastrous siege. In the west local forces turned their attention to Plymouth. The king, in the centre, became obsessed with Gloucester and in August commenced a long and, in the end, futile siege. All of these plans had a logic of their own related to regional security and the mastery of local resources, but it may also be argued that together they dissipated the energies of the Royalists and would have done so even if they had ended in victory. In the end it may have to be assumed that there was no grand strategy at this point. Some historians have argued that this effectively meant that the Royalists lost the war in September 1643; others believe that the political war was certainly lost when the king's dealings with the Kilkenny Confederation prompted the Solemn League and Covenant that month.[52] Militarily, it may be argued that the Royalists had a few months' grace, despite losses in the sieges and at Newbury. Some of the Royalist forces were still in fine shape.[53]

In many ways the idea of stalemate is reinforced by the events of the king's campaign against Gloucester. This is one of the sieges where archaeological work has made an important contribution to modern understanding by demonstrating the nature of the fortifications with which the city defended itself in 1643.[54] Men and women were equally determined to keep the king out. As one commentator wrote, the women and children acted their parts in making up the defects of the fortifications . . . it was admirable to observe . . . the cheerful readiness of yong and old of both sexes, as well the better as inferiour sort of people by day and night.[55]

Faced with this determined effort, the king was held outside the town for four weeks. During this time Essex, with reinforcements from the London trained band regiments, dashed westwards in late August and by 5 September threatened the rear of the king's army, forcing it to withdraw. A day later, Essex put supplies and men into Gloucester and turned about to get back to London. The king chased after him, but he was largely outpaced until Rupert slowed the Earl at Albourne Chase, allowing the king to overtake him before he could get to Newbury. As the earl approached the town, the king's army drew up between Essex and London, and on 20 September the king and Essex fought each other to a standstill at their third battle. The king, his ammunition exhausted, withdrew during the evening and left the route to London open to Essex, who promptly took it. On his return to London with the trained bands, Essex was regaled as a hero, and the demands for his replacement were temporarily silenced, even though in his wake his main army failed to hold on to Reading. If this was resonant of the end of 1642, so was the rest of the year in the south-east. Waller was given a new army, with which he launched a new campaign in the south, first attacking Basing House and then turning on Hopton, who was sent to tackle him. He drove the Royalists out of Winchester, occupied Arundel and opened a siege of the castle there. As winter set in, a temporary lull affected some areas of England and Wales but eluded others. As it became quiet in the south, the northern Welsh marches burst into life. Leven gathered his new army north of the Tweed, and the Marquis of Newcastle's subordinates began to galvanize the north-east. In East Anglia, the Earl of Manchester was completing the creation of his new army, which was to play an important part in the new year's war. At this point it is appropriate to ask the question, where were all of the resources coming from?

7

The Costs of War

Be marcifull to us & bless us and all ye ends of ye earth shall feare us[1]

In October 1643, the husband of Jane Kitchen from Upton in Nottinghamshire died. Within three months of John's death, Jane was embroiled in the war efforts of both sides. Constables and other officials in Upton were put into office through the houserow system, with principal householders taking office by turn. On 1 January, it was Jane's turn. She was now embarking on what a great number of men and some women across England and Wales were to be involved in throughout the war and interregnum – the administration of a series of wartime and extraordinary duties which went beyond the normal offices of the constable. Constables in England and Wales were responsible for the administration of a parish or constablewick, which could vary in size and form from a nucleated village to a string of scattered settlements to a district or ward of an urban settlement.[2] Constables were the bottom rung of local government in England and Wales and had a range of duties relating to the military, financial and legal administration of the counties. Because the constables were also responsible to their own community, many of these duties resulted in conflicts as constables fell foul of either the law or their neighbours as a consequence of this dual responsibility.[3] Such problems increased dramatically during the wars, as additional layers of financial and political complications were forced upon the offices. One constable, John Worsdale of Branston in Leicestershire, expressed this when he wrote on his accounts during the civil war period:

Mount not up to the place of honour for prosperitie is more dangerous than adversitie, and more perish at the rite hand of prosperitie than one at the rite hand of loe and poore degree.[4]

Ship money and coat and conduct collections had already exposed them to attack from all ranks of society: Sir Arthur Hesilrige had arrested a constable in Leicestershire, thereby intimidating the rest. Wartime collections of taxation carried some threats of military sanction. As if the implied threat of the collection of money and goods from the community by a group of heavily armed and mounted men on a regular basis were not enough, there was undoubtedly some threat of violence on occasion. This chapter explores the universality of the war's effects across the four nations, using relatively fresh evidence to provoke further research into those regions which have not as yet been thoroughly examined. There has been a good deal of work on the nature of the war in some regions of England, but little similar work has been undertaken for Wales, Scotland or Ireland, and even in England coverage is patchy.

Even so, local studies have a long tradition in this field. Many of the antiquarian histories of England contained some studies of the civil war. In the early twentieth century books dealing with Hampshire and Sussex were dedicated to the war, and in the 1930s Cornwall and Nottinghamshire were examined in a way that set trends for the future.[5] In the 1950s and 1960s a further stimulus was given to county studies by historians seeking to examine the role of provincial gentry in the long-term causes of the civil war. Following one study of Yorkshire gentry in the late 1960s, Alan Everitt studied the county of Kent in great detail in a ground-breaking publication in 1973, and Clive Holmes undertook an important examination of the Parliament's Eastern Association a year later. In 1973 David Underdown looked at Somerset; this work was enhanced by John Wroughton's book on the north of the county published in 1992.[6] In the Midlands, Anne Hughes has examined the county of Warwickshire in an important book, and Philip Tennant has subsequently placed part of her study into a wider context by looking at the issue of wartime exactions in the south Midlands. In 1974 R.E. Sherwood attempted to analyse the effects of the war on the Midlands region using a series of primary source extracts which make it clear that the burdens imposed on the civilian population were heavy and problematic.[7] He was not the first historian to do this. Many such documents were contained in older county histories, notably an exciting book by D.R. Guttery published in 1950.[8] Subtitled *The People Pay*, this book was written for the 'general reader' using parish account books to examine the effects of the war on the west Midlands and producing a stirring description of them. Unfortunately, the lack of references makes it quite difficult to explore the book's conclusions and assertions. Any idea that the general reader is not to be entangled with such things as footnotes or even explanations within the text is problematic, for it imposes limitations on the reader and leaves problems for the historian stirred by provocative books like Guttery's to probe the issues raised in them. Sherwood made no such mistake and thus made it much easier for a wide range of historians roused by him to examine the subject further.

There is a debate about the level of violence involved in taxation collection. It has been argued that the collection of taxation was accompanied by threats; contemporary examples from the continent indicate that the collection of taxation in England was undertaken in the manner of *Brandtschatzung* (burning-money). This form of collection carried the threat that if levies or taxation were not paid then some part of the village would be burned down.[9] More recently the argument has been modified somewhat: 'In addition to their collection of regular payments of the assessments and contribution, troops also carried out raids in order to levy irregular payments, expressively known in continental warfare as *Brandtschatzung*, burning-money.'[10] This statement refers more clearly to the irregular nature of the proceeding. Either way, there is no doubt that taxation could be a major problem. Some scholars believe that historians in general have largely ignored the burdens war imposed on local communities. Rural communities may have been the most vulnerable, because towns and cities possessed recognized authorities that were in a position to present the town's interests to the outsider. Rural communities could be more easily subjected to 'demands for money, for food, for forage, for winter quarters; and these were often still enforced . . . by very brutal means'.[11] In 1986 north Midland evidence was used to suggest that the fire-raid was not common and certainly not regarded as legitimate. The debate continued with other historians supporting the view that such threats were common.[12] After a reassessment of the evidence in the light of nationwide studies, the weight of the evidence nevertheless seems to demonstrate that in terms of the regular collection of the assessment and contribution in England, there was little actual violence and little incidence of it.

Emergency raids are evident in the sources discussed below, but punitive raids were very different affairs to general taxation; and contemporaries make that distinction in their narratives. The analogy to continental affairs is pertinent, although it is possible to find comparisons much nearer to home than contemporary authors did: Ireland offered several examples of a brutality that went beyond the English experience.

With the Parliamentarian war effort we are on surer ground, as it has been explored relatively extensively. In general the Parliamentarians were organized, if not always efficient. They imposed taxation systems, which it is claimed 'intensified trends already apparent in the English economy', stimulating the end of subsistence agriculture by driving on the need for surplus cash to pay assessments and excise.[13] The effects of the war in Kent were different to those in other areas: 'in Kent as in other counties remote from the fighting, the Civil War was not a "total" war', in contrast to Warwickshire, where taxation, especially in places where Royalists sometimes were able to collect money too, presented the economically weakest with "unimaginable burdens"'.[14] This has been taken up and contextualized by an examination of the damage to the infrastructure of poor relief, communications and education provision. One estimate is that for the gentry in East Anglia, between a fifth and a third of the income from rentals was used to pay for the war. For those further down the economic ladder, there was less opportunity to recoup their losses from something as comfortable as the rest of the rental.[15] However, research in north Somerset suggests that '[l]ocal people in general therefore were able to absorb the costs of the war comfortably without permanent hardship or distress'.[16] This may not be a universal proposition, for in marginal areas where survival was already a problem, there may have been no way of producing surplus to fund taxation.

There is less material available regarding Royalist taxation, and even recently it was said that '[t]he Royalists had to find money in a much more sketchy and ad hoc manner, by voluntary contributions, involuntary fines, and downright looting'.[17] This is patently untrue, however. Evidence from the parishes of England and Wales actually demonstrates that the rival systems mirrored each other in their structures, their methods and in their success at favourable moments.

In both England and Wales, the central bodies for collection within the counties had their origins in the summer of 1642, when the Royalists created a council of war at Oxford. For local government purposes they resurrected the commissions of array late in the year, despite their failure to galvanize the trained bands.[18] Their functions now became important and they were given financial responsibility over their counties. Sums to be allotted around each shire were discussed at meetings, though the records for these have generally disappeared. The main examples of commission material come from the Glamorganshire Order Book, the minutes of the Worcestershire Committee and the dockets of patents and commissions kept by the Clerks of the Chancery.[19] Transcripts of the latter, which were made by William Dugdale, provide the names of those appointed to commissions and committees by the king during the war and also contain some of the operational instructions handed to them.[20] However, considerably more evidence is available if one looks farther afield, though the material referred to below is clearly not comprehensive and a great deal remains to be done. Evidence from private papers, such as those of Richard Herbert for Monmouthshire, adds significantly to our understanding of the operational processes of the Royalist war effort. Furthermore, the constables' papers, and even those of churchwardens and, sometimes, overseers of the poor, can offer more material on the processes and effects of the collections of Royalist and Parliamentarian taxation.

At the core of the Royalist administration was the commission of array, often subdivided to deal with different areas of a county, and sometimes peripatetic in nature in establishing meetings throughout a county to demonstrate control as much as to deal with local issues. Problems arose because the commissioners had to work with the military commanders. Some commanders held commissions that predated the rebirth of the commissions of array, whereas others felt, with some legal justification, that their own commission did not oblige them to work with the commissioners of array. Conflict could also arise when other commanders were excluded from the commissions of array for political or religious reasons. In Staffordshire for example, the renowned Catholic Thomas Leveson, colonel and governor of Wolverhampton (until May 1643) and Dudley, was excluded from the commission and was at loggerheads with the county commissioners throughout much of the war. His subsequent appointment as High Sheriff in 1644, instead of bringing him into the fold, gave him authority over armed forces through his officeholder's power to raise the posse comitatus, which he used to challenge the commission of array.[21]

There were further formal and informal subdivisions of the commission of array. For instance, the JPs on them were charged with examining complaints about taxation levels. This was a traditional role, although it had been somewhat attenuated by the weight of indictments for non-payment brought before the benches in the period of ship money and coat and conduct money. In 1644 a new committee or series of committees was established in the counties under Royalist control. The Parliament assembled at Oxford established an excise tax in England and Wales, which was serviced by commissioners in each county through offices in the market towns. There is little evidence for the collection of this particular Royalist tax, and anything which is said of it tends to be provisional. One general point can be made, and that is that the excise was likely to generate little income. In the north and the north Midlands, for example, it came into effect just as the Royalist cause and Royalist territorial control declined dramatically. Moreover, we can say little about excise committee membership, although some county excise commissions are referred to in the Chancery Clerks' register. The commissioners of array could be very successful in their dealings given favourable circumstances, but as most were opposed by at least some localized Parliamentarian opposition, their freedom of movement was often restricted. Two neighbouring commissions demonstrate the vagaries of the situation. At the end of 1643, the Leicestershire commissioners were able to tour the county without being interrupted by their enemies based at Leicester. When the Parliamentarian county committee attempted to follow their example, Royalist troops caught it at Melton Mowbray. The Parliamentarian forces were defeated and several of the committeemen were captured.[22] However, at about the same time, Rutland commissioners of array were forced into seeking refuge at Belvoir Castle, after troops under Colonel Waite (or White) captured headquarters at Burleigh House near Stamford, preventing them from returning to the county.[23]

The Parliamentarian war effort was invigorated as the campaign season of 1642 drew to a close in the south and Midlands. At the centre Parliament created a military executive in the form of a Committee of Public Safety, which following the alliance with Scotland was superseded by the Committee of Both Kingdoms. This committee in turn dealt with the Lord General and established a series of financial committees in the City, utilizing buildings belonging to prominent companies. They were composed of MPs and lords and extended through them to chains of governance stretching into the counties. Committees were nominated at county level, probably from names of proven activists. Certainly in Derbyshire and Nottinghamshire, Sir John Gell and John Hutchinson, the two men most responsible for establishing a Parliamentarian military presence in the region, were at the centre of the administrative effort too.[24] Although these committees handed assessment collections to the central committees in London, they were answerable only to Parliament itself, which caused considerable difficulties if there were arguments and factional fighting in the local bodies. The county committees, known as militia committees or – more realistically – general committees, were subdivided. Smaller committees dealt with the sequestration of delinquents' estates, scandalous ministers and – after July 1643 – an excise tax. If the creation of sub-committees from the membership of the main committees had been intended to try to prevent arguments, it did not succeed in some places. The squabbles of the Warwickshire committees suggest that although some of these disputes appear petty, the principles of financial accountability that lay at their core were important. Such questions of probity and trust between the taxer and the taxed were fundamental issues of early modern government.[25] By 1645 accounts committees were also set up in the counties, precisely to deal with matters of financial management.

The problems inherent in this system have been clearly demonstrated. The committees funded the armed forces, largely through their weekly assessment; but they had little control over the army commanders, who were in principle responsible to Essex. Even the major generals who commanded the forces raised in the county associations were technically distant from the control of the county committees or their association committee. Members of the lieutenancy who led the county forces were incorporated into the committees, 'thus easing friction', but the overall division of control over military forces was to remain problematic.[26]

Both sides passed their orders on to the local communities, using warrants from high sheriffs incorporated into the commissions and committees. This resulted in there being two serving sheriffs in a county at the same time as long as both sides could maintain some form of presence there. The instructions passed through the usual chain of government – through the high constables to the constables. In England the Royalists seem to have allowed the traditional ad hoc meetings of the constable and his or her neighbours to decide upon the collection within the constablewick, but Royalists in Wales and Parliament ordered the appointment of assessors. The Constables' Accounts of Great Staughton in Huntingdonshire yield a good deal of information about the Parliamentarian process in action.[27] Levies there were assessed by the constable and four nominated sub-collectors. They had to publish the details of their levy so that aggrieved villagers could accompany the five men to Huntingdon when they handed over payment to lodge complaints to the committee. If there was any failure on their part the collectors were to pay a fine of 40 shillings each. The publication of the levies was considered important; a levy in May 1649 carried the rider, 'The neglect of which publication in time hath bred many inconveniences'.[28] The assessment and levy of taxation also entailed the development of bureaucracy and the attendant printing industry. Civil war papers in Bridlington, the Public Record Office and at Bedfordshire County Record Office contain a few examples of printed receipts with appropriate gaps for amounts, the parish name and the collector's name.[29] As well as stating the amount to be collected, the receipt also includes the promise that the money was to be repaid at 8 per cent interest by both nations. This is the chief value of the receipt for the taxpayer, that it marks his or her entitlement to reimbursement. Most surviving receipts are handwritten, and many relate to the contribution or assessment levies. They were particularly important to the constables, as they detailed what had been paid in cash and what had been handed over in the form of goods and provisions.

THE NORTH MIDLANDS[30]

In some ways the north Midlands offers a model for civil war records. The region has the highest concentration of surviving constables' accounts from the period, although few central Royalist documents are available and only slightly more exist for Parliament's local administration. The accounts from these counties nevertheless show how the Royalist war effort worked in relation to its Parliamentarian counterpart. Moreover, the military history of the region offers a model for understanding the way in which areas of England and Wales at one time in Royalist hands passed into Parliamentarian control. By the end of 1643, Royalist forces firmly controlled the north Midlands. There were pockets of Parliamentarian resistance, and these were to be crucially important in 1644, but for the time being they were cowed. The Royalists' success was undoubtedly due partly to the work of Lord Loughborough, who had been in command of four counties since the end of February. His task had not proved an easy one, and he owed the strength of his position at the end of the year to the fact that his immediate commander, the Marquis of Newcastle, was based in Nottinghamshire and Derbyshire. In each region the possession of a series of minor garrisons was important, not only as routes of communication and bolt-holes in difficult times, but also as quarters and taxation collection points. By the end of 1643, Lord Loughborough's forces and those in Nottinghamshire, over which his control was largely theoretical, held no fewer than eight major and sixteen minor garrisons in Leicestershire, Derbyshire, Nottinghamshire and Staffordshire.[31] These garrisons, the villages in their vicinity and a collection of less fortified towns, including Leek and Uttoxeter in Staffordshire and Chesterfield in Derbyshire, housed about 5,000 men of the north Midlands army. These forces regularly collected taxes from the surrounding area. The Leicestershire garrison and the county committee based there, on the other hand, were largely ineffective. At the end of 1643 they were unable to collect their assessments or even the rents of the committeemen themselves, and the county of Kent's contributions had to be used to subsidize the Leicestershire Parliamentarians.[32] The counties were divided up among the garrisons on the basis of hundred or wapentake divisions, and there seem to have been no qualms about cross-county boundary divisions. The Asbhy-de-la-Zouch garrison, for example, collected money from Leicestershire, Derbyshire and Warwickshrie hundreds.[33]

Sources from around villages across the region suggest a fairly uniform pattern of collection, with assessments adjusted or announced quarterly. Rating in this region was not just on acreage or annual income, as in the south Midlands and marches discussed below, but also on livestock grazing the pastures.[34] At Stathern in Leicestershire, for example, 1643 assessments were levied at 8d an acre, 8d a score of sheep, and 4d a pasture beast. At Coddington in Nottinghamshire, the same year's levies were set at 2d per acre, 2d per score of sheep and a penny each per pasture beast or dwelling.[35] Thus in both cases, the work of both men and women, the pasture and the field were all taxed. In this region, it would also seem that the collections were made regularly by touring troops of horse with defined circuits. Surviving evidence for one set of circuits from Newark for Colonel William Staunton's regiment, on the other hand, suggests a very unclear and difficult course through villages strung out around Nottinghamshire rather than grouped together.[36] In fact these may represent not collection points but merely the sources of the revenue for these particular units. However, the account book of

Staunton's lieutenant, Gervase Hewet, fails to clarify this. Certainly the villages on the list paid money to him as treasurer, and it is clear from the Upton constables' accounts that representatives of Staunton's regiment visited the village to make collections. This may have been because Upton was close to Newark, but there is no indication in Hewet's account book to distinguish Upton's payments from any others, some of which were well to the south of Newark and others well to the north.[37] After the middle of 1644, the region passed into the hands of Parliamentarians. One remarkable aspect of the situation is the way in which the two sides tried to ameliorate the problems of power sharing in the region. Clearly, on some occasions the two sides collected taxation on consecutive days when a community fell within reach of garrisons from both sides. The accounts of Mavesyn Ridware in Staffordshire in 1645 show that when both sides were collecting money there, each dropped their assessments to about two-thirds of normal.[38] As Parliament gradually assumed power, it appears to have begun to tax the communities at more or less the same levels as the Royalists had; only the method changed, as they seem to have expected constables to travel to specific collection points. There is little material evidence of the method of collecting money within the boroughs of this region. Borough papers for Leicester and Nottingham demonstrate that these town governments were keen to maintain discipline and order; but in the case of Nottingham, friction between members of the council and the governor, John Hutchinson, features in the entries.[39] The minute book of the committee at Stafford demonstrates, amongst other things, the urgent need to keep the town market and its services going in time of war. It also shows the way in which the committee was involved in a range of duties stretching from wartime taxation collection and military administration to the keeping of moral order.[40] For Royalist towns there is much less material. The account book of Gervase Hewet shows some minor details of urban wartime life in Newark, a major Royalist garrison. He recorded a series of payments in 1644 or 1645 to Don Kerchival as follows:

picking of hey	0-1-0
For clening ye yeard at ye Angell	0-2-0
For clening street against widow Tylers	0-2-0[41]

The 1643 account book of Lichfield garrison illustrates changes wrought in the town when, after the siege of April 1643, it became a major Royalist garrison. As the walls were repaired and the defences enhanced with artillery platforms and a reworked moat, the townspeople witnessed the construction of brass foundries, ammunition works and gunpowder mills.[42] The 1645 account book for the garrison, too, demonstrates the efficacy of the Royalist system in the late months of the war. Even at this stage the Lichfield Treasurer was collecting money from the hundred of Offloe right up to the outskirts of the enemy garrison at Stafford and was also able to cover seven-eighths of his expenditure even then.

THE NORTH OF ENGLAND

In April 1643, with the queen at York and Cholmeley now in the Royalist camp, the Earl of Newcastle issued the warrants for what became commonly referred to as the Great Sesse. Initially a total sum of £90,000 to cover three months was imposed. It was divided among the Ridings and then between each Riding's wapentakes, amounting to £6,000 in the West Riding's Claro wapentake.[43] The sum was further subdivided within Claro, with one division bearing £2,950, and the village of Timble alone paying some £35 towards this. The Great Sesse was reissued throughout the year at the rate of £30,000 a month, as Thomas Smith of Whorlton testified in the North Riding; and if Chief Constable Matthew Ward's memory can be trusted, it continued until the following spring, when the Scots army reached the region. From then on Royalist taxation took the form of less regular collections in the vicinity of garrisons such as Skipton and Helmsley.

Some communities in the county were faced with large sums to pay. Bridlington Town and its daughter settlement Bridlington Quay between them paid £95 to Cholmeley on 1 December 1643, a further £24-15s-4d the following month and then £33-9s-2d in May 1644, in what was to be the last major payment to the Royalists. At Bridlington in 1633, the four constables had required only £8-19s-1d to cover their charges in office, and only slightly more, £9-4s-2d, in 1641. However, by 1643 this sum had more than doubled to reach £22-10s, and of course it had to be borne in a time of massively increased central taxes.[44]

At nearby Scarborough, the income from the customs duties charged by the port was diverted to the Royalist cause, even though there was still some £200-0s-9d owing on the amounts collected between 10 October and 30 December 1643. A total of £313-4s-3d had been paid in duties, of which Sir Hugh Cholmeley's treasurer claimed £200 and two Royalist officers, members of Sir Hugh's family, claimed another £31 out of the total £302-4s-10d worth of disbursements by the Customs House. The first recorded assessment for the town dates from 7 December 1642 when Cholmeley held Scarborough for Parliament and was paid £50 to erect gates and 'other works' for the town. Scarborough consisted of four quarters, each administered by a bailiff responsible for tax collection. The second recorded levy, dated 25 July 1643, was to raise £60 for the town's use. Some 9 per cent of the 322 taxpayers were women, and together they paid 8 per cent of the collection in 1643.[45] The amounts of cash leaving some smaller Yorkshire communities were still very great. At Tankersley near Doncaster a warrant signed by a local man, Sir William Saville, along with Sir William Widdrington and Sir George Winkworth, elicited £24-1s-4d.[46] In the north of the county, at East Rounton, six months' assessments alone took £108 out of the village, and three subsequent collections in 1644 totalled £72. Furthermore, over £100 in billeting and other charges was not counted in the levies.[47]

It is clear from the accounts which Chief Constable Matthew Ward submitted to the Committee of Accounts after the war that the high and petty constables were inundated with paperwork. The first assessment he recalled, the Great Sesse of April 1643, involved keeping receipts for billeting and the commandeering of horses. For several weeks all of the paperwork and cash were left with the chief constables until army officers began to collect it from them. The February 1644 levy did not allow for the remission of billeting charges being collected 'in money without allowance of ticket or billet'. This strict ruling obviously made the levy more onerous and it may have been opposed, as by the end of the month the Yorkshire commissioners relented and allowed up to one-third of the amounts to be rebated on production of tickets or receipts.[48] Matthew Ward recorded a great shortfall that month, although winter conditions and the possibility of protest against the initial refusal to allow rebates may explain this.[49] Ward claimed that he paid over £169 to Sir William Carnaby and that the rest of the levy on his division – £814-6s-9d, or 83 per cent of the total – remained uncollected. Even allowing for the one-third of this sum that could have been rebated against this shortfall, it is clear that the discrepancy was significant.

Despite its size, the county of Yorkshire provides no great wealth of information about the local collection of taxes, making the picture of rural charges there difficult to discern. The uncollated nature of the material in the Public Record Office also presents problems. Indeed, some of the evidence is practically fragmented. A working book for some collections made in the York area exists, but it lacks a cover and is in poor condition. It would seem to cover 1643–4, but it is difficult to bring order to the figures jotted in it. It does show that the small communities north of York, Wigginton, Haxby, Earswick and Huntington, were faced with large tax bills during this period. From February 1643 to April 1644 Wigginton, a parish of 1,900 acres owned by the Parliamentarian Lord Howard of Escrick, paid £143 in tax at a rate of roughly £2-15s a week. Neighbouring Haxby, a smaller village split between the parishes of Strensall some three miles away and Driffield some twenty miles away, laid out £113 in the same period. Both parishes had alluvial soils and were later given over to root crops; both were also dependent to a significant degree upon use of the pasture and contained unfarmed moorland in their boundaries. Neither, therefore, was a particularly wealthy community.[50] Some places attempted to evade as much of the tax as possible, as in previous years, by challenging the allocation. The occupiers of the site of Fountains Abbey objected to their inclusion in the ratings imposed on nearby Markington; it was 'A Libertie and Constablery of themselves And have never contributed to Markington in any charges'. The landholders were then separately assessed, Mr Richard Evans was charged 6s-8d, and the tenants of Mrs Ann Martine were to pay 'fowertie shillinges' between them towards the 'General Ease of the whole Wapentake of Claro.'[51]

For the vast majority of the men and women of Yorkshire, the personal cost of the Great Sesse is largely lost to posterity. The returns made to the Committee of Accounts give some indication of these costs for the villages of Whorlton and its associated settlements of Rudby, East Rounton and Hutton juxta Rudby. These villages in the Cleveland area of the North Riding were parishes of mixed husbandry, with less than half of the land used for agricultural purposes and much of that being set aside for pasture. At Whorlton four hundred acres were described as pasture and five hundred as waste. Except for the Meynell and Constable families, which held significant parts of the manor, and Sir Arthur Ingram, who held some land in Whorlton, the inhabitants were not rich. Thomas Smith's assessments for the Royalist tax ran to a total of £2-4s-9d between

Michaelmas 1642 and Michaelmas 1643, as certified by Constable Robert Smith. Under the next constable Thomas paid £2-8s-4d before March 1644, when the system broke down and smaller and less regular sums were paid.[52] Evidence in the south of the county paints a similar picture. At Tankersley the amounts paid by individuals to the May 1643 assessment of the Great Sesse of £90,000 ranged from Lord Araford's (*sic*) £9-6s-8d to Widow Savile's two shillings.[53]

SCOTTISH AND PARLIAMENTARIAN TAXES

For the people of some of the northern counties, 1644 brought the second foreign military occupation in four years. At Whorlton the Scots arrived in April 1644. Unlike parts of the rest of England that funded the Scots, payments to the Scottish army represented continuity with the superseded Royalist regime in the north, rather than a supplementary levy. For Thomas Skenna of Whorlton, the Scottish burden was a great one. In 1643 he had paid Constable George Hunter £29-11s-10d towards the Great Sesse. In 1644–5 he paid £67-0s-10d towards the support of Bailey's and Hume's regiments of Scottish horse and over £70 the following year. The drain on the people of Whorlton lasted a long time and is shown in a series of accounts. Robert Burton claimed that he paid levies to the Scots for twenty-four weeks in 1644, and levies continued for all in 1645. In his claim for redress, Roger Lerder referred to twenty-four weeks of assessments in 1646. The East Rounton's total layout during the twenty-one weeks of Scottish occupation in 1646 cost £302-0s-8d 'besides quartering'. The small community of Rudby paid £107-4s-6d to the Scots during 1645 and continued until 25 January 1647, by which time the total sum paid since Martinmas 1645 came to £714-6s-0d.[54]

Receipts kept by the Roman Catholic Salvin family of Croxdale, County Durham, confirm the lasting nature of payments to the Scots. Surviving receipts exist in an unbroken sequence from 4 July 1646 until 28 January 1647. The system was a consistent one; all of the Salvin payments were made to the Earl Marshal's regiment and were signed by the major, Andrew Leslie. The amounts paid were fairly consistent too, being £2-0s-3d, £2-4s-0d or £2-0s-6d a week. From 3 October 1646, with the exception of a £4 assessment to cover two weeks on 29 October, the amount remained at £2-0s-3d

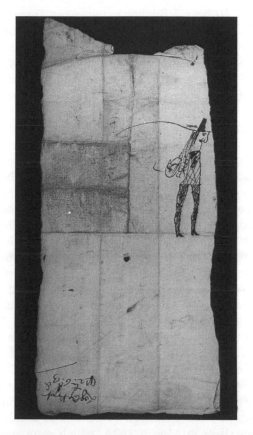

Plate 7 Drawing of Andrew (Andro) Leslie from the back of a
tax receipt (ref. D/Sa/E585.6), reproduced by permission of
Captain G.M. Salvin and the Durham County Record Office.

until 16 January. A final payment of £3-2s-0d followed. Leslie's
constant visits may have been an irritation to the family, but it was
his appearance which probably caused the strongest reaction. On
the reverse of one receipt is a drawing of a long-nosed man in tartan
trousers and a preposterously broad-brimmed and befeathered hat.
Croxdale as a whole was also paying the levies for the British army
in Ireland and for the garrison at Raby Castle. Additional billeting
charges at Croxdale from May 1645 until the following November
cost the village a further £9-5s-8d.[55]

In nearby Hullam, the inhabitants also paid money to the Scots and to Colonel Robert Lilburne's regiment from the Northern Association forces. Between April 1644 and Martinmas 1645 the village paid out £9-3s-11d to them both. As this is only one part of the £139-9s laid out by the community since the war had begun, we may here be seeing a settlement beset by quartering charges far greater than the cash levies that occurred in some areas of Somerset.[56]

At the beginning of the war, while they held the ports of Scarborough, Hull and Bridlington Quay, the Parliamentarians could collect taxes from the east coast and most of the East Riding. It is clear that in each of the Riding's wapentakes the subdivisions were used as a basis for allocations. Evidence from Harthill wapentake, the largest in Yorkshire, shows that the four administrative districts known as Beacons were used to subdivide taxation allotments. These four groups of parishes had been united to provide the warning beacons from which their name was derived – Bainton, Holme on Spalding Moor, Hunsley and Bishop's Wilton.[57] Despite the Parliamentarians' initial military supremacy in the region, it would appear that the effectiveness of the collection of weekly assessment was limited. As early as May 1643, arrears amounting to 30 per cent of the expected total had developed in Bainton Beacon, and Captain Remington was assigned to collect late money. In Hunsley Beacon arrears seem to have been smaller; Lieutenant Colonel William Boynton was given a list of only a third of the parishes in the beacon that were in arrears.[58] Developing cash problems would only have been exacerbated by the defection of Sir Hugh Cholmeley and the Scarborough garrison in March 1644, which removed the valuable income from the town and port as well as opening the way for the loss of Bridlington and Driffield. The town and Quay paid the Great Sesse into 1644, when the spring offensive launched from Hull resulted in the payment of money to Boynton's regiment, part of which was based at Bridlington Quay. Part of Boynton's family was lodged in the town in May, suggesting at least temporary occupation of the dual settlement. From May onwards taxation in the East Riding was almost exclusively Parliamentarian, except in the immediate vicinity of Scarborough.

THE SOUTHERN MARCHES

Material from Worcestershire and Gloucestershire can be used in this sample. In the former county, Prince Rupert had set the Royalists' assessment at £4,000 a month in February 1643; the money was supposed to go to Lord Herbert directly to support his forces in the region. There was also the additional burden of supporting the Parliamentarian garrison at Gloucester under Massey, forces from which were being left at free quarter around the town from February.[59] There is no evidence in the few surviving accounts from Gloucestershire villages that this money was ever collected. However, the accounts of Sir Nicholas Raynton of Maugersbury do show the effects of Hertford's presence and of the contribution made by collections in the early part of the war.[60] Hertford's 'first coming' resulted in five days' quarter, costing £25. A contribution, presumably part of the £4,000 per month, was collected by Lord Percy and Colonel Gerrard and amounted to £3-3s-4d. Money was collected for fourteen months, possibly from February 1644, followed by a series of contribution payments paid to Royalists. These accounts are also particularly important for examining extraneous costs of the war. In conjunction with contributions payments were made to the various forces sent to attack Gloucester in 1643, and Essex was paid when he relieved the town at the beginning of September. Further attempts to restrict the movement of the Gloucester garrison, which involved Lord Wilmot and Lord Wentworth blocking access to the town the following year, cost Raynton £28, and the campaigns of Essex and Waller that summer cost him dear. Waller demanded £27-10s in money and £30 of corn. Sometime in the summer of 1644, Massey was able to extract a 'contribution' from the Maugersbury estates too, but payments to the Royalists did not stop.

The most useful village records from Gloucestershire come from Hartpury. Here a series of levies covering the period from 1645 to 1651 can be used to assess not only civil war levies, but also changes in landholding patterns in the community during the war period.[61] A series of assessments shows that women in the village held about 25 per cent of the land in 1645 and paid a proportionate amount of the levies. The land value in the village in 1645 was £842, of which men held £648-5s and women £213-15s. Men, who made up some 71 per cent of taxpayers, paid 75 per cent (£16-11s-0d) of a levy made on 4 March 1645 for the monthly pay and 70 per cent (£10-8s-0d) of a levy on 5 June towards the British army in Ireland. By 1649 women were paying a lower proportion, largely owing to the death of Mrs Dorothy Compton, who had held land worth £50 per annum. The proportion of income here in the hands of women is significant; it is greater than that seen in parts of neighbouring Worcestershire or in the rural community of Salwarpe. There a smaller

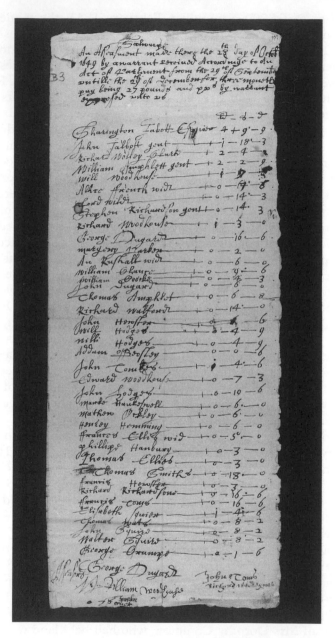

Plate 8 Detail of a Rating Document for Salwarpe, Worcestershire (ref. BA 10/54/2), reproduced by kind permission of the Rev. David Vince; photograph: Hereford and Worcestershire County Record Office.

proportion of women taxpayers contributed between 8 per cent and just over 15 per cent of levies exacted between 1647 and 1650.[62] Nevertheless, apart from an October 1649 levy, women never paid less than 10 per cent of the taxes, and at no time did they represent fewer than 11.6 per cent of taxpayers in the community; in 1649 they represented 12.5 per cent (five of thirty-five) and in 1650, 16 per cent (six of thirty).[63]

Material from Worcestershire, this time from the Hartlebury Royalist garrison in the Bishop's Palace, the meeting place of the county commission of array for part of 1644, further demonstrates women's involvement with the war effort. The returns to the Exchequer after the war suggest that the main incidences of loss in the war were a raid by a Captain Hitchcock before 1645, the arrival of the Scots in 1645 and the brief siege of the castle in 1646.[64] The goods taken from forty claimants suggest that the part of the rural economy managed by women suffered heavily, if not more than that managed by men.

Thomas Brooke:
Plunder by Captain Hitchcock's company took
in linen, apparel, bedding, pewter, and other
necessary to housekeeping   10-00-00
House plundered by the Scots, took linen, bedding,
pewter and other things fit for housekeeping   04-00-00
Plundered at the siege of Hartlebury Castle, linen,
bedding, pewter, brass, beer and provision   08-00-00

There are problems with this and other entries in the Hartlebury accounts. Clearly there is an element of formula; the repetition or near repetition of the words 'necessary to housekeeping' suggests some standardization of entries. Second, there is a suspicious amount of rounded figures, except where specific amounts would be available, such as Emanual Ives's loss of twenty sheep, which had an easily determined market price, and Fidkin's taxation, for which receipts would exist. The rest may well represent rounded-up guesswork. The accounts do show important features: the theft of linen, apparel, blankets and bedding demonstrates that the produce of women's labour was valuable, both for the plunderer – it would be necessary for quarters – and for the claimant. We can see the sorts of values placed on it, and this is important, because as much of this produce, probably all of that listed here, was for domestic consumption, its cash value is normally lost. Moreover, beer production –

which may have been the reason the brassware was stolen – the porkets and bacon, the bread and perhaps even the kine were items from the female sphere of economic production. The civil war is the cause of much information about the availability of women's work, and the taxation returns illustrate just how central women were to the rural economy.

DYSFUNCTION: THE PRICE OF WAR IN WALES

The system of taxation adopted by both sides, and the process by which it was implemented in Wales, was similar to that in England. After the money Charles appropriated from the Welsh contributions to the £400,000 raised for Ireland had been used up by the beginning of 1643, the need for regular sources of income impelled Charles to collect contributions through the agency of the commissions of array. For Wales, there is not enough primary evidence at the community level to paint a full picture of collection in rural areas. Apparently no constables' accounts for any Welsh community have survived, and very few of the later returns made to the Committee of Accounts in London amongst the Exchequer papers are extant.

The civil war administrations of both the Royalists and the Parliamentarians fitted the Welsh sphere of local government as they did the English. Levies passed down to the local communities through the sheriffs, where they were incorporated into committees and commissions, and then through the commotal or hundredal chief constables down to the petty constables in the rural communities. Like their English counterparts, the Welsh hundreds seem to have been ascribed to certain garrisons, although in the smaller and poorer counties, entire shires were subject to one garrison. The evidence from Monmouth clearly demonstrates the weakness of this system, whereby the garrisons required sums that were not easily divisible by the parish and hundredal allotments. In order to cover the expenses of the county's four major garrisons – Chepstow, Monmouth, Abergavenny and Newport – several hundreds had to be subdivided amongst them. Furthermore, a complicated arrangement of payments between the governors supplemented garrison income. The garrison of Abergavenny received a contribution from Coveth Meredeth, Bassaleg and Henllys from Newport hundred, and a further payment of £31-14s-10d from the governor of Chepstow to make up the £390 required – only £266-13s-4d could be got from the

Abergavenny hundred itself.[65] The governor of Abergavenny, moreover, received his personal expenses from the hundred and areas assigned to Monmouth.

There is little evidence relating to tax collection at the county level generally. In Glamorganshire, although there is more detail on this aspect than for elsewhere, there remains little at grassroots level.[66] The Glamorganshire commission of array order book shows that the constables were collecting the majority of the levy in Glamorganshire, and it can be assumed that the tax collection in Wales was no less successful than in the Eastern Association, given the same degree of stability. The papers of Richard Herbert and those of Walter Powell of Llantilio Crossenny provide a good impression of the Royalist collections in Monmouthshire in 1644–5. Those of Herbert detail the complex payments worked out by the commissioners of array, whereas Powell's combine this aspect with papers from his own locality.[67] However, the most substantial set of papers, which originated in Welsh villages themselves, come from the Radnorshire commotes of Colwyn and Rayader. There are still not many papers in this collection, which is to be found amongst the Exchequer papers in the Public Record Office.[68]

Surviving taxation records from central Wales clearly demonstrate the effects of Sir Thomas Myddleton's 1644 campaign, both in personal and strategic terms.[69] Much of the information turned in by the constables refers to Parliamentarian levies, but there is some information about the early taxation established in the county by the Royalists. When the constables of St Harmon in Rayader Hundred pieced together the details some five years later, the first levy of 'contribution towards the maintenance of the wars that we can understand hath been paid' was for £12-10s, levied by Chief Constable John Lloyd in late 1642, part of a county-wide sum of £300. This was followed by some £30 assessed on the parish of Nantmel, part of St Harmon, towards a levy of £600 on the shire. The sum of £600 per month is similar to that which was being paid in Anglesey, Denbighshire and Flint later in the war.[70] At St Harmon the initial payment soon became part of a constant levy of contribution, charged quarterly upon the shire by the commissioners of array in a period of stability. War taxes were collected alongside the normal quarter duties for maimed soldiers, as was 'sicke money' for the county hospital. The parish's contribution, amounting to £25 each quarter, was collected for half of 1642 and throughout 1643 according to the constables' returns. The records may mean that the first

£12 paid represented one and a half months' money, due before 25 December 1642, and that the second quarter payment was to cover the three months from then until Lady Day 1643. There then followed four quarterly payments of contribution and four collections of billeting money to raise the sum of £88 levied quarterly in the county between Lady Day 1643 and 24 March 1644. Two further quarterly collections of contribution took place before the system seems to have broken down.

In August 1644, the village suffered a greater degree of arbitrary collections from outsiders at Abbey Cwm Hir. The garrison was, at least in part, composed of English forces driven out of the Midlands by local Parliamentarians after the battle of Marston Moor.[71] The garrison began to take horses from the villages and promised recompense, but in the final analysis they were unwilling or unable to do so. Edward ap Rees lost a red mare and £4 in goods and chattels and Edward ap Stephen Meredith lost a white horse to the garrison valued by him at fifty shillings. Such losses were disastrous to some of the inhabitants at the time. Griffeth ap Stephen, a badger or small trader, lost both his stock and his means of carrying on his trade when his two horses and all the oats in his barn were taken. There is little doubt that Griffeth ap Stephen's losses were potentially catastrophic, turning his family of a wife and six children from one of independent means to one probably incapable of supporting itself. For the rural small traders like Griffeth, the arbitrary aspects of the war must have been most damaging. Whereas the richer sort could draw on reserves, and even in the last resort sell land to cover such exactions, and the very poor would be covered by the village (if charged at all), there was simply no mechanism for providing Griffeth with new horses. For the community as a whole this personal disaster must have had consequences too. The village may have had to provide him with poor rate money and initially step in to cover his assessments as well.

After the payment of fifty shillings towards a county levy to pay for the siege of Newtown, Montgomeryshire, payments to the Royalists, or rather, 'money collected without the authority of Parliament', came to an end. The changeover did not greatly affect many people in the parish, and Griffeth ap Stephen remained uncompensated until at least 1647. Exceptions to this rule included tenants of Sir Robert Fisher, whose lands fell under the power of the sequestration committee of Montgomeryshire. The constable made it plain that the new system enforced by the committee, based perhaps at

Presteigne, exacted the same sum, £600 a quarter, from the county as the general weekly assessment. There were also levies for the support of the British army in Ireland.

Campaigns in south Wales too affected the efficacy of the collection of taxes. When Monmouth was recaptured by the Royalists in November 1644, the commissioners of array began to reconstruct their disrupted administration. They wrote to the high constables expressing their belief in the need for a stronger effort to 'prevent any inroad or violence from the malice or power of the Rebells now in arms against his majesty'.[72] This was in reality an instruction to begin the collection of contribution, and the Skenfrith Hundred chief constables were told to hand over £166-13s-4d to Walter Powell within eleven days.[73] During those eleven days the chief constables had to oversee the appointment of assistants to each of the petty constables in eleven parishes, as well as supervise the collection itself. The assessment was to be levied on 'every tenant, inhabitant, occupier of land and tithes, clergy as well as laity'. Distraint was to be applied to each person who refused. Powell evidently met with some problems; the treasurer at war, William Lawes, wrote on 26 December to remind him that he was four days late with the payment.[74] This was just the first of the payments. The hundred was thenceforth to pay £256-13s-4d monthly for a four-month period starting in January 1645. One half of the regular levy was to be cash, the other in kind, a balance reflected throughout the county's £1,760 monthly bill. By February, some £65-18s-4d was in arrears and Powell was threatened by Lawes with having to quarter a party of horse on the parishes if the hundred did not pay up. When they did not do so, the threat was carried out; on Palm Sunday (30 March), thirty-three men and horses arrived under Captain Christopher Laythorne and stayed until the money was paid over some ten nights later. Powell was still having to use threats against the Skenfrith chief constables after the horse left, and on 15 April orders were issued for their arrest.[75] Skenfrith Hundred's contribution was matched closely by Wentlloog Hundred's £266-13s-4d a month, divided unequally between the two divisions and also paid half in money and half in goods.[76]

We are left with little evidence of the exactions as they affected the individual parishes in Monmouth, even less for Radnor and nothing for the vast majority of the communities of Wales. Fortunately, amongst Walter Powell's papers are rating papers from his own parish of Llantilio from 1645, tabulated according to the goods collected within the community: bread, cheese, butter, beef, oats and straw. The papers also give the prices paid by the Royalist commissioners:

Bread 526lb @	1d per 1 lb
Cheese 150lb @	2d per 1 lb
Butter 56.25lb @	4d per 1 lb
Beef 93lb @	1.25d per 1 lb
Oats 84 bushells,	
1 peck and a half,	
(2,700 quarters) @	2d per quarter

It is unlikely that these prices fully reflected the local market prices; they did not in England. Evidence from Upton in Nottinghamshire suggests that the official price was lower than the normal market price and that constables may sometimes have paid the producer the difference between the two. These accounts indicate that women controlled a significant section of the rural economy. In a later assessment women provided 25 per cent of the bacon, 16 per cent of the oats and 12.5 per cent of the wheat; and a group of widows in the parish was also recorded as providing butter and bread.[77] Whilst this does suggest that women in Wales were playing a major role in the economy and thereby the war effort, it still gives us little with which to make a full assessment of their part.

In the wake of Myddleton's attack on central Wales, Radnorshire accounts show that the Royalists were unable fully to resurrect their taxation system. As stability returned to the region in summer 1645 Parliamentarian taxes dominated the scene at approximately the same rates as the Royalist taxes which they had superseded. At St Harmon three quarter payments were recorded in 1645, with smaller payments being made to support the garrison at Presteigne. However, evidence from Llansantffraed-in-Elvel in Colwyn Commote shows that although nine months' payments dating from May 1645 were levied, they were not actually collected until October. After that, levies were made every two months, each one covering a three-month period. Thus, May, June and July 1645 were paid in October; the August, September and October levy was paid over in December; and so on until June 1646, when the levies caught up and became advance payments. The parish of Llansantffraed-Cwmdeuddwr probably also used this means of catching up, but the information recorded does not confirm this fully, merely recording the commencement of payments in October 1645. Returns from Betws Disserth in Colwyn Hundred do bear out the demand for arrears, and the pattern there mirrored that in Llansantffraed-in-Elvel, with arrears dating back to May 1645 and payments commencing in the following October. The villagers of Betws Disserth were most scrupulous in also recording their billeting charges, which amounted to over £13 during the period when the county was between administrations. Myddleton's capture of Abbey Cwm Hir in the autumn did not automatically entail the county's collapse into Parliamentarian hands. Even the Parliamentarians who seem not to have fully established themselves until October deemed the obligations of the Radnorshire people to date only from May, some six months after the fall of the garrison.[78]

THE WAR IN SCOTLAND

The most important and informative piece of work on the general nature of war effort finances in Scotland remains David Stevenson's 1972 article on the financing of the Covenanters' cause. Hazlett's work some thirty years earlier is still important for detail regarding the experience of the Scottish army in Ulster.[79] More detail on the deprivations imposed on some of the Scottish people is provided in Stevenson's later work on Alasdair MacColla, which contains some of the most accessible work on Gaelic culture in its early sections. The Scottish invasion of England in 1644 was financed on a new basis. There were to be two parts to the payment, although they were to be levied in approximately the same manner. First, a loan of £800,000 or 1,100,000 merks Scots (c. £66,666 sterling) was initially raised to cover the war in Ireland; this was then diverted to the army for England when Westminster offered to pay for the war in Ireland and set about raising the money for the British army in Ireland. Second, there was a tax of £100,000 Scots (c. £83,333 sterling) for the defence of Scotland against rebellion or invasion. In October 1643, meetings at county level were established with newly appointed commissioners and chief landholders from the shire. They looked again at both rental values and what were termed 'casual rents', earned income from sales of produce such as coal or fish. Income from other trades was probably also included in the assessment process.[80] The amounts to be paid, either as a tax or as a loan, were drawn up by the Collector-General, Sir Adam Hepburne of

Humbie.[81] Sub-collectors were appointed, and it was to them that the monthly maintenance was paid. The officers responsible at grassroots level were factors on estates or bailies or bailiffs in communities and burghs. In early 1644 an excise was also created because the loan and tax money was not coming in at the levels required.[82] In general taxation in Scotland was levied by the committees of war in the sheriffdoms, as in the bishops' wars. Throughout the period revenue was behindhand, and this shortfall became exacerbated by the war against Montrose and the plague that accompanied it.[83]

To administer the forced loan of £800,000 Scots each county was assigned a sub-collector, and new ratings were devised to allot the levy. The burghs paid a sixth of the total, and the provosts and bailies collected the money and handed it to the county sub-collector. The English Parliament agreed to pay £30,000 sterling a month to support Leven's army, even though it still owed part of the brotherly assistance from 1642 and the instalment due at mid-summer 1643 had been postponed. The initial costs of setting an army on foot were still to be borne by Scotland, with England promising recompense after the war. Although £100,000 (c.£8,333 sterling) of the monthly salaries was to be paid in advance, mobilization costs were a major problem and this prompted the use of the sum originally intended for Ireland. By March 1644 most of the loan money earmarked for forces in Ulster had been used for the mobilization at home, but the war committees levied more for local forces. The money was slow to come in, and when Montrose began his first campaign in Scotland the shortage was acute, even though by this time the Scottish forces in England were levying money directly upon the communities in the north-eastern English shires.

In Scotland evidence of collection at the local level is not available in the same way as it is in England or even Wales. Muniment papers in the Scottish Record Office probably still hold undiscovered material in the form of factors' papers, but there may be no equivalent of the constables' books. Similarly, in Scotland there was no centralized policy of assessing local communities' losses as in England and Wales. Nevertheless, following the ruin caused by Montrose's rising in 1644–5 and the plague that hit Scotland towards the end of that period, many communities and individuals tried to secure exemption from further levies on hardship grounds. There were too many for army treasurer and Collector-General Humbie, who complained that 'many' were exempted 'upon some pretended reasone or uther'.[84] The four-year account of losses at Crathie in Aberdeenshire compiled in July 1649 is one of the few remaining fully detailed complaints.[85] In structure it is very similar to the constables' returns for England and Wales, but there are differences. It was drafted by the minister, witnessed by ministers from the nearby communities of Glenmuik and Logie Coldstane and passed on first to the committee of war for the sheriffdom of Aberdeen and then to the committee of moneys.

The Losses of marjorie Mitchell wid . . .
Item george Lord gordone his forces killit 6 hir
ane elbe and a w[edder]
[a wether – castrated lamb] . . . at   5lib 6s 8d
Item taking frome her be Midleton his forces
two bolis vict[uals]   13lib 6s 3d
Item killit by his forces twell sheepe &
thrie lambes at   32lib
Item two ponnis & a corne stack at   3lib 8s 8d
Item they killet two . . . at   8lib
Item the levtenent gnrall [David Leslie] his forces
in April 1649 killet a plent
[?Pluet – pluech – plough] oxe at   26lib
Item taken frome hir at ye same time a girles
plaid at   5lib 6s 8d
Item four elnis whyit cloathes at   53s 4d
mor ane pone at   13s 4d
Item his forces took frome hir thrie foletis bear at   7lib 10s
Item a forlet brofit oatis   25s
Item be his forces takin when he camit in
ye penult. of April 1649 . . . at   20lib

suma   119lib 8s 4d[86]
                                     (c.£9-19s
                                     sterling)

This extract shows that Crathie's experience of war was concentrated into three periods: Lord Gordon's occupation in 1645; General Middleton's in 1647 and Leslie's in 1649. In April 1645, many of Lord Gordon's forces left Montrose at Dunkeld and returned to Aberdeenshire. Their presence in Crathie can hardly have been very welcome; they killed thirty sheep belonging to Edward McHardie and also took the wool. McHardie also lost five young goats, five old goats and ten kids – a total value, he reckoned, of £115-6s-8d Scots (about £9-12s sterling). John Abernathe lost three goats, three kids, a wedder and a lamb. Crathie was a community dependent

upon pastoral agriculture. Sheep and goats represented the main-
stay of the farming, supplemented by the spinning of wool for the
production of plaid. Middleton's forces commandeered cloth in large
quantities. Worse, in the case of John Fleming, John McHoyhue and
Fleming the cottar, was the loss of spinning wheels burned by the
soldiers. This action went beyond the taking of victuals, especially
when coupled with the theft of sheep and their wool, and it caused
problems similar to those suffered by people like Griffeth ap Stephen
who lost their means of gaining a livelihood. It may have been a
retributive act – punishment for 'entertaining' the rebel Gordons.
Certainly, later occupations saw more widespread exactions, and the
forces camped on the town may have been there specifically for such
a punitive purpose.

Scottish burghs were rated for the tax and loan too. As a result
of Edinburgh's levies, the city incurred a debt in 1644 to cover the
advance payments. The costs of the Edinburgh regiment serving in
England amounted to £5,166 Scots (£430 sterling) per month, a
total of some £30,996 Scots (£2,583 sterling) between 1 March and
31 August 1645. In Glasgow 'outreiking' (clothing and arming) the
soldiers in February 1644 had cost £2,296 Scots (£191-6s-8d sterling). The monthly maintenance was in arrears by some six months
by the end of 1645, and collectors were ordered to use their dili-
gence to collect the money 'according to the stent'. People who quartered dragoons were offered a rebate on their contribution, although
it would appear that they had to pay first and then claim a refund
from the town's excise income.[87] In Aberdeen the process by which
levies were collected is slightly clearer. There, no fewer than fifteen
people were appointed as stentors to assess the levies of 18,400
merks Scots (£2,740 Scots and *c.*£228-6s-8d sterling) and were
instructed to

> stent the foursaid soume on the nichtbors of the town justlie, but any
> respect of persons, and sould give out and deliver to the magistrats
> and clerk of this burghe the taxt roll thairanent under their hands,
> and that with all convenient diligence possible.[88]

Another problem in larger urban areas was the massive cleaning
programmes needed to keep down the levels of dirt accumulated by
an overcrowded population. In Newark, England, soldiers swept
streets and yards, while in Edinburgh a tax of 50,000 merks Scots
(*c.*£7,575 Scots and £631-5s sterling) was levied on 'inhabitants

and heritors of whatever quality' in May 1646 to keep the streets clean, to care for the sick and to build huts for stabling.[89]

Little research has been done on the financial implications of the war in Ireland, but a new study of the armed forces is being undertaken, and the general economic issues have recently been tackled.[90] The financial systems employed by all sides have been explored to some degree. The Confederates were able to exact some form of tax, generally the great applotment from Ireland, and in theory they should have been able to collect tax from all but the pockets around Dublin in Leinster and Cork and Youghal in Munster and the more substantial areas around Derry in the north and the Scots' bases in the east of Ulster. Material in the surviving account book in the State Papers of Ireland, however, does not entirely support this view.[91] Most material relates to Leinster and Munster only; there are no receipts left from Connaught despite Confederate military control. As a result of this and the fact that much of Sligo was involved in heavy fighting, little evidence of taxation there remains at all.[92] The historian is at the mercy of the poor survival rate of the material – much of the local material was destroyed in two fires, and a good deal of the central government material went with it.[93]

Nevertheless, it is possible to gain some idea of the Confederation of Kilkenny's financial administration. As contemporary critics pointed out, it was certainly an expensive system. There was a 'world of clerks, and attorneys, a set number of commissioners in every county, receivers and applotters'.[94] It is clear that in the period March 1646 to January 1647, the Confederation's principal levy, general applotment, was coming in a reduced amount from nine of the twelve counties of Leinster, the exceptions being Dublin, Louth and King's (Offaly), and from three of six counties in Munster, the exceptions there being Cork, Kerry and Clare. Moreover, seven boroughs in the two provinces were also paying applotment regularly. Excise receipts were coming in from a greater area. All the counties of Munster and four boroughs, Limerick, Cashel and Fethard in Tipperary, and Waterford, were paying something to Kilkenny. From Leinster, counties Meath, Kildare, Wicklow, Carlow, Wexford, Kilkenny; and boroughs Kilkenny, Callan and Wexford contributed something, with Wexford and Kilkenny counties demonstrating that they could pay higher amounts than the others.[95]

Little is known about how Confederate, English or Scottish levies were collected within the communities of Ireland. On the estates of the Earl of Antrim, it can be assumed that the factors were involved, as they would be in Scotland. The fact that the Confederation seemed to be constructing a model of English government below the level of county council suggests that in counties under their control, constables were collecting taxes to pass on to the collectors. In English-held Dublin town and county, the constables were being used too, and evidence from Youghal shows that bailiffs collected the levies there.[96] The effects of devastation were felt across Ireland when emergency measures were taken on a scale unseen across the Irish Sea. The Dublin government ordered the burning of crops around the city in November 1641, and Ormond had to be ordered to stop burning corn and hay in north Leinster in March 1642 to prevent a famine being caused through lack of seed crops. Replanting policies then had to be undertaken to keep the city supplied.[97] Ulster was perhaps the worst affected of the four provinces. It was claimed that Antrim and Down had been ruined before the army of 16,200 Scots arrived in 1642 and proceeded to use these counties as its base. Other Ulster shires – Fermanagh, Londonderry, Donegal and Tyrone – were also devastated.[98] The reasons behind this destruction are not difficult to trace, and New English and Scots colonists and officials were swift to apportion blame. Londonderry was 'brought into a most miserable and lamentable case' by 'the cruelty of the natives stirred up by the popish priest and Jesuits'. A more balanced yet apocalyptic view was that of Owen Roe O'Neill;[99] he commented on his arrival in Ulster in 1642:

> Unless I saw it I would not believe it; for on both sides there is nothing but burning, robbing in cold blood, and cruelties such are not usual even amongst Moors and Arabs.[100]

Destruction gained official sanction. In August 1642 the Lord Justices recommended to Lord Conway that counties Longford and Westmeath in Leinster be laid waste to damage the rebels' war effort in Ulster.[101] As a result, Confederate armies operating in Ulster took with them creaghts, cattle herders and their herds, to provide food for campaigns. These were people used to travelling long distances with their herds who had adopted the farming technique known as transhumance, whereby large parts of rural communities moved to pastures seasonally with their herds. There is no indication of the gender of the creaghts, and they are usually referred to as men; however, it is possible, given that many of the herders in Connaught were traditionally women, that both men and women were involved in this aspect of the war effort.[102] Herding was one of the features of Irish society which English observers regarded as uncivilized, and they wrongly described communities involved in transhumance as nomadic.[103] This view in turn led both Scots and English forces to regard the creaghts and their slow-moving herds as fair targets for violence; even the Confederate General O'Neill treated them harshly. Non-combatants also saw the creaghts as a threat and the inhabitants of northern Leinster resented their presence, probably because their herds used up pasture.[104]

There are some details of war taxation available for Youghal in County Cork and for Dublin. Evidence of rating in Youghal is contained in the borough records. A rate to collect £200 in December 1643 for Inchiquin's forces in the county was assessed by John Galwan and Nicholas Bagbeer and was levied on seventy-six men and ten women; two of the women paid jointly with a son and a husband. The women, representing some 10.2 per cent of the taxpayers, paid 13.5 per cent of the tax, and assuming joint and equal responsibility in the two cases of joint registration, women paid 15 per cent of the levy, an amount similar to rural payments in Worcestershire.[105] The monthly rate assessed on 4 February 1643 was levied on thirty-seven men and six women who paid a total of £614. The women, representing only about 15 per cent of the taxpayers, paid some 18.15 per cent of the total. One month later forty butts of seck, valued at £17 each (a total of £680) were levied on sixty-nine men and eight women. The women paid a total of £138-10s-0d of the levy, a proportion of almost 20 per cent. From then on the changeover of tenancies was rapid. On 26 July 1644 Lord Broghill expelled all 'papists' from the town with half an hour's notice. They could take with them only the clothes they were wearing, although their goods were later restored. The justification for this act was that the Catholic presence in the town posed a threat to the security of the Protestant hold on County Cork. The dramatic effects of this are noticeable in the levies imposed on the town thereafter. An influx of new tenants, some of them army officers, filled the vacated properties and increased the number of taxpayers to ninety-eight by September 1647.[106]

In Dublin the churchwardens' accounts for St John's parish continue throughout the war. Of particular interest are the sesses collected

in 1638, 1640, 1643, 1644 and 1646. These indicate the changing
composition of the population in the town during these years by
giving us access to the names of tenants. In 1638, 214 people paid
a total of £75-8s towards the sesse, with women tenants paying
10.5 per cent of this amount. In 1643 the number of taxpayers
had increased to 242 and the rate to which they contributed was
£75-2s-4d. By this time women represented 14 per cent of the tenants
and paid some 12.46 per cent of the levy. The incomplete levy of
1644 suggests that the proportion of women taxpayers remained
constant, although their contribution fell to only 6.7 per cent of the
tax. By 1646 evidence of the wartime depopulation of Dublin is
seen in the accounts. A number of tenancies had changed hands,
again probably due to the expulsion of Catholics who had relatives
in the Confederation's territory. The total numbers of taxpayers had
fallen dramatically to only 167 people paying a levy of only £47.
The proportion of women had fallen to the pre-war level of around
10 per cent, with their contribution to the levy being £3-19s-8d or
8.46 per cent.[107] Although the material from Youghal and Dublin
represents only a small amount of evidence, there is no reason to
doubt that women in Ireland were contributing to the war effort just
like their sisters in England, Wales and Scotland.[108]

IMPROMPTU LEVIES

It is clear from the evidence of corporate bodies such as parish or
urban accounts that the resources of the four nations were being
exploited to the hilt during the war, even before more sporadic and
impromptu levies began to be exacted from the communities. Personal accounts yield the same information. Rentals from Toton in
Nottinghamshire show the constant interference of war levies in the
running of the estate of Lady Stanhope. They also show how when-
ever the Royalists took possession of Trent Bridge, a mile south of
John Hutchinson's garrison at Nottingham, they were able to tax the
otherwise inaccessible parts of south-west Nottinghamshire.[109] One
largely untapped source for examination of the war effort is probate
material. Given that it has been used in other areas of historical
study, notably gender history, this gap is surprising. Wills and inven-
tories show what the war meant to individuals, and how some never
shook off its effects during their lifetime. Humphrey Billinges of
Witchenford in Worcestershire left his servant Margaret Rosse 40

shillings 'towades recompense of her losse of cloathes she sustained and lost by souldiers'. The inventory of the late George Goodman of Croft, Leicestershire, listed £25-16s-6d worth of 'Plundered Goodes', including not only two maps, thirteen pictures, one corselet and a musket but also brass and pewter from the kitchen, three beds and a looking glass. Joseph Wilmore of Ashby-de-la-Zouch died a creditor to no fewer than eleven officers in Lord Loughborough's army as well as the commander of the Duke of York's regiment. At Mansfield in Nottinghamshire in 1645, the uncle and guardian of two orphan brothers, William and Thomas Dand, was faced with debts due to him out of their estate after they had both died. The debts included payments made to the Earl of Newcastle and the Newark garrison on behalf of the elder brother. The war was to prove expensive in more than just financial terms to the Dand family; the younger brother Thomas had died before the war, but the elder, was killed in February 1644 at the age of 16 defending the Derbyshire commissioners of array at Ashbourne.[110]

Fear of tax collections drove people in the four nations to take precautions against loss. For many people this entailed burying hoards of coins. A systematic study of hoarding has suggested that a range of factors induced people to hoard coins. Hoarding is of course not unique to the war period. In an age when there were no banks, cash sums were routinely hidden, to be used when necessary. During the war, the approach of armies, the recruitment of soldiers, and nearby fighting or the proximity of garrisons all influenced the hiding of money. Fighting is believed to have been a major influence, and the Newark, Oxfordshire and Gloucester regions are thus areas where coin hoards are numerous. Five Midland hoards can be dated to the aftermath of the king's defeat at Naseby in 1645. Coin hoards in the south-west clearly define the limits of the Earl of Essex's campaign in the summer of 1644. Coin hoards in Ulster can be dated to the early period of the rebellion, which gives a very obvious impetus to the burying of cash, and this evidence seems to confirm the view that fighting was a major influence. Of course hoards were also found where there was little or no fighting. However, the propensity for the war to reach into the lives of people of all ranks provides a general explanation. The incidence of fighting may explain why some hoards were never collected; the owner may have been killed or, if the hoard was hurriedly buried in an emergency, its location forgotten. The general pressures of war taxation and the powers of distraint given to the agents of tax collection must have inspired the hoarding of coinage across the four nations, while death and destruction may have left some hoards uncollected.[111] This was a war which affected everyone in the four nations. The needs of the war machines reached into the fields and the yards of the rural community and into the homes of everyone. They mobilized the resources of the industrial regions and even took the mirrors out of the chambers of the people. To fight the wars in four nations required the resources of the whole people of Britain and Ireland. The personal costs of the civil wars is an issue that will be explored further in the succeeding chapters.

8

Victory and Defeat

> Wee are bothe well thanks be to God and our greates want is your company which we extremely long to see but wee must wait with pations tell it please God that we shall be so happy in the meene time my earnest Prayer to god for to preserve you in this dismall time[1]

On 27 December 1643, John Sayer of Rudby in the North Riding of Yorkshire paid £1-4s-8d to Constable Robert Smith for the second month's tax of the assessments levied since Martinmas. Smith was on his rounds that day collecting from those who paid levies fortnightly like Sayer. On Epiphany he returned, collected a further £1-5s from Sayer and returned again two weeks afterwards for a further sesse. After that collections became less regular, as old arrears were now paid off. By 6 March Sayer had paid six months' levies in four months. Collections then appear to have stopped until the following November, when Constable George Hunter began weekly collections. The situation in the north was on the verge of change when Sayer made the first of his payments to Smith. By the time he had made the last, the military map of the north had already altered radically, and when he made his first payment to Hunter the military map of the four nations had changed dramatically.[2] The political landscape had changed too, and it is these changes that form the basis of the first part of this chapter.

At the end of 1643, whatever the state of the Royalist cause and its potential for victory, there was some sense of a need for a new initiative. So as the Scots entered the war to disrupt the daily lives of the people of Rudby and hundreds of towns and villages in the north-east, Charles I initiated an attempt to increase the base of support for his cause. On 22 December 1643, Charles summoned the Long Parliament MPs who had left Westminster to a Parliament at Oxford, which assembled in Christchurch College on 22 January 1644. Before Parliament, Charles, '[f]orgetful of his own transactions

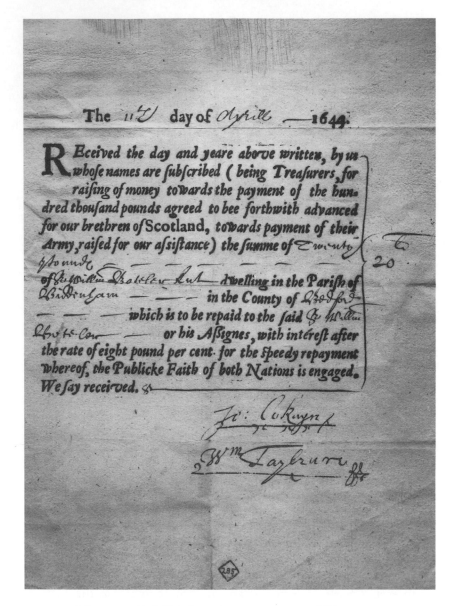

The 11ᵗʰ day of *Aprill* ——— 1644.

Eceived the day and yeare above written, by us whose names are subscribed (being Treasurers, for raising of money towards the payment of the hundred thousand pounds agreed to bee forthwith advanced for our brethren of Scotland, towards payment of their Army, raised for our assistance) the summe of *Twenty* *pounde* — — — — — — — — — *of Mr William Boteler Esqᵗ* — dwelling in the Parish of *Bidenham* — — — in the County of *Bedford* — — — — which is to be repaid to the said *Mr William Boteler Esqᵗ* — or his Assignes, with interest after the rate of eight pound per cent· for the speedy repayment whereof, the Publicke Faith of both Nations is engaged. We say received. —

Plate 9   Civil War Taxation Receipt (ref. TW 1006), © Bedfordshire County Record Office.

with the Irish . . . was prepared to stand forth as the champion of English nationality, and to call the loyal Houses to express their indignation at the invitation given to the Scots to invade England'.[3] On the letter the Oxford Parliament sent to the Earl of Essex protesting against the Scottish invasion were the signatures of forty-four Lords and 118 members of the Commons. It has been suggested that service elsewhere prevented the inclusion of a further thirty-eight Lords and fifty-seven MPs. Charles was thus able to call on a third of MPs and most of the Lords. However, one of the king's problems was that although some of the Lords were new men, raised to nobility because of their military achievements, like Sir Ralph (now Lord) Hopton or Henry Hastings (now Lord Loughborough), and intensely loyal, not all were automatically Royalists.[4] Some, like Loughborough's own brother, the sixth Earl of Huntingdon, had been critics of Charles's rule in the 1630s, and they soon began to ask difficult questions about taxation and the way in which military commanders were fighting the war.[5]

Staffing in the Royalist regiments was called into question, and the ratio of horse to foot in the armies was also criticized. These issues were related to financial matters at least as much as to military ones. The regiments of foot and horse were generally undersized. Some foot regiments struggled to reach 500 men, and many numbered between 100 and 200; troops of horse consisted of twenty men in some cases, though often having near full complements of officers. As officers' pay, which was dramatically higher than that of private soldiers, formed the bulk of regimental wage bills, this was a great drain on resources. The example of the Parliamentarian Eastern Association shows that for nine regiments of foot at 9,340 men, the monthly wage bill for officers represented about 28 per cent of the total. Research on the Royalist north Midlands army of Lord Loughborough suggests that at its height there were only enough men to fill five regiments of horse and fewer than two of foot at the very most. Yet these men were organized into seventeen regiments of foot and fifteen of horse.[6] At the same time, although contemporary military practice suggested that the ratio of horse to foot should be around 1:5, in some Royalist forces it was 1:1; and it cost twice as much to billet a trooper and his horse than it did to billet a footsoldier.[7] Little wonder that the Oxford Parliament was concerned at the cost.

January 1644 saw the first major involvement of the other two nations in the war in England and Wales. After the cessation, regiments from Ireland landed in ports in Wales and England and moved to join forces across the country. By March 1644 17,600 troops had arrived. Many had come into the country via Flintshire and Chester serving in Cheshire and were grouped in five regiments under John, Lord Byron. Byron had been sent into the marches and north Wales to strengthen the weak Royalist hand there. His predecessor, Arthur, Lord Capel, had failed to prevent local Parliamentarians Sir William Brereton and Thomas Myddleton from breaking into north Wales and establishing garrisons in Cheshire. As noted in chapter 6, two of them, Beeston in the south and Nantwich in the centre of the county, could block the exploitation of Chester's hinterland. Byron was originally given a post under Capel, but when Ormond was appointed commander of the Irish forces in the region and Capel retired to Oxford, Byron became the effective commander in chief of the region.[8] He rapidly began to take control of the area, using the Irish regiments to force most Parliamentarians to abandon north Wales and going on to besiege Nantwich.[9] The town was so important to the Parliamentarian hold on the region that help was organized. Sir William Brereton had withdrawn to Manchester, but Parliament asked the Fairfaxes to help. Sir Thomas Fairfax accordingly left Hull, skirted around the Earl of Newcastle's army as it prepared to march north to take on the Scots, and joined Brereton. Together they attacked Byron on 15 January in a fight that lasted about two hours. At the end of it the Royalists, also attacked by part of the garrison which sallied out, were defeated. Some 1,500 Royalist soldiers, including many of those from Ireland, surrendered, another 200 were dead, and only one Royalist colonel managed to get off the battlefield. Byron retired to Chester with a much reduced force, and was unable at least for the present to go on the offensive. In his wake, Fairfax recaptured a number of minor garrisons, but Beeston nevertheless remained in Royalist hands guarding access to north Wales.[10]

Before Newcastle's army marched northwards, preparations had been made for the expected invasion of the Scots. Sir Thomas Glemham began to prepare the defences of Newcastle town and reorganized Northumberland regiments to meet the threat from the north. On 18 January Leven's army of 18,000 foot, 3,000 horse, 500 dragoons and 120 cannon arrived at Berwick. To meet them Newcastle drove north with 300 horse and perhaps 5,000 foot.[11] His low numbers were to be supplemented by levies of conscripts in the northern counties and forces gathered by Sir Charles Lucas from

Lord Loughborough's Midland garrisons. Glemham maintained a watching brief at Alnwick as the Scots picked their way slowly down the east coast. The Marquis of Newcastle got to the town of Newcastle with just twelve hours to spare. After driving off Leven's attack, he prepared the town to withstand siege before withdrawing to hold the Tyne. It was a further nine days before Leven, assisted by the weather, was able to push the marquis back and cross the river. Newcastle wanted to bring the Scots to battle. He had left Northumberland in their hands, but the port was safe and ready to be rescued if Leven were driven back over the Tyne, a fate that looked imminent when Leven withdrew to Sunderland after the battle of Howden Hills. Newcastle attempted to attack him there but was repulsed. In turn he now withdrew to the River Tees to make a stand. For over two weeks the armies faced each other on what is believed to be the marquis's intended 'last line of resistance'.[12] Disaster in Yorkshire brought this situation to an end.

In the Midlands and south Yorkshire Parliamentarians had gone on the offensive. Sir William Constable drove up the east coast, took Bridlington, defeated Royalists at Driffield, skirted Scarborough and captured Whitby. In March John Lambert left Cheshire with part of Sir Thomas Fairfax's forces and captured Bradford. John Belasyse, the Royalist commander in Yorkshire, was torn in two directions by these attacks. To his south, Lord Loughborough was held up by Sir John Meldrum's siege of Newark. With Prince Rupert's help he defeated Meldrum on 21 March. While the prince immediately returned to the Marcher counties, Loughborough attempted to help the Yorkshire Royalists, sending Major General George Porter with the Newark horse to Belasyse's aid. On 25 March Porter joined Belasyse in the attack on Bradford. Porter was in part responsible for the defeat of the Royalists when he failed to support Belasyse's actions, and he then promptly marched back to Nottinghamshire, ignoring Loughborough's order to return north. As a result, on 11 April at Selby Belasyse was denied valuable support. Sir Thomas Fairfax returned from Cheshire, along with Lord Fairfax, collected Meldrum's remaining soldiers and descended on Selby, trapping the Yorkshire Royalists. In the wake of Belasyse's crushing defeat, historians have joined with the Marquis of Newcastle in condemning Lord Loughborough for his failure to send help. In truth, however, the blame should lie more heavily on Porter and Rupert, who supported Porter's inactivity by allowing him to stay in Nottinghamshire after Bradford.[13] News of the disaster in his rear forced

Newcastle to give up his idea of holding out at the Tees. On 12 April he abandoned his defensive lines and sent his cavalry south under Lord Goring. As Goring skirted the victorious Fairfaxes and camped in Nottinghamshire, his commander led the foot to York, where it was soon bottled up by the Scots and local Parliamentarians. A third army, the Eastern Association forces under the Earl of Manchester, joined them after reoccupying those parts of Lincolnshire abandoned after Rupert and Loughborough had relieved Newark. The Royalists in the Midland region also came under renewed pressure when the Earl of Denbigh moved into the west Midlands and threatened Lord Loughborough's garrisons. The Royalist collapse in the north was so rapid that the inhabitants of Whorlton, not to mention John Sayer and his fellow taxpayers in neighbouring Rudby, paid no sesse to Newcastle after March. Royalist administration in that area had been completely swept away.

There was a growing sense of doom at Oxford. Waller had defeated Lords Forth and Hopton at Cheriton on 29 March.[14] Waller's victory forced Hopton and Forth to withdraw first to Basing House and then retreat to Reading. This marked the end of the Royalist push south of the Thames, for the king drew Forth and Hopton's army into the Oxford field army. In April Waller was ordered to join Essex and put pressure on Oxford. It was an uneasy relationship: the two did not get on, and Essex disliked Waller's independence as much as that of the Earl of Manchester, who had also been expected to join Essex in the Midlands but instead had marched north. Despite their mutual distrust, the combined armies of the two commanders had a decisive impact. Reading and Abingdon were abandoned and Oxford placed under pressure. The queen, heavily pregnant, was evacuated with her court and sent to Exeter to be ready for escape to France. As Waller closed in from the south and Essex from the east, Parliament reinforced Waller's army and set about creating another under Richard Browne. Charles suddenly darted from the capital with a tiny force and lodged himself at Worcester on 6 June. This surprise marked the end of the uneasy relationship. Essex met Waller and told him that he was free to pursue the king while the earl himself would attack the south-west. The Committee of Both Kingdoms was aghast, but Essex did not care. He dismissed most of the committee's campaign plan, concurring only with the parts which sent Waller after the king.

As Waller followed the king towards the west Midlands, Charles, with a surge of strategic sense, dodged him and relieved the pressure on Lord Loughborough by driving Denbigh's forces from south Staffordshire. The king then turned eastwards, leaving Waller at a loss to keep up as Charles picked up reinforcements from Oxford and marched towards the now undefended Eastern Association counties. Parliament hastily scraped together as many extra men as it could, abandoning the idea of the third army but sending Browne to join Waller instead. Again the king surprised them, turning back at Buckingham and waiting for Waller at Banbury. The two commanders then engaged in the military chess at which Waller excelled, until on 29 June Charles set off with Waller after him. As Charles's army began to straggle out on its line of march, Waller pounced. Pushing his army across the River Cherwell over the bridge at Cropredy and via a ford to the south at Slats Mill, he sought to cut the Royalists in two. It was a good idea, but the execution was lacking. Because Waller's forces did not cross as swiftly as they needed to, the king was able to turn back the vanguard and attack the forces crossing the bridge as the rearguard dealt with those coming over at the ford. Waller was defeated, his army mauled and his artillery lost. Charles hung off a little way when he heard that Browne was approaching, and then retired to Evesham. In his wake the Parliamentarian armies became embroiled in a spate of mutinous behaviour and desertions, and both Waller's and Browne's armies disintegrated. The king, still worried for the queen's safety, was presented with an unimpeded chance to take on Essex, who was heading towards Devon and Cornwall, perhaps lured by the possibility of a popular rejection of Royalist forces.[15]

Meanwhile, York was enduring a siege that was to last eleven weeks. Life in the city had become dangerous for the civilian population, and intermittent bombardment of the city had gone a long way to destroying the semblance of normal life. At first the besiegers had set up position some way out of the city in outlying villages such as Acomb (now swept up into the city's suburbs). They captured satellite forts early in the siege as the net tightened around York.[16] The early effects of the siege were therefore felt more by the inhabitants of the surrounding countryside than by the townspeople. The normal taxation system in Wigginton, Haxby and Earswick had collapsed when the Scots arrived, which probably accounts for the neglected state of the Royalist account book covering their area. A new and, in some cases, foreign system of levies was being imposed. At Acaster Malbis the tenants 'had all their corn wasted, and the sheep, kine and swine eaten by the Scots'.[17] However, the pressure on the city was great. On 29 April York council reckoned that there were 4,000 soldiers billeted in the town, at the standard price of 4d a day for diet. Food was distributed to the billets where officers lodged, and 'the names of soe many soldiers as are alooted to every house shall be delivered to the house holder that he may pay them accordingly'.[18] This was the last entry in the council book until after this first siege was over. When the Earl of Manchester arrived with the Eastern Association army, there were enough Parliamentarians and Scots to surround the city closely. Gun batteries were placed close to important sections of the wall, but more devastating to the inhabitants of the straggling suburbs was the destruction wrought on their properties. The besieged Royalists razed the buildings outside the walls to prevent them from being used as cover for attacks by the enemy. At least one Parliamentarian observer wrote of the sadness of this:

> had thine eyes yesternight with me seene york burning, thy heart would have been heavie. The lord affect us with the sad fruits of wasting warres and speedily mercifully end our combustions, which are carried on with high sinnes and heavie desolations. Truly, my heart sometimes, is ready to breake, with what I here see.[19]

The attack on the King's Manor, formerly the grounds of St Mary's Abbey, followed the explosion of a mine under Marygate Tower which ripped through the weaker walls of the former abbey.[20] Manchester's forces rushed into the breach, but when Royalists sallied from the water tower down the road from St Mary's Tower, they found themselves trapped. In the fight which followed, the Royalists killed some three hundred of Manchester's attackers and pushed his forces out of the city.

Prince Rupert's forces relieved York on 1 July after crossing the Pennines and coming into Yorkshire via the Royalist garrison at Skipton. He tricked the allies into thinking he was marching on York from the west, got them to draw off in that direction and instead dodged back and approached the city from the north. In the early hours of 2 July he led the Royalist army over the Ouse at Poppleton, using a bridge constructed to maintain contact between Manchester's army and Leven's.[21] Some parts of the Northern army arrived late onto what became the battlefield of Marston Moor, forcing some last-minute shuffling of regiments to incorporate them. Some had not reached their allotted positions when, after a rainstorm, the

Plate 10 Lodge, *The Ancient and Loyall City of York*, a 17th-century etching, reproduced by courtesy of York City Art Gallery.

Parliamentarians attacked, driving Lord Byron's wing into retreat.[22] Cromwell was injured in this attack and retired briefly from the field while Leslie pushed on into the rear and flank of the Royalist army. On the Parliamentarian right, Sir Thomas Fairfax's horse was soundly defeated by Lord Goring and a large part of the Northern horse. The battle was becoming something of a seesaw, with its fulcrum in the centre of the lines of foot, until Fairfax urged Leslie and the newly returned Cromwell to swing around the rear of the Royalist army and attack Goring. The layout of the ground which had earlier given the advantage to the Royalists now worked in the lieutenant general's favour. Goring was defeated, and the Royalist army began to retreat to York.

Rupert now reassembled much of his own horse and the Northern army horse and led them north-west for a campaign in Lancashire. Newcastle was considering his position; he had spent a fortune building up the army and had now seen most of it destroyed, with no possibility left of reconstructing his war effort in the face of the three victorious armies. His future looked bleak, and he decided to leave the country. His wife justified it in the following way:

> My Lord being a wise man and foreseeing well what the loss of that fatal battle upon Hessam Moor, near York, would produce, by which not only those of His Majesty's party in the northern parts of the kingdom, but in all other parts of his Majesty's dominions, both in England, Scotland, and Ireland, were lost and undone, and that there was no other way but either to quit the kingdom or submit to the enemy, or die, he resolved on the former, and preparing for his journey, asked his steward how much money he had left: who answered, that he had but £90.[23]

The Royalist cause had collapsed almost completely. Several garrisons still existed; although Constable had captured Whitby and Bridlington, Scarborough still held out, as did garrisons at Skipton, Helmsley and Pontefract. York itself remained defiant for two weeks in the face of a new siege. On 12 July the corporation received a letter from Fairfax, Leven and Manchester which prompted the opening of discussions on the following day. On 15 July articles of surrender were agreed.[24] Parliamentarian control ensured that the council and government of York changed slowly after the town's surrender. No one was purged in 1644, although it has been suggested that elections in December for empty places on the council added more Puritans to town government. Only in January of the following year did Parliament instigate the removal of five men identified as 'disaffected'; they were replaced by members of the lower hall – the 'twenty-four'. This did not change the city government's social composition, except for putting it in the hands of a wealthier merchant class, but it did strengthen the Presbyterian outlook of the council. Presbyterian religious reform was introduced in the city, and imposed throughout the parishes. This new religious and political face was implemented both through a combination of central and local government pressure and the support of Lord Fairfax in his role as governor of the city.

The devastating effects of losing the north were not fully understood in Oxford for some time. Indeed, it has been argued that the cause was not yet completely lost; there remained some potential for revival if an outside force could inflict military defeat upon the Scots and local Parliamentarians, or if the Scots could be drawn away.[25] Nevertheless, the mood of the Skipton garrison was transformed from confidence to insecurity, despite an influx of veterans from Northern army regiments into the garrison.[26] After its taxation area was reduced when Parliamentarians occupied surrounding parts of the county, the garrison changed tactics, becoming more belligerent and mounting long-range attacks across Yorkshire until well into 1645. Across the county at Scarborough the issue of the garrison's survival was gloomily discussed. A crossed-out comment in the minute book's entry for 20 July 1644 reads: 'Sir Hugh [Cholmeley] stand by the towne and so long as possible they cann'. The garrison had lost much of the strategic reason for its existence: trading networks once controlled from York had collapsed after Marston Moor and the neighbouring ports fell into enemy hands.[27]

It the south-west, Essex had made a terrible trap for himself; ploughing onwards toward Cornwall, by 14 June he had reached and taken Weymouth, forcing Prince Maurice to abandon the siege of Lyme the following day. The chance of driving the Royalists out of the region seemed to possess the earl and he bypassed Exeter and went on through Devon into Cornwall. His army was well behaved and it had smooth passage through the region and was welcomed in some places, but there was no rush of recruits. Essex continued to weaken his army by leaving garrisons behind him as he pushed on to Tavistock by 23 July and forced local Royalists to abandon the siege of Plymouth.[28] Nemesis dogged his step: only four weeks after Cropredy Bridge, the king had reached Exeter, where Maurice joined him. Together the prince and the king led 16,000 men; the earl had only about 10,000.[29] At the beginning of August the king reached Liskeard, only twenty miles from Essex at Bodmin.

At this point Charles suggested that he and Essex join forces to drive the Scots out of England. The earl remained loyal to his cause, however, even though Parliament, in despair at the appalling news of the race to the west, was preparing to dump him, telling the king that Essex could make no treaty without its consent.[30] At the same time, belief in the possibility of an outright victory was waning within the Royalist army. Lord Wilmot, the lieutenant general of horse, was starting to have doubts, and he was not the only commander who had begun to believe that the war was becoming futile and ruinous. Rupert too was soon to come to this conclusion. Parliamentarian Generals Manchester and Essex would probably also have preferred a negotiated peace.[31] Wilmot may then have correctly gauged Essex's mood when he proposed that they should unite and force peace on both king and Parliament, but the earl rejected Wilmot's overture too. The reaction in the Royalist camp to Wilmot's action was dramatic: the king had Wilmot arrested, but he was then faced with angry horse regiments from the 'Old Horse' which had fought in the Oxford field army since the war had begun. These regiments petitioned the king and expressed their 'great amazement almost to distraction' over Wilmot's very public arrest. Eventually the king had to allow eighty officers, along with Maurice and Lord Forth, to petition Essex themselves along the lines of Wilmot's proposal to him. The result was the same, as Essex's loyalty and sense of propriety again stood firm. Wilmot was replaced by Lord Goring, the former commander of the Northern horse.[32]

The Earl of Essex was by now trapped on the Fowey peninsula, with no hope of rescue. The Parliamentarian fleet that had shadowed his march, providing supplies and ammunition, could not get near enough to be of service. The earl conceived a daring plan to get his horse out under cover of darkness through the tightening net of Royalist forces. On 31 August Commissary General Hans Behre and Sir William Balfour escaped with 2,000 horse. Essex's next idea was not so praiseworthy. In the night he took a boat and sailed down the Fowey to join his cousin the Earl of Warwick at sea, prompting the Royalists to ask why the Parliamentarians had vowed 'to live and die with the Earl of Essex, since the Earl of Essex hath declared that he will not live and die with them'.[33] On 2 September the final stage of the dismal battle of Lostwithiel took place when Sir Phillip Skippon surrendered the foot. While it appeared splendid, the Royalist victory was seriously flawed. Essex's horse was safely away and the foot was released under arms and only bound not to fight until it reached Southampton or Portsmouth. Once there it only needed rearming. Nor was the Royalist west entirely free of Essex's army, for it now had several more Parliamentarian garrisons to contend with. The policy that had shrunk Essex's force along the way now tied up pockets of former Royalist territory.

Parliament was thrown into such a panic, however, that desperate measures were undertaken. Waller was given the funds to reconstruct his army, and the Earl of Manchester, who had captured much of the north Midlands bordering on Yorkshire, was brought south. After Essex's forces were rearmed and reconstructed, the three armies united between the victorious king and London. The king was not even thinking along the same lines. While in Westminster it seemed clear that the capital was under threat, to the king it was his capital, Oxford, that seemed in danger. Far from planning to march on London, his army, now only 10,000 strong again, was to concentrate on strengthening the garrisons at Basing House, Banbury and Donnington Castle. Basing was in the most difficulty, but the king could not reach it once the three Parliamentarian armies had united at Basingstoke, so instead he put supplies into Donnington north of Newbury. When his army was grouped between the town and the castle, the Parliamentarian Leviathan moved in on it. The unification of the three armies brought problems with it, requiring as it did the co-operation of three men who could not work together. Essex resented the commissions given to Waller and Manchester and would not subordinate himself to either of them. They in turn would not accept commands from him. The compromise was a committee made up of the three commanders, their lieutenants generals and two civilians. The decisions of the committee were then published under the signatures of the three generals. Fortunately for this difficult process, Essex became 'ill' and remained in bed out of the way, allowing the committee to decide to attack the king.

The second battle of Newbury began as a brilliantly conceived strategy. As the main army approached the king from the east, Waller set off to march right around it and attack from the west, crushing the Royalists in a pincer. The first part of the plan went well, and on 27 October the pincers began to close. However, lack of coordination in the later stages of the attack allowed the king to get out of the trap, deposit his artillery in the castle, and march to

Oxford. Parliament's discomfort was complete when an enlarged Royalist army under Rupert's overall command returned to Donnington and removed the guns on 9 November. The Parliamentarian army, starved of money, food and effective leadership, was simply powerless to intervene. It all served to brighten the atmosphere at Oxford and obliterated much of the gloom caused by Marston Moor.

The Parliamentarian leadership was in a state of confusion, and Cromwell found himself the only one in favour of an attack on the king. Sir Arthur Hesilrige warned that should they be defeated, there was no other Parliamentarian army nearer than Newcastle, an assertion which was only a slight exaggeration. Manchester reinforced this air of despondency and exaggeration when he declared: 'If we beat the King ninety and nine times, yet he is a King still, and so will his posterity after him; but if the king beat us once we shall all be hanged, and our posterity be made slaves'. He had a good point, which would be proved later when the folly of having no clear political war aim became apparent. But at the time Cromwell correctly deduced that 'if this be so, why did we take up arms at first?'[34] Such arguments did little to maintain unity. Manchester and Cromwell were not united in their military understanding, and their religious outlook was polarized along the lines of both Houses of Parliament. Cromwell was a Congregationalist or Independent, Manchester a Presbyterian; and as the campaign drew to a close in bad weather, the commanders began a new war amongst themselves at Westminster. Cromwell and Waller, although the latter was a Presbyterian too, united in an attack on Manchester's behaviour in the campaign. Manchester responded by launching an attack on Cromwell in the Lords. It was a thinly veiled challenge to the lieutenant general's Independency, which Manchester associated with a dangerous democratic tendency, although he framed it as a charge of disobedience on the field. The Lords backed Manchester and took up the complaint that Cromwell was staffing his regiments with Independents, a charge backed by the Scots through Manchester's major general, Lawrence Crawford. The Scots were angry that Cromwell had disparaged the efforts of Leslie at Marston Moor and had claimed all the glory, with the help of favourable press reports.

This period of debate both inside and outside Parliament provoked a major shift in military politics. Shifting political groups in Parliament now saw the Scots as allies of the Peace Party, while members of the fragmented Middle Group drifted into the other factions. In the Commons, the War Party and its Middle Group adherents held a tenuous sway. The religious divisions in Parliament were not as clear as they were in the army leadership. The War Party embraced Presbyterians such as Zouch Tate, whose investigation of the Parliamentarians' recent ill fortune was reported on 9 December. The fault, according to his report, was 'pride and covetousness'; and Cromwell humbly agreed. Tate's resolution was that men should deny their ambitions, and therefore that no one could be both an MP and an officer in the field armies or the lieutenancy: all who held both positions should resign one or the other. Some historians see this decision as a victory for the War Party because it ensured the dismissal of Essex and Manchester, who, unlike members of the Commons, could not resign their seats in the Upper House. The aristocracy was thus deprived of its traditional automatic right to lead the military forces of England and Wales. This issue formed the basis of the opposition to the self-denying ordinance in the Lords.[35] Another view is that an aristocratic faction, centred on Northumberland, simply replaced the rivals Essex and Manchester with its own clients. It was a 'baronial solution', replacing Essex, who was thought to be close to an agreement with the king, which would enhance his own political power, with Northumberland, who was appointed guardian of the king's children. Northumberland was set to become a Protector in all but name, with precedence in the House of Lords and vice-regal powers.[36]

The aim of the War Party was the creation of a New Model Army, with a new 'purged leadership'. Although plans for the new army were afoot before the self-denying ordinance was drafted in January 1645, the War Party took it up with new vigour to try to circumvent the Lords' refusal of the ordinance. According to at least one view, the army was not an apolitical creation. When the new army was designed and its leadership appointed, Sir Thomas Fairfax, a moderate Presbyterian, was named commander in chief and Sir Phillip Skippon was commissioned major general. The lieutenant generalship, traditionally the commander of the horse, remained vacant for some time. By naming the commanders, the block on the ordinance was circumvented and the Lords outmanoeuvred. A newly drafted ordinance, which did not directly ordain that all MPs should resign their military commissions, was reluctantly accepted by the Peace Party and the Lords in April. It did not matter so much now that there was no army for either Manchester or Essex to lead, since both their forces and those of Waller had been absorbed into the New Model Army. The final principal command, the leadership of the horse, was eventually settled in May. Because he was in the field, the Commons had allowed Cromwell temporary commissions once the period of grace allowed for resignations under the self-denying ordinance ended. The Lords objected, although it was 'their' clause which made this possible, but they could insist only that he remain on temporary commissions. There was soon to be no time to discuss the issue further.

The winter was not entirely quiet throughout the country. Cromwell and Waller had spent some time trying to keep the Royalists from recapturing some of the garrisons Essex had left behind in the west. When Waller resigned under the terms of the self-denying ordinance, Cromwell, who did not, concentrated on disturbing the Royalist garrisons between Oxford and Worcester. The Royalists meantime sought to re-establish control of the approaches to the south-west. In December 1644 William Phillips of Salisbury lost 'in the firste place a hate from my heade worth 0-6-0'.[37] The Northern horse had burst into the town on 31 December 1644 and plundered the inhabitants for three days. In all the citizens claimed to have lost over £1,300 in goods and cash from houses and shops when they totted it up for Parliament. The indignity of it is apparent, for as well as William Phillips's hat, the Royalists went off with various types of cloth, coal, shoes, shoe leather, wine and personal items such as those Thomas Evans identified as 'the mony out of my wife purse and my servants things'. From Richard Bilby, yeoman, they also took a petticoat. Tools of the trade were not safe: Thomas Hamond, a barber, lost his equipment. The nurse attending Widow Rawlinson was robbed, as was her patient. Denis Simon was particularly angry because he

> lost his coote being taken to guide them to Bishopton his coote was worth 5/-.

Not all the losses were incurred through theft; there was of course the billeting to account for, and the soldiers left behind a 'poore sicke soldier' with John Russell and he was 'not able to releafe him'.[38] Popular anger, such as that which can be detected in the complaints from Salisbury, was about to burst onto the wider stage shortly afterwards. As the king progressed eastwards after Lostwithiel, he had issued a call to the people of the southern counties to rise up, place themselves under gentry leadership and march with him to London to force peace on Parliament. This move inspired a peace petition in Somerset which was directed to Parliament. But the suggested terms were clearly Royalist ones, and the response was correspondingly patchy. In Dorset the king's call was not heeded, and in Wiltshire it was used only as a cover to raise more Royalist support. The Wiltshire petition was avoided, if possible, because people detected its Royalist intent – especially after a churchwarden at West Camel who was suspected of Parliamentarianism was imprisoned for refusing to garner signatures.[39] The belief that petitions were the correct avenue for resolving problems continued to bubble away over the autumn and winter. The king went on to devise the 'One and All' campaign, which he hoped would mobilize the substantial number of freeholders to present petitions to Parliament in their thousands, effectively forcing a peace upon the country. In Worcestershire the gentry called a meeting to debate the issues of peace and order in December 1644. The people who met had been drawn from the county elite and all had a 40-shilling freehold; therefore, they had a fixed interest in the community and some role in its government. What they wanted above all was peace and order, but they also wanted an end to the military burdens. Initially they opted for a Royalist stance, calling first for a negotiated peace. Only if necessary would they go through with 'One and All' and raise the county against Parliament.[40] The situation changed completely when the commissioners of array at Worcester proved unable to quell military misbehaviour. The county grand jury became a focus for the county gentry and it presented both the armed forces and the commissioners in January 1645 for disorder before the January sessions. The goodwill of the movement had been lost, and discontent in other quarters was now tapped.

As early as the previous October, there was a marked reluctance to pay the required contribution to the Royalist garrisons in Shropshire. In December an estimated 1,500 people took up arms against both sides but focused on the unruliness of Royalists in general, and one of the garrison commanders, the Dutch Colonel Van Gare, in particular. Protests grew, and demands became more sophisticated. The protesters believed that the army should be under civilian control; that the powers of the commissioners of array and the justices, not garrison commanders, ought to be paramount; and that taxes should be raised in the county only to cover the number of troops within the county. Moreover, there should be no free quarter imposed on taxpayers, and resistance offered to plundering soldiers should not be illegal. This movement largely petered out in the county once the Royalists against whom it was chiefly directed were defeated early in the year and lost effective military control with the loss of Wem. At the same time, however, the inhabitants of the Woodbury Hill area of Worcestershire began to meet in large numbers. Towards the end of February, the people of Herefordshire followed suit. What became known as the clubman movement was being born. It became an important phenomenon and has been discussed by many historians.[41] On 5 March 1645 the Worcestershire clubmen and women drew up the Woodbury Hill Declaration setting out their aims. They wanted protection against unruly soldiers, regular and legal taxation, and the traditional forms, structures and officers of government. They presented their petition to the (Royalist) high sheriff rather than the commission of array as a whole. Clubmen rejected arbitrary rule and broadly supported the monarchy and the Protestant religion. Some historians have proposed that the movement was a reaction to the heavy burden of Royalist taxation generally; others have suggested that the Worcestershire protesters were instead opposed to the formation of the Marcher Association, which had grown out of earlier discussions among the gentry in the region.[42] As a result of the gentry's demands for some degree of autonomy, an association among Worcestershire, Herefordshire, Staffordshire and Shropshire had been established for regional defence. The king insisted that Prince Maurice should nominate officers for forces raised in the association and demanded that some association forces be drafted into the main field army, but it remained a local initiative. It has been argued that by accepting the creation of the association, Charles cut himself off from sources of funding, which in turn led to the Royalists' inability to compete with the New Model Army's new funding system.[43] Other historians, however, believe that the creation of the association had the effect of tying the region more closely to the war effort, for the first time mobilizing all the resources of Worcestershire, including those of the Woodbury area. It was this and the appointment of the Catholic Earl of Shrewsbury as leader of the association that prompted the clubmen's Declaration.

In Herefordshire, clubmen risings began in March 1645 and were directed, like the popular risings in Shropshire at particular targets. The unpopular governor of Hereford, Barnabus Scudamore, was the main cause of their anger. Following attempts to levy taxes on Broxash Hundred, fighting broke out between soldiers and civilians. Within days Hereford was besieged by as many as 16,000 angry civilians, about half of them being well armed.[44] Parliamentarians were not slow to take advantage of this. Edward Massey, the governor of Gloucester, tried to inveigle the clubmen into joining the Parliamentarian cause, only to find them adopting a neutral stance. This position can be seen as evidence that the club movements across England sprang from localist sentiments rather than national grievances. On the other hand, their leadership may have been politically motivated. One of the leaders in Herefordshire, Thomas Careless, had goods seized by Royalists after he opposed the collection of contribution. Moreover, Careless and two other prominent clubmen became Parliamentarians, and they were perhaps acting in Parliament's interest at the time, even if those who followed them were not.[45] Princes Rupert and Maurice put down the Herefordshire rising when they moved into the county with their forces, but other disturbances followed. As the Woodbury Declaration was being prepared and Careless and his colleagues drafted their petition, 4,000 people assembled in the south-west to oppose local Royalist forces. By the summer they had drawn up petitions to both king and Parliament following the collapse of local agreements with Royalist commanders, including Lord Goring.

One of the most striking things about the club risings is their sophisticated pyramid organization. The church provided the focal spot within the parish as a meeting place, and church bells were used as an alarm and a communications system. After Sunday church services club activists would drill, in a way reminiscent of Sunday archery at the village butts. Each village also mounted a watch built upon the tradition of watch and ward. Parish contingents of clubmen and women would be summoned to general assemblies on high ground, or in old hillforts in the south-west, by the ringing of bells. Message runners could also be used to raise a hue and cry. The structure owed much to the tradition and custom of local government. An analysis of the social composition bears this out. The gentry was heavily involved in some places, clergy were involved, and there were a good number of yeomen too. All of these people had some experience of local government and organization. They would serve as grand and petty jurymen, constables, overseers, churchwardens. Some would vote in elections, a majority would participate in local decisions which concerned them, as 'neighbours' assessing levels of taxes and lewns in what would later become known as the 'Vestry'. Women club activists would be drawn from the same groups, different mainly because they may in some cases have been excluded from office on gender grounds. However, they may well have formed part of the pool of neighbours even if they did not hold office themselves. The women would all be versed in domestic economics and management, and at times they held power as a 'deputy husband'. There was nothing surprising about what any of these people were doing; they were only using their experience to protect that which accorded them the status to gain that experience in the first place. Research on fenland disturbances has demonstrated that the local social structure made the organization of the riots possible 'with the gentry of substantial peasantry often providing leadership or direction, and servants following their masters, sons their fathers, wives their husbands'.[46] Smaller risings show similar levels of organization. During 1604 a series of riots involving enclosure breaking at Shepshed in Leicestershire developed out of a dispute over common land between tenants and the Earl of Rutland. The tenants' action involved a sophisticated three-stage protest of petition, 'riot' involving a relay of two-person teams and answers to the Star Chamber response.[47] On the one hand the Shepshed rioters confirm the importance of local social structures; these people farmed marginal land where wastes on which they had a variety of common rights formed an essential part of their agricultural system. But there are differences too: the women at Shepshed constituted the majority of those charged with riots and conspiracy. They were not following their husbands, they were there side by side with them as people holding joint interest. One, Alice Mitchell, referring to one of the nights when women alone were out demolishing the enclosures, claimed that the women were defending their own rights. Many cases of riots also involved local officeholders, the same sort of people who were deeply embroiled in the clubmen risings at an organizational level. But they were not the only social groups capable of leading such movements. In the western risings of the 1620s and 1630s in the forests of Gillingham local artisans contributed leadership and a major commitment to the riots. Again it was the crown which sought to 'improve' the condition of the agriculture in the area, and this time the local yeomen and husbandmen were drawn in and offered substantial compensation for the restriction or abolition of common rights. It was the poor and the artisans who used the forests for raw materials to supplement their smallholdings who lost out. It was they who had no need of leadership, who provided the momentum for riots.[48] For the clubmen and women, the threat to stability posed by arbitrary taxation mingled with the political dissatisfaction of the gentry. It was a case of different social groups with related aims coming together.

At the same time interesting questions are raised precisely because no clubman risings took place. The reason for this may lie partly in the establishment of order in the regions. In those with the most effective military control, and thus the most regular system of taxation, order was preserved, and there was no need for any expression of popular outrage. Garrisons in these areas effectively minimized minor military incursions from outside too. It may be argued that alongside the calming effects of garrisons, the regular presence of armed forces collecting taxes had an intimidating effect. But this explanation fails to address the disorderly element of marching armies passing through regions, which had been a problem in Worcestershire. It was no less of a problem in the supposedly orderly Midlands, where the armies of Newcastle, Prince Rupert and Lord Goring in succession travelled through or even stayed for a considerable amount of time, causing a good deal of hardship.[49] Nevertheless, it is important to consider the geography of these risings, even though its implications are not fully understood.

Not every region free of clubmen was entirely quiet. In late 1644 the people of Chester rejected the Royalist excise levy imposed in July when Rupert marched his defeated army back from the north. The lieutenant governor, Sir Francis Gamull, stood for election as mayor, only to be rejected in favour of a man opposed to the excise.[50] In Derby the following May, two unnamed women

> went up and down the town beating drums and making proclamations . . . that such of the town as were not willing to pay excise should join with them and they would beat the [excise] commissioners out of town.

Attempts by the county committee to negotiate with them failed, and as the committee sat at the mayor's house, one of the women stood outside the window banging her drum, drowning out the debate. This tactic worked; the excise was not collected again until July. When it was levied again, the townspeople seized a soldier and fastened him to the bull ring in the market while 'the women did beat the drums as before'. It still proved impossible to collect the money, despite orders from London. When the excise commissioners could do their work again, the tax was this time used primarily within the county and not sent to London. Partly for his own ends, Sir John Gell, the governor of Derby, probably persuaded Parliament that this compromise was more acceptable to the rioters.[51] If indeed this had been an aim of the rioters, and of Gell, it fits in with some of the club movement's demands and the gentry petitions, which a few months earlier pressured the king to keep locally collected taxes within the area for regional use.

In the meantime the New Model Army had been formed. On paper it consisted of 1,000 dragoons, 14,400 foot and 7,000 horse. But combining the armies of Essex, Waller and Manchester had produced only just over half the number of infantry required. Recruiting was proving difficult, and the new funding system based on the monthly pay raised in the seventeen counties under Parliament's control that year was behindhand, although it was to be collected efficiently later. Fairfax was given £8,000 to pay new recruits two weeks' wages, but few were forthcoming.[52] Perhaps because farm labourers could earn a footsoldier's pay without the attendant danger, impressment soon had to be employed to fill up recruits from the ranks of the poor aged between 18 and 65. It was not to be a landholding army like the trained band; any man or son of a man with £5 in goods or £3 in land could not be made to join. Scholars, clergymen and students at the Inns of Court or at either university were exempt. Peers and MPs were likewise free of obligation, as were sons of esquires. Certain professions and trades were also exempted; mariners, fishermen, watermen and tax officers had little to worry about.[53] The poor men dragged into the nets of the committees in the home counties were marched under guard to the new army, but the Kentish conscripts escaped, and the Hertfordshire ones robbed and looted on the way. Eighty conscripts from Bedfordshire ran away after reaching the army, but fortunately before they had received their uniforms or weapons.[54] The problem of desertions dogged Fairfax for over a year, and they continued even after the death penalty was extended to recruits who ran off and powers to execute deserters were given to the county committees. As recruitment continued, the New Model Army moved on the west, directed initially by the Committee of Both Kingdoms, which was dominated by Essex and Manchester. It was an uneasy first few weeks. No sooner had Fairfax reached Dorset on his way to deal with Goring, who himself was trying to undo what Essex had achieved in the west, than the Committee told him to turn around and head to Oxford.

Despite efforts by Princes Rupert and Maurice and Lord Loughborough to recapture the Marcher counties, Chester was still besieged by Sir William Brereton. Because the Scots refused to budge southwards to tackle the king when he moved on Chester, Brereton was suddenly left exposed and had to withdraw northwards. In the meantime the king, with no immediate northern target, turned eastwards. He was undecided as to what course of action to take. There were several possibilities open to him; he could have gone northwards in an attempt to retake Yorkshire; Langdale had led a lightening march there to relieve Pontefract in the spring and had easily outmanoeuvred his enemies. There was even the lure of Montrose's victories in Scotland to allow consideration of a strike farther north. He could also have attacked the exposed Eastern Association, or joined Goring in the south-west.[55] Instead he decided upon a short-term goal; an attack on a Midlands garrison to frighten London. Leicester, with its badly designed defences, was chosen. Of its immediate rivals Nottingham, which had held off several attacks so far, was too difficult; Stafford was inconsequential and cramped; and Derby was too dilapidated to hold onto afterwards. Leicester was stormed on 31 May after brief negotiations. The street fighting, though brief, was vicious; townswomen and men fought hand to hand with Royalist forces in the streets and threw tiles off the roofs onto their attackers. The next morning tens of civilians lay dead, and the mayor's mace had been looted. Lord Loughborough was confirmed in his regional command and given Leicester to govern, with Sir Matthew Appleyard, who had served in the same capacity at Youghal in County Cork, as his deputy governor. Loughborough was also given his own lieutenant general, Sir George Lisle, to be in command in Leicestershire. All of the local Parliamentarian garrisons had been abandoned as a result of the siege, creating something of a renaissance for local Royalists.[56]

In the aftermath of the fall of Leicester, a shocked Committee of Both Kingdoms allowed Fairfax a free hand, and he left Oxford in search of the king. Charles apparently had become mesmerized by the predicament of his wartime capital. Instead of pursuing any major project, Charles had simply gathered cattle in the Midlands and forwarded them to Oxford. His inertia so angered the Northern horse that they threatened to leave for the north on their own. This forced the king to promise that when Oxford was safe, he would go north with them. He then sat around Daventry for six days awaiting the return of the cattle escort. No such dilly-dallying impeded the New Model Army, which found the king's army in Northamptonshire. Charles set off north, dodging westwards in a vain attempt to shake off Fairfax, but on the night of 13 June 1645 the two armies met in the vicinity of Naseby south of Market Harborough. On the morning of 14 June the two armies moved towards each other. As Charles's main forces marched from around Market Harborough, Fairfax positioned his forces north of Naseby. Cromwell, lieutenant general of horse, was placed on the right, with Skippon as major general in charge of the foot in the centre and Henry Ireton as commissary general commanding the left wing on ridges north-east of the village and awaiting the Royalist approach across Broad Moor.[57] The king was in ebullient mood – and so was Lord Digby, who during the night had urged Charles to attack. Prince Rupert had strongly disagreed, favouring instead a withdrawal northwards to collect forces from the Midland garrisons. During the battle he ceded responsibility for overall command to his uncle, preferring to lead the right flank rather than stay in the centre as commander in chief. The battle was lost and won quickly. It was all over in under three hours, and right from the early stages the relative size of the two forces was critical. The king's army consisted of somewhat fewer than 8,000 men, whereas Fairfax had over 14,000. When Cromwell attacked and defeated Langdale on the Royalist left, he used only a fraction of the forces under his command. The rest were then able to wheel left and attack the Royalist foot. On the opposite flank, although Rupert drove straight through Ireton's flank, his smaller force failed to push all the Parliamentarian horse before it. Some of Ireton's men thus remained and were able to attack the flank of the king's centre. Although the veteran footsoldiers in the king's army had driven back the front lines of the New Model Army centre, they were eventually stopped by sheer weight of numbers and then over-whelmed by the attacks of the Parliamentarian horse. The king at-tempted to counter-attack with the reserve, only to see his order misunderstood and his reserves join the flight of his left flank. When Rupert, who had gone on to attack the rear of the New Model Army, returned to the main fight, there was little he could do but escort the king off the field and try to ensure the escape of as many Royalists as possible. For many of the foot escape was impossible; surrounded on top of the ridge, death or surrender were their only options. With resistance on the field ended, more of the Parliamen-tarian horse joined in pursuing the retreating Royalists until they reached Leicester. On the way part of the Parliamentarian army ran into the baggage train. There they found the camp followers – mainly wives, lovers and girlfriends of the Royalist soldiers. To defend themselves against marauding troopers, some of the Welsh women grabbed knives and shouted at the soldiers. The Parliamentarians then slaughtered these women wholesale, claiming that they were armed Irish whores and witches, shouting out in Irish. One account of the battle read: 'we heare that the number of whores that were killed, were about three or four hundred'.[58] The differences between Gaelic Welsh and Gaelic Irish meant nothing to the troopers.

The defeat was little short of catastrophic. Many of the king's veteran footsoldiers were killed or marched into captivity, although some changed sides and entered the New Model Army. In the wake of Charles's retreat with the horse, Lord Loughborough found himself with a town full of wounded soldiers, and the walls battered down in the siege were not yet repaired. With the advice of a council of war he negotiated a surrender allowing all the soldiers to go to garrisons or join the king rather than be captured. Since the terms did not allow the Royalists to keep their horses, the night before the surrender Loughborough sneaked them out past his unwary besiegers. On 18 June he surrendered and rode off to join the king, who promptly arrested him for giving up the town.[59]

Once Fairfax had retaken Leicester, he turned southwards to deal with Goring in the south-west. He took only fifteen days to reach Somerset, some 136 miles distant.[60] Goring was waiting for him, preparing to retreat towards Wales and eventually join the king to help create a new Royalist army. He tried to draw Fairfax away from the intended line of retreat by sending Porter back towards Taunton, but only a detachment of the New Model Army was dispatched along with Western Association forces to defeat Porter. Goring then prepared his withdrawal towards Bridgwater by trying to hold Fairfax out of Lagport while the army slowly withdrew. On 10 July Fairfax attacked Goring's very strong position and defeated the main Royalist forces. Such a victory against these odds not only opened the west to Parliament, it convinced the New Model Army commanders that God was with them. The minister Richard Baxter was present and wrote of the final stages of the battle: 'I happened to be next to Major Harrison as soon as the flight began, and heard him with a loud voice break forth into the praises of God with fluent expressions, as if he had been in a rapture'. Cromwell, who had already detected the hand of God at Naseby, said of Langport: 'To see this, is it not to see the face of God!'[61] With this sort of conviction behind the New Model Army officers, perhaps it is true that '[t]he war had been effectively won in less than four weeks'. At least as far as

Plate 11 Jan Wyck, *The Siege of Oxford*, in the collection of the Earl of Dartmouth presently on loan to the Museum of Oxford.

England and Wales were concerned, the major campaigns ended at Langport.

After defeating Goring at Langport, Fairfax set about clearing the west of Royalists. In August he captured Bath, and while besieging Sherborne Castle encountered local clubmen, who were in contact with Royalist officers. In early August clubmen moved on the New Model Army near Shaftesbury, and although Cromwell persuaded some of them to depart, a large menacing group opened fire on the Parliamentarian army. Cromwell attacked them with a party of dragoons and drove them off, ending their effective participation in the war and all hopes of using them to forge a popular Royalist army. In August Fairfax began the siege of Bristol. After two weeks he stormed the town and forced Rupert to surrender. This disaster effectively ended Rupert's role in the war and forced Charles to try to maintain Chester as the main port through which hoped-for Irish forces could come into England. The war in the south-west did continue into the new year, when Lord Hopton was recalled to the Royalist colours and charged with forming a new army to hold the south-west. However, on 19 January the New Model Army defeated him at Torrington, and the war in the region was more or less concluded.

As will be seen in the ensuing chapters, the need to hold on to Chester dictated much of the Royalist strategy in England and Wales in the later months of 1645, and the first task of the new army created at the end of the year under Lord Astley was to secure Chester's hinterland. The success of this policy was limited, and in February 1646 Chester surrendered. Astley's army was trounced at Stow-on-the-Wold in March 1646 as it made its way southwards towards Oxford. This defeat ended the last hopes of forging a Royalist field army at Oxford. Charles surrendered to the Scots in May at Newark. This did not end the wars of the four nations, and before we can return to the consequences of the king's defeat in England, it is necessary to set it in the context of the wars across Britain and Ireland.

9

War in the Celtic Nations, 1644–7

You remember the place called the Tawny Field?
It got a fine dose of manure;
not the dung of sheep or goats,
but Campbell blood well congealed[1]

During the years 1645–7 the war took different courses in the four nations. This chapter is concerned principally with the war in the three Celtic nations. While in 1646 the first English civil war could be said to have come to an end, war continued in the three other nations for a considerable period. Royalist groups held out in Wales into the following year, and in Scotland a different agenda was pursued under the guise of Royalism. In Ireland the needs of Royalism sat very uneasily with the Catholic Confederation, forcing the pace of political negotiations there.

WALES

After mid-1645 Wales witnessed the continued decline of Royalist fortunes. The geographical layout of Wales meant that the war almost followed three separate courses. Central Wales was slipping under the control of the Parliamentarian commissioners, north Wales became embroiled in the attempt by the king's forces to hang on to Chester, and in south Wales incursions from Pembroke and western England began to destroy Royalist control. We turn first to the north where in September the king had led his dwindling forces to Chester, only to be caught by the Northern army of Sydenham Pointz. This attack was unexpected because it was known that Pointz was hovering in the north as David Leslie led a section of the Scottish army north to deal with Montrose and MacColla in the campaigns discussed later in this chapter. The battle of Philliphaugh in September

1645 relieved Pointz of this duty, and he turned southwards in time to lead an attack on the Royalist forces under Marmaduke Langdale as they attempted to defeat the small force under Michael Jones which was besieging Chester. The resulting defeat of the Royalists' best cavalry regiments on 23 September forced the king to abandon Chester and flee again into Wales. The Royalist commander Sir William Vaughan made another attempt to rescue the city, because after Bristol had surrendered to Fairfax on 10 September, Chester was the only Royalist port suitable for landing troops from Ireland, and also because the king was expecting a final agreement between Ormond and the Confederates. Vaughan and other Welsh leaders, including Archbishop Williams on Anglesey, recruited and coerced as many men as they could for a rendezvous at Denbigh. As the Royalist forces converged, Brereton and Michael Jones organized a counterstrike. On 30 October, their forces reached Mold and on the following day approached Denbigh, where on 1 November the Royalists mustered 1,700 horse and 400 foot. The Parliamentarians attacked and defeated the mustered recruits and drove them off into north Wales, while they themselves briefly occupied Denbigh town.[2] They also occupied Wrexham, where the Flint county committee took up residence and began work. Relief plans were still being drawn up by Royalists hoping to reach Chester, but Brereton and the other local Parliamentarian commanders were now well able to hold back any attempts to march on the city or to supply it with food. On 3 February 1646, Chester surrendered and much of the purpose of Royalist strategy in north Wales fell apart. What followed was a series of sieges to dislodge the remnants of the Royalist army. Chirk was taken at the end of February, Hawarden on 16 March. Ruthin Castle succumbed to a siege of six weeks and surrendered on 12 April. The Parliamentarian forces were thus able to isolate Denbigh Castle and Flint, while moving around the coast to take on Caernarfon, Conwy and then Anglesey, which submitted in June.

In south Wales, where Charles had once hoped to forge a new army in the wake of Naseby, the Royalist cause was defeated as much by a reaction to the length of the war as by military opposition. Charles had gone there in the wake of Naseby and had issued ambitious instructions for raising a new force. These plans were somewhat dented by the defeat of Goring at Langport, but Parliament was nevertheless worried enough to persuade the Scots to march out of the north and mount an attack on this new Welsh army.[3] This was no easy task, as Leven and Leslie were at this time very concerned about the campaign Montrose and MacColla were waging in Scotland. Indeed, at this point Montrose had just defeated Baillie at Alford and was heading into the Lowlands. Nevertheless, south they marched, pressing on Hereford in mid-July. On 25 July the Scots began a close siege of the city. In the meantime, Charles met the commissioners of array in Glamorganshire, where he gave them and their Monmouthshire colleagues instructions for raising 1,000 men apiece and for raising the taxation levels to £1,250 a month in Glamorganshire and £1,200 in Monmouth. In Monmouthshire the commissioners came up with an alternative – a county-based force of irregulars whose principal task would be to harass the Scots if they moved westwards from Herefordshire. Charles accepted, but the initiative was passing from his hands. On 29 July he went back to Cardiff to be met by 4,000 armed men demanding autonomy: a reduced taxation level, a local man to govern Cardiff, local gentry to command the soldiers in the county, and the right to elect their officers in their Peaceable (or Peace) Army, 'implying their separation from the Royalist cause'.[4] Parliament suggested that it was the impetus from the local people that forced the gentry to adopt their stance, but some historians believe that the gentry had enough incentive for their action themselves. The taxes were unpalatable to them too, and they were aware that the Royalist cause was on the wane. They were simply taking this opportunity to register their own opposition to the way Charles was shamelessly exploiting their county (and their country) in order to right the disaster in England.[5] There was a difference between the Peaceable Army and the clubmen of 1645. These angry Welshmen were not opposed to the war, as were the clubmen of the Marcher counties; rather, they were firmly opposed to the king's war effort as a result of the declining Royalist fortunes. Moreover, the army was led by the gentry of the region who wished to salvage their lands and their political control from the wreckage of the king's cause. It was an attempt to secure the peace and quiet of the county in the face of a destructive war, with the gentry playing their traditional paternalistic role.[6]

On 1 August the Royalists in Pembrokeshire were defeated three miles outside Haverfordwest at Colby Moor, and the port was taken. It was the end of a brief Royalist resurgence led by Charles Gerrard, who only in June had captured most of the country from Rowland Laugharne's Parliamentarian forces. Now the Parliamentarian commander not only swept through the county, he went on to invade Carmarthenshire in October. With Gerrard called south-westward in the wake of Langport, Laugharne was able to complete the occupation of the south-west unimpeded by the king.[7] Back in Cardiff, Charles, under pressure from the Peace Army, replaced Charles Gerrard with Sir Jacob Astley. He chose Astley in the face of a demand for a local man, or at least a Welshman, but it was almost Charles's only gesture. Although he refused to reduce the tax burden, he did acquiesce in its non-collection. He replaced the unpopular governor of Cardiff, Sir Timothy Tyrrell, with a local man, Sir Richard Bassett. And then he left, marching through Brecon, volatile Radnorshire, Staffordshire and on towards Doncaster.[8] He had thought to join Montrose, hoping to make use of the Scots' absence from the north, but found Pointz and the Northern army too much of a threat. He was soon to return to Wales, after what has been referred to as his 'aimless wandering in the Midlands'. It wasn't an entirely useless wandering, however. In the north Midlands, there was a brief reconstruction of Lord Loughborough's war effort, taxes were collected again from a wider area and two garrisons which had fallen in the summer of 1644 were recaptured by daring Royalists.[9] The king's presence on the fringes of the Eastern Association had frightened Parliament, which suddenly realized that the creation of the New Model Army had left the region undefended. However, the king's forces were too small for him to be able to exploit his presence there, and on 4 September he returned to the west.[10]

As the king approached Hereford, the Scots army withdrew. Some had already left the area under David Leslie, heading north to return to Scotland and deal with Montrose in the campaign that was to culminate with Philliphaugh. This boosted the king's confidence, and he and Astley began to deal with the disaffected south Wales gentry. Langdale forced the Peaceable Army to disband when he confronted it at Cardiff and co-opted 1,000 of its members into the king's forces. But all of this effort came to nothing when Bristol surrendered to Fairfax and the New Model Army. The prince had promised to hold the city for as long as possible, his surrender looked precipitous, and his uncle dismissed him. Maurice and Gerrard resigned in protest. They knew, as Charles did, that the town was at best ambivalent concerning the Royalists; a large section of the population, including a prominent group of women, were hostile, and the defences were so far stretched as to make defence difficult. In south Wales, the king's fortunes changed again. He was forced to gather his soldiers together and head north, out of the way of Fairfax's New Model Army. As soon as Langdale left Glamorganshire, the

Peaceable Army re-formed and went over to Parliament. On 17 September, Bassett had to hand over Cardiff. Parliamentarian forces were shipped over from Bristol, and more were raised in Monmouthshire. The king, with no hope of help in south Wales, moved north in an effort to hold Chester, but his army was defeated at Rowton Heath within a week of the loss of Cardiff.[11] The Royalist cause in the south and south-west of Wales was now almost at an end, although within six months there was a Royalist reaction to what has been termed the 'rapid puritanizing' which followed the elevation of many hitherto covert Parliamentarians to positions of military and civil power. The tax burden, which had inspired the creation of the Peace Army, had increased rather than decreased after the fall of the Royalists. Sir Edward Carne led an armed force to Cardiff and demanded that the governor surrender in the king's name. Laugharne had to be called from the far west to deal with the rising. These issues were soon to lie dormant but resurfaced within a few years to embroil Laugharne and his lieutenants, Colonel Poyer and Powell.[12]

In mid-Wales, Major General Thomas Myddleton wrecked Royalist control in 1644 by opening a route into Wales in the wake of the capture of Oswestry in Shropshire. Although Myddleton's first attempt to break into mid-Wales had ended in his being driven back to Oswestry and besieged there, rescue by Sir William Brereton's forces enabled him to start again. Brereton and Myddleton pressed back towards Montgomery, and in a pitched battle there on 18 September 1644 defeated a combined Royalist force of Irish troops, Welsh regiments and part of Lord Byron's army from Chester. At Conwy, Archbishop Williams surveyed the scene, suggesting that the Montgomery defeat was as serious at that of Marston Moor. Indeed, within the Welsh context it was: 'It reduced the Royalists to the condition of remaining in their garrisons awaiting siege'.[13] This situation produced the state of anarchy discussed in chapter 8. No side could exercise overall control there, though Parliament was able to do so the following year and collect back taxes. In the wake of the battle, Myddleton took possession of Newtown, Montgomery and the Red Castle. He then began to raid the neighbouring counties, passing through Radnorshire – where he captured the only Royalist garrison, Abbey Cwm Hir, on 4 December – and on into Brecknock; by the end of the year he was in Cardiganshire. The reason Myddleton took so long is that his campaign was not given high priority. He had wished to go on into north Wales, but Brereton, the nearest commander of any magnitude, wanted to concentrate on taking Chester.

This struggle for strategy can be interpreted in several ways. First, it can be seen as a conflict of localism. Brereton was acting within his own county, and Myddleton was concerned to regain control of his own native county and his home, Chirk, which was a Royalist garrison. It can even be regarded as a conflict between English and Welsh interests, with an Englishman placing priorities firmly in an English context and a Welshman concerned to free his own country from the enemy. In reality it may well be simply a conflict over limited resources. Myddleton's aim of splitting the Royalist control of Wales in two by driving a wedge through it required a greater depth of perception to attract support than did the taking of Chester, which acquired an obvious and immediate priority in the context of Royalist reinforcements from Ireland. The centre of fighting in Wales switched in 1645 to the north and the far south-west, but the seeds of self-destruction for the Royalist cause had already been sown, and the events of the summer began to influence the people of mid-Wales. In the wake of the defection of the Peaceable Army, the gentry of Breconshire and Radnorshire finished the Royalists off in central east Wales, leaving Aberystwyth as the only Royalist garrison in mid-Wales. By the end of the year, Aberystwyth was besieged by Laugharne.

SCOTLAND

Scotland was for some time the source of the king's greatest hope. In late 1643 a party of Macdonnells under Alasdair MacColla had begun a war which was to grow beyond his clan's ambitions for redress after years of pressure from the Campbells. It was not surprising that Argyll, the chief Campbell, was sent to deal with the invasion of this small group of men on Islay. Indeed, the campaign against them was quite brief; after some seven months it was reported that the 'rebels' were all dead – those not killed in the actual fighting were dealt with later: in the words of Sir James Campbell of Arkinglass, 'I took them and causit cut of[f] above ane hundredth and ffyifteine of them'. Other incursions, a raid by Montrose on Dumfries and a rising in the north-east led by Huntly, had also been quelled by the middle of 1644. However, even before these defeats a new Royalist plan was afoot. Antrim, who had escaped once again, spent late 1643 and 1644 negotiating Confederate help for the Highland Scots. The result was the creation of a force of some 2,000

Irishmen, led by officers who were Macdonnells or MacDonalds. They embarked for the Isles from Waterford at the end of the June, and on 4 July they anchored at Islay before moving first to Mull and then to Morven. After a campaign which saw the capture of several garrisons in Kintyre, MacColla met with Montrose, who with a few followers had sought him out.

Even if able to strike fear into local Covenanters, the Clan Mac-Donald/Mcdonnell, led in the Highlands by MacColla, was incapable of meeting head on any Covenanter force which was currently heading towards it. MacColla's meeting with Montrose and his small, almost fugitive band was important to the clan's fortunes.[14] Montrose brought a 'veneer of respectability' to this war-band, and in return they gave him a fighting force with 'love of and skill in, fighting' with 'zeal for the causes they fought for (for Ireland, for the Clan Donald, for Catholicism, and last and least, for the king)'. Essentially, they were fighting an anti-Campbell war, a war that was aimed at restoring lost lands in Kintyre and the Isles to the clan. This aim brought with it a war against the people with whom the Campbell chief, Archibald Campbell, Marquis of Argyll, was associated. Indeed he was their immediate enemy. MacColla's failed campaign of the previous year had been defeated by Argyll's subordinates, and it was soon to be up to the marquis to defeat this second campaign. In a larger theatre, the Irish forces had been sent to the Highlands to try to draw the Scots forces back from Ulster, where they were continuing the war during the cessation. Initially these aims were the limits of MacColla's war plan, but his new ally wanted something different, and this divide was to lead to problems later. Montrose held the king's commission as lieutenant general for Scotland, which was to prove important in gaining active support from hitherto quiescent Royalists. He also brought a Protestant veneer to the cause, crucial in converting it from a Catholic struggle to an ecumenical Royalist one; although this posture was not thoroughly convincing to everyone, Montrose could pose as a Royalist first and foremost, over and above religious considerations. His appeal was not universal; he was an ex-Covenanter leading Irish Catholics and Scottish Highlanders in rebellion against a Scots Protestant government based on Lowland culture. The cultural conflict at the heart of the Ulster/Highland internal struggle was now part of the British war in Scotland.[15] What Montrose wanted was a war in Scotland beyond the Highlands and, ultimately, the creation of a new administration in Edinburgh which would withdraw the Covenanter Scots army from

England, rather than Ireland. Finally, a new Royalist Scots army would invade England and restore Charles to power. This scenario was not particularly appealing to the Irish soldiers, as Charles had never demonstrated the loyalty to them that Montrose demanded they give to the king. Moreover, once out of the Highlands, the campaign seemed to them to be irrelevant.

Indeed, as soon as they had moved from their original base, their fears seemed grounded. Argyll moved on their garrisons at Mingary and Kinlochaline, which they had taken upon first landing in July 1644.[16] Yet by August, Montrose and MacColla's actions had changed the attitude of the government in Edinburgh. Hitherto, it had been content to concentrate on English affairs, leaving Argyll to get on with defeating the small band of rebels, but after the Royalists marched into Atholl, everything changed, and Lowland Scotland looked vulnerable. Forces of fencibles, the local forces equivalent to trained bands in England and Wales, were mustered in Perth, Angus, Stirling and Fife. At one point Stirling itself appeared in danger, and troops were sent there quickly. The Edinburgh council spent 900 dollars 'outreiking' three companies of soldiers heading that way on 11 September 1644.[17] But it was too late. Montrose had instead headed to Perth, where a store had been set up to supply the campaign against him. The first pitched battle of the campaign was at Tippermuir, west of Perth. Montrose attacked the assembled 'peasants and burghers' in the fencibles under Lord Lothian. As he had no cavalry to speak of, Montrose placed the Irish in the centre to face the Lowland foot, with the Highlanders on the flanks. They were armed with bows, which had a much higher firing rate than muskets and would, it was hoped, bring down a withering hail of arrows on the horse deployed by Lothian. As the Lowlanders rode forward with this forlorn hope, the Irish fired their muskets twice and charged in the method employed in Ireland during MacColla's early campaigns there: the Lowlanders fled. Montrose should not be given credit for using this creative method of attack with outgunned forces; as MacColla had already used these tactics successfully in 1642, the credit probably belongs to him. It has recently been suggested that there was probably little in the way of a 'Highland charge' in any case, and that the fighting in the centre of the field may have been a more conventional fire-fight. This view accords with another currant study, which indicates that the so-called Highland or Gaelic charge was only a response to the shortage of ammunition in the early months of the war in Ireland.[18] In any event the slaughter that followed was massive. Glad to get their revenge for the defeats inflicted on them in their homeland, the Irish killed every fleeing soldier they could find along the three-mile route to Perth. Montrose was probably taken aback, and he was certainly worried that his force had disintegrated into a vengeful horde before his eyes, but order was restored somewhat after the soldiers reached Perth itself.[19] The Covenanter forces at Stirling were now led by Argyll himself and eleven Lowland shires were sending forces there. Montrose moved on to Dundee, but when the town would not surrender, he continued north, having no time to waste because Argyll was moving up behind him. He proceeded to Aberdeen, where on 4 September all 'frie and unfrie' in the town were placed under arms. The Erin, Greine, Futtie and Cruikit quarters had been instructed to choose lieutenants, ancients and other inferior officers.[20] Such part-timers could not withstand the onrush of angry and vengeful Irish soldiers, nor could the levies from clans of the Forbeses, Frasers and Crichtons gathered under Lord Burleigh. On 13 September, at the battle of Justice Mills, west of Aberdeen, Montrose's forces defeated the Covenanters, who had rejected his offer to surrender the town. Montrose did allow the town to evacuate women and children, because he intended to sack Aberdeen if it refused his summons. In the event the victory was followed by a pursuit into the town itself and awful devastation. The council register contains details of prominent citizens who were killed, including the baillie, the master of the hospitals, two advocates and two merchants, and eight score others:

> for the enemye, entring the toune immediatlie did kill all, old and young, whome they fond on the streittes, amongst whome were two of our tounes officiares, called Breck and Patrick Ker. They brak up the prisone hous doore, set all warderis and prisoneris to liberyties, enterit in verie many houssis and plunderit theme killing sic men as they fand within.

Montrose himself left the city that night, but the Irish stayed there over the weekend

> ... killing, robbing, and pludering of this toune at their plesour. And nothing hard bot pitiful hovlling, crying, weiping, mvrning, throw all the streittis ...
> ... Sum wemem thay preisseit to defloir, and vther sum thay took perforce to serve thame in the camp.[21]

The dead remained unburied over the weekend – and unmourned too, for the weeping widows were murdered if they uttered a sound. The wealthy were undressed before being killed, to preserve the condition of their clothes. It was unleashed hell, but all permissible under the strictures of military law which allowed the sacking of a defeated, defiant town. It went on too long, however, for good discipline to be maintained, and some Irish soldiers remained behind as Montrose strove northwards to elude Argyll. The scenes at Aberdeen, which have a reasonably reliable provenance, did little to help Montrose establish his army as the legitimate face of Royalism is Scotland: many of the accounts from Aberdeen came from Royalists, a great many of whom were murdered in the town during that awful weekend in mid-September. It is easy to see why the Gordons under Huntly remained aloof, especially when we remember that they were charged with degaelicizing the Highland areas of Aberdeenshire in a manner akin to what the Campbells had done in the west. As he moved through the region, few of the Gordons joined Montrose.[22]

The Royalist forces split up shortly after Aberdeen, and MacColla went westwards to try to secure the castles of Mingary and Kinlochaline, which were still under siege. Montrose returned eastwards to try to continue the Lowland war, which inspired the burgh of Aberdeen to send commissioners to him to 'expose and declaire to him the present desolation, misrie and distresse of the said burghe'.[23] Argyll, although worried about MacColla's activities in the Campbell lands, was under Edinburgh's direction and thus forced to keep his attention fixed on the Lowlands. He was right to be worried. MacColla relieved Mingary Castle, and the Clanranald rose to join him, as did some of the Donalds of Glengarry under Donald Gorm MacDonald of Scotus. The Keppoch men under Donald Glas MacDonald joined him in Lochaber, and so did the Stewards of Appin and the MacIans or MacDonalds of Glencoe. He then rejoined Montrose by mid-November.[24] It was not long before the harsh winter should have put the campaigning season to an end.

However, while Argyll thought it was safe to send some of his men into winter quarters, the Clan Donald had other ideas. In the deep of winter the Royalists entered Argyllshire and began to devastate the Campbell lands. Villages were burned and men and boys of military service age were killed if caught. Cattle were looted or killed where they stood. MacColla gained the name *fear thollaidh nan tighean* – the holer or piercer of houses – meaning in effect the destroyer of houses. Three groups led by Montrose, MacColla and the captain of the Clanranald together terrorized the region: one group chased Argyll himself from Inveraray and celebrated mass there. But few recruits were coming in; there were not many more Donalds still living there, and the MacGregors with their banned name were also few in number because of the policy of extermination waged against them. By the end of January, the campaign was over. Montrose came to rest in the north-west in the friendly lands of the Stewarts of Appin and the MacDonalds of Glencoe, the priests with him happy at finding fertile ground for their religion. Many of the Highlanders disappeared home with their spoils and their exciting tales of conquest, leaving Montrose with possibly fewer than 2,000 men. Moreover, he was now between two armies, the mainly Campbell force led by Argyll to his south and the forces of Ross and Moray at the north end of the Great Glen. He then turned on Argyll, who had moved up to Inverlochy. Manoeuvring through snow, Montrose attacked and defeated Argyll on 2 February. The slaughter that began after the battle left up to half of Montrose's opponents to die there in the wet, thawing snow.[25] Most of the dead were Highlanders, killed in a Highland civil war which had been fomented in the first place by the Stuart monarchs eager to establish order and a Lowland cultural hegemony in the region. It is significant, as has been pointed out, that at the 'start of the battle the Lowland infantry had been driven from the field; they were almost irrelevant, cleared aside so that the real business of the day, the slaughter of the Campbells, could begin. Montrose himself, indeed, was almost an irrelevance in Gaelic eyes'.[26] Much of the Gaelic poetry dealing with this campaign ignores Montrose completely and refers to the whole affair as being a MacDonald issue. Indeed, in the poem of Ian Lom Mac-Donald, there is only one reference to one other clan with MacColla: the MacLeans of Duart, who had sent only a few men, were dismissed as pale-faced kale eaters. The bloodshed and the devastation of the Campbells, on the other hand, was dealt with in detail:

> To Hell with you if I care for your plight
> as I listen to your children's distress
> lamenting the band that went to battle
> the howling of the women of Argyll[27]

Several women wrote poems on the effects of the battle at Inverlochy, dealing with bereavement and divided loyalty. Florence Campbell was married to Ian MacLean of Coll, who fought with their son for Montrose; but her brother, Sir Duncan Campbell of Auchinbreck, was killed by MacColla after the battle. She remained a Campbell in outlook, writing, 'were I at Inverlochy, with a two edged sword in my hand, and all the strength and skill I could desire, I would draw blood there, and I would tear asunder the MacLeans and MacDonalds, and I would bring the Campbells back alive'.[28]

The news of Inverlochy spread quickly, and the forces gathered at the northern end of the Great Glen evaporated, their leader, the Earl of Seaforth, eventually meeting with Montrose and offering his loyalty to the king. More important, some of the Gordons joined him, and though only a few, they were cavalry. Nevertheless, Huntly himself still would not throw in his lot with the Highlanders, Islanders and Irish. His sons, Lord Gordon and Nathaniel Gordon, had fewer qualms, but even so when Montrose moved south of Aberdeenshire in April, many Gordons stayed back; and by the middle of April most of the others had returned with Montrose's permission. In the meantime Montrose and MacColla attacked and captured Dundee. In the fighting on 4 April, in the wake of which part of the town was burned and plundered, the city estimated its losses at £162,229-15s-8d Scots (*c.*£13,519 sterling). But as his men rested, news reached Montrose that the forces led by William Baillie and James Hurry (who was again fighting against the king, after being captured at Marston Moor) were fast approaching the town. Quickly Montrose's army escaped into the night. It was hardly a creditable action, but the Scots and English treated the affair as if it had been a great victory, even if Baillie and Hurry fell out with each other in allocating the blame for letting so many of the Royalists escape.

In the weeks that followed, Montrose tried to build up his forces, but the three main groups remained separate. Montrose waited in the Trossachs, while MacColla and the Gordons remained in Aberdeenshire. It seems that regular tax collection was initiated. The Aberdeen minutes make it clear that although the town paid Mac-Colla to leave his Irish men outside with bribes of money, fine clothing and furniture for his captains, the Royalists established monthly maintenance levied at the same rate as the burgh's monthly levies for Edinburgh.[29] During that month Gordon forces were in Crathie taking the food and supplies from the villagers referred to in chapter 7.[30] Hurry left Baillie in the south to shadow Montrose while he went north to Aberdeen. The Royalists took advantage of this division and united in the north, chasing Hurry through Banffshire and Moray towards the Covenanter garrisons in Inverness. This move again affected the loyalties of the wavering Seaforth and persuaded him once again of the virtues of the Covenanter cause.

At Auldearn on 9 May, Hurry turned on his pursuers.[31] He attacked from the south-west with 4,000 men moved in from the direction of Cawdor and almost caught Montrose's 2,000 men by surprise.[32] First into action was a small force led by MacColla, which was almost overwhelmed but held out until the Gordon cavalry arrived and helped stem the advancing tide. When the Gordons charged into the left and right wings of Hurry's army, Montrose was at last able to support the centre with foot and begin driving Hurry back. As soon as Hurry's men broke, the slaughter began. The Campbell regiment of Lawers was treated particularly brutally. It was a devastating defeat that had to be explained, and Hurry has been accused of heaping a lot of blame on one cavalry commander, Drummond, who was later executed for treachery.[33]

Next, Montrose had to deal with Baillie. A deadly dance proceeded around the Highland regions of Banff and Aberdeenshire as Baillie and Montrose attempted to manoeuvre each other into fighting. In the meantime, both Montrose and MacColla attempted to recruit clans to the Royalist cause, offering to restore lost lands to Patrick Roy MacGregor of that Ilk and enemy estates to John MacNab the younger of that Ilk in return for their support. Eventually Montrose drew Baillie on to attack him while MacColla was detached in the West Highlands. On 2 July Montrose defeated Baillie at the Bridge of Alford after a brief fight in which Lord Gordon was killed.[34] Following this, with no Covenanter army behind him, Montrose marched south to rescue the king, now defeated at Naseby. If the king was to be completely defeated, Montrose's strategy of creating a Royalist government in Scotland would be pointless, as it would be too late to intervene in the English and Welsh war. MacColla rejoined Montrose with reinforcements at Foundon in Kincardine, and by the time the army had based itself in Dunkeld, it numbered in the order of 5,000 men.[35] Passing Perth and Stirling, Montrose headed towards Glasgow and on 14 August reached Kilsyth. Opposing him was a reconstituted Covenanter army under Baillie, but he was not alone. His failures had allowed a committee of Parliament to exercise sway over his movements, but the committee too was influenced by the defeated Argyll and Hurry. Eagerness to get to grips with the rebel earl and the Royalists led this committee both to override Baillie and to concoct what has been described by some as an awful tactical blunder. On 15 August, Baillie moved on Montrose from the east, but as the army began to deploy to Montrose's west, the committee decided to move it all slightly to the north onto higher ground. It can be argued that there was no blunder at this point; since Baillie's original position was not a strong one, the move towards the hills north of Montrose made tactical sense. As the army shuffled onto this high ground, for some reason a section of Covenanter cavalry under Major Haldane attacked Irish outposts, which was indeed a blunder, as it prompted a counter-attack.[36] In the ensuing slaughter perhaps half of the 7,000-strong Covenanter army were killed. This was the defeat of the last Covenanter army in Scotland; there were no more left to face. 'It was also the culminating victory of Gael and especially the Clan Donald, over Lowlander'. It should be noted that the war in 1645 bore little relation to anything that could be covered by the umbrella title of the English civil war.[37]

For many Lowland Scots in the summer of 1645 a killer more dangerous than Montrose was loose. Plague had begun the previous year and affected the Lowlands through the season. In Glasgow the construction of fences was ordered, and all close-fits (alleyway ends) and yairds (yaird-dykes were garden or enclosure walls) were to be built up to stop plague carriers getting into the town.[38] As a result of Glasgow's foresight, Montrose intended to set up his seat of government there, because Edinburgh was heavily afflicted with the plague. His army, basking in victory, began to plunder the town when they arrived a couple of days after leaving Kilsyth. Montrose withdrew to Bothwell Castle and took the army with him. There he was courted by prominent politicians, for the Covenanter government had collapsed and Montrose appeared to be the most promising power broker. He himself was promoted to Captain General and Deputy Governor of Scotland, and in turn he knighted MacColla at Bothwell. On 18 August he summoned a Parliament to meet at Glasgow on 20 October, However, at this point the alliance between Clan Donald's aims and Royalist strategy began to weaken. This breakdown was partly due to the inherent conflict in aims present when the alliance was first formed, but it was also partly due to Montrose himself. Just as the Gaelic poetry neglected to mention him, he neglected to refer to MacColla or the Highlanders and Irish in his despatches to the king. It was as if he was ashamed of them. He was also faced with the need to win allies at a politically unstable time in Scotland, causing him to hand out favours to those who pressed in on him at Bothwell rather than to those who had served him loyally during the past year. At the beginning of September, many of the Clan Donald left the camp for the Highlands, and Lord Aboyne, disgusted at Montrose's behaviour, took the Gordons home. Writers and historians have accorded MacColla a principal role in this desertion, but he was in Ayrshire attempting to break up a potential gathering of Covenanter forces when most of the Highlanders, MacLeans and men of Atholl left. MacColla even took a small party into Argyllshire to try to recruit replacements. The situation was desperate: at Kilsyth he had led 5,000 men, and there were probably only 1,000 under arms at Bothwell. Hopes of a massive recruitment campaign were not matched by reality.

To Covenanters in Edinburgh the home country was now a priority. Accordingly, 6,000 men under David Leslie left the Scots army now operating in the English south-west Midlands. Leslie hurried north past the king, who was contemplating advancing to join Montrose, and crossed the border into Scotland. On discovering Montrose's army at Philliphaugh, Leslie attacked, and by the time Montrose himself arrived it was to find his army defeated.[39] Since it was impossible to rescue the foot, Montrose fled. Most of those left behind were Irish, and the racial implications of the war again became apparent at Philliphaugh. Half of the Irish died fighting or trying to escape; the others surrendered on quarter but were then executed, their wives and lovers murdered along with them. The leaders Montrose had left behind were taken to Edinburgh and executed publicly, accompanied by a vengeful and murderous sigh of relief on the part of the tarnished Covenanter regime, which now crawled back into the light. In the wake of Inverlochy, Campbell leaders had reconstructed their commands and regained control of the centre of Argyll's lands. It was there that MacColla returned in the autumn of 1645 to complete the Clan Donald campaign. He assembled a force of some 2,000 men, who then went on the rampage, slaughtering any men of military age and taking what they needed. It was clear from the Campbell recovery that the local Campbell leaders were not going to side with the king, and MacColla's policy seems to have been simply to exterminate the Campbell military might. Indeed, in December a band was drawn up and signed for rooting out Campbells, and by the end of the year the Campbell military might was restricted to several scattered garrisons.

As the Royalist fortunes in England went into terminal decline, MacColla continued to attack the fortresses of the Campbells in the

Highlands. But not one of the major garrisons fell to him, and Campbell forces tried to avoid an open battle because of MacColla's formidable reputation in the field. When MacColla caught them at the battle of Lagganmore, they were beaten. After the battle the surviving Campbell soldiers were herded into a barn along with the women and children from the area. Then, on MacColla's orders, the barn was fired. Only one woman and one of the commanders, John Campbell of Bragleen, escaped the flames. The sight of this horrendous atrocity became known as the *Sabhal nan Cnamh* (the Barn of Bones).[40]

In April the Campbells made an attempt to retake their lands, but it was a 'dismal failure'. Much of the campaign appears actually to have consisted of brief raids which secured two castles. Essentially Argyll and Kintyre remained, if not in MacColla's complete control, then certainly no-go areas for the Campbell forces. The MacDonald forces were joined in June by the Earl of Antrim and a force which has been estimated at fewer than 2,000 men.[41] Montrose's forces were not to be supported by the reinforcements; instead, Antrim moved to reinforce MacColla's control of the Highland area. It may have been an important moment for Antrim, who returning to the MacDonald ancestral lands of the Clan Ian Mor. But it was only days before the king's order to lay down arms reached Scotland. Charles was now a prisoner of the Scottish forces that had been besieging Newark in Nottinghamshire. He had surrendered himself to them in order to perpetuate what he believed to be serious divisions between the Scots and the English and Welsh Parliament. He was soon being escorted north to Newcastle, where the first in a series of peace proposals was presented to him. His initial order to his forces in England, Wales, Scotland and Ireland to stop fighting produced a mixed response. Some English garrisons fought on throughout the summer, and Harlech in Wales kept going well into 1647! In Scotland, Huntly and Montrose gave up the fight, but the MacDonalds did not do so immediately. In the pause which followed, the Campbells counter-attacked, with the Lamont lands in Cowal as their target. The surrender of two castles was achieved, possibly through trickery; and a large number of the garrison soldiers were butchered in the kirkyard at Dunoon – some shot, some part-hanged and buried alive, others hacked to death. There appears to have been a concerted effort to make it clear that the soldiers and the Lamont leaders were fighting not for the king but only for the MacDonald clan, and were therefore exempt from any of the terms which the king and the Scots commissioners in England had agreed on to end the war in Scotland.[42] As Antrim and MacColla toured the garrisons in Kintyre, urging the commanders of the garrisons to hold out in the face of the horrifying news from Cowal, a letter was delivered to MacColla from the king ordering him to surrender. He and Antrim refused, on the grounds that there was no guarantee of safety for the soldiers who did so. But when a second message arrived, Antrim did withdraw. Strangely, he did so after being promised that he would be given possession of the estates of the Marquis of Argyll. How Charles hoped to secure them, when he was in effect the prisoner of a political group largely in Argyll's sway, is not known. Even more unusual is the fact that Antrim felt able to believe the promise. MacColla stayed put, but for a while during the summer, Antrim did leave, returning towards the end of the year. Antrim probably cherished some hopes of playing a major role in Ireland, where, as was related earlier, the Ormond faction in the Confederation had been overthrown.

MacColla's hold on the Highlands was to remain steady over the next months. It is clear that a great deal of Campbell territory was in his hands, which was seriously affecting the pocket of Argyll himself. However, the Synod of Argyll did deal in these months with people who were abandoning the MacDonalds, probably in response to the king's orders. 'Thes that com off the rebelss before they be imployed in the service, professe repentance'. At the same time, a great religious crusade was still going on, as the priests accompanying MacColla seemingly won converts from all social groups. The Synod also had to deal with these people; on 11 March 1648 it referred to

> these who brought their children to be baptised by priests and these that were mayed by them in Kintyre be censured as the highest degree of complyers.[43]

In February 1647 the net was drawn tighter about the MacDonald forces. An army led by David Leslie and drawn from the forces which had now left England progressed up the east coast, securing the fall of the last Royalist garrisons which had hung on after the conquest of the region in 1645. By March the Huntly garrisons had all surrendered. In April Lieutenant General Middleton and part of the Covenanter army visited the community of Crathie.

his forces destroyit wt horses sevin bollis victuall at 46lib 13s 4d
Item they killit fyve elvis wt thair fyve lambes at 15lib
more they tooke wite them pannies at 31lib 6s 8d
Item mor twe corne stuckis and trie short pockis at 3lib

from John Fleming. From John McKenzie, they took and killed

a cock, and a stucke at 20lib
Item they destroyit 6 hny 4 bollis victuall at 26lib 13s 4d[44]

Although the people of Crathie were burdened with a level of destruction which seems to suggest a punitive attack on village resources, they escaped lightly in comparison with what happened to the people of the east coast when Leslie turned towards them. Already in the west, anyone of Irish origin was executed without trial, and men of Scottish birth but with significant Irish connections – like Captain John Mortimer, who was associated with the Irish garrison of Lesmore Castle – were treated likewise. As Leslie began to head west, MacColla began to devastate the lands through which they were to pass. Inveraray was burned, and the parishes of Kilmartin, Kilmichael and Kilberry were destroyed. Nevertheless, Leslie reached Dunblane in late April and in mid-May moved on Kintyre. On 24 May he defeated a force at Rhunahaorine Point and pursued them. By the end of the month he was at Dunaverty Castle. Here Leslie attacked the garrison after it refused to surrender and took the defensive ditches. When the castle surrendered, 300 members of the garrison were massacred, possibly by relatives of the victims of the *Sabhal nan Cnamh* massacre. After a pause while he awaited ships, Leslie crossed the sea to Giga and then to Islay in pursuit of MacColla. Alasdair's father Coll Ciotach was captured when Leslie lay siege to Dunyveg. When the castle surrendered, Leslie offered generous terms to the Irish soldiers within. They were shipped home after promising not to fight again in Scotland. MacColla had already sailed to Ireland, and in his wake, his father, Donald Gorm and Ranald MacDonald were hanged, probably by a vengeful Argyll in his capacity as Justice General of the Isles. The summer of 1647 brought peace to most of the west of Scotland, but it did not bring ease. Death and disease both preceded and followed Leslie into Kintyre. Leslie had complained during the campaign that he could get little food and no cattle in Kintyre. His forces themselves assisted in the process of denuding Kintyre and Islay of cattle, and they left plague in their wake. Large sections of the Isles were left empty after this last part of the war, an emptiness which Argyll himself was not slow to exploit. Now that the MacDonalds had died in war or of diseases on the lands they had populated which Argyll had received earlier in the century, he colonized the region with Campbells and other 'loyal' people. The Campbell–MacDonald war had brought Argyll this partly unexpected boon.[45]

IRELAND

The cessation did not end the war in Ireland for everyone. In County Sligo in the province of Connaught, the rule of the Confederation is hard to determine. It is possible that the town of Sligo was not represented at the Kilkenny General Assembly. However, the county was, and in common with other counties in the province, it was represented by principal landowners. Concern for order in the wake of rebellion was paramount and one of the representatives, Luke Taffe, was given responsibility for enforcing peace in the county. It is clear from recent research that although the Confederation had been born of rebellion, it was now determined to eschew some of the very men who had propagated rebellion in the shire. Taffe was asked to arrest, amongst others, Tahg O'Connor Sligo and his brothers, all involved in the capture of the castles of Sligo and Templehouse in late 1642. They were henceforth to be excluded from the decision-making process, a step which was to create rival power factions in the future.[46] Even so, war continued here after the cessation because it was not all-embracing. Many of the English soldiers in County Roscommon were not in favour of the peace, and the publication of the treaty between the English Parliament and Edinburgh formalized this unhappiness into support for the Solemn League. When Parliament urged the English and Scottish forces in Ulster to sign the Solemn League and Covenant, the result in Connaught was a series of raids by the English and Scots from the garrisons in Roscommon against which the Irish forces, bound by the cessation, could not retaliate. The Earl of Antrim attempted to persuade the Scots commander in Ulster, Robert Monro, to join the king's side before creating the army which he sent over to Ireland under MacColla. Monro would have none of it, and when Antrim tried to threaten him with forcible expulsion from Ulster, the Scot defied him to defeat him in battle.[47] Antrim's army made no friends before it left Ireland: Clanricarde threatened to destroy it, and Lord Taffe complained that Antrim's men had wiped out his tenants. Antrim himself was the cause of some of the problems in Ireland. Of the many power struggles in the country, Antrim's was one of the more important; for he challenged the right of other commanders to lead the Confederate armies, and as he created the army for Scotland, he threatened to invade Ulster himself. This threat was of great concern to the Supreme Council, as Antrim could destroy at a stroke both the expedition to Scotland and the attack on Ulster, to be led by the Earl of Castlehaven and Owen Roe O'Neill. This was a crucial time, for the two campaigns formed the two prongs of an attempt to get the Scots to abandon Ulster, first by causing problems at home and then by defeating them in Ulster.[48] The Council's response was first to try to placate Antrim by obtaining for him the fleet he needed to ship the army over to Scotland and then to enlist Ormond, who had a good working relationship with the marquis, to calm him down. Because the expedition to Scotland was a Royalist adventure, the Lord Lieutenant was providing the shipping from the fleets at Wexford and Waterford. The army was marched all the way to the south coast to be embarked at Ballyhack in County Wexford, where they embarked on 24 June 1644. The aim of forcing the Scots to withdraw from Ulster was not achieved. Of the 9,000 or so Scots in Ireland, only about 1,400 of Monro's army and the Earl of Argyll's regiment returned to Scotland from Ulster.[49] On the other hand, the removal of Argyll's regiment was a political success for the MacDonald/Macdonnell cause, since the soldiers had been quartered on Antrim's own lands in Ulster, and represented the Campbell claims on the Irish Macdonnells.

The cessation's difficulties were not helped in Ireland by the attitude of Murrough O'Brien, Lord Inchiquin in the Munster enclave. He held the triangle of territory which stretches along the coast from Youghal to Brandon and Kinsale and north to New Market and Churchtown. Before the cessation he had held off the attacks of the Confederate forces in Munster, and once the cessation was declared, he was unhappy. Although he was an Irish chieftain, he was an ardent Protestant and as such denounced the treaty with Catholics. After Marston Moor, he threw in his lot with the English opponents of the cessation and went on the offensive against the Confederation, breaking the cessation in south Munster. Westminster sent shiploads of supplies and arms to the ports under

Inchiquin's control, happy to secure the south-west coast for its shipping. Inchiquin instituted the removal of all Gaels not loyal to him from his territory, ostensibly to improve internal security. At Youghal, this affected the composition not only of the population generally but also of the government. On 10 October the council recorded the importance of the changes with the note that the session was the 'first after the expulsion of the Irish inhabitants'. Perhaps for the benefit of new members, the duties of the officers and the freemen were rehearsed. The changes in tenancy holdings within the town can be seen by the massive changeovers evident in the rating lists, from which most of the Irish names disappeared.[50] Ormond was angered by Inchiquin's move, and although Inchiquin suggested that Ormond eschew the cessation himself and lead the Protestants in Ireland against the Catholics, the Lord Lieutenant was more concerned with the loss of customs duties which the loss of the south-west ports entailed.

By the summer of 1644 Monro was again taking the offensive, and after capturing Belfast he began to move into Cavan in the direction of the expeditionary force being established under the Earl of Castlehaven. Castlehaven's forces were the second prong of the attempt to drive the Scots out of Ulster. The ensuing campaign was hindered by Castlehaven's timidity and ultimately achieved little. Moreover, O'Neill had been offended when he was not offered the command, and the relationships between the two generals remained cool. Castlehaven squandered time building a large military camp at Charlemont. When Monro approached, lack of supplies, forced the Ulster Confederate army to withdraw to Leinster.[51] During 1645 Owen Roe O'Neill was unable to establish any firm hold on the province, because his forces and those of the Scots were fairly evenly matched. No major attempt to unseat the Scots in Ulster was made that year. Instead, the Scots were at times able to push Owen back into Connaught and Leinster. The political picture in Ireland changed suddenly in late 1645, when a double thrust of international politics broadened the conflict. In that year the king considered offering a secret treaty to the Confederation which would in effect undermine Ormond's attempt to drive a wedge between the Catholic Irish and the Old English. The war was having major international repercussions as it became bound up in the Counter-Reformation. Rome was represented in Kilkenny by Peir Francesco Scarampi, sent by Pope Urban VIII, who had arrived just before the cessation, and the Vatican was putting itself firmly behind the Irish clergy, who had made great strides in the establishment of the Confederation and wanted to reinvigorate the Catholic church in Ireland. Rome rejected approaches from Charles I in favour of an open and public re-establishment of the Catholic faith. With Scarampi's backing the Catholic Irish resisted Ormond's attempt to persuade the Confederation to concede to anything less. This crucial issue more than anything else prevented the cessation from developing into a full peace treaty.

In July 1645 Lord Herbert of Raglan, once the king's general in south Wales and now Earl of Glamorgan, reached Ireland. Unaware of Glamorgan's secret mission, Ormond welcomed the earl and was glad to have him represent the king's desperate plight to the Supreme Council at Kilkenny. While the Lord Lieutenant believed that Glamorgan was meeting with the same limited success that he had had, in reality Glamorgan was offering very different terms to the Confederates. He promised full satisfaction of the Catholic demands by way of a secret treaty to be published after the Irish sent an army of 20,000 to England. Not all of the Confederates accepted the offer; the Old English believed that only an open treaty with Ormond would carry with it any guarantees. The European implications again surfaced when the new pope, Innocent X, sent a nuncio, Cardinal Giovanni Battista Rinuccini, to Ireland to replace Scarampi. When Rinuccini arrived in October 1645, his perception of the state of affairs cut through some of the problems posed by Glamorgan's offer. Negotiations between Rinuccini and Glamorgan in late 1645 set clear terms: there would be a full restoration of the Catholic church, with bishops in the House of Lords. Political changes involved ensuring that the next Lord Lieutenant would be a Catholic too.[52] Whether or not the king actually sanctioned Glamorgan's offer remains questionable. Some historians believe that he had, and that Rinuccini had a letter confirming that Glamorgan had the king's trust. However, the terms of the previous discussions and those of Glamorgan and Rinuccini were suddenly exposed and rendered useless.

In Sligo, the anarchy that followed the cessation and its rejection by the forces in Roscommon was exacerbated in the next two years by the imposition of taxes by O'Neill's forces in periods when they were driven out of Ulster. Moreover, at the provincial level, there were bad relations between the provincial general and Viscount Mayo, who reckoned that he, not John Burke, should hold the post. In the end, Mayo refused to co-operate with Burke and declared unilateral separation from the Confederation. When he took possession of the castles in County Mayo, the Earl of Castlehaven was sent to deal with him. Castlehaven recaptured the seized castles and arrested Mayo in April 1644. However, by the time Mayo escaped in early 1645, unrest in northern and western Connaught had spread throughout Leitrim and Sligo. Sir Charles Coote, who had led the English forces in Roscommon until the cessation, finally publicized his dissatisfaction with the peace and declared his support for the Westminster Parliament. He returned to the west of Ireland and captured Sligo in June 1645, without much of a fight. The divisions in the Sligo Confederate leadership were exacerbated by the control exercised by Taffe. The politically marginalized Tahg O'Connor Sligo was in Sligo at the time and may well have assisted Coote out of pique at being sidelined. More castles in the county fell to Coote, but these setbacks did tend to galvanize the previously divided Connaught leadership into a united effort against the English.[53] During one of the skirmishes in the Sligo area, the Archbishop of Tuam, Malachy O'Queely, was killed. On his body were found details of Glamorgan's August discussions with the Supreme Council. Copies were sent to Dublin and London. Ormond, shocked to the core at what he saw as betrayal, arrested Glamorgan and charged him with treason. But somehow Ormond must have been convinced that Glamorgan was telling the truth when he declared that he was acting on the king's orders. When the Supreme Council threatened to end the cessation if Glamorgan was not released, on 22 January Ormond obliged.

By the beginning of 1646, the situation was further complicated by a new set of proposals, even more generous than those offered by Glamorgan, sent to Rinuccini from Rome. They were terms agreed by the queen and Sir Kenelm Digby with the pope. In February the sixth session of the Assembly headed off attempts to agree terms with Ormond, and Glamorgan hoped to persuade the king to accept the queen's treaty. In his desperation to get military aid to the king before it was too late, Glamorgan persuaded the Irish to agree to prolong the cessation until 1 May to give the king time to agree. All of this effort came to nothing. Glamorgan's military plan to rescue Chester fell apart when he ran out of money, and his political plans collapsed when the king disowned Glamorgan's August treaty, which the earl had hopes of resuming once the copy sent to Westminster was published. In the wake of the seeming collapse of the Royalist cause in England, Ormond came to terms with the Confederate delegates at Dublin. The treaty, however, offered only vague references to the king's grace and favour with regard to religion, and following the king's public disavowal of Glamorgan, it could hardly satisfy the Irish Catholics. When the king surrendered to the Scots in May 1646, Ormond had to persuade the Confederates to agree to a treaty, for he was now effectively on his own. The Old English were keen to come to terms, but the nuncio was not. Rinuccini was determined to keep pressing for a fully free Catholic church in Ireland, something Ormond still could not countenance.

The determination of the Catholics was strengthened during the spring of 1646 following General O'Neill's success in Ulster. Rinuccini had brought with him funds for the Confederation's cause, and he directed much of them towards O'Neill's forces, thus offsetting the effects of the Supreme Council's denial of funds to him for the previous three years. In a renewed campaign in the province using weapons brought to Ireland by the nuncio he caught an exhausted Scottish army led by Monro himself. The Scots had planned a major rendezvous at Benburb as a preliminary to a sweep through south Ulster. The two armies skirmished along the River Blackwater throughout 5 June. Monro expected O'Neill to withdraw, but O'Neill drew the Scots eastwards in an attempt to provoke Monro's attack. But at 7 p.m. it was O'Neill who attacked the Scots' left flank, supported by 1,000 horse returning from an attack on forces from Coleraine. Monro's army was decisively defeated in the battle which ensued.[54] This defeat of a significant Covenanter army at Benburb was heralded as a 'Gaelic apex', with the defeat of both Scottish and English forces categorized in the following poem as painted Picts and devils:

> Whiles neere Benburbe, three diverse nations fought,
> And thundringe Mars, to rage theire captaines brought,
> The English, Irish and the Scottish wives
> Could not discearne theire loves that lost theire lives
> And when the mangled face could not be knowen, They turned
> The stript deade bodies upp and downe.
> The taile behind made knowne the English race,
> The blew chop yarde bewrayed the Scottish face,
> But where they found non such, nor strange signe,
> The Irish women saide, the man is mine.[55]

Militarily, the battle was crucial, for it seemed to offer the chance to inflict further defeats on the Scots throughout the province.

However, O'Neill soon realized that that was not going to be possible, and he withdrew to Cavan. In the international arena, the
battle was of great importance. It strengthened the pope's resolve to
send financial aid to Ireland, and a *Te Deum* was sung in the Vatican.
Moreover, Innocent X requested that the banners captured from the
Scots be sent to Rome to hang in St Peter's. Thanks to the publicity
sent to Rome by Rinuccini, it was clearly perceived as a major
victory in the Counter-Reformation abroad, but hopes of military
victory at home proved illusory. The Scots at Benburb did not represent the majority of the Scots in Ulster, and O'Neill was still in
no position to tackle many of the Scottish garrisons. He was possibly still suffering from being long deprived of necessary weaponry;
in any case the political situation was about to deflect him from
Ulster.[56]

At the end of July Ormond published the treaty agreed between
him and the Confederates in April, and on 4 August the Confederation published it in Kilkenny, believing that it had convinced Rinuccini
of its value. The nuncio did not agree. He was at Waterford hosting
a legatine synod of the Irish church when the treaty was announced.
On 6 August the synod rejected the peace, and claimed that those
who signed it had by doing so broken their oath of association to
the Confederation. Anyone who assisted Ormond was to be excommunicated. This action initiated a political battle which soon embroiled the military commanders. O'Neill was called southwards by
the clerical party from Ulster and his army moved on Kilkenny.
The synod placed an interdict on towns and priests that accepted
the Ormond treaty and on 1 September excommunicated everyone
who favoured it. Under such pressure, even the Old English general
Thomas Preston, commander of the Leinster army, acquiesced in
the renunciation of the treaty. Ormond, present in Kilkenny to prom-
ulgate the peace, was forced to leave in mid-September. The nuncio
returned to form a new Supreme Council, which he presided over
himself, in the wake of the imprisonment of the treaty's supporters.
To strengthen the new council's questionable credibility, the revamped Confederation decided to attack Dublin. The Ulster army
and the Leinster army, led by the intense rivals O'Neill and Preston,
were sent to conduct a winter campaign. The divided command was
not a good omen for success, and although they closed in on Dublin
and forced Ormond to consider terms with the Westminster Parliament, it was to little avail. Ormond then turned his attention to
the issue of Preston's loyalty. He sent Clanricarde to meet him, but

Preston committed himself only to a pause in hostilities.[57] Rinuccini distrusted Preston's motives and recalled his army under threat of excommunication. This was a military and political embarrassment for the nuncio, which 'exacerbated the divisions amongst the confederates'.[58] Although the General Assembly of January 1647 repudiated the Ormond treaty, it renounced the excommunications issued the previous year, and the Supreme Council members arrested in September were released. In March a new council was created, incorporating members opposed to Rinuccini's position.

The summer of 1647 saw many strains imposed upon the Confederation. Ormond finally came to terms with the Westminster Parliament and handed the city of Dublin to a force under the command of Michael Jones in July. While Ormond concluded the final arrangements for handing over the city, Preston moved in on Dublin. However, on 8 August he was defeated by Jones at Dungan's Hill near Trim. O'Neill had to be called into Leinster to defend the province, even though his Ulstermen were resented. His Catholic forces had been unpopular when they had camped in the Leinster counties in previous years, and now the bitterness the Old English felt towards him was increased by their realization that they were dependent upon him.

In Munster, Inchiquin too had gone on the offensive and pressed hard on the Munster army. He pushed eastwards through the province, capturing Dungarvan and Cashel and then threatening Waterford. The disaster was complete when on 13 November Inchiquin defeated the Munster army at Knockanuss. At this point the assembly was riven by panic and irresolution. There was only one effective army in existence, led by a man many of them mistrusted. Moreover, some suspected that O'Neill wanted the crown of Ireland for himself, and a diatribe attacking the Old English was published in Lisbon in 1645 and circulated in Ireland in autumn 1647. Conor O'Mahony, a Jesuit, suggested that Ireland should throw off the British monarchy and elect its own. The return to O'Neill of the great O'Neill's sword by the pope did nothing to calm fears of his ambition, which by 1648 even the nuncio was beginning to suspect. In November 1647 the Confederation had sent envoys to treat with the queen and with the pope, with the aim of securing the terms of the Glamorgan treaty. But by then the king and Ormond were already planning a renewed war as part of the king's bid to return to power by force of arms in all four nations. We shall return to this matter in chapter 11.

PART III

A Revolution in the Making

10

The Radical and Conservative Impetus

This was the Lord's doing and it is marvelous in our eyes

10. The great reward of honour here, and glory hereafter, that shall be given to everyone that is valiant for the Lord[1]

Largely through the way it had used their labour and their incomes, the first civil war in England and Wales deeply involved the people of these two nations in the struggle for the political future of the country. This involvement forms the basis of the succeeding chapters, which examine the development of revolutionary and counter-revolutionary impulses. At the end of the war in England and Wales the inhabitants of the two nations surveyed a physically damaged world. Roads were blocked in places by earthwork forts like those constructed outside York, while bridges had been broken up to hamper the movements of armies. The school at Ashby-de-la-Zouch had been destroyed, probably because it lay so close to the castle, which had been held by Lord Loughborough's forces during the war; it may well either have been garrisoned as an outwork or demolished because it was too close to the castle walls.[2] It was not alone. Great houses and humble town houses alike had been destroyed or severely damaged during the war. Trade, too, had been interrupted, and was still subject to interference where Ireland was concerned. Cattle markets had been disrupted through the fragmentation of the drove routes across England, Wales and Scotland. It was time to put things back together, although the situation was not yet stable and the most pervasive of all the effects of the war, financial exactions, were still in place. After the first civil war, two distinct responses developed in England, both of which influenced the position in the four nations to some extent. We must be wary of using modern political labels to tag movements of 350 years ago, but broad terms can be used here as long as their drawbacks and limitations are understood. The fundamental response, perhaps of the majority of English and Welsh men and women across the social spectrum, was an overwhelming need to return to stability. This broad category, which we may call conservative, encompassed a variety of political positions. It could embrace Presbyterianism, which was soon to embrace a monarchist perspective, and unreconstructed Royalism itself. It could also include a strand of the neutral response to the war, including third-force politics and the club response, which had embraced both a desire for order and stability and a moderate anti-war stance. For most people the desire for a recognizable form of order may well have dominated their hopes in the years after the war ended in 1646. And for the majority this may also have entailed a monarchy, but as most people were never asked, we cannot really know whether they felt that the restoration of the king to his traditional powers was a necessary precondition for order. Just how much the king's political body meant in everyday life and how much stability was really represented by the organs and features of government at the local level is unclear. We can, of course, refer to the theoretical politics of the period and acknowledge that in that sphere the monarch was seen as the fountain of all order. From this it can be ascertained that all government was at the monarch's behest, but what did this really mean to the defendant in the quarter sessions court or the trained bandsman in the county armed forces? At certain times the English peasantry definitely expressed their belief in the king as an arbiter in inter-class disputes, such as the Midland Revolt of 1607, but counterbalancing that is the western rising or the fens, where the king acted as an aggressor rather than an arbiter. These episodes cannot have left unchallenged the view of the king as the fountain of all justice and order, since they themselves threatened social order and peace. Whether or not the majority of people perceived Charles, restored to pre-1640 powers or post-1641 powers, as a necessity, they did desire stability and a reduced taxation burden. These factors were important in events leading up to the second civil war in England, Wales and Scotland and became a basis for direct action by conservative groups.

Some, probably a minority, of the people in England and Wales sought a radical approach to the post-war issues facing the two nations. For some radicals this meant readjusting the existing system, for others it entailed sweeping the system away altogether, constructing a brave new world, embracing a democracy (probably limited to men), and ending the monarchy. Other radicals wanted even more – the abolition of titles and property and the establishment of a common treasury. For many people from all of these progressive groups, God was important. It was God who had presented the forces of Parliament with victory, and therefore everything enacted afterwards had to be to His glory. There was an important qualification here. God had, in His own mysterious way, favoured the Presbyterian cause, which was soon to be diametrically opposed to much of the radical agenda. One other reservation should be noted here. There was a difference of approach between those who sought God's glory through the improvement of the lot of the common people and those who sought the same end through the establishment of a state church system. One was almost secular in its approach, the other almost theocratic. Naturally, in relation to politics these two motives were not mutually exclusive. A major part of this chapter is devoted to establishing the political shifts in England and Wales which led to the second civil war, and their relationship to the other two nations. This chapter first explores the background to the desire for stability, order and lower taxes.[3]

We can gain some impression of the financial aspects of governance in the period from a case study of Great Staughton in Huntingdonshire, where copies of county committee orders were made in the constables' book. Great Staughton, a parish of 6,047 acres, lies on the south-western border of Huntingdonshire in Toseland Hundred, about eight miles south-west of the county town. In the mid-seventeenth century the town had a population of about 600, and three constables took care of the secular administration. One looked after the south of the parish, which contained most of the town itself; another took care of the manors of Gaines, Dillington and Perry; and the third looked after Beechamstead. Only the accounts for the southern ward survive.[4] The parish was an arable area specializing in beans and wheat. In the middle of the century it was owned by the Wauton family; the manors of Dillington, Perry and Gaines hall were held by Robert Baldwin; and Beechamstead was held by Sir Lodovick Dyer.[5] The accounts consist of three useful sections: the accounts themselves; a set of orders issued by the Justices of the Peace at the end of the war; and, finally, the warrants sent out by the county committee from 1646 until the 1650s, plus related orders continuing until the 1660s.[6]

At the Epiphany quarter sessions held on 12 January 1647 the Huntingdonshire justices of the peace issued a series of instructions aimed at establishing order in the county. The inclusion of copies of the order in the constables' book is important. Records of justices of the peace are rare for this period, and in many counties they do not exist. In Nottinghamshire, for example, the sessions minute books recommence only in 1652, and there are only shadowy references to the sessions in other sources. The parish books show that the JPs were concerned with all forms of order. The first three deal with potential food shortages and refer to brewers. Not more than three bushels of malt were to be used in the production of a hogshead (fifty gallons) of beer, not only to prevent waste 'in these times of feared security' but also for 'wholesome and good beire for temperate men', and no one was to produce malt without a licence. The constables also had to watch for people ingrossing corn or victuals and to ensure Sunday observance by stopping 'all travellers with cattell or carriages on those days'. They were similarly ordered to

> punish all beggars wandering persons and rogues by whipping them according to law and passing to their last habitations or place of birth. And if the constables be remiss therein suffering any to pass unpunished they pay the penalty of the statute.

Some instructions dealt with work and unemployment, enjoining churchwardens and overseers to maintain the poor by the usual methods of rates, not to let any person starve, and to ensure that all who were able to work did so on pain of imprisonment. Wages were to be regulated and those who paid excessive rates were to be imprisoned. Order nine related to the maintenance of highways and instructed constables to make sure wagon owners took care not to damage roads. Order ten started by confirming that constables make presentments at the quarter sessions as usual, with specific regard to the ten orders.[7] These are generally conservative instructions relating to traditional practices, mirroring orders given out during times of dearth. Only references to 'fearful security' and delinquents mark these instructions out as anything other than traditional methods of local government.

At the other end of the account book, recorded upside down, are the orders from the county committee, beginning with an order for £3-13s-4d in British army tax levy dated 22 September 1646. Three days later a levy of £17-0s-0d a month for four months for the Scottish army appears, backdated to 4 March 1644. In Huntingdon three separate collectors were responsible for these two levies and for the monthly pay; in the village, three collectors were responsible for all taxes. The first reference in the account book to the monthly pay is on 2 December 1646. The amount levied was £99-4s-0d, to cover four months backdated to 1 June 1646. A later assessment for £20-6s-4d shows the proportional distribution amongst the three wards at 50 per cent for the town, 17 per cent for Beechamstead and 33 per cent for Gaines, Dillington and Perry. The problems caused for the village collectors and constables, as well as the villagers themselves, become clear when one realizes that the money had to be collected and paid over in sixteen days' time. Although the next warrant, dated 24 March 1647, was levied on 'equal rating on those suitable to pay', there is no further detail about the way in which levies were assessed. Because constables' lays in the townside ward were rated on land at 2d in the pound from 1646 until 1649, it is probable that this was the basis of other assessments too. These figures can be extrapolated to provide some sense of the cost to villagers of the war levies. To raise the monthly pay of £16-15s-5d would require a levy in the order of 4¹⁄₄d in the pound. Later levies of £20-6s-4d would require a levy of over 5d in the pound.

On 9 February 1648 a warrant for joint tax for the New Model Army and the British army set out the full instructions regarding collection. The collectors were the three constables and William Fothergill, gent., William Berrage, William Peacock and Edmund Pakle. They were to collect £50-6s-5d to cover three months' tax, which represented approximately the same rate. The order they were working to, an ordinance dated 23 June 1647, called for the levy to be publicized before 13 February,

> so if any find fault they maie make their complaint to the committee att Huntingdon upon 15 instant upon which day you are to deliver yor assessments with a copy there fairly written and your names subscribed there.

The seven men were warned that if they failed in any part of the task, they would be fined 40 shillings each.[8]

A similar pattern followed this demand. The money needed for Ireland continued to be collected in Great Staughton at the rate of £33-11s-0d for the six months from 1 February 1648. As part of the £60,000 per month for the New Model Army from 29 March until 29 September 1648, the community was charged another £16-15s-6d. The war of 1648 was to impose more problems for the community, as an additional levy of £23-18s-3d was imposed on 9 August, to be paid to Francis Bloodwicke at his house in Huntingdon within five days.[9] Even when the fighting was over, except in Scotland and around Pontefract Parliament was required to continue paying the New Model Army, and the monthly levy was again raised at the same rate. When this six-month assessment ran out in June 1649, the new three-month levy was higher, at £90,000 per month. Of this, Huntingdonshire paid £800 per month, Toseland Hundred £200-7s-0d a month, and Great Staughton £20-6s-4d each month. The only respite for the town in this period came in June 1649, when the taxes on the county were reduced to allow for the payment of outstanding billeting charges. At the same time the committee asked the county to 'give notice of such persons who had an tax money taken from them about Bartlemasstide 1645 by cavaliers'. This referred to the king's march through the county in August 1645. At the time the Royalist forces rounded up 700 head of cattle and seized all available horses.[10]

The weight and burden suffered by Great Staughton was mirrored around the rest of the country. War continued in Ireland and Scotland, and even around Harlech, well into 1647. Even where fighting had ended, the burdens of war did not disappear. Indeed, it was pointed out that the amount of Parliamentarian levies grew from £54,000 a month to £60,000 after the war and, as we have seen, to £90,000 in 1648–9.[11] The excise tax continued to elicit more protests than did the monthly assessments, but the issues which affected people's perceptions of the post-war years can be understood only if we remember that excise and monthly pay were only two parts of a burden which also included money for Ireland, payments to the Scots until 1647, and billeting. The costs addressed by these levies were not negligible; in some cases billeting cost more than any of the other assessments. In some regions there were local additional taxes – such as those levied by commissioners Laugharne, Poyer and Powell in central and southern Wales – to support garrisons.[12]

Excise taxes led to riots in various places, for example in Derby during 1645. At Droitwich in Worcestershire violent opposition greeted Captain Prescott's attempts to levy the tax. A mob threatened to burn down his lodgings, and as he escaped he was beaten and shot at. In the ensuing fight a rioter was killed, and Prescott was indicted before the assizes before the indemnity committee could deal with the incident. At Norwich during November and December 1646, a riot was sparked by excise collection, and in London in

1647, a riot in which participants drew heart from the Norwich incident was to have important consequences. At Smithfield on 15 February 1647, a fracas caused by the refusal of one purchaser to pay excise on livestock developed into a full-scale riot, resulting in the excise office being burned down. Parliament was concerned by the proximity of the riot and ordered the Middlesex JPs and sheriffs to proceed rigorously against rioters. At the same time MPs tried to ease the burden on the poor to try to make the tax more palatable.[13] When the political crisis deepened in the summer, Parliament again reconsidered the excise and began to remove some of the levies on home-produced salt (the spark for the Droitwich riot) and meat (the spark for the Smithfield riot). The popular pressure to end the excise was perhaps less influential in prompting change than was a Presbyterian desire to drum up support through passing a 'popular' act in summer 1647. The riots of autumn and winter resulted in minor changes in February 1647 compared with the more fundamental changes in the summer.

In the summer of 1647 a major political crisis developed, prompting one historian to comment that 'England was more clearly on the verge of anarchy than at any time during the century'.[14] Alongside anxiety over the excise social instability across England and Wales coincided with a fundamental political breakdown. The Earl of Manchester's statement about the king still being king even if Parliament's forces defeated him ninety-nine times now appeared absolutely accurate. The king had decided upon a series of points of principle, which can be classified into three defences: religion, his friends and his powers. Naturally, these contrasted with his erstwhile enemies' wishes for the establishment of a new church, the trials of prominent Royalists and the maintenance of parliamentary control over the militia. These goals formed the basis of proposals presented to Charles by the English commissioners at Newcastle. Had there been no major political split in the Westminster Parliament, Charles would have had little chance of defeating a politically united opposition. But the English and Welsh MPs were not united, and the army and Parliament were growing estranged. Charles hoped to make use of these divisions to win back power and intended to drive a wedge between the English and the Scots. In England the division between Presbyterians and Independents was moving beyond Parliament and into a wider sphere. By 1647 the Westminster body was largely dominated by the Presbyterians, who could present something of a united front with the Scots, even if Charles detected a potential political advantage in seeking to divide them. The Independents, on the other hand, were stronger in the army, and the situation polarized when Parliament began to discuss disbanding the New Model Army to save money. When the Newcastle propositions were presented to the king in June 1646, they were warmly received by both English and Scottish Presbyterians. In August the Scottish commissioner, the Earl of Loudoun, pressed Charles to accept the propositions in their entirety on the grounds that failure to so do would encourage anti-monarchist sentiment in England. But Charles prevaricated, hoping that Independents would see a glimmer of hope in his stance for their opposition to a Presbyterian church. Charles himself would not stomach Presbyterianism, which he saw as the product of rebellion and as odious as Catholicism. However, Henrietta Maria, who perceived all Protestant sects as heretical, seems to have made little distinction between any of them. She therefore advised her husband to sign the Covenant. In the end Charles would not do so, and the propositions remained unsigned. Charles had objected to other proposals too: the twenty-year control of the militia by Parliament; the nullification of peerages awarded since 1642, with which Charles had rewarded his supporters; and the extensive lists of people barred from pardon for their part in the civil wars.[15] The Scots soon tired of the king's failure to agree terms and of Westminster's inability to settle remuneration of their expenses during the war. By the end of 1646, the Estates had decided that the future form of government in Scotland would have to be decided without the king, if he refused to sign the propositions then on offer. As soon as an agreement on payments to the Scots was reached, the Scottish army prepared to leave English soil. In January 1647, Charles was left at Newcastle as the Covenanter army returned home. He was then collected by English soldiers and escorted through England to Holdenby House in Northamptonshire, where his arrival coincided with a dramatic political crisis.

Much of the popular resentment against the taxes focused on the presence of the army and transcended the provincial–metropolitan divide. An invaluable analysis of this issue is based on the proceedings of the indemnity committee set up to examine cases lodged in local courts against soldiers. The majority of complaints related to the theft of horses and provisions, including arms, by the provincial forces, rather than by the New Model Army regiments. Some 17 per cent related to debts incurred, including quarter charges built into soldiers' wages, because of a disruption in army pay.[16] Communities particularly resented quartering, especially when its cost represented a significant addition to regular taxation. In fact, people resented the soldiers being there at all, and the village of Linton in Cambridgeshire attempted to prevent the New Model Army soldiers from billeting there in 1647 by prosecuting the constable who tried to allocate billets.[17]

From amidst some of the grievances caused by the religious, economic and government dysfunction emerged groups with radical solutions to some or all of these factors. Perhaps the one with most potential, at least in the secular field, was the Levellers, who developed demands for liberty of conscience and political liberty. To understand the Levellers, it is crucial to unravel their relationship with the New Model Army. The army has been variously portrayed as radically politicized or as largely politically inert. Support for Leveller politics from the army was to be critical to Leveller potential, but some historians challenge the extent of this backing, and even the existence of any support at all, playing down the political effects of the whole period or viewing the New Model Army as no more political than any of the other civil war armies created by a distinctly unradical aristocracy.[18] On the other hand, recent work suggests that a core of radicalism did develop amongst sections of the army, fostered by religious belief and understanding.[19] The Parliamentarian armies had been accompanied by radical preachers since the war began, and religious conviction permeated the issuing of tracts and guides such as *The Souldiers Pocket Bible*, which made it clear to the soldiers that their duties were spiritually bound up with God's work.[20] Moreover, it is difficult to argue that the army was politically inert; in works like *The Souldiers Catechisme* of 1644, Parliament had involved soldiers in the reasoning behind the war, uniting them in a cause which was clearly political. Following a disclaimer rebutting the idea of fighting against the king himself, in the form of an ambiguous claim to be fighting for 'King and Parliament', the catechism replied to the question of what the soldiers were fighting for with less ambiguity:

> 2. I fight for the Lawes and Liberties of my Countrey, which are now in danger of being overthrowne by them that have long laboured to bring into this Kingdome an Arbitrary, and Tyrannicall Government.
> 3. I fight for the preservation of our Parliament, in the being whereof (under God) consists the glory and welfare of this Kingdome; if this foundation be overthrown, we shall soone be the most slavish nation in the Christian World.

4. I fight in the defence and maintenance of the true Protestant Religion, which is now violently opposed, and will be utterly supprest in this Kingdome and the Popish Religion again advanced, if the armies raised against the Parliament prevaile.[21]

These statements do not automatically mean that the army was radicalized and fertile ground for Leveller political ideology *per se*. However, those arguing for a rigorous Protestant community saw the catechism as a principal means of imposing religious ideology on the nation, and therefore one which could be used to create a common identity. Moreover, the catechism clearly involved the soldier in saving not only the political nation but also the soul of its people. Expectations of social and political dividends as just reward for involvement in the political war would resonate with many members of the New Model Army.

The leaders identified by historians as formative and as principal actors are John Lilburne, William Walwyn, Richard Overton and John Wildman.[22] There were others – Colonel Thomas Rainsborough and Edward Sexby amongst them – who surfaced to give a broader edge to Leveller politics. Rainsborough, for example, is the man who at Putney voiced the Levellers' broadest aims. However, the original ideas and actions seem to have been generated by this 'gang of four'. Lilburne is credited with being a champion of justice, and it is this theme which lent his political thought a strain of consistency throughout the years of the group's political importance and explains apparent contradictions in his approach to politics – including the uncomfortable alliance with Royalism in 1649. Although a younger son from the ranks of the minor gentry, he learned politics and religion as an apprentice to a cloth merchant in London. There he imbibed Presbyterianism, and by the age of 22 he was associated with Bastwicke and Burton. In 1637 he was pilloried and then imprisoned for circulating their banned works, thus receiving his first lesson in injustice. He was released only after the Long Parliament sat thanks to the action of Oliver Cromwell. His Presbyterian nurturing wore off, and conflict between him and Presbyterians developed during his military career, culminating in his imprisonment under sentence of death at Oxford. He served first under Lord Brooke and then, after his release from Oxford (engineered by his wife, Elizabeth), in the Eastern Association army. Naturally, he and the Earl of Manchester did not share common religious views, or even military aims. At this stage in his career he was closer to Cromwell largely because the Lieutenant General saw him as a useful weapon against the earl, rather than because of compatible political views. By July 1645 enemies from within the Eastern Association plotted his downfall, now possible because Lilburne's anti-Presbyterian views had angered his former patrons, Prynne and Bastwicke. These two were not only rigorous in their Presbyterianism, they were also conservative and neo-Royalist in their politics. Unfounded allegations resulted in Lilburne's being dragged before the Commons and imprisoned without a legal trial by the parliamentary Committee of Examinations. Lilburne saw this treatment as an example of the new arbitrary rule imposed on England and Wales. He used the experience of his imprisonment to develop his ideas on England's new form of tyranny.

Lilburne met Walwyn some time during 1645, around the time that Walwyn had produced new works on religious toleration. Walwyn was a humanist, widely read in classical writings as well as in Puritan ideology, but he rejected predestination. He did not reject humanity's sinfulness, but for him God was a loving being, offering the chance of salvation to all. This view led naturally to toleration for any pathway to God, whether Independent, Congregationalist, Presbyterian or even Roman Catholic. His spiritual humanity led him to use humorous rebukes as a political weapon rather than the vilification favoured by opponents like Thomas Edwards or the heavy satire employed by some of his own associates. For Walwyn, religious toleration and God's spiritual assistance to humanity had to be matched by social reform, and it was this feeling which brought him into the coterie that developed Leveller thought. Walwyn joined Richard Overton in writing the anti-Presbyterian tracts. Recalling the Elizabethan Puritan tracts produced under the name Martin MarPrelate, Overton began a series of Martin Marpriest pamphlets criticizing the conference of the Westminster Divines and their secular supporters, creating such characters as Sir Simon Synod, Sir John Presbyter and Mr Persecution. Lilburne's involvement with Overton's writing, which extended to using the same illegal press, was responsible for part of the accusations against him when the Commons imprisoned him in 1645.

Lilburne and Walwyn began to develop their linked attacks on the political state of the nation. In *England's Birthright Justified* Lilburne attacked Parliament's arbitrary powers, as well as going on to challenge some of the fundamental principles of the people's exclusion from governance, such as the use of a foreign language (Latin) in legal proceedings. He also began to attack the tax burden, a theme on which Walwyn expanded in *The Ordinance for Tithes Discounted*, which disparaged the hypocrisy of the Presbyterian ascendancy in hanging on to the system of church funding which had been attacked earlier. Of course any challenge to tithes was more than an attack on church funding; it also called into question lay or appropriated tithes that had been assumed by the owners of former church lands. Such a position was thus perceived to be an attack on property, for if tithes went, what about rents, and the benefits of land ownership? It also raised the whole question of taxation.

In 1646 Lilburne began to identify clearly with issues related to the army when he attempted to win his arrears of pay. Thus, in that year the two disparate groups, soldiers and civilians, were linked by the future Levellers, albeit in a sometimes uncomfortable relationship. In the course of this argument with Parliament, Lilburne attacked Manchester's Presbyterianism. As the earl was now Speaker of the House of Lords, Lilburne was dragged before the bar of the House, where he infuriated the Lords by refusing to accept their authority over him and failing to remove his hat. In their anger the Lords had him imprisoned in the Tower, fined him £2,000 and had his pamphlets burned by the common hangman. Lilburne declared to his persecutors: 'All you intended when you set us a fighting was merely to unhorse and dismount our old riders and tyrants, that so you might get up, and ride in their stead'.[23] If he was right, then the sentiments of the *Souldiers Catechisme* had misled the soldiers: there was to be no share in the new state for the Lord's servants. Whilst the Levellers' 'party' really developed only in the coming months, already their enemies lumped them together. Prominent amongst their opponents was Thomas Edwards, who in 1646 published *Gangraena*. As the name suggests, Edwards saw that England and Wales were not only weakened by the wounds of war but that those very wounds had become infected. This infection took the form of a collection of religious and political sects which had sprung up in the latter days of the war. Edwards gave details of these groups, their beliefs and their practices. A broadsheet produced in January 1647 continued the theme, using rhyme to summarize Edwards's points. It castigated the Independents, who could be said to include the Levellers and many of the army, as preventing peace.

The Saints Communion Christians do professe,
Most Necessary to the life of Grace,

But whilst some shrowd them by this bare notion,
Condemning all the rest for Antichristian,
Preferring much confused sad distraction:
They thus disturb a settlement in the nation.[24]

Even allowing for the bias incorporated in this piece of verse and in Edwards's own work, neither really provided a sociological study. Edwards hoped to provoke horror in his readers, particularly those in Parliament, and thus to prompt action against the sects. He grouped together the future Levellers – Walwyn, Lilburne and Overton – in contrast to the way in which he attacked preachers as individuals. Walwyn's response to Edwards was far more subtle: he turned the concept on its head and suggested that rather than England being sick and infected, Edwards was ill and suffering as a result from a jaundiced view of life. What he needed to help him recover and become a good Christian was love.[25]

Already, Presbyterians saw the future Levellers as a threat. Indeed, it was they who coined the name Levellers in 1647, as an insult based on the notion of levelling enclosures. This label had originally been attached to people during the Midland Revolt in 1607. Historians date the effective formation of the political 'party' to summer 1646, when Walwyn and Overton drafted *A Remonstrance of Many Thousand Citizens* as Lilburne was being tried in the Lords. Here, the revolutionary nature of the group was revealed. Developed out of the arbitrary nature of the Lords' dealings with Lilburne, the tract attacked the king and the House of Lords, hinting at the abolition of both. The Commons, though acknowledged as the supreme body because it was the only organ of government embodying any aspect of the will of the people, was derogated for betraying the trust of the people and was urged to dissolve itself. Overton was arrested quickly for his assault on the Lords, but he and Lilburne continued to write. Lilburne attacked the Presbyterian oligarchy in London and the king in *Regal Tyranny Discovered*, published in January 1647. Here, he highlighted the incompatibility of a monarchy with the concept of power deriving from the people, just in time for the king's return from Newcastle. By March 1647 the 'Large petition' with signatories organized on a ward-by-ward basis was the embodiment of Leveller thought at that time. It was addressed to the House of Commons as the sole representative of the people's power, although Walwyn's subtle text did not specifically call for the abolition of the Lords.

The March submission of the petition coincided with the sudden
fury of the army on learning of Parliament's plans for it. It was this
which conveyed power to the Levellers, in much the same way as
the Scottish army had been the muscle of the earlier revolution.
Parliament's own low popular standing and rising costs left Westminster almost powerless. Even so, Parliament voted to commence
disbanding the army three days after the Smithfield riot. Only 5,400
horse and 1,000 dragoons would be kept under arms besides the
garrison forces. The New Model Army foot would be recruited for
Ireland or disbanded. An attempt to replace Fairfax with a Presbyterian officer failed by a margin of only twelve votes. The parliamentary Presbyterians, supported by a Presbyterian City government
and confident that the army was unpopular across the country, felt
certain of their decision and continued attempts to exclude Cromwell,
Ireton and Colonels Fleetwood, Rainsborough and Harrison from
military commands.[26]

Levellers in the city drew up their *Petition of Many Thousands* and
canvassed the London population for signatures, calling for the retention of the army as the main defence against the undoing of the
'good works'. This move may have opened wide fissures in the London political scene, for at the same time the London justices were
encouraging Parliament to hurry up with disbandment. Soldiers
began to make their voices heard; they were politically aware and
had a fine sense of being part of a crusade. However, the army was
not in tune with the Levellers, and for the group of anonymous
soldiers who circulated their statement the preservation of religion
came first, liberty of the people second and parliamentary freedom
third. This situation has to be set in the context of the debate over
the payment of the army.[27] Petitions circulating amongst the rank
and file were gathered together by officers, who deleted the political
demands and framed a set of five demands: a general act of indemnity, payment of arrears, no conscription for volunteers serving in
the army, and no conscription of cavalrymen into the foot for service abroad. They also claimed compensation for maimed soldiers,
widows and orphans and regular pay for themselves. These demands
provoked Presbyterian MPs into ordering Fairfax to suppress the
petition, and as Fairfax reluctantly complied, Holles went further
and drafted a motion which would make a traitor of anyone continuing with the petition. This measure, passed in a 'thin house',
marked an open breach between the Presbyterians and the army.[28]

Plans to create the new army for Ireland widened the breach

further. Waller and Massey were ordered to undertake the work. Although a convinced Presbyterian, Waller was shrewdly aware of how unpopular he was and stepped aside. Skippon, the former major general of the New Model Army, was forced into fronting the operation. It was too late to put a different face on affairs. The creation of the new army was seen for what it was and, coupled with Holles's motion, created a 'revolutionary militancy' in the army, although as has also been pointed out, some sections of the New Model Army were composed largely of former Royalist soldiers who had enlisted late in the war and were diametrically opposed to the radical factions. They were intent on demanding the restoration of the king and committed acts of violence on people who ignored their loyal toasts. But they were a minority, and served to provide the army's opponents with propaganda against army violence, rather than presenting a concerted political consciousness to challenge radical soldiers.[29] In the end only about 7 per cent of the officer corps enlisted for Ireland, and they have been identified as a Presbyterian hard core, with the colonels among them proving unable to persuade many of their subordinates to join them.[30] Historians differ in the extent to which they think Leveller influence pervaded the army. For some the 'thinking' soldier was imbued with Leveller pamphlets, but others believe that although some soldiers were citing Lilburne during this volatile period, they were probably radicals of a different mettle who shared some common ground, as opposed to completely like-minded political creatures.[31] The distinction is important, for it demonstrates the potential for radical politics to develop in ordinary people. Some historians have made much of the relationship between the army and the Levellers, whereas others deny that the army was anything other than self-interested in its relations with radical civilians. As for the Levellers, it has also been suggested by J.P. Kenyon that they were entirely hostile to the army, considering it the root of all ills until late summer 1647. This view is not quite accurate, however. The *Petition of Many Thousands* had called for the retention of the army, and the army for its part was using bits of Leveller philosophy when it suited its needs. In late April soldiers for the time being rejected the more extreme political notions of the Levellers and took the advice of John Rushworth, who suggested that they largely restrict themselves to army concerns. But the army's radicalism cannot be seen purely in terms of its demands for pay and arrears; the Levellers probably used it only to defend themselves against political attack in the summer of

1647.[32] Although it is difficult to discern fully the nature of relations between army radicals and Leveller radicals, some form of relationship definitely existed. By the summer a shared set of ideals had developed, neither imposed by one side on the other nor simply the result of one set of political sophisticates (the Levellers) co-opting a mass with an essentially non-political agenda (the army).

In the spring of 1647 events moved quickly. In the face of the failure to create an army for Ireland, the Presbyterian majority in the Commons forced through a bill awarding the army six weeks' arrears of pay. Parliament continued to act in a high-handed manner, calling three soldiers to account for their language in a leaflet called *Apologie*, in which the authors seemed to imply that Parliament had 'degenerated into tyrants'. The troopers who handed the paper to Skippon implied that few officers had been involved with the drafting of the work and that it was the work of the common soldiers. The army contained a developed organization to support petitioning; regiments had elected representatives, called agitators, to meet with other regiments and discuss political activity. The officer corps reacted by appointing officers drawn from the same regiments to shadow the agitators. Collectively this group of agitators and officers became the General Council of the Army and began to meet together from July 1647. The army regiments were being angered by proceedings against the three trooper commissioners in London. There were thirteen trooper commissioners at Westminster altogether while these three were questioned by the Commons, and through their links with their regiments they stirred up army anger at the Presbyterian threat to imprison their comrades. The Commons as a whole did not agree with Holles's attempt to lock the men up and instead ordered the army leaders at Westminster to return to the army and calm the regiments down. When the colonels and generals followed this instruction, however, they found the army already in an almost mutinous state. The line of communication between the troopers in London and their comrades had been effective, and the news of their treatment had spread. Agitators elected in the regiments of horse appealed to Fairfax for help.

The Presbyterian majority in the City government began to reorganize the leadership of the London trained bands, and Parliament asked the Scots to supply an army to help put down the New Model Army's challenge. London forces were given new trusted leaders, which effectively meant that they were purged of Independents and replaced by sound Presbyterians. There was a ready-made officer corps already to hand in London. Willing volunteers could be drawn from amongst the cadre of unemployed officers discharged from disbanded Parliamentarian forces. These men had gravitated to Westminster to try to secure their back pay and had formed a vocal pressure group, which Parliament now sought to pay off with a grant of £10,000.[33] As the New Model Army managed to secure petitions of support from the counties in which parts of it were based, Parliament began to man the defences of London in an unprecedented manner. Secure in their citadel, so they believed, on 25 May the Presbyterian Parliament announced that disbandment of the New Model Army would begin on 1 June, with eight weeks' back pay issued to the men. Fairfax, trying to strike a balance between the Commons and the disorder threatened by his near-mutinous army, decided that it was necessary to take the army's side for a time. He publicly reaffirmed the order for a general rendezvous of the scattered forces at Newmarket. On 4 June a band of 500 troopers, led by Cornet George Joyce, marched to Holdenby in Northamptonshire where the king was being held and took him into their custody. Neither the king, who may have feared that he was going to be murdered, nor subsequent historians have determined fully the nature of Joyce's authority for this act. There have been attempts to pin responsibility on Oliver Cromwell, but as Charles was taken to Newmarket, where the whole army was gathered, Cromwell was only one beneficiary. The army leaders had gained a major card in their hand, but then so had the radical politicized soldiers, who were not aligned with the army leadership. Cornet Joyce may well have acted out of the soldiers' interest and at the behest of the agitators; he later claimed to be acting as the elected representative of those he led.[34] According to Joyce's own account, the king was about to be seized by a group of Presbyterian officers and his men arrived in the nick of time. Regardless of what Cromwell thought, Fairfax had misgivings and tried to send the party back to Holdenby, but the king himself urged them to press on to Newmarket. Even with the trump card, Fairfax continued to stress the necessity for order and got the army to agree at Newmarket both to a solemn engagement to stand together until their financial demands were met and to continued loyalty to Parliament. Politically, Fairfax had gone about as far as he could or would go. He could not be a part of a revolution, but as long as the demands were just, he was a formidable supporter of the soldiers. The army began to move on London, despite the passage of generous indemnity acts in late May and mid-June by a slightly more tremulous Parliament. At St Albans the army declared:

> We were not a mere mercenary army hired to serve any arbitrary power of state, but called forth and conjured by the several declarations of Parliament to the defence of our own and the people's just rights and liberties. And so we took up arms in judgement and conscience to those ends, and have continued them, and are resolved . . . to assert and vindicate the just power and rights of this kingdom in Parliament, for those common ends premised.[35]

If Fairfax had gone as far as he could at Newmarket, it is clear that others had progressed beyond him. He could read and agree with the statement; as an heir to a noble title, a candidate for the Commons, and a future member of the Lords, he had a clear stake in government. His just rights and liberties were pretty secure by comparison with the vast majority of society, who had few rights and many more duties. Descending through the ranks of the New Model Army, claims to liberties and rights became very different concepts. Beyond the ranks of esquires like Cromwell, gentlemen officers and perhaps even tailors like Joyce – who if fortuitously placed would have a vote in borough elections – stood the great mass of the politically disadvantaged. Some of the horse troopers were husbandmen and may have voted in elections; many more would not, and the footsoldiers would have been almost completely without rights to vote or choose even local government officers. Yet the declaration was on behalf of the whole army, conscious of its part in the ongoing political and religious struggle.

Parliamentary resilience began to crumble. One month's pay was sent to the army at St Albans, but in response the soldiers returned not thanks but instead the demand that eleven MPs, including Holles, be excluded from the House. Protestations of loyalty to the House were giving way to a belief that MPs should deserve loyalty rather than simply expect it, and that the governed should have a contract with government. It was a theory of ascending power put into sharp practice. When Parliament did not reply, the army moved to Uxbridge. On 25 June Parliament rejected the army's declaration, but the eleven MPs withdrew voluntarily. Things calmed down a little, and the army moderated its pronouncements in a manifesto written in the wake of Holles's withdrawal. When Parliament promised to act on pay, Fairfax withdrew to Reading and then Bedford, from where he began to send some of the more radical regiments out to quarters across the south Midlands. Any hopes that Parliament had of outside help faded dramatically when part of the Northern army turned up at Bedford with its commander Pointz a prisoner. All Parliament could do was give Fairfax general command of all the forces in England and Wales.

It was now London that went into a state of apoplexy. Mobs angry at the concessions to the army broke into Parliament. Parliament had been right in thinking that its hard line was a popular one, but it had been powerless to enforce its will, for the very issue which rendered the army unpopular, namely, finance, was the same one which made it angry. The army was unpopular because of the heavy and inefficient tax burden it imposed on citizens. And if Parliament were to concede to the people, the army would not be paid and would instead be disbanded. The army could not be disbanded without some pay, but pay could not be raised in sufficient amounts from an unwilling people. The Presbyterians were straws in the face of two hostile winds. Concessions to one whistled up the other, which was just what happened at the end of July. The mob wanted Parliament to offer the king generous terms so that some form of normality could be re-established, without what they saw as a rebellious army setting a new agenda. In a temporary strengthening of Presbyterian resolve, Holles and his cronies returned to the Commons, defences were manned and Massey was given command. Of course this provoked the army, which promptly reassembled and marched on London. Independent MPs and both Speakers flung in their lot with Fairfax and declared that Parliament was no longer free. As the Londoners pushed into Parliament and brought Westminster to a standstill again, the army leaders drew up a document of their own designed to end the impasse and presented it to the king. These *Heads of the Proposals* were given to the king on 23 July, after the Army Council had accepted them six days earlier. Often acknowledged as the best opportunity yet presented to the king, the document represented only some of the demands of the radical army.[36] Parliaments were to be biennial, called 'as in the late Act was made for triennial Parliaments'; they would sit for a minimum of 120 days and no more than 240 days. Executive government would be in the hands of the king and a Council of State chosen by Parliament, and members' service would be limited to seven years. The Council would have power over the militia and foreign policy for England, Wales and Ireland; although power over the militia was deemed to be in the hands of Parliament, power to 'direct the several and particular powers of the militia' was to be in the hands of the Council. After ten years, the king would again be given power to appoint leaders of the militia. The disestablishment of the church was confirmed, and the Book of Common Prayer was not to be enforced; but although treaties between England and Scotland were to be reaffirmed, the Covenant was not to be compulsorily imposed. There was to be an act of indemnity for Parliamentarians but not for Royalists, although the massive list of proscribed persons included in the Newcastle propositions was scaled down. Essentially, it was a conservative, if Independent, document, firmly grounded in the achievements of the political revolution of 1640–1 in which Cromwell and his colleagues had been involved. It did not travel far along the path sought by the agitators.

As for the king, he was already discussing alternative strategies with different parties, including Parliamentarian Presbyterians and Scots. It was to be his hopes which guided his attitude to the army in the latter discussions – and he filibustered. At the heart of his reply of 9 September was the remark, 'His Majesty. . . finds them the same in effect which were offered to him at Newcastle'. He added that perhaps Parliament should discuss them and try to represent them in a manner 'more capable of His Majesty's full concessions'. But he could not resist an attempt to divide his opponents. Referring to the sections relating to the treaties with Scotland, which were fairly innocuous, and much as they had been when Parliament and the Scots commissioners had agreed upon them at Newcastle, Charles declared, 'His Majesty will very willingly treat upon those particulars with the Scotch Commissioners'. He was behaving in a way which was now quite natural to him when negotiating with any one of his appellants: he was duplicitously playing for time. As Manchester had said, he was still king, and he did not yet see himself as the defeated party. Rather, Charles saw himself as only temporarily devoid of practical support.

While the king considered the proposals, Fairfax pressed on to London and paraded the army on Hounslow Heath on 3 August. Next day he took peaceful possession of the western section of the London lines of defence north of the Thames. Two days later, the New Model Army entered Westminster, where the MPs welcomed Fairfax, and then London, where he took possession of the Tower. Holles and the other ten members most hated by the army had fled the city, and now they were formally expelled. With them out of the way, army business began to dominate much of the proceedings, urged on by the presence of the soldiers in the London area while Fairfax kept a watchful eye on Parliament over in Chelsea. Demands for indemnity were dealt with by the reinforcement of the Indemnity Committee, followed in December by the creation of sub-committees in each county to deal with the cases currently being taken through civil courts. Arrears of pay were attended to, although the money was not easy to raise. Parliament dealt severely with inefficient assessors and collectors, but 'it dared not proceed against the taxpayers themselves'.[37] Doing so would have destroyed any vestige of support which Parliament hoped to retain amongst the hard-pressed people. A month's pay at a time trickled in. It took a long time to reach the pockets of the soldiers, but it did serve to placate many of them, and disbandment of the Northern army, now of course under Fairfax's command, was undertaken, with only six weeks' arrears being handed out. Now that the army felt that it was being listened to, it was willing to put up with previously unacceptable conditions. More radical soldiers, however, were not satisfied with this, nor with the *Heads of the Proposals*, which had been offered to the king largely without their consultation. By October, as the discussions with the king at Hampton Court dragged on fruitlessly, the radical soldiers and the Levellers united on policy and printed the *Case of the Army Truly Stated*. This document, variously described as 'not one of the most readable of the Leveller-Agitator pamphlets' or as a 'lengthy diatribe', accused the grandees of not being able to secure the liberties of the people, because they had so far been unable to secure the arrears of the army.[38] It also questioned how the army leaders could be expected to fulfil the aspirations of the agitators and their constituents if they could present such a set of proposals as the *Heads*. It was this challenge which Fairfax felt the Army Council should debate at a meeting to be held at Putney. Before the meeting convened, however, the Levellers put forward their proposals for a new constitution: *An Agreement of the People for A Firme and present Peace, Upon the grounds of common-right and Freedom*.

The different *Agreements of the People* represents another crucial area of debate. What exactly did the Levellers mean when they referred to the 'freeborn Englishman'? Did they, for instance, ever envisage women having voting rights on a regular basis, rather than irregularly, based on a capricious combination of land ownership and a compliant sheriff? Much of the debate in recent years has concerned the definition of 'freeborn'. At one extreme, it has been suggested that the reference in the later *Agreements* to an electorate of those who did not have to work for somebody else for a living express the original intention of the Levellers.[39] If this is the case, the electorate might have changed very little; perhaps the only impact would have been a more equitable distribution of the vote across the classes already accustomed to voting. In other words, it would have had the effect of ensuring the consistent application of the same qualifications across the country and in every borough. On the other hand, some historians see a more radical approach, opening up the franchise to all men who were not imprisoned or debarred from voting by past Royalist activity.

Proponents of the limited franchise have advanced the theory of possessive individualism. At its core, this means that a person had to be in full possession of himself or herself and not 'owned' or 'directed' by an employer in order to qualify as 'freeborn'.[40] Probably, most women were thus automatically excluded, as the feme covert was under the legal guardianship-tutelage of a male, father or husband. On the other hand, widows or spinsters who had economic independence – women like Jane Kitchen, for instance, or the powerful women in Salwarpe – may well have been eligible. Self-possessed individuals had to derive a living independent of anyone else, so they could not be wage labourers or servants. These assertions have been questioned by a number of historians, who argue that the definition of servant may not have referred to all wage labourers.[41] The Levellers may effectively have restricted the vote to gentry, yeomen, husbandmen and artisans. However, the notion that the Levellers never argued for a greatly expanded electorate contradicts evidence from the Putney debates and the first *Agreement* itself.[42] The terms of reference in the text, which mentioned only the freeborn Englishmen, are unfortunately vague. However, Colonel Rainsborough recognized no such restraints when he argued that every person bound by a government's laws must first have given his assent to such laws. The Levellers, as suggested earlier, believed that power moved upwards to the governing body from below, not downwards from God.[43] Indeed, the Levellers continually deferred to this theory of ascending power, as when they declared that the Commons was the only body enjoying the will of the people. The Lords and the king himself certainly did not agree with this theory; to them, power descended from God through them to the people. There were qualifications to be made, and functions of government which depended on power coming from below – election of MPs and appointment of constables, churchwardens and overseers – could generally be covered by the proviso that all these bodies and officers were called at the behest of the monarch, or were only there to do the monarch's will. Henry and Mary Stewart, who had been dragged before the Dublin courts back in 1640, had been at the receiving end of the 'official view' of the nature of power.

The first *Agreement of the People for A Firme and present Peace* was probably the result of work by the three principal Levellers and a fourth, John Wildman, who arrived late on the political scene. What attracted him to the other three is not easily understood, as he had a less defined political past. He was not a religious man but used the Bible as a source for political argument because it was in effect a standard political text in the period. His republicanism was probably a major factor, and the Levellers were moving towards a republican stance by default through their use of the ascendancy theory. Maurice Ashley declared that Wildman was actually an incorrigible conspirator.[44]

The *Agreement*'s four principal clauses claimed that the government should be in the hands of a unicameral assembly. This assembly, known as the Representative, had certain duties and limitations to its power. Duties included the protection of religious toleration, responsibility for dealing with crimes committed during the war, and equal application of laws without any advantage being accrued by anybody from estate, tenure, social status or charter. Amongst its limitations was the inability to impose conscription of the freeborn.

The Levellers saw presenting the *Agreement* to the army as a positive step towards gaining the consent – the agreement – of the people. The army was a cross-section of male society, and the Army Council was a cross-section of the army. The earlier Leveller text, signed by soldiers and civilians, had been presented to Fairfax, inspiring the idea that Leveller proposals should be discussed by the Council at a meeting to be held in Putney church. In the last days of October, the Council met with representatives of the Levellers. Fortunately, minutes taken at the meeting have survived, providing a near-verbatim account of their democratic demands. Here the Levellers – Wildman, Rainsborough, Edward Sexby, John Allen and Maximillian Petty – were confronted by the grandees – Cromwell, who chaired the meeting, and his son-in-law Henry Ireton. From the very start Cromwell questioned whether they could even discuss the *Agreement* at all, arguing that the army could not possibly enter into any form of agreement or engagement because it was already bound by the engagement to Parliament made at Newmarket, and the *Agreement* committed them to dissolving the present House and creating a new government. Eventually this blocking tactic was circumvented, but Ireton then launched an attack on the first principles, particularly the vague suffrage reference. Clearly, to him it was not obvious that 'freeborn' meant a fully self-possessed individual. Rather, to Ireton it spelled anarchy through the eradication of the fundamental political relationship between franchise and property. Rainsborough turned the principle around by making the following declaration:

> for really I think that he that the poorest he that is in England hath a life to live, as the greatest he; and therefore truly, sir, I think it's clear, that every man that is to live under a government ought first by his own consent to put himself under that government.[45]

Nevertheless, discussion of the *Agreement* centred on the first clause. Cromwell and Ireton successfully prevented the agitators and Levellers from being able to secure the army's agreement to the propositions. The Putney meeting broke up without any movement towards revolutionary change. The rendezvous that was to follow for the soldiers to give their consent to the *Agreement* was cancelled. Instead, the army was summoned to three different places where Fairfax addressed the soldiers and rejected the Levellers, declaring in his pamphlet *Remonstrance concerning the late Discontents and Distractions in the army . . .* that the Commons was as near an equally elected body as possible. Regiments which did turn up at the Corkbush Field rendezvous against orders on 15 November were harangued by Fairfax and Cromwell. Leveller sea-green ribbons and copies of the *Agreement of the People* were torn from the soldiers' hats by loyal officers, and one of the 'ringleaders' was shot. In the face of this onslaught the soldiers' resistance collapsed. The radicals were caught off guard, while the more conservative soldiers were cowed into obedience, perhaps shocked that their radical colleagues suddenly appeared to be out of step with the seemingly sympathetic leadership. It has been argued that in any case a divergence of interest between the army radicals and the Levellers was apparent long before Ware, and that sympathy towards the shot Leveller soldier may have been slight. This split had arisen partly because the Levellers and the army disagreed on the need for a strong central authority. In the army's view a strong authority, as within the army itself, was necessary for good government, and specifically for the efficient centralized collection of taxes for army pay. By autumn, although the tax was only trickling in, it was beginning to reach soldiers. Suggestions that this be dealt with by decentralized bodies with a greater emphasis on consent, which if asked for now would almost certainly not be given, sat uneasily with the soldiers' need for money.[46] However, the soldiers' inaction at Ware could also be explained by their awareness that the situation had suddenly changed dramatically. On 11 November, the king escaped from Hampton Court. The last thing that the New Model Army needed now was disunity. There was little point in discussing a new England if the old defeated England of Charles I was about to raise its head again. The Leveller–army relationship had not faded, but the army leaders were on the defensive at Putney, and they realized that their minority group was being reduced, not increased, by Ireton's long-winded defence of property. It may be that it was the frightening time alone which secured army support for Fairfax, for radicalism was still strong in the army, and was to reappear dramatically within a year.[47]

11

Engagement to Execution

Sufferings . . . under the tyranny and cruel oppressions of those that pressed ye late unlawful ingagement[1]

Relations between the Scots and the Westminster Parliament declined after the defeat of the king, and this was one of the main factors which drove the four nations on to their next series of crises. Although they had been consulted over the negotiations at Newcastle and were pleased to press the terms on the king, the Scots realized that the arrangements for intervention in England were not reciprocal. When they had asked for English aid at the time of Montrose's and MacColla's greatest triumphs, they received short shrift.[2] No help was forthcoming, and some of the English had even encouraged them to withdraw from England altogether, even though the Scots had offered to allow the Committee of Both Kingdoms to direct actions north of the border, as it did in England and Wales. Whilst the Scots may have had a four-nations view of the conflict, the English Parliamentarians seem to have been preoccupied only with two. No really open breach occurred until after the English civil war was over, even though the king was hoping to negotiate with leading Covenanters after Kilsyth. Although there was little chance of that, rumours circulated in England while the king was at Newcastle that he was negotiating a separate treaty with the Scots commissioners. They were based on misunderstandings; the king had embroiled the French in discussions through the agency of the queen in late 1645. These had been a contributing factor in the king's journey to Newark and his surrender to the Scots there, even though he believed that he would get a better reception than he actually did. The proposals on offer to the king through the agency of the French via their intermediary Montereul were distinctly different. If the king agreed to a religious settlement in both countries, the Scots would press for compromise on the civil issues. This position may help us to understand the Scots' perception of their role as a religious one. They may not have considered civil matters in England important and probably regarded them as beyond their proper concern. The religious issue alone was the one in which the Scots felt they had a role, so if the king and queen agreed to a religious settlement with them, then the Scots would present their proposals to the English. The French offered to help 'with banners unfurled,'[3] if war came about between the Covenanters and the English as a result of this secret negotiation. The English proposals to the king had offered no leeway on the civil issues and were actually less stringent than the Scots would have liked on the religious ones. To the English, the Scottish belief that the religious issues were paramount, while the rest were negotiable, was worrying and undermined the political aims that had been at the root of the war. For their part, behind Scots fears about the English attitude to religion lay the debate over the nature of the post-war church. They were not convinced of the fortitude of the English Presbyterians, who appeared willing to compromise on the control of the church and let it remain in the hands of Parliament rather than be separate from the state as the Kirk was.

Views of the Scottish attitude to the Newcastle propositions differ. On the one hand, it has been argued that the Scots urged the king to agree to the Newcastle propositions, whereas on the other, the Scots' disappointment with the king's failure to sign the treaty has been emphasized.[4] It is possible that they were more disappointed at the king's refusal to come to a settlement at all either with them or with the English. New negotiations between the Scots and the king got off the mark quickly after the king was abandoned at Newcastle at the end of January 1647. These were spurred on later in the year because leading Covenanters were worried that the *Heads of the Proposals* were the work of the Independent faction and offered no firm religious guarantees for Scotland. Leading Covenanters, including the Earls of Loudoun, Lauderdale and Lanark, were concerned when they heard that the king had praised the *Heads of the Proposals*. It was praise made for their consumption; for as we have seen, he had actually likened them to the Newcastle terms he had rejected. The three Scottish lords met the king at Hampton Court, where he had been moved as the army had advanced on London. Charles authorized them to discuss with Ormond a plan to lead a Royalist revival in Ireland. The former Lord Lieutenant was prepared to return to Ireland if the Scots invaded England in the king's name. The Scottish lords tried to persuade the king to flee north to Scotland, but although he agreed to go as far as Berwick, he was put off by their demand that he sign the Covenant, and that unless he made some concessions he would be a virtual prisoner there too.[5] Instead, when the king did escape on 11 November 1647, he 'showed his lingering distrust for the Scots by turning south'. Charles fled to the Isle of Wight, possibly in the hope that the governor of Carisbrooke Castle would help him reach France.

From what turned out to be just a new prison at Carisbrooke, the king offered terms to the English Parliament, which included the establishment of a Presbyterian system for three years, pending a final settlement. He then wrote to the Scottish lords claiming that his offer to the English was only an opening proposal which might be altered later. In an effort to win back their favour, Charles suggested that his flight to the Isle of Wight had not changed his position regarding their discussions in October.[6] In the meantime the Westminster Parliament had drafted new proposals, to be known as the Four Bills. These in effect consolidated the main civil issues of the previous treaties it had offered the king. The first gave Parliament a twenty-year control of the militia, the second dealt with the renunciation of the king's wartime proclamations against Parliament, the third annulled wartime ennoblements and the fourth removed most of the rest of the king's control over assemblies of Parliament which had not already been eroded by the Triennial Act and the Act against Dissolution. If the king agreed to these proposals, a series of supplementary issues would be opened up for discussion, including the establishment of a Presbyterian church and the king's acceptance of Anglo-Scottish treaties made during the war. The Scottish commissioners did not like these bills, however, and in their eyes the reduction of ecclesiastical matters to a supplementary issue seemed particularly worrying. Surely, they argued, they should 'build the House of God before our own'.[7] The Westminster Parliament reacted angrily to such criticisms, and MP Henry Marten suggested that the Scots were making more exorbitant demands than the king, and that the Solemn League, but a temporary expedient, was no longer applicable to the relationship between England and Scotland.

When the English commissioners left Westminster to present the Four Bills to the king at Carisbrooke Castle, the Scottish lords followed, hoping to negotiate a separate treaty with Charles under the guise of presenting their objections to the Four Bills. By the end of the year the king was able to play the English and Scottish treaties

Plate 12 Charles I imprisoned on the Isle of Wight,
© Hulton Deutsch Collection Ltd, London.

off against each other, and the Scottish lords came to a hasty agreement with him. Known as the Engagement, it ensured that the king would only confirm the Solemn League and Covenant in England through Parliament, but it did not compel either the king or his subjects to sign it. This represented a major concession, probably reluctantly made, by the Scots negotiators, because the king had pretended that he liked the Four Bills. On the other hand, the king agreed to further political union between the southern and northern kingdoms, involving such practical measures as having Scots on the English Privy Council and Englishmen on the Scottish Privy Council and ensuring equal representation in discussions of foreign policy (Welshmen were probably being included as Englishmen in this case). Free trade between Scotland and England (this presumably included Wales too) was also to be introduced. As with many of the political matters, this was in line with the ambitions of James VI and I. Of more immediate consequence was the Scottish promise that if the Westminster assembly did not agree to such terms, Charles would be restored to his English and Welsh throne by force of Scottish arms.

Charles then rejected the Four Bills. The Westminster Parliament, struck by his duplicity, decided that it could no longer sanction discussions with the king. Though ignoring calls from Sir Thomas Wroth that the king be impeached, on 3 January the Commons took the Vote of No Addresses. No one from then on could hold discussions with the king without Parliament's sanction. Parliament itself would not hold any more talks with him and, furthermore, would receive no messages from the king. The Lords demurred, convinced that at the back of the proposal was an intention to abolish the monarchy, and along with it the House of Lords itself; as Northumberland had worryingly pointed out, by holding no discussions with the king Parliament had already divorced the monarchy from government. It was unwise, as the upper chamber pointed out, to dissolve one form of government without having another to put in its place.[8] However, the deployment of the army in Westminster persuaded the Lords to accept the vote, but two of the stalwarts of the first civil war, the Earl of Stamford and Lord Robartes, withdrew from the House. The recalcitrance of the Scots, too, demanded action, and the last political vestige of a bi-national executive, the Committee of Both Kingdoms, was abolished. In its place the existing English members along with three newly nominated Independents continued the meet at Derby House; they became known as the Derby House Committee.

The Scottish lords had conceded a great deal without the sanction of the Estates or the Edinburgh Parliament, and when they told the Committee about the Engagement on 21 January, they lied about it, suggesting that the king had satisfied Scottish demands. As the Scottish nobles returned to Scotland, they opened negotiations on military preparations with English Royalists and dissatisfied Presbyterians. In France too, the queen began to raise money for a renewed war. By mid-February, the Committee of Estates had swung around behind the Engagement, ignoring the way in which it did not meet the earlier requirements. The Kirk was not so sanguine, however, and before Parliament met, it declared the religious provisions inadequate. This view held sway amongst the Covenanter grandees – Argyll, Balermino and Lothian – but they were now in a minority. A pacific movement amongst ministers encouraged the Scottish government to try to restore the working relationship with England, which had deteriorated rapidly since the signing of the

Engagement. Argyll and his supporters, on the other hand, suggested using David Leslie and the army to overawe the Committee, just as the New Model Army had overawed the English Parliament, but little came of this notion. Despite Argyll's attempt to pack his own supporters into the new Parliament, there was a majority for the Engagement of about thirty-five, with about half of the shire and burgh members and three-quarters of the nobles backing the treaty.[9] Moreover, Engagers packed the executive committee created to direct the constitutional and religious implications of the treaty. This had been established as a sop to calm the fears of the Kirk, but was largely emasculated by the removal of three of Argyll's original five supporters nominated to it. However, the Engagers could not command control everywhere, and they could not win over the army. Leslie refused to accept the Engagement, as did Leven; but Middleton, who had worked with Leslie in Scotland, refused to sign a petition condemning the Engagement. Opposition to the Engagement within the army was not united however, and any plan to use the army as muscle to force Parliament to abandon the Engagement collapsed. In April 1648 the Scottish Parliament passed an act condemning the English Parliament for not imposing the Covenant and suggesting that the New Model 'sectarian army responsible for such actions' was a threat to the security of Scotland.[10] The Kirk quickly, and with little difficulty, pointed out that it was ironic for Parliament to criticize its English counterpart for not imposing the Covenant on the country, since it had singularly failed to impose it on the king. Royalist nobles like Traquair also refused to accept the logic of going to war in defence of a Covenant which they themselves had refused to sign. Hamilton, of course, could happily support the actions of the Parliament, being both a Royalist and a Covenanter. At the end of the month, English Royalist soldiers who had travelled to Scotland in the wake of the Scottish commissioners had been banded together and sent to capture Berwick and Carlisle. The Celtic kingdoms were now in the forefront of a second civil war. In Wales Pembroke Castle was already held against the Westminster Parliament and the New Model Army.

In Scotland the act creating a new army was passed on 4 May. It was to be about 30,000 strong and was to incorporate the already existing Covenanting army. Leven, whose opposition to the Engagement was known, had been passed over as commander at an early stage. The command was offered to Leslie, even though he was also known to be an opponent, but he refused. Hamilton was then given the command; Middleton, Leslie's lieutenant in 1646–8, was put in charge of the horse, and William Baillie was given the foot. The levies for the soldiers were in the hands of Edinburgh Council within four days. The levy of 1,200 men was identical to that of 1643, when the Covenanting army for England was raised. Four days after that a levy of £40,000 Scots was being raised in the city. By 9 June the full implications of the new war began to be clear. The levy for a year's monthly maintenance came to £53,475 Scots (£4,456-5s sterling), on top of which were four months' quartering charges of £6,000 Scots (£500 sterling), with the expenses of collection computed at £15,525 Scots (£1,293-15s sterling). This whole sum was subdivided amongst the three divisions of Edinburgh within the walls. Canongate, the Pleasance and North Leith, and South Leith. The former bore the brunt, with a total of £46,913 Scots (c.£3,909 sterling); the two latter divisions paid £9,043 Scots (£753-10s sterling) each: speedy collection was urged. At the same time, perhaps in an attempt to minimize the disorder in the town caused by the arrival of so many Royalists of different ilks and political and religious outlooks, the burgh declared that:

> noe person quhatsumere efter publication heirof sall take upon hand to weir any plaids about their heides in such commoun streits or open mercattes under paine of confiscatioun thairof and farder punishment.

Officers who neglected to enforce this order were to be imprisoned.[11] There was opposition to the Engagement and its implications in the city. That it entailed accepting the Marquis of Hamilton as a military and political leader so enraged Alexander Denholme, an Edinburgh baxter (baker), that he accosted Hamilton in the streets late at night. There he abused the marquis with rash words and behaviour.[12]

In Glasgow, too, the implications of the war became apparent.[13] The order for the levy from the Clydesdale shire war committee reached the city on 16 May 1648. The Engagement was not popular there either. The town made a supplication to the shire committee a week later, claiming: 'we find a general unwillingness to engadge in this war through want of satisfactioune in the laufulnes thairof'. Parliament, the council suggested, should look into the 'laufulnes of necessitie of [the] engagement'.[14] Nevertheless, the burden continued, with the excise being levied in the town and landward areas of Lanarkshire, as well as the 'pendicles and liberties', at £1,000 Scots

(£83-6s-8d sterling) per month.[15] In the rural Lowlands, too, the war effort was making itself felt by the early summer. At Dolphinton a party of horse under a Captain Baillie descended on the town to get people to sign the 'unlawful engagement'. After the war the account of the sufferings was sent to the Committee of Accounts and Monies, listing 'the sufferngs of the parish . . . under the tyrany and cruell oppressions of those quch pressed ye late unlawful Ingagement And also the damages . . . by them and by yt army ye english forces and Colonel Montgomeries' Regiment'.[16] Baillie's troopers took one horse, worth £9 Scots, from William O'Bryan while also costing the village £100 Scots. They were followed by Captain Maxwell's party of horse, which cost 30 shillings Scots a day each, amounting to a total of £88 Scots. Maxwell then sent another troop which charged the same rates, for a total of £96-13s-4d Scots. Further quartering of troops preparing for the invasion of England, including a troop of horse from Ireland, cost a further £962-16s-0d Scots. More horrendous was the attack on three men by soldiers from Captain Smith's Irish troop:

> it. ye horse troop did mutilatt ad disable ane man of the fingers of his right hand and cittit Robert Sim and yrby still will be unable to labour for his living and pitiful is woundit and other cutt Wm Andersone both in hed and armes.

There is an implication that the wounds inflicted upon the first man were politically motivated and related to an unwillingness to sign the Engagement. The document does demonstrate that the community was worried about the longer-term implications of the visitations. The wounded men were included because their disabilities were likely to cost the village in welfare provision; the sum estimated at the time was £40 Scots. There was also a concern that the meadow was being destroyed. Six separate parties of horse were alleged not only to have eaten the corn in the fields but also to have destroyed the meadows.

In Wales seeds of discontent amongst certain groups were seen in 1647. In June the county of Glamorgan had been wracked by a revolt led by prominent Royalist gentry, including men like Sir Henry Stradling (former governor of Carlisle) and Sir Richard Bassett (the last Royalist governor of Cardiff), who had been displaced by the Peaceable Army in 1645. Their rebellion was said to be an attack on the work of the county committee and its alleged failure to submit accounts. Other fears contributed to their reasoning: as the rising got under way in early June, they also claimed that the abduction of the king from Holdenby House on 4 June caused many to fear that a new revolution was afoot.[17] The insurgents' principal excuse for the rising, however, was that the committee was oppressive and burdensome. Taking their cue from the Parliamentarian Colonel Edward King's attack on the Lincolnshire committee, they claimed to be rising not against the government itself but against the committee. Indeed, they suggested, they were acting in the name of the king and Fairfax. Their opponents believed differently. Colonel Rowland Laugharne said that they had rebelled because the committee had been lenient towards the Royalists. The rebels countered by claiming that the committee had abused its power when deciding who was a delinquent, criminalizing the wealthiest in the county in order to extract taxation from them. The committeemen did this, they suggested, to make themselves wealthy rather than for the good of the state or the county. The revolt broke out when some members of the county gentry, who it was later alleged were about to be imprisoned by the committee, sent out warrants on 13 June to the high constables for a general muster at Cowbridge. Some 1,500–2,000 men were raised and led to Llandaff. The leaders of the insurgents then appealed to the local Parliamentarian leaders – Laugharne at Carmarthen and Colonel Pritchard, the governor of Cardiff – to join them. They then moved on Cardiff, where Laugharne advanced upon them. At Laugharne's approach, large numbers of the rebels began to return home, and the leaders fled the county. It was an easy victory, and rebel claims that the whole of south Wales might have risen in revolt are questionable. After all, the rebels' appeal to Monmouthshire to join them was unsuccessful.

However, underlying dissatisfaction with the way committees were running Welsh counties, which had provoked the leaders of Glamorgan into rising with their armed force, continued into the next year and provided the support for the rebellion of a very different kind of rebel leader. Laugharne, the man at the very centre of quelling the Glamorgan revolt, himself went into active opposition in 1648. His rising set off rebellion across south-west Wales in the spring. The focus was Pembrokeshire, the heartland of Welsh Parliamentarianism. The instigator of the rebellion was one of Laugharne's closest military associates, his brother-in-law Colonel John Poyer, at that time the governor of Pembroke Castle. Poyer, a local merchant, was opposed by other prominent families in town, whose loyalty to

Parliament had not been as constant as his own. Members of the Lort family and John Elliot claimed that Poyer had misappropriated profits from the demesne lands of Carew Castle. This created in Poyer a certain degree of paranoia. He began to believe that people were out to kill him and became so frightened by this propect that when ordered to surrender the castle to a section of the New Model Army under Adjutant General Fleming on 22 February as part of a routine handing over of fortresses, he refused. His men, like so many other soldiers, were owed back pay, money which had not come to them as swiftly as it had to the New Model Army troops. Poyer refused to hand over the castle until arrears had been settled, but he also craved indemnity for himself against any attacks by his local political enemies.[18] Almost as soon as he did this, Royalists preparing for the fruits of the Engagement began to encourage Poyer's stance. Parliament may well have exacerbated the problem by passing an ordinance declaring him a traitor if he did not immediately render the castle to Fleming.[19] Effectively, there was now no way for him to turn. The more hostile Poyer became towards Parliament, the more the Royalists' hopes grew. What began as a legitimate set of military grievances, and perhaps paranoia on the part of Poyer himself, became transformed by propaganda and Royalist encouragement. Perhaps Poyer too began to see himself as standing not for his own and his soldiers' rights but for something greater. 'Great England's honour lies in the dust and little England lends a hand to raise it up', wrote Royalists, referring to the Pembrokeshire 'rebellion'.[20] When attempts were made to disband Laugharne's own forces, many of the soldiers began to drift towards Pembrokeshire, identifying with Poyer's demand for back pay. This prompted Poyer to drive Fleming from Pembroke town, where he and his men had been billeted during the dispute.[21] On 10 April Poyer declared for the king. As he did so the loyalties of Laugharne – already in London at an inquiry into his supposed Royalist leanings – and his second, Rice Powell, wavered. Powell led his men in an attack on Carmarthen, and then seized Swansea and Neath.

The forces now gathered around Poyer and Powell – and Laugharne, after he had raced back to Wales – numbered 8,000 and consisted of a mixed bag of Royalists, Presbyterians angry at the emasculation of the Presbyterian faction in Parliament, former clubmen and disgruntled soldiers. They did not constitute an effective force, however. Many may have been pressed into service, and few substantial Royalists with the ability to command loyalty amongst lesser Royalists had joined the revolt.[22] In any case the revolt was not able to spread far enough for this to become a recruitment problem. Although Fleming's forces were defeated and he was killed when trying to curb rebel advances, Colonel Thomas Horton's forces met with greater success. Laugharne and Horton clashed on 8 May at St Fagans near Llandaff, scene of the dispersal of the Glamorgan rebels in 1647. A hard-fought battle, it has been claimed to be the largest on Welsh soil during the period, bigger than the battle of Montgomery in 1644. In the end the Parliamentarian forces won; the hastily assembled groups of disparate rebels may have represented a wide political spectrum of opposition, but they lacked resolution and training when pitched against New Model Army regiments. Oliver Cromwell arrived in Horton's wake to take over the campaign in south Wales and follow the retreating Laugharne to Pembroke, while Horton tackled Powell at Tenby. By this time, however, the new war had spread into England.

Discontent over taxation had not evaporated during the latter part of 1647; indeed, other anger had fed into it. Royalists had latched on to a series of riots over Christmastide, and Glamorganshire's criticisms of county committees had not been isolated. Committees were disliked across the social spectrum, for reasons ranging from dislike of the taxation levels to dissatisfaction with their social composition. Towards the end of the first civil war, several counties had claimed that the committee set over them was of low social standing. In Leicestershire in 1644, a probably Royalist-inspired petition claimed that the committeemen had few Leicestershire connections: the committees' 'defects of number, acquaintance amongst us, and interests in the county, cannot afford us any probable hopes of preservation'.[23] Although some of the committeemen there continued to hold some substantial estates in the county, they were certainly not well versed in administrative experience when put on the committee.[24] In Warwickshire, both the upper and lower echelons of county government were affected by the declining status of the participants. Of the forty-two men appointed to the commission of the peace between the war and the Restoration, only four had been JPs before the war, and eighteen post-war justices were not even from amongst those identified as gentry in a study of Warwickshire society.[25] A study of Kent has mapped out the decline of the status of governors via committee statistics. The number of *nobiles minores*, titled gentry like knights, declined, while the number of esquires, coincidentally the backbone of the Royalist war effort in the Midlands, increased on the committee throughout the war years and after.[26] As property, status and government went hand in hand in the seventeenth century, this perception is important. Conflicts after the war between traditional elements of county government and the committees were crucial to the groundswell of popular resentment. One of the reasons the New Model Army soldiers felt persecuted in 1647 was that sufficient members of the old elites, including quiescent Royalists who had eschewed public involvement with the cause from 1642 to 1646, were still involved in county government. Such people, acting as JPs, were able to see to the prosecution of soldiers in civil courts for their own political motives, at a time when their attitudes should have been out of step. Not every county was dominated by a traditional governor-versus-committee split. In Somerset, for example, the grip of the Parliamentarians in the county was so firm in the years after the war that the committee was able to influence the creation of the first commission of the peace. There the conflict was between radical Independents, centred on Colonel John Pyne, and Presbyterians, led by Sir John Horner and William Strode. It was to be Pyne's men who packed the bench from 1646 onwards, minimizing dissent.[27]

Attack on the legality of the regime and its organs of administration was multifaceted. At one level Judge David Jenkins, claimed by Parliamentarians to be the major influence behind the Glamorgan revolt, was claiming that the law courts in London had no legal basis, because Parliament had assumed kingly power with no legal right. On another level, traditional meetings such as quarter sessions were being used to formulate county petitions against county committees. On a third level, the mob itself was still attacking the function of the new government. Into this series of oppositionist stances Royalists, for direct political motives sometimes only tenuously linked to the motives of the other three, attempted to insinuate counter-revolution.

In Devon inexperience of governance led the committee to make mistakes. Some members were merchants who not only had their own business in Plymouth to attend to, but were not acquainted with the techniques of county government. One excellent study of administration in Devon has argued that the committee was very much Plymouth-based and that the north of the county was 'least-governed'.[28] Moreover, these men were not those who ran the quarter sessions, and since they were based in Plymouth, they were geographically divorced from the centre of county government and the seat of the sessions in Exeter. Inexperience was partly responsible for failures in administration during the post-war years, which involved the county in difficult civil–military relations in early 1648. In February a petition drafted by some members of the committee and two JPs to complain about the assessments and about the quartering of soldiers in the county was circulated, but although many people signed it, it was never sent on to Parliament. Instead it was headed off by the intervention of Sir Hardress Waller, military commander in the county, who explained diplomatically that defaulters, not the officials, were to blame for the incidence of free quarter. The petition came to rest in the quarter sessions papers.[29] Even so, Exeter demonstrated considerable civic resistance to billeting troops sent during May 1648 under Waller's command to guard the west as Cromwell's forces moved into south Wales.

In Norwich it was the abolition of the Christmas holiday which acted as the inspiration for rioting. Presbyterians felt that Christmas was an unnecessary holiday period, not sanctioned by the Bible, and given over to disruptive feasts and social licence of all forms. General clamour for religious reformation, even after the Solemn League had bound England to further godly reform, had tended to concentrate upon the many saints' days still littering the Reformation calendar, but as a result of unofficial action in 1644, some London shops stayed open on 25 December. The holiday was abolished with the issue of the Directory of Worship, published on 4 January 1645, which allowed only Sundays as holidays and sanctioned monthly fasts. However, that year Christmas was observed by many people, and many shops remained closed. The following year more people ignored the traditional holiday, but at the end of 1647, dissatisfaction with the regime caused popular festivity to combine with rebellion.[30] At Norwich, as Christmas 1647 approached, the mayor was presented with a petition asking that Christmas be observed in the city. John Utting could not agree to it, nor did he take much notice of a second petition demanding that he enforce the use of the Directory of Worship, which a faction in the town felt was being ignored. When he took no action to stop unofficial celebrations, the Puritan faction complained to Parliament, which finally summoned the mayor the following April to explain his inaction. On 23 April a crowd gathered in the city and locked the gates to prevent the mayor from being taken to London. The crowd shouted that it would purge the town government and throw 'roundheads' out. They then attacked the houses of leading aldermen. When it was rumoured that troops were on the way, the crowd attacked the committee house, where an arsenal was stored. As the troopers from East Dereham arrived in the town, fighting developed, and in the confusion the committee arsenal was blown up, killing about forty people. It is clear that the men, women and children of Norwich who were fighting the troopers came from a range of political alignments, and that only some of them were genuine Royalists, even if the king's name was shouted by a good many during the day. Local interests, particularly the insult felt by Parliament's summoning of the mayor, have been suggested by one historian of the county as having provided the spark for the rebellion.[31] But it is surely the case that there was widespread objection to the post-war administration of the town, even if the committee house itself was only attacked because it held ammunition. As the papers of the committee were ransacked and burned, the interests of the people may have been served in other ways too.

In London and Canterbury too, Christmas was the occasion for rioting. At Canterbury the day saw traditional football games played and holly bushes set at doors in the usual manner in contravention of the Christmas ban by the county committee.[32] Disobedience spread over the ensuing days, during which the Puritan ministers were mocked and pelted with mud, the aldermen driven from their homes and the magazine seized. Royalists seized their opportunity, claiming that Charles I was about to be restored to power with the aid of the Scots and that he would soon be in Kent. It took several days for the committee to restore order in the county once the rebelliousness in Canterbury had spread through the region. The members of the city committee had wavered in their loyalty; although not prepared to support the Royalists in their attempt to hold the city against the county committee, they had offered mediation. Sir Anthony Weldon and the county committee were in no such mood. The trained bands were assembled and confronted the rebellious town. Isolated from any outside support, the Royalists were forced to surrender, and Weldon took his revenge. The rebel leaders were incarcerated in Leeds Castle, and the defences of Canterbury were slighted.

In London, Christmas Day celebrations at St Margaret's, Westminster, provoked the MPs into arresting the churchwardens and a clergyman. Holly and ivy decked the city streets, and the mayor was insulted as he tried to remove it all. Despite the raising of the militia of London and Westminster, Christmas was treated as a holiday, and few shops opened on 25 December. The same pattern was witnessed at Ipswich and Bury St Edmunds, where youths wandered the streets armed with spiked clubs to ensure that shops stayed closed.[33] Christmas riots represented two things: a general dissatisfaction with a regime that seemed incapable of returning England and Wales to normality, and a specific dislike of the Presbyterian system. Both probably represented reactions to symptoms rather than a deeply held opposition to either Parliament or Presbyterianism. Both were very closely associated with unpopular features of post-war life. The heavy and continuing burden of taxation and/or the billeting of a seemingly overweening army were associated with Parliament. The prohibition of festivities was blamed on the Directory of Worship. It has been argued that the effects of the changes wrought by the Directory were likely to be limited. Traditional Book of Common Prayer services continued to be held in a large number of East Anglian parishes in the 1650s, despite the issue of the Directory. On the one hand, it has been suggested that this happened largely because the new religious regime did not create any alternative festivals to replace those that it proscribed.[34] Conversely, a monumental survey of churchwardens' accounts from across England and Wales provides evidence that the Directory of Worship was having a major effect on the practice of the church, with a steady decline in festival services, especially in the post-war years.[35] Both these points of view rely on evidence of a degree of popular support for the traditional church in the post-war years and continuing into the 1650s, even if the Directory was succeeding in changing the religious landscape. The war and Christmas therefore caused a very noticeable change in society, providing both a religious and political symbol with which to taunt the regime. Support for the traditional church may well have been fading, and it may well have become less politicized in succeeding years. It certainly was no longer universally bound up with Royalism, no matter how much the Royalists in the winter of 1647–8 wanted it to be or tried to make it. Riot and Royalism made for strange bedfellows, but these were adverse times for Royalists.

Nevertheless, the attempts to capitalize on the discomfort people were feeling towards the regime were abundant. Rumours of Royalist landing circulated in Kent and in south Wales. Farther north, the gathering Scottish and English forces which were causing so much disruption in the Lowland shires were looked on either as ominous signs of a new war or as beacons of hope. In England and north Wales, rebellion broke out from the same mixture of motives as it did in south Wales, with the Royalists trying to make it somehow all look related to a general desire for the return of the king to power. The small amount of actual plotting that had occurred produced a series of mistimed revolts: seizures of ports like Deal and Walmer and castles like Pontefract, and risings like that in Kent and the Midlands. If the New Model Army had been disbanded, then these pinpricks might have succeeded in destabilizing the regime sufficiently to cause it either to collapse or to waver enough to offer lenient terms to the king. But if the New Model Army had been disbanded, many of these revolts might not have occurred at all. In the end the New Model Army not only existed, it was also too well organized for these mistimed risings to cause it much trouble. 'Kent exploded' on 11 May, just as a significant part of the New Model Army reached Chepstow on the way to deal with Pembroke, just in time for the opening stages in the trial of the Christmas rioters at the assizes. Here the Grand Jury, charged with its usual task of deciding whether a case was a *billa vera* (true bill) or *ignoramus*, decided the latter, effectively setting the prisoners free because there was no case to answer. This prompted rejoicing and petitioning. On 24 April, Parliament had received a petition from Essex, signed by 30,000 people, calling for the army to disband. The people of Kent now drafted a similar one, and the people of Surrey followed suit on 12 May. Rioting spread over the south-east, and the youths of Bury St Edmunds went on the rampage again, causing the Suffolk trained bands to be called out to deal with them. In Kent rioting spread over the county, reaching the environs of London by the end of the month. On 29 May 10,000 people gathered at Burnham Heath and elected the Earl of Norwich as their leader. Fairfax was soon there with a sizeable force, even though Cromwell had taken 5,000 to Wales and John Lambert had gone to Yorkshire with another three regiments of horse and two foot regiments. On 30 May he captured about 1,000 of the Burnham Heath rebels and pursued the rest towards Maidstone. The rebel forces now held Rochester Castle, as well as Deal, Walmer and Sandwich. Dover was besieged, but Fairfax did not linger; while setting troops to watch the garrisons, he pressed on after Lord Norwich. At Maidstone he caught up, and on 1 June the heart of the rebellion was crushed, only three days after it had really got going. Those forces that were not defeated in the streets of the town melted away – some men to their homes, others to the garrisons on the coast. A hardier group gravitated to Canterbury, but since Weldon had destroyed its defensive capability, it could not be held against an attacking force, and Norwich led most off to Gravesend. The city then surrendered to Fairfax.

The fleet, which had almost completely sided with Parliament in 1642, was also embroiled in the events of 1648. In late 1647, when the Independents gained ascendancy at Westminster, the admiralty commission was reconstituted to reflect the new balance of power. It then summoned Vice-Admiral Sir William Batten to answer general charges that he was disaffected, but also to explain his conduct regarding fleeing Presbyterian MPs in August 1647. His vessel had stopped the ship hired by the MPs, but after examining their passes had allowed them to proceed. By threatening to bring charges against him, the commissioners persuaded Batten to resign, but he had already received 'a dramatic indication of his popularity' when a hundred naval officers publicly supported his action in letting the MPs go.[36] In Batten's place the Commons nominated the Leveller Colonel Thomas Rainsborough, who had good naval credentials but poor political ones, at least according to the Lords, who refused his appointment after the Ware mutiny. The Commons gave him the command anyway, and Rainsborough took up the post energetically. He was reappointed when the summer guard fleet was created in the spring. However, he was not particularly popular, and Parliament's treatment of Batten still rankled with many commanders at sea. This fact, together with the implications of the fleet being sent out in Parliament's name in the wake of the Vote of No Addresses, probably accounted for the ensuing revolt. When the Kent revolt broke out, captains in some ports allowed rebels to take possession of their vessels. Furthermore, when dock officials at Chatham rebelled, ships there joined the rebels too. Worse was to come. When Rainsborough went ashore to inspect some forts in the Downs, his flagship and three others mutinied, inspired by propaganda circulated by William Batten's chaplain. These sailors went on to take control of the remaining ships in the Downs. The mutineers professed that they were not Royalists, but they endorsed a treaty with the king, adopting mostly the same aims as the Kentish rebels. They also demanded that the first civil war admiral, the Earl of Warwick, be returned to his command. Warwick did set out to treat with the mutineers on Parliament's behalf, and Rainsborough was recalled to the army, but although this action seems to have prevented the revolt from spreading along the south coast, it did not attract the loyalty of all of the fleet. Some ships settled for the dumping of Rainsborough, but others sailed to Holland, where despite their protest that they were loyal to both king and Parliament, they became in effect a Royalist fleet under the command of the Prince of Wales. As Prince Charles took command of his small fleet, he was joined by Batten, who very publicly changed sides and took his ship, the *Constant Warwick*, with him.[37] It was not an entirely happy relationship, for the prince appointed his own leaders for the fleet, including Lord Willoughby of Parham, Parliament's commander in Lincolnshire at the opening of the civil war. Because he was a Presbyterian, Batten was disliked by other Royalist leaders, including Prince Rupert and his brother Maurice, who were about to begin a naval career of several years' duration. With Royalists despising turncoats and sailors despising landlubber Royalist commanders, the fleet was riven with dissent, limiting its ability to mount successful operations.

In Kent the rebellion was almost over, and the clearing up of small garrisons began. The main, but shrinking, rebel party had thought of attempting to take London from the south, but the southern approaches were barred to them. Instead, a few hardy Royalists crossed the Thames and joined a Royalist party in Essex which had staged a rising in Chelmsford on 4 June. Here were assembled Lord Loughborough, former general of the north Midlands; Lord Capel, former general in the northern marches; Sir George Lisle, sometime Lieutenant General to Loughborough; Sir Charles Lucas, who had reinforced Newcastle in 1644; and an Italian soldier, Sir Bernard Gascoigne. Pursued by Fairfax and the New Model Army, the collected leaders and their soldiers retreated into Essex to the town of Colchester, where they hoped to be able to forge links with the mutinous fleet. Fairfax almost caught them and the rush for the gates at Colchester became a nail-biting race, which the Royalists won with seconds to spare. The fighting in the suburbs cost the New Model Army a thousand men, and the Royalists locked out a hundred of their own when Lucas slammed the city gates. Fairfax then sat down for a siege, sent for heavy artillery and awaited more troops. But he did not have enough men to seal off the town immediately, and Royalist horse was able to scour the seaward areas of the county for forage.[38] By 20 June Fairfax had established a line of circumvallation around the town, and foraging raids became more and more restricted. As they did, the townspeople found life harder, and the bay makers of the town managed to get Fairfax to allow them to sell their goods at Lexden Heath once a week. By 1 July the town was completely encircled, and the fighting was already becoming nasty. Fairfax complained that chewed bullets and poisoned bullets were being fired by the garrison. This practice was considered outrageous, as chewed, distorted bullets could inflict horrendous wounds on victims. He threatened that no quarter would be given if the practice continued. By mid-July, the Royalist horse regiments, now penned in, began to slaughter their mounts for food. As August approached the townspeople's houses were searched for food stores.[39] Hopes of relief from the sea were dashed when the Prince's Royalist fleet was unable to break into the mouth of the River Colne; indeed, attacks on the south and east coast in general proved largely fruitless.[40] As it became clear that help could not come from the sea, the besieged Royalists had to hope instead for a victory in the north.

The Engager army had entered England belatedly, and in much smaller numbers than the Edinburgh Parliament had envisaged. In the end Hamilton led some 9,000 men over the western border on 8 July and then lingered at Carlisle for six days. There he was joined by Marmaduke Langdale, and 3,000 more men and another 6,000 from Scotland reached him at Penrith on 14 July. Another contingent of Scots from the Ulster army was also attempting to cross the Irish Sea, in the face of dogged patrolling by Parliamentarian ships. Lambert, in Yorkshire with a watching brief just before the Kentish revolt, crossed the Pennines and began to harass Hamilton's progress. After Pembroke surrendered on 11 July, Cromwell marched north, joining Lambert on 27 July.

Hamilton had now stopped for a week at Kendal, and by the time Lambert and Cromwell were united, he had progressed only as far as Hornby in Lancashire. Monro and the Ulster Scots were approaching to his rear. Hamilton had the larger army, some 20,000 all told, but his men were ill disciplined and undernourished, supplies from along their route had been spirited away when they approached, and they were very unpopular. Cromwell led at most 9,000 men, including 2,000 recent levies who were less well disciplined than the core of New Model Army regiments. Cromwell and Lambert crossed the Pennines in mid-August and found Hamilton's army stretched out along the roads from Westmoreland to Wigan. While the foot were in Preston, the horse were twenty miles ahead at Wigan, and Langdale was in the vicinity of Settle.

On 17 August Cromwell chased Langdale into Preston. There he caught the main infantry forces under Hamilton himself, attempting to cross the River Ribble. He captured the bridges over the Rivers Ribble and Darwen, thus forcing the Scottish leader to cross the

River Darwen by small boat and lead the foot down the road to Wigan via Standish. In the meantime the Scottish horse under Middleton charged up the Chorley road to Preston, missing the foot altogether and instead running into advance parties of the New Model Army. Realizing what had happened, Middleton then turned south and followed Hamilton down the Standish road. When the Scottish army assembled at Wigan the next morning, it was still larger than the New Model Army advancing towards it, but it was demoralized. Hamilton's next move was a retreat, even though the army was really still moving further into England.[41] On 19 August the Scots rearguard waged a spirited resistance, but it was now a defeated army. After days and nights of pouring rain, the saddened, soggy soldiers had no dry powder and no supplies. Their ineffectual commander abandoned them at this point, taking some of the horse with him but leaving Baillie to surrender the foot. Cromwell received Baillie quite kindly, arranged for the prisoners (as many as 4,000) to be guarded and turned north to defeat Monro. Lambert pursued the fugitive commanders. Middleton was caught at Stone in Staffordshire, Hamilton at Uttoxeter, and Langdale was captured at the 'battle' of Willoughby Field in Nottinghamshire.

In Scotland the news of the defeat of the Engagers was greeted with enthusiasm. A massive popular Covenanter rising began in Ayrshire, Clydesdale and Galloway. This Mauchline rising was the natural extension of the radicalization of the south-west over the past thirty-odd years. Presbyterianism was a populist religion in the region, providing the support for the creation of this 'extremist' Covenanter 'army'.[42] Thousands of people assembled and were led by Leven and Leslie to Edinburgh in what was to become known as the Wiggamore raid. There was some fighting in the Lowlands between the assembled Wiggamore forces and the Engagers who sought to hold on to power and the garrisons of Berwick and Carlisle. The Committee of Estates abandoned the capital as Leven and Leslie approached, but their forces defeated Argyll's Campbell clan at Linlithgow and captured Stirling. This success inspired the Engager clique with confidence, and they returned to the capital. It then dawned on the two groups that there was a worse issue to deal with. For the first time since the wars had begun, an English army with the ability to invade Scotland was approaching. Cromwell, having now defeated Monro, was advancing northwards.

News of the defeat at Preston dashed any lingering hopes of succour that the Colchester rebels had, and on 29 August they surrendered the town. Fairfax had three of the leaders tried by a court martial, accusing them of having broken the terms of their surrender in the first civil war by having taken up arms again. Gascoigne, Lisle and Lucas were sentenced to death. Gascoigne was reprieved when it was realized that he was Italian and that his execution might provoke a nasty international incident just when England needed stability in foreign affairs, but Lucas and Lisle were shot. The noble leaders – Norwich, Capel and Loughborough – were sent to Windsor Castle to await Parliament's pleasure.

The north Wales rising was similarly short-lived. The six northern counties had been placed on alert the day after Horton had defeated Laugharne. On 9 May the sheriffs and JPs from the north met at Wrexham and agreed to put the country 'in a posture of defence'. Some £6,000 was to be raised among the six counties, and they were bound to help each other. Arms for Denbighshire and Flint were to be stored at Denbigh Castle. Other castles, like Ruthin and Rhuddlan, were slighted to prevent them from falling into the hands of the Royalists. Sir Thomas Myddleton was at the forefront of local defence, joined by the turncoats Sir Thomas Ravenscroft and Colonel John Aldersley, who had handed Hawarden Castle to Brereton back in 1643.[43] In Caernarfon Thomas Mytton was based at the castle, but when he tried to visit Beaumaris, his former troop captain shut the gates in his face. The local Royalist leader, Sir Thomas Owen, assembled a small force of Royalists and attempted to take on Mytton at Caernarfon. However, Mytton gathered a force from the garrison at Caernarfon, the north Wales shires and Chester to confront Owen. On 5 June, after a sharp fight at Y Dalar Hir, the Royalists were defeated and Owen captured.[44] This did not quell the Royalist zeal, and attempts to rescue Owen from Denbigh were made, but the centre of Royalist activity in the country now switched to Anglesey, where Lord Byron was in charge.[45] He forced a pledge of loyalty on the adults of the island, and when Hamilton invaded England, the Royalists' hopes rose. However, they were left alone for some time, and hopes of victory faded after the battle of Preston and the surrender of Colchester, as the Parliamentarians began to deal with the rising. On 15 September Myddleton crossed the Menai Strait, but it was another fortnight before he and the Royalists came to battle. Byron had by this time left the island, because the Welsh officers decided that they should be led by one of their own countrymen and appointed Sir Richard Bulkeley instead. The Nottinghamshireman believed that whatever the motives of the Welsh, a military mistake had been made, and he went on to join the Earl of Derby in his splendid isolation on the Isle of Wight. On 1 October Bulkeley was defeated, and the final resistance on the island ended the following day. In the southern two nations the war settled down into the sieges of Pontefract and Scarborough, seized by indomitable Yorkshire Royalists.

Back in Scotland, Cromwell was unimpressed by the sudden discussions between the Wiggamores and the Engagers, even when on 26 September they abandoned their claim to rule the country. In the face of his hostility they were purged from the administration and Monro, now at Stirling, was ordered back to Ireland with the remains of his Ulster forces. Cromwell summoned Berwick on 15 September and then requested the Committee of Estates to hand over it and Carlisle. Negotiations with Argyll and the Covenanters at Mordington led to the surrender of the two garrisons at the end of September, but Cromwell's forces had entered Scotland on 21 September and Lambert pressed on to Edinburgh. Quite without parliamentary authority, Argyll's faction constituted themselves a Committee of Estates. Kirk Party rule began, with Cromwell's political support, and when he had ensured that they would purge the government of Engagers, he left for England, with the military support of Lambert and two regiments of the New Model Army.

The English presence on Scottish soil was as unwelcome in Dolphinton as had been the oppression of the Engagers. When the New Model Army soldiers arrived, they took corn and found quarters in the town, for which the people claimed £607-8s-0d Scots. Cromwell's return to England brought little relief:

> Itt at ye removing the plunderit and tooke money and horse and sustenant to £126-0-0.

In all, the enterprise of the Engagement cost the community of Dolphinton £4,220-3s-0d Scots, according to their own estimate, and the auditors said that 'we . . . find clearly yt ye suffering of ye parish are no less no above the account'.[46]

In Ireland during 1647, the renewed activity of the English Parliamentarian forces under their new leaders – Jones in Leinster and George Monck, working with Monro, in Ulster – was bearing fruit. By the end of October, Jones captured Portlester, and Monck and Monro had taken Athaboy and ten other garrisons. Owen Roe O'Neill concentrated his efforts on an attack on Dublin itself that autumn.

As usual he was being kept short of supplies, and he had to take great quantities of provisions from County Meath. The new assembly at Kilkenny had only nine representatives (out of the total seventy-three) from Ulster, and was therefore packed with those opposed to O'Neill; it was also packed with those opposed to the clerical faction which he and Rinuccini led. As a result of the assembly's tardiness, O'Neill had to withdraw from his attack on the Dublin area pursued by Jones's horse. Worse followed as the Confederates turned on themselves. At the end of December 1647, the General Assembly broke up, leaving behind the Grand Council, which was itself now dominated by representatives of the Old English still willing to do a deal with Ormond. Negotiations were also opened between them and Lord Inchiquin, who had extended his control over south Munster by defeating the Confederate army at Knockanuss on 27 November. This defeat effectively destroyed the Confederate military presence in Munster, and Inchiquin went on to capture most of the major towns in the province, with the exception of Waterford, Limerick and Clonmel.[47] As a result of Inchiquin's reluctance to discuss terms, the Confederation decided to overthrow the clerical faction to encourage him. The nuncio and the general were in any case no longer on such good terms with each other. Rinuccini had been persuaded that O'Neill truly did have ambitions for the crown of Ireland, and in early 1648, when the envoy Luke Wadding sent Hugh O'Neill's sword from Rome as a gift to Owen Roe, it was rumoured that the pope had sent it to him as a preliminary to sending him the crown.[48] The Kilkenny government responded by seeing to it that the general's commission was rescinded.

While the king's cause was being fought in England and Wales during the summer of 1648, in Ireland the fight against the king's enemies was largely cast aside, as the Irish factions opened up into internecine strife. During the spring, when affairs in England had deflected Westminster from attending to the logistical needs of its commanders in Ireland, the situation in Munster changed complexion. A Confederate army pressed in on Cork, preventing Inchiquin from supplying his army. Under this double pressure, in April Lord Inchiquin changed sides, taking south Munster over to the side of the Confederation. The agreement with Inchiquin was signed on 20 May.[49] Despite the cooling relationship with O'Neill, Rinuccini attempted to block the treaty. When it was clear that he was powerless to influence policy, the nuncio left Kilkenny, alleging that there had been an attempt on his life, and went to join O'Neill. Many Irish people must have been unable to stomach the agreement with Inchiquin. After all, he hated Catholicism as a creed and had expelled all Catholics from the English territories in Munster back in 1644. In the north, Rinuccini tried to forestall a rumoured attack on O'Neill by Preston's army by threatening to excommunicate anyone who supported this 'new cessation' with the Protestants.[50] The Irish Royalists, too, were less than happy, and in the light of the Engagement wanted to try to persuade the Scots under Monro to join them. The general and the nuncio then moved their forces into County Kilkenny and confronted Preston for about a week in midsummer. Withdrawing first into Tipperary and then northwards, O'Neill was pursued by Confederate forces. In the wake of Rinuccini's proclamation, Inchiquin's army joined Lord Taffe's and Clanricarde's Connaught forces, as well as Preston and the Leinster army, in an attack on the Ulster forces in the vicinity of Athlone.[51] There followed a war of manoeuvring as Owen Roe O'Neill sought to avoid being crushed by the four armies descending on his forces. The four armies pursued this game of cat and mouse for eight days until they despaired of catching him, split up, and returned to quarters.[52] This in-fighting prevented the unification of the Irish nation behind Charles I, and since there was no opportunity for Ormond to exploit, he remained in England for the summer.[53]

The end of the internecine hostilities gave Ormond the opportunity he needed, and he returned to Ireland in an effort to retrieve something of the cause now defeated in the other three nations. A century ago it was believed that the queen in France thought that Ireland was now to play the role into which Scotland had been forced at the beginning of the year.[54] If this is true, then Charles was applying what has been called elsewhere a 'Celtic solution' to his problems. Since the conflict began he had tried to mobilize three countries against one. In the later stages of the first civil war, he had tried to defeat his increasingly powerful enemies in England with support from Wales, Scotland and Ireland. In some respects, the conflict in 1648 was a repetition of this, but by the end of the year Charles had only one nation to turn to. When Ormond arrived, the situation did change, not so much because of him but because of what had happened over the Irish Sea. The Confederation knew it could hope for nothing from the English Parliament, for the peace treaties offered to Charles had referred to a range of punishments and prohibitions that would apply to the so-called rebels of Ireland; essentially, the Catholic Irish were proscribed from any amnesty. To throw in their lot with the Royalists seemed their only prospect of saving Ireland from the wrath of the Westminster Parliament. This idea had dawned on O'Neill as well, and he too entered negotiations with Ormond. Only Rinuccini stuck to the belief that even if they were victorious, the king could not be trusted, because of his position as the monarch of three Protestant nations, to give Catholicism equal status. The nuncio left Ireland in early 1649. Other Catholics seemed not to hesitate in joining the Royalist cause. John Bellew, who had caused Lord Moore so much trouble at the beginning of the rebellion and had led an artillery guard during the war, returned to arms when Ormond arrived. In 1661 Ormond recalled that Bellew had served loyally after the marquis returned to Ireland. As well as bringing £100 for the cause, he also brought in a company of foot 'in His Majesty's pay', which then became an artillery guard. By the following year, the company was serving as the Terroghan fort garrison.[55]

In the wake of O'Neill's approaches to Ormond, the Supreme Council approached the general and proposed a settlement of the religious difficulties. However, there was little chance that the general would be able to convince the Old English-dominated council of the clerical case, though he did not limit his opportunities. O'Neill used his discussions with Michael Jones over routine issues such as an exchange of prisoners to test the waters for treating with Westminster. The realities of the political situation over the Irish Sea dictated that terms agreed with the Westminster Parliament might well have had a greater guarantee than any negotiated with a powerless king. Jones was willing to discuss matters, since at the time Owen tried to talk to him, the governor at Dublin was starved of supplies because of O'Neill's success in wrecking the local economy in the Dublin area.[56] Jones was able to benefit from these discussions; Owen Roe O'Neill sent supplies to Dublin, and in return the creaghts accompanying the Irish army were allowed to graze in areas held by both Jones and Monck at Dundalk.

At the same time Ormond offered terms to the Confederation which did not offer the security for the Catholic church that even the Old English wanted. Priests were to have only quiet possession of the churches in their hands until a 'free Parliament' could determine the issue. The term 'free Parliament' could mean many things; without a guarantee that such a Parliament would have adequate representation for the Catholic people of Ireland, such promises were meaningless. As for any guarantees that the Catholic church would have a recognized existence, structure and funding, nothing was forthcoming from the Lord Lieutenant. At first the assembly rejected the offer, whereupon Ormond pointed out that its members were quite powerless to request anything else of him. The alternative, as the governments in England, Wales and Scotland wanted, was the extirpation of the Irish nation.[57] When this was brought home to them, the Old English caved in and at the end of December reversed their decision. The articles of peace were publicly proclaimed on 19 January 1649. Owen Roe O'Neill was fully isolated by the peace. He held no rank recognized by any faction in Ireland except his loyal Ulster army, and even this was disintegrating. Some of his officers, worried by his insistence that the religious terms of the peace were wholly inadequate, left him and made peace with the government. Other officers fought each other in political arguments, and Owen's son Henry killed a fellow officer in a duel. The common soldiers, short of supplies and caught in the middle of the religious and political debate, also began to desert. O'Neill fished around for help, trying to open discussions with the government in London, with the royal family, and with Prince Rupert, to little avail. Ormond also tried to win over the leading English commanders, Jones at Dublin and Sir Charles Coote in Connaught, but they were more willing to talk to Owen Roe O'Neill than to Ormond. All three Englishmen could gain short-term practical advantages from any terms which allowed them grazing rights and supplies. Both politically and in the long term, however, they wanted to continue the split between Ormond and O'Neill as long as possible, because they were confident that help from England would arrive. Coote was the one most desperately in need of food supplies, and he knew that Derry could not hold out long unless he entered into a local arrangement with O'Neill to exchange weapons for food. Coote also wanted O'Neill to help him drive off the Covenanter Scots, who were now loyal to Charles and were attacking his garrison. Although O'Neill called a provisional council of Ulster and obtained its consent for aiding Coote, the discussions eventually came to nothing. Monck too opened discussions with O'Neill, because he was also under attack in Ulster from the Scottish forces there. He and Jones agreed to a cessation with O'Neill, partly because of the threat of an Ormond –Scottish alliance but also because it kept Ormond and O'Neill apart. The cessation, which was to last three months from May, brought censure on the heads of the Englishmen and made Ormond determined to undermine O'Neill's power in Ireland. While devising a new campaign against Dublin, which he feared would soon be welcoming reinforcements from England, the marquis had Lord Castlehaven capture O'Neill's three garrisons in Leinster at Maryborough, Castlereban and Athy and thus confine the general within Ulster. Ormond then moved on Dublin with Inchiquin. Ormond himself concentrated on besieging the capital, while Inchiquin moved north to Drogheda.[58]

In England and Wales, the end of the second civil war brought a great clamour for justice. Sir Thomas Wroth's call for the king to be impeached was no longer a lone voice. Charles was now being referred to as a 'man of blood', and he was being blamed specifically for so many deaths in the ensuing wars that it was averred he had blood-guilt upon him. His death was now linked to the spiritual survival of the kingdom of England. The victories won against Charles in the four nations were God's work, argued many preachers and soldiers, and also a sign that He had judged against the king on account of his blood-guilt, and the time of reckoning had now arrived.[59] On the other hand, some people were not so sure; Parliament actually dropped the Vote of No Addresses and reopened discussions with the king in August 1648 in an attempt to forestall a political revolution backed by the army, which would sweep away the monarchy, the Lords and Parliament itself. The ten surviving secluded members were restored to their seats in the Commons. In the Upper House, the Lords had been very lenient towards the seven members impeached by the Independents, although by now one, Lord Willoughby of Parham, had gone over to join the Prince of Wales in Holland.

London Levellers had presented a petition calling for the abolition of the Lords, while Parliament pressed on with talks at Newport on the Isle of Wight. However, the king was now switching his hopes to Ormond's mission in Ireland, and once the marquis had gone there in October, he refused to budge from his offer of a limited Presbyterian system and a ten-year period of parliamentary control over the militia. The army had begun to call for the abandonment of the Newport treaty talks, and in any case, Parliament soon realized that they were fruitless, because the king's eyes were again elsewhere. On 27 October the treaty was at an end. It was now the army's turn to dictate the pace of political change. In October Cromwell's son-in-law, Henry Ireton, proposed that the army should occupy London and purge Parliament. Fairfax, now a lord himself since the death of his father, did not respond. With the army based at St Albans, Ireton withdrew to Windsor and began to frame a Remonstrance. This became the *Remonstrance of the Army*; 25,000 words long, it called for an end to negotiations with the king and argued that he should be brought to trial. The arguments were powerful and clearly related to the events of the past year. Ireton demonstrated that there were no treaties to which the king would adhere, because all of the treaties presented to him over the past nine years, beginning with the discussions at Berwick in 1639, had infringed upon some of the rights Charles regarded as inalienable. If he had agreed to any treaty, there was no guarantee that he would abide by it. It was well known that the king was duplicitous and would shamelessly discuss different and contradictory terms with several bodies at once. As a result, Charles might well become involved in party politics if he were restored at all, playing conflicting parties against each other as they competed for his support. Instead, Ireton suggested that power lay with the people. It was the ascendancy principle that power flowed upwards from the people, in whom rested the true sovereignty, and was exercised on their behalf by their representatives in Parliament. Exactly who constituted the people is at issue, but Ireton probably meant those whom he had labelled at Putney as having 'a fixed interest'.[60] Fairfax now realized that debate was unavoidable, and on 7 November called a Council of Officers to discuss the *Remonstrance*. For four days the officers debated the document, but in the end few felt they could support such a radical statement of political aims, and they therefore eschewed it. They preferred instead to contact the king directly, only to see him reject their approaches as he had others. The result was a series of uncomfortable alliances. Ireton, disappointed by the St Albans discussions, turned to the Levellers, whom he met at The Nag's Head in The Strand. Lilburne and the Levellers rejected the execution of the king. What Lilburne had been saying since the beginning of the year was that there was little point in displacing one tyrant in exchange for another tyranny, that of the army. Nevertheless, the discussions at the inn created a committee to draft a new *Agreement of the People*.[61] As for Fairfax and his more conservative officers, they were again thrown back into discussions with Ireton when the king rejected their approaches. The *Remonstrance*, which the Levellers disliked, was now adopted by the Council of the Officers, and presented by them to Parliament.

When the *Remonstrance* was presented to Parliament, the Commons set it aside for the time being. This was a mistake, for the impulse for a solution could brook no delay, and the army acted instead. Fairfax ordered the king to be brought to London from the Isle of Wight and occupied London with the army. Even though the most notorious Presbyterian MPs left the House again, the Commons still tried to hold back the onrush of change. On 5 December, it announced that the apprehension of the king was illegal. On 6 December, having rejected the demand for a complete dissolution, Fairfax was not involved in the next stages because he would not sanction the purging of the Commons planned by Ireton. Accordingly, Colonel Thomas Pride and Lord Grey of Groby, a general of the first civil war, and the son of the Earl of Stamford who had opposed the Vote of No Addresses, stood at the door of the House and kept out the Presbyterians, content with simply secluding some 186 but imprisoning another forty-one. Fifty-six more MPs stayed away. Fairfax was furious, but Cromwell, whom he had recalled from Pontefract (where he had taken over after Rainsborough had been murdered in a kidnap attempt), approved of what had been done. Now there were only 154 MPs left in the House, and they proceeded to debate the king's future.[62] At the same time, the Levellers completed the second draft of the *Agreement*. The Whitehall meetings between them and the army had never been harmonious, and the *Agreement* published on 15 December was principally the work of the Levellers rather than a co-operative effort. In it, the precise redistribution of seats was detailed, and relationships between the legislative and the executive were more strictly defined. Qualifications for franchise were restricted, possibly as an indication that there was some attempt at compromise with Ireton's stance on 'fixed interest'. Another personal agreement was produced by Lieutenant-Colonel John Jubbes, perhaps as a suggested compromise between the Levellers and Ireton. It was noted some time ago that the *Agreement* was most noticeable for the breadth of religious toleration it offered; even the Catholic Irish were encompassed.[63] Ireton and his officers in turn produced a further *Agreement*, which it has been argued actually represented a true joint effort between him and the Levellers. In any case all three versions faded from sight; the last was presented to Parliament on 20 January 1649, but by then the Commons was too busy to discuss it.

On 1 January the Commons established a High Court. On 4 January the Lords rejected it, and the Commons responded by declaring itself the supreme representative of the people and reprocessed the ordinance for the High Court as an act. The court was to consist of 150 members and was to try the king. Secret sessions which Fairfax attended in the early stages devised the charge and the manner of the trial. On 21 January the king was brought to the first public meeting. If there was no doubt that the king was to be found guilty, there certainly was a hitch in the procedures. Charles, who had resigned himself to being a martyr, decided he would stand on principle and refused to recognize the court. He would not reply to the charge, and as a result the witnesses who had been drawn from around the country to swear that they had seen the king committing acts of war upon his people could only be heard *in camera*. The public spectacle of the king being proven guilty could not take place as planned; instead Charles attracted sympathy for his dignified stance at the three public sessions where he refused to recognize the court's legality or the veracity of the power which had created it. Moreover, Charles did make some valid points about what protection a subject could expect if even he, the king, could be called to account by a body with no legitimate origin. It was a point hammered home by Lady Fairfax, who also attended the session. On the first day she bellowed, on hearing her husband's name read out as a commissioner (he had not attended), 'He has more wit than to be here'. At the last session, when it was asserted that Charles was arraigned in the name of the people, Lady Fairfax shouted 'Not half, not a quarter of the people of England'.[64] It did not matter a whit; the trial was a show, and its main act was always going to be the sentencing of the king. Despite Charles and Lady Fairfax's pointed remarks, this was still the outcome. On 27 January Charles was sentenced to death. There is little point in debating the legality of the proceedings. They were plainly illegal; there was nothing in the constitutional structure of the country which allowed for the trial of a monarch. England, Wales, Scotland and Ireland were all governed on the basis of a descending theory of power, the idea that authority came through the monarch from God above. The trial, whether all the participants believed it or not, was conducted from the position that power ascended; Charles was at one point referred to as an elected king. That, as he replied sharply at the time, was absolutely not true. 'England was never an elective Kingdom, but an hereditary Kingdom near these thousand years'.[65] Nor was Charles being tried under any new constitution. There was no *Agreement* in force, and there had been no decision on the nature of the state once the king was dead. Indeed, it was only when the king was on the way to the scaffold on 30 January that the MPs realized that they had not prepared for the moment of his death, when by custom his eldest son would become king. The execution was delayed for two hours while the Commons made it illegal for anyone to proclaim the Prince of Wales king. But when Charles died outside the showcase Banqueting Hall, the monarchy survived him.

12

The People's Reaction

Annus Infamus 1649 delicti et facinoris
1649: the infamous year of the wicked crime[1]

The year 1649 was a crucial one in the history of the four nations, for major decisions were made about the structure of government. This chapter examines those forms which were adopted and those which the king's executioners firmly rejected. The execution of Charles I had not solved all of the major political problems facing England and Wales. Moreover, it had created new ones. Scotland had not been invited to participate in the decision to execute the king, and the ruling Kirk Party was not happy. One of the reasons for shuffling off the king had been to achieve stability. Ireton's *Remonstrance* the previous October had more or less argued the point that there could be no peace while the king was alive. But his death had apparently not lessened the potential for conflict. War was still being fought in Ireland; the Scots were now fighting the English commanders Monck and Coote, Jones was isolated in Dublin, and the forces nominally fighting for the monarchy were growing in strength. Moreover, in England there were a number of rival propositions for the new England which could possibly be forged in the wake of the king's execution.

It was clear that the nations had to be stabilized. The Levellers were difficulty enough, but the general problem of instability throughout the four nations also had to be dealt with. The immediate problem was to create a framework that would foster the creation of a constitutional settlement. But there was also the question of how to proceed against some of the principal actors of the 1648 rebellions. In addition, Ireland had to be dealt with to prevent it from being used as a base for Royalist attacks on England and Wales, and looming somewhat further off lay the disgruntlement of Scotland.

The Commons began to debate the legal basis of power, which in turn involved discussions on the position of the monarchy, the Lords and the form of executive government. The House of Lords was almost defunct since the Commons' claim in January to be the sole representative of the people. On 6 and 7 February decisions were taken to abolish the Lords and the monarchy, although the bills were not passed until 17 and 19 March and it was to be May before England and Wales were proclaimed a 'Commonwealth and free state'. No less than a political revolution had occurred. Moreover, it went beyond the limits of the Scottish and English Revolutions of 1640–1. Those two revolutions had radically altered the balance of power between the executive and the legislative, and had changed the monarch's role in the creation and management of the executive. But in 1649 the very bases of these relationships were swept away: there was no longer to be either a monarchy or an automatic position in government for the aristocracy. The revolution had in effect removed 'two-thirds of the components of the national legislature' and had altered 'the source of sovereignty for both the executive and the judiciary'.[2]

Some historians are unwilling to accept the arguments interpreting the events of 1648–9 as *the* English revolution. They see the events of 1649 as a *coup d'état* and as just part of the revolutionary process which had been in place in England since late 1640. But this argument surely needs to be broadened to include the revolutionary processes in Scotland, where the somewhat earlier revolution clearly provided a model for the early stages of the English revolution. That potential for revolutionary change was ingrained by 1648 is evident; why else could it have taken only some six months to move from a position in which only the Levellers had a complete constitutional programme to one in which the development of a new system of government was acknowledged at Westminster? Continuing with the argument that 1649 was a military coup, we can see that although the army forced revolution upon the surviving elements of the traditional system, what it did *not* do was to supersede the civilian government. To do so, as has been pointed out, would have amounted to the fourth stage of a coup. According to one analysis, revolution consists of four stages.[3] The first and second stages in this case involved the armed forces influencing and then coercing a civilian government into acting in their interests; in the third stage, which can be seen as a model for 1648–9, the military supplants the ruling group of civilians and puts in their place its own nominees. We could also perhaps argue that the third stage is similar to what happened in 1648 in Scotland, when the Covenanter army leadership initiated the Wiggamore revolt against the Engager government. In the fourth stage, which did not take place in England (or indeed in Scotland), the army takes power into its own hands. Instead, in both countries the creation of the new constitution was left in the hands of the remainder of the purged Parliament – until 1651 in Scotland and 1653 in England. When the army again intervened with a repetition of stage three at Westminster, it did so again without really progressing to stage four.

Other historians have argued that the revolution of 1648–9 was a conservative revolution, forced on its participants and principal actors only by the instability caused by the second civil war and Charles's failure to accept defeat. In short, the revolution was taken to stop further radical change being forced on the country by, amongst others, the Levellers and their allies.[4] It is a powerful argument, reinforced by the fact that those who took over desired to hang on to elements of the traditional system such as the House of Commons and were in no rush to complete restructuring after the changes of March to May 1649. Speed in the creation of the new state was no longer a priority, and over time the purged House of Commons came to regard itself as the end, not the means, of constitutional change in England and Wales. The stability it created by doing so was arguably necessary to ensure the destruction of both internal enemies (the radical and political groups) and external enemies (the Confederate and Royalist alliance in Ireland and the Kirk Party in Scotland). Nevertheless, this viewpoint presupposes that those imposing the revolution had strong vested interests in perpetuating much of the status quo of governmental machinery. If we rule out some of those groups with such interests from the process of change, perhaps we can explore this scenario farther. Monarchists and aristocrats, whose role in government was destroyed, can be excluded straight away; in the Commons, MPs and the electorate would have had to be the driving force of any conservative revolution. Even then, the purged Presbyterian MPs must really be ruled out, and the Commons cut down to the Independent core. Within this group, the principal men at the heart of the driving force of change still lend support to the conservative argument. Both Ireton, who did more than any other Independent to legitimize the revolution, and Cromwell, who consulted his conscience in the north and around Pontefract before throwing his weight behind Pride's Purge and the trial of the king, could be seen as having conservative intentions. To

Ireton, tampering with the relationship between the right to elect the legislative and the right to own property was out of the question, at Putney in 1647 and at Whitehall in 1648. Even the most radical coherent programme with which Ireton was involved, the second *Agreement*, did not break that relationship. If Ireton saw further radicalism, represented by Lilburne and his Leveller clique, as threatening essential relationships within government, he may well also have seen the execution of the king as necessary to restore the stability needed to conserve this fundamental part of government. It was Ireton who pressed for a purged House of Commons rather than total abolition in 1648, and Cromwell favoured this step too because he believed that government should be carried out not by the sword but by a legitimate Parliament. This philosophy of course serves to explain the lack of the fourth revolutionary stage.[5] For both Cromwell and Ireton, any new government had to receive sanction from the old. The retention of the Commons as the body to draft this new constitution was essentially a conservative step.

However, Ireton and Cromwell can also be seen as men who, although both voters and MPs with fixed interests in government before the revolution of 1640–1, were changed fundamentally by their experience of war.[6] While this interpretation may serve only to explain their actions in overthrowing parts of the existing system, it could also contradict the notion that the revolution was just a conservative reaction and support a more radical analysis. According to some, the influential drive to revolution came from elsewhere and Cromwell was pushed further than he may have wished, or at the least had to run in a slightly different political direction, to remain ahead of the political impetus in late 1648. Pressure to execute the king came from army units raised in and spread over the country: 'Units stationed in Yorkshire wanted him brought to justice just as strongly as those in the London area.'[7] Demands and ideas for revolutionary change came from a group of people who may have represented only a tiny proportion of the country but who came from outside the traditional political order. In other words, the people who demanded revolution were those who had no stake in the maintenance of the political system, for whom a conservative revolution would have been no revolution at all. It is thus not improbable to argue that even if the actions of 1648–9 had the effect of denying a protracted voice for the Levellers and others, they were essentially a progressive phenomenon, especially as they ultimately turned England's polity from one based on the notion that power descended from God into one based on a belief that power ascended from the people.

With the basis for the new polity in place, it was time to deal with
the enemy within. It was decided that the defeated Royalists were to
be tried by a new High Court of Justice. One of the seven great
delinquents had escaped; Lord Loughborough had absconded – rather
dramatically, it is suggested – from Windsor Castle on the eve of the
king's execution. Five of the others – Hamilton, Holland, Norwich,
Owen and Capel – were still in captivity and were dragged before
the court in early March. Of them, only old Norwich and Owen
were spared. The trials were, of course, controversial and clearly
motivated by revenge, even if we accept 'blood-guilt' as a genuine
religious and political belief. Lilburne and the Levellers continued
to question the legality of the army regime, restating their position
of a year previously when they argued that to exchange one tyranny
for another was unacceptable. Lilburne, who sent Capel and the
others books on law as they awaited trial, saw the High Court in
particular as a new and frightening tyranny. As it had no basis in
known laws, it was worse than any feature of the late king's government.

The Levellers also constituted an enemy within. Their solution to
the post-war crisis was not to be reopened for discussion unless it
was in the form that had been approved of in the second *Agreement*.
During the first weeks of 1649 the Levellers engaged in criticism of
the High Court of Justice, but when on 22 February an Order of the
Day forbade soldiers meeting to discuss political affairs, Lilburne
took up his pen. Four days later, he produced *England's New Chains
Discovered*, attacking the Council of State created to sit between sessions of Parliament. It also set out the form of government Lilburne
had now developed, which had an executive committee composed
solely of members of the legislative body, unlike the existing Council
of State, which embraced army officers. Parliaments were to be
annually elected, and the whole scheme was devised to minimize the
power of any executive, which since the end of the previous year had
been the greatest fear of the Leveller politicians. At the same time
the paper attacked Parliament for not having delivered the promised
freedoms:

> For where is that good, or where is that liberty so much pretended,
> so deerly purchased? If we look to what this House hath done since
> it voted it self the Supreme Authority, and dithburdened themselves

of the power of the Lords. First, we find a high Court of Justice . . . The Next is the censuring of a Member of this House, for declaring his judgement in a point of Religion . . . Besides the Act for the pressing of Sea-men . . . Then the stoping of our mouths from printing.[8]

In the Leveller journal, *The Moderate*, the article was printed alongside an attack on the current social evils, unemployment and high prices; and to attract the soldiers, Lilburne appealed to the Commons to sort out arrears of pay and other grievances. When soldiers sought to respond to this approach with a petition, five of the eight men who presented it to Fairfax were humiliatingly cashiered. Although there were scattered instances of discontent in the army, Fairfax's severity managed to keep most of the army in line. The Levellers responded with a pamphlet drafted by Overton, *The Hunting of the Foxes from Newmarket and Triploe Heath to Whitehall, by five small Beagles (late of the Army)*. Written as if by the cashiered soldiers, it was aimed at tarnishing the grandees by making it appear that they had betrayed the other ranks. It was followed by a second version of *England's New Chains Discovered*, presented along with a petition to the Commons, in the same vein as *The Hunting*. . . Both tracts effectively declared war on the grandees.[9] This time the Commons and the army acted in concert and Lilburne, Overton, Walwyn and Thomas Prince (a party treasurer) were arrested on 28 March. The day before, the Commons had declared them guilty of trying to incite a mutiny in the army. Dragged to prison by two regiments of the army, the four were brought before the Council of State. When they refused to recognize the court's jurisdiction and demanded that they be taken before a justice of the peace, the Council committed them to the Tower.[10]

Reaction was dramatic: petitions were drafted in London demanding the release of the prisoners, and most important, the Leveller women activists too intervened at centre stage. Prominent amongst them was Elizabeth Lilburne, who had married John after his release in 1640. The women were following in the tradition established early in the revolutionary period of women petitioning Parliament and objecting to the excise taxes. The Lilburnes must have long ago agreed on their political positions and stances; in 1646 John had asserted equality of men and women

who are, and were by nature all equall and alike in power, dignity, authority and majesty, none of them having (by Nature) any authority, dominion, or magisterial power, one over or above another.[11]

This statement was in direct opposition to current theories of patriarchal power, which suggested that every man was a petty king with authority over his wife. It struck at the fundamentals of social structure. It has been suggested that Lilburne's statement rejected 'not only distinctions of class but the patriarchal family also', amounting to 'social dynamite'.[12] As we might expect, other historians (see arguments reviewed in chapter 8) disagree. Women were not classed as self-possessed individuals and, being under the protection of men, would thus have sacrificed their birthright.[13] If this is the case, what was Mrs Lilburne's interest in the blatant injustice executed on the four men? Could it have been purely personal? This is unlikely. As a ground-breaking study of women and property points out, we still tend to see laws and social injunctions as monolithic when viewed backwards over time. Subtleties, which contemporary men and women would have readily acknowledged, made it possible for women to pursue property matters through the law, though they often go unnoticed by later historians. As demonstrated by the case studies referred to in chapter 7, women in their own right held, and paid taxes on, up to 30 per cent of real estate in England and Ireland; in Wales and Scotland women were substantial producers, probably equalling their sisters in the other two countries. If men were dispossessed of what the Levellers called birthright by the current political systems, and understood that they were so deprived, then surely women did so too. The Levellers' 1647 petition indeed argued that women had suffered in the war just as much as men had. In late April 1649, Elizabeth Lilburne and the most influential Leveller woman, Katherine Chidley, organized two petitions and a series of demonstrations to demand the release of the prisoners. They used the parochial structure of Leveller organization created during the previous two years to good effect. Signatures from across the city were collected in churches and at religious meetings in every ward and division. On 25 April the first petition was spurned, and the women were sent home with the injunction

> That the matter you petition about, is of a higher concernment then you understand, that the House gave an answer to your Husbands; and therefore you are desired to go home, and looke after your own businesse, and meddle with your huswifery.

Housewifery was as misunderstood by men then as it is by many historians today; the MPs failed to recognize that it embraced the very things that encouraged a political stance by women: labour, income and taxation.[14] The second petition, presented on 5 May, referred to this ignorance. Katherine Chidley, its most probable author, referred to the attempt by Parliament to silence their earlier efforts:

> Since we are assured of our creation in the image of God, of an interest in Christ equal to men, as also of a proportionate share in the freedoms of the commonwealth, we cannot but wonder and grieve that we should appear so despicable in your eyes to be thought of as unworthy to petition or represent our grievances to this honourable House. Have we not an equal interest with the men of this nation in those liberties and securities contained in the *Petition of Right*, and other the good laws of the land?

Chidley was implying that women, as property holders and tax-payers in their own right, were beneficiaries of the *Petition of Right* just as much as their male counterparts. The Commons thought otherwise, continuing to view women generally as subject to men in the home. They contemptuously refused to receive the petition, with its 10,000 women signatories, from the hundreds of green-beribboned women who presented it. In 1650, the Commons changed the word 'persons' to 'men' during the debate on the Act of Subscribing the Engagement, and went on three years later to reject another of Mrs Chidley's petitions on the grounds that 'they being women and many of them wives, so that the Law took no notice of them'.[15] If they truly believed this, it suggests ignorance on their part, and as many were lawyers, it is more likely that they knew very well that the law was far more subtle than they made out. The Commons was really setting up barriers against women's attacks on its political supremacy. The revolution had clearly gone far enough for MPs after the pass-ing of the Acts abolishing the monarchy and the Lords: there was no room for debate on gender relationships within Westminster.

At the same time, other Levellers were trying to provoke unrest in the army. In April a minor mutiny over pay at the Bull Inn, London, resulted in the execution of a soldier, Robert Lockyer. Lockyer in-stantly became a martyr, and at his massive public funeral in the City the streets, people and his coffin were all bedecked with swathes of sea-green and white ribbons. On 1 May a third draft of the *Agree-ment of the People* was ready. Walwyn, in *The English Soldier's Standard*, called for the reconstruction of the General Council to discuss it. Again the Levellers offered their *Agreement* as a salve for the nation's ills, proffering what has been called a 'generous' electorate (it excluded servants, those in receipt of alms and ex-Royalists) to choose a 400-strong unicameral assembly as the supreme body, to be called the Representative, in a secret ballot. No Lords or monarchs were mentioned, and the electoral divisions were organized according to population distribution. There was to be religious toleration, although Catholics were denied access to public office, and the church was decentralized, with parishes electing ministers. The law was to make no distinction with regard to class and was also to be decentralized, with local courts ensuring the principle of judgement by peers. Local government would be staffed by officers chosen locally rather than centrally. In effect the *Agreement* constituted the disestablishment of government and church.[16]

Six regiments of horse elected new agitators in the wake of publication of the *Agreement*; Colonel Scrope's horse, on its way to Ireland, stopped at Salisbury and refused to continue its journey. A group of frustrated and angry soldiers assembled around William Thompson at Banbury. Thompson was the author of *England's Standard Advanced*, a pamphlet calling for a general mutiny against the army grandees. He also called himself captain, although as a recent attempt to court-martial him had discovered, he was not a member of the army at all. Thompson declared his solidarity with the mutinous regiments and invited soldiers to join him in fighting for the *Agreement*.[17] As the unrest began to spread, Cromwell and Fairfax led regiments loyal to themselves to Oxfordshire, where they surprised the Leveller soldiers near Burford. There was little fighting. The generals had moved so fast and so far (fifty miles on 14 May alone) that many rebels were caught in their sleep. As a former agitator sent by the grandees offered negotiations, the army and the wrath of the generals descended upon the rebels. Most surrendered, although some, including William Thompson, fled to Northamptonshire. Three or four hundred men were locked in Burford church, all of them liable to be dealt with as mutineers.[18] On the morning of 15 May, four only were tried and sentenced to death; three – Corporal Church, Corporal Perkins and William Thompson's younger brother – were shot, passing into history as the Burford martyrs and still commemorated each 15 May with a political rally at Burford. Thompson himself made it to Northampton, where he released three prisoners from the gaol, took the excise money and distributed it to the poor. Eventually, troopers from the army caught up with him, and he was killed at a fight near Wellingborough.

The defeat at Burford marked the end of the Leveller promise. The movement's leaders were thrown into despair by Burford, and it never recovered the status of power broker achieved in 1648–9. It did not fade away, however; the male and female leaders kept writing, petitioning and demonstrating throughout the next decade. To some extent there were attempts to extend the power base of the movement. The following year Wildman and Lilburne were involved in the drainage disputes in the Isle of Axeholme, possibly with the intention of introducing wider political ideals into the already politicized struggle between drainers and tenants. However, both principal historians of the riots argue that the Levellers were probably not doing anything other than putting their legal abilities and expertise to use in return for land.[19] The whole notion of wider political issues being bound up in the fenland revolts is open to argument. It has been suggested that the relationships indicate that opponents of the drainage were sufficiently knowledgeable about political affairs to believe that the Levellers may have had common cause, or at the very least shared ideals, with themselves. It was the fenmen and women who saw the advantage of Leveller support, rather than the Levellers who sought merely to exploit discontent.[20] This sort of relationship certainly does raise questions about the supposed lack of appeal to the rural sector traditionally attributed to the Levellers.

The True Levellers, or Diggers as they became known, appeared just as the Leveller cause entered its crisis. They offered an entirely original and practical solution to the nation's troubles, although their written manifesto drew on Genesis for justification and they were not original in their vision of rural utopianism. The Digger solution did not propose fiddling about with the electoral system or trying to introduce equality into an existing system, but rather aimed to introduce a completely new system, derived from first principles. We know little of the Diggers as individuals, and we are uncertain of their gender breakdown. We know that women were amongst them, but no women's names survive on their tracts and papers.[21] Chief amongst the leaders were Gerrard Winstanley and William Everard, the chief authors of *The True Leveller's Standard Advanced*, a remarkable document published in March 1649, which informed the world that it had failed to live up to what God had intended when creating the earth.

> In the beginning of Time the Great Creator, Reason, made the earth
> to be a common treasury, to preserve beasts, birds, fishes and man,

the lord that was to govern this creation. For man had dominion given to him over the beasts, birds and fishes. But not one word was spoken in the begining, that one branch of mankind should rule over another.

As the authors explained, mankind had not fulfilled this promise. Men and women had instead given away their personal power to others – monarchs and other governors – in exchange for protection. Those leaders thus became powerful and rich and eventually gained sovereignty over other men and women and over the world itself. As a result some people had become landowners, whereas others became the dispossessed poor.[22] The solution, the Diggers explained, was to begin to restore the principles of the common treasury by taking over unowned waste ground, cultivating it and living communally on its bounty. On 1 April, just before the tract was written, this plan had been put into effect at St George's Hill outside London, and throughout the year other colonies developed in the Midlands and Home Counties. Contemporaries were either confused or angry. When he met the Diggers, Fairfax was bemused by their insistence on keeping their hats on in defiance of social convention. In his opinion and that of Captain Gladman, the Diggers were mad. Others were not so convinced. As Manning argues, the Diggers may have appeared a negligible problem from Westminster, but from the proximity of Cobham and other places adjacent to colonies, it was a different matter.[23] Local landowners realized that the colonies posed a threat, not only to their land but to the concept of property itself. The Diggers were not advocating violent or sudden revolution, but rather gradual change inculcated through example. To landowners, this philosophy was worrying because of its possible effects on their own tenants. There is no doubt that the message was being spread through a variety of means. Alongside Winstanley's tracts, poetry and song echoed his philosophy. In *The Digger's Mirth*, Winstanley referred to the story of Esau and Jacob and the deceitful assumption of birthright, making the point that it would not always be that way:

> And when the Father seeth it good
> and his set time is come,
> he takes away the tyrant's food
> and gives it to the Son

The *Digger's Song* is even more robust in its condemnation of property and status:

You noble Diggers all, stand up now, stand up now
You noble Diggers all, stand up now,
The waste land to maintain, seeing Cavaliers by name
Your digging does disdain and persons all defame[24]

Local landowners could not abide the settlement at St George's Hill and instituted a campaign of violence and disruption against the Diggers. They also had recourse to law. Digger cottages were destroyed, their crops trampled and many of them dragged into court and given punitive fines. By the following year both the colonies at St George's and the settlement at Cobham to which the St George's pioneers had gone had been destroyed. Even the Wellingborough colony, which had received widespread support, had been abandoned because of opposition from some powerful local landowners.

The Digger solution had a number of origins. Winstanley's personal philosophy is undoubtedly important: his communalism derived from the Bible as well as from radical Levellers' groups such as those who produced the pamphlet *More Light Shining in Buckinghamshire* on the eve of the establishment of the colony at St George's. He was almost certainly a pantheist, believing that God permeated everyone and everything. For him the Fall marked the abandonment of the common treasury of God's earth, rather than mankind's expulsion from the Garden of Eden. According to one recent historian of his philosophy, he was also an early ecologist. As well as living in harmony with one another, men and women had to 'live in community with the globe and the spirit of the globe' to restore the primeval agrarian communism that had existed before the Fall and had characterized the Garden of Eden.'[25] Winstanley's views have been defined by one historian as anarchistic. He envisaged no need for magistrates or lawyers, largely because there would be no landownership. In such a nation, Winstanley expected the state 'in Marxist phrase, to wither away immediately'.[26]

Winstanley was not the only influence on Digger thought and action. The field has also been referred to as the seminar of the agrarian people. The struggle on St George's Hill was an extension of the rights of the commons. Other historians view the Diggers as invaders of the commons who were taking something which was not theirs and were thus stealing from the agrarian poor. Their presence would be unwelcome in areas where rights to the commons were intrinsic to economic survival.[27] On the other hand, the Northamptonshire colony demonstrated the potential of the Digger movement to benefit the rural community; no fewer than 1,169 people there were in receipt of poor relief, and since the colony offered work, some local landowners supported it. The Digger solution dealt directly with the important issues which affected the majority of the population: poverty, landlessness and common rights. Although it may have been an already outdated appeal to a rural utopia, it did offer a solution to deadlock at the heart of the state, which could usefully help the 'poorest he' in the country.

IRELAND: O'NEILL'S DEATH AND CROMWELL'S WAR

By May 1648, Ormond had begun to construct a new war effort in the country as a whole to pay for the new armies. Evidence from the Ormond papers suggests that the three forms adopted by the Confederation were restarted or continued in three provinces. On 10 May instructions for the sequestration of enemy estates in five out of the six Munster counties were issued. Delinquents were defined as any persons in arms, against the king, absent from the country, anyone who had consented to the 'execrable murder of the late King', those who aided the enemy and those who opposed the treaty between him and the Confederation. Excise taxes were also established, although as a letter to Ormond from Galway shows, these may well have been difficult to collect. Galway merchants suggested that the excise

> would be an absolute and unrecoverable decay of trade, and discourages all our merchants, whereby the daily danger of their lives and all their fortunes convey unto this corporation (as they have done since the first erection thereof) all the means they have to serve His Majesty or defend themselves.

It is also clear that a general applotment was in place alongside levies of food. A petition of the gentry of King's County (Offaly) in Leinster, dated 29 August, demonstrates that this was something of a burden, especially when extra burdens were imposed, possibly without warrant. They referred specifically to Lord Dillon's levy of an extra £312-10s-0d on the county for soldiers not covered by the payments of the applotment of £210 per week, which went to three regiments of foot and a regiment of horse not under Dillon's command. Dillon's charges effectively doubled the total. It is also clear that although Westmeath was charged £200 a month, not all of this was forthcoming.[28] Together, the latter two petitions suggest that these were both organizational problems, even if King's County could afford its initial applotment, and given the catastrophic military situation that followed the letter of the King's Countymen, it is likely that these issues were never resolved.

After leaving Ormond at Dublin, Inchiquin had gone on to capture Drogheda on 11 July 1649 and then threatened Monck at Dundalk. In accordance with the cessation agreed with O'Neill, Monck requested the general's help. Not surprisingly, Owen now vacillated because he was holding discussions with Ormond. However, he had promised Monck aid, and in return for a promise of ammunition in exchange for supplies, he marched towards Dundalk. The supply column that he despatched to the town delayed its return journey, and the foot became drunk before leaving. On their march back to O'Neill, Inchiquin attacked and defeated them. Panic spread through the newer recruits to the Ulster army, and O'Neill himself, now faced with a desperate ammunition shortage, withdrew to Clones, County Monaghan.[29] Inchiquin then surrounded Dundalk, whereupon the garrison promptly changed sides and surrendered to him. Monck was sent home to England, where he was censured for his treaty with O'Neill.

The Royalist–Confederation alliance was now ascendant in Ireland. In Connaught, the Earl of Clanricarde, commander of the provinces' Royalist and Confederate forces, not only captured Sligo but also established forts in the area, which protected the small port from being attacked successfully by English parliamentary forces and enabled it to hold out until 1652.[30] The Scots under Monro had captured Belfast, Carrickfergus and Coleraine, and now only Derry and Dublin were held against the Ormondists. Derry was soon threatened by the Scots, and O'Neill was now called on to fulfil the obligations of his cessation with Coote. Accordingly, in late July he relieved the city, and in an ironic celebration the province's principal Gael was toasted by one of its principal colonists.[31] At this moment of strange triumph, affairs in Leinster came to a crashing conclusion. On 2 August Jones attacked Ormond's forces at his base at Rathmines and defeated them. This prompted an immediate retreat to Kilkenny by the allies. John Bellew, who was captured there along with the other officers and soldiers from Ormond's army, was allowed to 'pass into Irish quarters without let or disturbance'. The concession was probably made because Jones still did not have enough resources to guard and feed prisoners.[32] It was an important victory, and it enabled Jones to make plans for retaking Drogheda and Dundalk. But most important, it secured Dublin as a base for landing troops from England. On 13 August, therefore, Cromwell set sail with 7,000 men. Rathmines changed O'Neill's position too. He now realized that there was little chance of any outside help for his stand against the cessation. Requests for help to European Catholic states produced no material aid, and negotiations with the English regime had come to nothing. In their need, he and Ormond turned to each other, but there was still no easy solution to the wide gulf between their respective religious positions.[33]

While they negotiated, Cromwell landed at Dublin and launched a campaign to retake Drogheda, whose governor was the Royalist Sir Arthur Aston, a former governor of Oxford. On 2 September, Cromwell arrived at Drogheda and settled down to besiege the town while awaiting the arrival of heavy artillery. No relief force could be gathered, unfortunately. Owen Roe O'Neill was too ill to lead a campaign himself and Inchiquin had returned south to Munster. Since Ormond could not reassemble his own defeated army, Aston was left alone. Once the guns had arrived, it took Cromwell only hours to make two breaches in the town walls. On 11 September, after further battering of the walls, the English forces launched an attack on the town and broke into the southern end.[34] The fighting in the town was particularly violent, and as it continued it became clear that no quarter was being offered to the defenders. Aston, his commanders and a few hundred soldiers were cornered on Mill Mount. Cromwell then ordered his soldiers to kill all of Aston's men. The governor himself was beaten to death with his own wooden leg, and savage butchery reigned in the streets of Drogheda, sanctioned by Cromwell. He was later to claim that these people were Catholic rebels and thereby in a different category from soldiers and not subject to the usual military 'rules'. In fact, what he was doing to the soldiers and the civilians who were also murdered was applying the same rules as had been applied to Charles I, because the people of Drogheda were tainted with blood-guilt for the Protestant victims of the 1641 massacres. It was a calumny. Cromwell had conveniently forgotten that the people of Drogheda had themselves been besieged by the rebels of 1641, and the soldiers of the garrison, placed there by Inchiquin, included soldiers from the English Munster forces, who had held out against the rebels too. What happened at Drogheda has to be seen in the context of the brutality of the war in Ireland, for example Coote's massacre of the Sligo garrison in 1645 and Inchiquin's actions at Cashel in 1647. Cromwell also needed a quick and frightening victory to overawe others. Finally, few civilians were killed; no contemporary sources suggested that soldiers killed unarmed civilians, and these have been extensively verified by modern historians. This suggests that the one report which made much of the massacre of women and children, that of Henry Wood to his brother Anthony, was a fiction.[35] Nevertheless, many of those that Cromwell called 'barbarous wretches, who have imbrued their hands in so much innocent blood' were not guilty of any such thing. Moreover, Cromwell thought he had done something wrong and felt the need to explain himself in a manner suggestive of an exploration of conscience.[36] The events at Drogheda did prevent him from doing the same thing again, however. His attempt to frighten other garrisons had the desired effect. Trim was abandoned quickly, and Dundalk, Carlingford and Newry soon followed. Owen Roe O'Neill began to move the Ulster army southwards to join Ormond, and on 12 October an agreement between him and Ormond was at last reached. On that night, the Ulster army reached Leinster, but it was too late for the general to be of much personal aid. He died on 6 November. His command was eventually taken up by Ever MacMahon, Bishop of Clogher, who began the task of recapturing the west of Ulster the following year. Cromwell had meantime marched south to Wexford and on 12 October, whilst negotiation continued, had stormed the town. Again, the attack was followed by the most appalling slaughter. Cromwell avoided mentioning civilian losses in his report, even though the boats sunk in the harbour, which he did refer to, were full; most of the 300 drowned as a result were civilians. He most closely associated the dead with 'blood-guilt', writing

> God . . . by an unexpected providence, in His righteous justice, brought a judgement upon them; causing them to become a prey to the soldier who in their piracies had made preys of so many of their families, and now with their bloods to answer the cruelties which they had exercised upon the lives of divers poor Protestants!

In one brief passage, Cromwell managed to link the more recent use of the harbour as a base for Royalist privateering with the blame for the 1641 and other atrocities committed upon his own co-religionists.[37] News of Wexford seemed to accentuate the trend of

Plate 13   Detail from William Petty's *Hiberniae delineatio* (1685)
showing the town of Wexford, reproduced by courtesy of
The National Library of Ireland.

garrisons surrendering to him quickly, and when Roos was invested on 17 October, the garrison surrendered to Cromwell within three days. But when Cromwell reached Waterford in Munster a month later, the walled town defied him. Disease, exacerbated by constant rain, began to cause heavy casualties in the army. Michael Jones himself died the following month. Despite this setback, much of Munster still fell to the English during the winter. Lord Broghill, once Inchiquin's lieutenant, had toured the garrisons in the province and persuaded them to declare for Cromwell. Amongst them was Youghal, where Inchiquin was the governor; the town's officers had written to Cromwell while he was at Wexford urging the 'happy uniting of us all'.[38]

Cromwell settled into winter quarters in south Munster, and in the spring he set off from Youghal and marched north to Tipperary before turning eastwards. He captured Kilkenny on 28 March. The Royalist–Confederate alliance had never really been able to mount an effective challenge to his invasion. Ormond's 1648 treaty had not overcome the deep problems that had riven the Confederation. O'Neill had overcome his deep-seated mistrust of Ormond and the Old English faction only because of the perilous state of Ireland when Cromwell had arrived, and his new army was far from wholly committed to the Royalist cause after his death. The Ulster army under Clogher had moved into north-west Ulster at the end of 1649 to secure the provincial border garrisons against Coote's aggression. In the summer of 1650 the army was caught in Donegal by Coote. When the Ulster army was destroyed at the battle of Scariffhollis on 21 June, Coote exacted a terrible price on its leaders, executing or brutally murdering every one he had captured, including Owen Roe's son Henry. The bishop himself escaped, only to be captured and hanged later in the year. The defeat at Scariffhollis marked the end of the last army Ormond and his Confederate allies could muster. On 10 April Broghill had defeated the last of the Munster forces at Macroom. Because Cromwell had captured Clonmel, the last effective garrison in the south, on 28 April, Clogher's defeat symbolized the end of the war outside Connaught. The province, still led by the Lord President Clanricarde, had escaped much of the destruction and disruption caused by the war of 1649. At the end of the year a good proportion of the applotment was coming in to the provincial collector, Ralph Parker. Money had come in from Roscommon, Galway and County Clare in Munster, and of £800 due to pay for the fleet under Prince Rupert at Limerick, only £127 remained uncollected. To make good the temporary shortfall, Clanricarde ordered Parker to buy cattle on credit when he went down to Limerick to pay and provision the fleet. Limerick town also provided money for the fleet, for which Rupert thanked the mayor at the end of January 1650, informing him that the 'prizes' that the Royalist fleet had won would be sold in the town by 'public outcry'.[39] Dealing with these last vestiges of Royalism was to take more than a year and cost Henry Ireton his life. Cromwell left the country on 26 May 1650, leaving Henry behind with the title of Lord Deputy.

SCOTLAND

Little evidence remains of the effects of the wars on individual rural communities in Scotland during these latter war years, although in Kintyre and the Western Isles, the devastation caused during the wars of 1644–8 was still being felt. The Campbells were moving new tenants into the land they had taken from the MacDonalds. Food was scarce in some regions, and there were double years of dearth; 1650 and 1651 were particularly harsh years. Several sectors of the economy had suffered badly; the cloth and the weavers' houses in Aberdeenshire were destroyed, and as already noted, plaid and spinning wheels were destroyed at Crathie. In the Lowland areas, the Fife communities of fishermen were devastated by the casualties they suffered at Kilsyth when the Fife levies were attacked. Dolphinton was probably not alone in having its meadow and corn destroyed in 1648.[40] The burghs were often preoccupied with the problem of the poor and social order. As in England and Ireland, the numbers of dispossessed had increased and regulation of the poor and disabled was carefully watched. In Glasgow at the end of 1649 the poor were expected to be self-regulating:

> item it is enacted and ordanit that all old able poore men who get maintenance sall be diligent in seaching the strainger poore in the town and to putt them out of the towne, and if they refusit to bring them, as alse any towne poore being goinge to the magitratis themselfis to lose thair pensions.

At the same time, all those refusing to pay their 'poores mentinance' had soldiers billeted upon them.[41] In Edinburgh in March 1650 there was concern that inns were disrupting the social order and a gender bar was placed on them:

> Taking into consideration the manifold evils that falls out within this burgh be woemen taverneris and the fearful sinns committed be them and the many actis and statuttis of this burgh maid agains the of old and the actis of the kirk of lait . . . all vintners to remove their women taverneris before Wittson and procure boys.

Baillie Robert Lockhart was appointed to meet with the ministers of the Kirk 'concerning the changing of women taverneris' on 13 March.[42] In Aberdeen there were still fears of the plague which had afflicted the area in the latter war years, and the wrath of the council fell upon Constable Patrick Watsone, a litster (dyer) by trade, who had concealed a sick person. He was ordered to stand at the scaffold on mercat (market) day with 'skekels' (shackles) on his hands for two hours. He also had to pay a fine of 200 merks (c.£11 sterling).[43] The problem of tax collection still affected the burghs. Threats to billet soldiers on the refusers were made in Aberdeen and Edinburgh in 1649 and 1650.[44] Cromwell's approach in 1650 was to increase the problems for the burghs.

ENGLAND

In England, too, there were general issues of disorder which claimed some attention. The wars and revolutions in Britain and Ireland had caused widespread displacement across the four nations. The first major cause of this was the rebellion in Ireland, which sent thousands of men, women and children of all social classes moving throughout Britain. After that, however, the destruction of some towns and cities through warfare and accidental fire sent other families wandering the roads to find succour somewhere, probably with relatives. This was not a new phenomenon; the roads of Britain were travelled by those who did not require stable housing – people generally referred to as geiptians, or Egyptians – seasonal workers and the unemployed.[45] War and civil war increased this social problem in England as well as Scotland. The village of Upton in Nottinghamshire, where Jane Kitchen had been constable in 1644, was not on a main road. People travelling north or south of that area could have used the Great North Road. In the year following the surrender of Charles to the Scots at nearby Southwell, fifty-eight Irish men, women and children and thirty-eight others passed through the town. In 1649 eighty-three individuals and twenty-two 'companies' of people passed through, all given small sums of money which totalled £2, or 3 per cent, of the community budget.[46] Most people were heading either north or south; York, London and Parliament were common destinations, but people were also heading to and from Kent, and to Edinburgh as well as more local destinations. Some of them were clearly avoiding the damaged bridges and roads around Newark and skirting what had long been a war zone by passing through the villages of Long Bennington, Cottam, East Stoke, Fiskerton Ferry, Upton, Norwell and Tuxford.[47]

In a village closer to London – Thundridge in Braughin Hundred, Hertfordshire – there were far more travellers for the community to cope with. Surviving accounts for 1650, 1651 and nine months of 1652 record a total of £36-08s-02d as having been spent by the constables. These accounts do not record the payment of the monthly tax, nor do they record billeting duties. What they do record are the 'normal' community charges, such as quarter duties and the constables' quarter sessions attendance expenditure. The vast majority of the recorded instances of expenditure related to people travelling through the community – singly, in groups, on foot or in carts. In all the community expended at least £19-08s-02d in payments to these people, some 54.18 per cent of the village expenditure. The actual numbers of people were enormous; in 1650, no fewer than 105 people described as 'poor', twenty-one soldiers, and seventy disabled people travelled through Thundridge. In 1651 the total number was 371 and several unspecified cartloads of people, a number greater than the total population of Upton. Even in 1652, no fewer than 224 people had passed through before October.[48]

At Great Staughton in Huntingdonshire, the figures for travellers rose and fell with the levels of violence during the post-war years. In 1643–4 the total was sixty-six people, including at least forty-six Irish people; in 1645–6 this rose to eighty-three people, only to be dwarfed the following year when it doubled to 173 people. The number fell to forty-one in 1648–9 but rose again to 116 in 1649–50 in the wake of the second civil war, falling to fifty-three in 1650–1.[49] There is a paucity of research in this area generally, so these examples have yet to be fully contextualized. But the figures raise several issues. Generally speaking there appears to have been a large increase in social mobility in the post-war years, but these numbers were rising before the war, and the number of Irish migrants had grown because of the economic depression there before the rebellion. Naturally, the large numbers of people passing through the urban and rural communities must have had a major impact on the perceptions of the social upheaval held by those who did not move, as much as on those who were travelling. Itinerant people have always excited fears amongst settled peoples. Gypsies, seasonal workers and 'vagrants' have given rise to fears of disorder for centuries. They were thought to spread disease and rebellious ideas, and to belong to armed bands involved in rebellion. Even in times of peace, fears abounded concerning those people who had no wish for a permanent home or, through no choice of their own, had no single place of abode. We must not exaggerate these fears and turn them into a universal social view. As far as governments were concerned, the most problematic group was the unemployed, termed vagrants, perhaps best described as the able-bodied poor. The view of this group held by the communities through which they passed did not always arouse such passions, and the compulsory whipping and fining of 'vagrants' was a source of conflict between the obligated officials, usually constables, and their communities. In war, fears that did exist must have multiplied, and apart from the obvious expense that they entailed, the vast numbers of moving people must have added to calls for social stability. More specifically, although the constables' accounts examined here are too few to confirm it, the numbers of travellers may constitute a trend. The Great Staughton accounts show a clear and perhaps logical pattern. The greatest phase of displacement occurred after the first civil war, before declining in the late 1640s to rise again briefly during the year of the revolution in the wake of the second civil war. This would suggest that the Thundridge accounts reached a peak in 1651, a year in which there was again war in England; the numbers in 1652 show a decline.[50] The Upton figures also show a marked reduction in the number of travellers after the end of the wars in England, following upon a sharp rise after the first civil war had ended. This pattern coincides with a marked decline in expenditure, which continued throughout the 1650s. Although the two factors are related, the drop in expenditure has other causes too, and could be taken to symbolize a return to order in the local community. Work on this aspect of the 1650s is largely beyond the scope of this book, however. More pertinent is the state of affairs in the communities during the period when the numbers were rising. A pioneering study of the Dorchester community demonstrates that there was a marked decline in charitable payments during the post-war years, and that poor-rate collection never returned to its pre-war levels.[51] It is clear that the increase in the number of licensed travellers who could call upon community coffers and village officials' time and resources came at the same time as the continued burden on communities was causing protest and unrest. The increase in demand for donations came just at the time when the communal ability to pay was limited. Worcester, just to take one example, was beset during 1649 by arrears which required a special measure to ensure collection for billeting money, monthly pay.[52] It is probable that Worcester and Dorchester were not alone in having such problems, although accounts for the period in the North Riding of Yorkshire show that they cannot be taken for granted. In some cases there was a decline in income or an increase in deficits, but it is not universal. In Thirsk the level of churchwarden levies was reduced from the 1630s rates of 2d per 10 shilling rental value and 2d per acre to 1d on each. This decline coincides with the first civil war, during which no record of the accounts seems to have been kept at all.[53] The churchwardens' accounts at Masham show an increased susceptibility during the war years to go into deficit. This tendency was very closely related to actual conflict, but it happened at other times too. Deficit years include 1638, 1643, 1644, 1645 and 1646. After 1646, the deficit disappeared, and the gap between income and expenditure increased favourably into the 1650s.[54] At Little Ouseburn, the 1640–3 accounts show a small deficit, but no figures before 1659 show a significant surplus, even though levels of taxation increased dramatically – from 45 shilling, in 1626, through £6-09s-10d in 1636 to £18-16s-9d in 1659.[55] At Kirkby Malzeard the accounts records skip seven years from 1641 to 1648 and reopen with a deficit of £2-4s-0d, above an income of only £8-5s-0d, which contrasts with pre-war incomes of between £24-19s-0d and £44-15s-0d. In 1649 only £8-13s-0d was raised of a cast or levy which should have raised £12, while at Wakefield sessions a warrant to distrain for arrears was obtained. Initially this had the effect of increasing the deficit, as just getting there entailed hiring a horse, subsistence payments and the cost of drafting the warrant, all of which came to £1-17s-6d, taking the expenditure up to £10-9s-2d. From then on fiscal matters improved, with arrears being collected and subsequent levies reducing the deficit considerably. Incidentally, one of the items paid for in 1649 was the defacing of the king's arms, which cost a shilling: they had been repaired only in 1640.[56] The state of village funding must be examined in far more detail before firm conclusions can be made, but we are probably looking at periods of instability rather than

decline and destruction in funding networks. Severe strain was put
on all areas in the late 1640s and early 1650s, but the effects of that
strain were more damaging to marginal communities than in other
places. The overriding concern of the period felt by those who lived
and worked through it may well have been insecurity, for which the
decisions at the centre and the radical propositions set out by the
various religious sects, the Diggers and the Levellers offered little
relief. Renewed war in 1650–1 exacerbated these issues further,
albeit temporarily.

13

A Crowning Mercy

Surely if it be not, such a one we shall have, if this provoke those that are concerned in it to thankfulness; and the parliament to do the will of Him who hath done His will for it, and for the Nation; whose good pleasure is to establish the nation and the Change of Government[1]

THE LAST CAMPAIGNS IN SCOTLAND AND ENGLAND

In Scotland, the Kirk Party had been angered by the execution of the king, in which they had had no say and which had formed no part of their political agenda. They had made serious objections during the trial, but no notice had been taken of their commissioners' objections. Two months after the execution of Charles I, Argyll and the Committee proclaimed Prince Charles king of Scotland, and representatives went over to meet him in Holland. The Estates were pre-empted around the country: in Glasgow the king had already been proclaimed at the Cross and bells rung between 11 a.m. and noon on 10 February.[2] Even so, the Estates did not wish to allow such enthusiasm to give Charles any false ideas: they insisted that he would not have any effective power until he had signed the Covenant. Charles agreed to do this in Scotland, but not in England unless a 'free Parliament' there agreed to it. At the same time the young king continued the same vein of diplomacy as his father: while he courted the Kirk Party he was surrounded by loyal Engagers like Lauderdale and the second Duke of Hamilton, brother of the executed duke, formerly Lord Lanark. Montrose was in the background too, but he was unacceptable to the Kirk Party and was still outlawed in Scotland. Nevertheless, while Charles toyed with the idea of joining Ormond in Ireland during 1649, he made Montrose Lieutenant General of Scotland. The marquis then proceeded to Scandinavia and raised a force of mercenaries, forwarding some to

Orkney in September 1649, where he himself arrived the following March. In the meantime, his king first forgot him and then betrayed him.

The king was no sooner crossing the North Sea than the Scots hardened their terms. Not only was he to sign the Covenant, but he was to eschew three things: his Royalist friends, Ormond's treaty with the Confederates and Montrose. The marquis had landed at Kirkwall in March and in April he and Sir John Hurry (once again a Royalist) crossed to John o'Groats. On 27 April their small army was defeated at Carbisdale. Montrose was captured three days later, and before Charles could do anything about it anyway he was taken to Edinburgh. On 21 May Montrose was hanged, beheaded and dismembered. The marquis's head was impaled on Edinburgh Tolbooth and his quartered body dispatched to the major burghs and placed on public view. It was Argyll's final revenge on one of the two men who had humiliated him in 1644–5.[3] MacColla had died in battle in Ulster in 1646.[4] The agreement between Charles and the Kirk was principally aimed at an offensive campaign against England. The Scots had remained 'sullenly but passively hostile to the Commonwealth'.[5] Nevertheless, they rejected the extinction of the monarchy and saw the Commonwealth as perpetuating religious instability in England. Whether we view the Scots as religious imperialists or as acting only in defence of the Covenant when they had invaded England in 1640 and 1644, this state of affairs was unsatisfactory. Their fears of sectarianism were only confirmed by the Commonwealth's unwillingness to establish a national church. Now sectarianism was replacing Episcopalianism as the biggest threat to the Covenanters. The Westminster Parliament had brought Cromwell home to lead an offensive counter-stroke to the Scottish threat. Fairfax refused to lead the army, claiming that an invasion would breach past agreements with Scotland. It is more likely that Fairfax would rather have reached accommodation with the king of the Scots than go to war against him.[6]

The army was assembled and ready by July 1650, backed by a levy, reduced by one-third, of £60,000 per month. This reduction can be observed quite clearly at the local level. The village of Croydon cum Clopton in Armingford Hundred, Cambridgeshire, was a community of around 140 people in the early seventeenth century, but the population fell steadily to fewer than ninety after the Restoration – sixty-five adults in twenty houses. In 1649 the assessments for the £90,000 cost the village £24-12s-10d for the three months, or

£8-4s-31/2d per month. There were fourteen taxpayers, and the levy was raised on land and livestock, the vast majority on land; only £1-7s-9d of the three months' total was collected on livestock. By 1650 the first quarter's assessment had fallen by a third,[7] but renewed war soon raised it to £8-4s-7d a month.

The war continued to intrude into the everyday lives of many people across the four nations through the imposition of high taxes. George Norton of Worton in Yorkshire kept very careful household accounts in a small *Accounts book of Household Expences* used solely for this purpose. In it he added up the cost of all domestic expenditure and offset it against the rents coming in to him. He duly recorded the expenses of his wife's lying in and the costs of food and herbs used in his kitchen. On page three, intruding into recipes and food bills, comes the cost of a dragoon and mount, £4-8s-0d, and for 12 September 1650, Norton's half of a monthly pay levy at £1-1s-1d. He also had to pay excise taxes bi-annually at 6s-2d, a seemingly small amount of his annual expenditure of £134-0s-0d.[8] In Scotland, too, in the collections of family muniments at the Scottish Record Office, there is evidence, probably much of it unexplored, to show that taxation continued at a high level in the shires, amounting for certain estates to very high proportions of county levies. A receipt dated 9 January 1650 shows that the Earl of Marr's estates contributed £378-6s-8d Scots (*c.*£13-10s sterling) for the Clackmannanshire levy, and a further 52 merks, 6s-8d Scots (£2-18s-3d sterling) for the Dundee garrison. By way of comparison, the taxation sum, which does not specify which levy it is going towards, can be compared with previous levies on the shire. For example it would have represented 72 per cent of the county's monthly maintenance in 1645, or 62 per cent of the tax levied that year.[9]

Cromwell crossed the border with an army of 16,000, and reached Dunbar by 26 July. The Scottish army was impressive in quantity, numbering some 26,000, but not in quality. It was put together quite quickly by David Leslie, and although many soldiers were veterans, the officer corps was weakened because ex-Engagers and Royalists were not permitted to enlist. Cromwell at first took the initiative and attempted an attack on Edinburgh on 19 July, only to be driven back down the east coast to Dunbar. There he found it hard to land the seaborne supplies because of atrocious weather. Leslie had followed him and was able to harry the English forces, which were soon riven with disease. The countryside was stripped of fodder and provender, and with every castle south of Edinburgh garrisoned, Cromwell found himself in hostile country. The casualties in his army mounted, and by the end of August 5,000 men were dead or ineffective. Leslie moved on the English forces at Dunbar, intending to cut them off from England by occupying the Doon Hills south of the town. On the night of 2–3 September he then moved downhill to attack Cromwell. In the early morning the English attacked, paralysing the Scots forces, while George Monck and John Lambert pushed across the Brox Burn at the main road and established a bridgehead for the rest of the army to cross. As more and more foot was pushed over the river, Cromwell mounted an attack on the Scots right flank. This was the decisive stroke which enabled the Scottish army to be rolled up from right to left and driven in retreat towards Haddington.

This victory allowed Cromwell to occupy the south-east of the country, and Edinburgh soon fell to him as well. It still took him the winter months to capture the castles in the region. But this did not yet finally dislodge the Kirk Party from power even if for Charles, the defeats and occupation of the Lowlands south of Glasgow and Edinburgh strengthened his position. The more radical faction lost control of the General Assembly. This group had concentrated hitherto on excluding Charles from power, refusing to have him acknowledged as king at Scone or to let him have an army command. In the meantime, a small faction of hard-line Covenanters from the south-west, where the Mauchline rising had occurred in 1648, rejected the attempt to make peace with Charles. On 17 October this group issued a Remonstrance, which caused a division in the unity of the church. In December the small army in the south-west was defeated by an English force, which then went on to occupy the region. While the western group saw Dunbar as a mark of God's anger at its alliance with Charles, the rest of the Party felt obliged to embrace Charles more closely. As for Charles himself, having witnessed the failure of a Royalist coup known as The Start, he had little choice but to move closer to the moderates.[10] On 1 January Charles was crowned by Argyll himself, the restrictions on recruiting Royalists were lifted and the army was re-created with Charles as its commander. Even so, the army continued in a defensive posture as Leslie tried to hold a line from the Clyde to the Forth, centred on Stirling. Cromwell's illness during the first half of 1651 meanwhile halted the campaign season until June, and Lambert was unable to prise Leslie from his base.

In June Cromwell returned to health and launched an offensive campaign by crossing the Forth at Queensferry and striking at the supply bases in Fife. As more English forces were brought across the border into south-east Scotland, the west coast route into England was left open for Charles Stuart. The young man took the opportunity, convinced that there would be a Royalist rising to greet him. It was a vain hope, and there were enough troops in England to hold the country in thrall even if there had been any popular support for the king. By the time the army reached Wigan on 15 August, only about 100 men had joined him, and these had been sent by the Earl of Derby, who was still ensconced in his petty-kingdom on the Isle of Man. A combination of factors limited support for Charles. The Royalist gentry were financially exhausted, and some were horrified by the way Charles stayed with prominent Catholic gentry. Many more regarded the presence of a Scottish army as unwelcome and opposed Charles's acceptance of the Covenant, which in England was taken at face value. Shrewsbury refused to open its gates to the Scottish king, and farther south, Gloucester was unimpressed by the pleadings of its former governor, Edward Massey, now serving with Charles, as he tried to get the town to open its gates. Otherwise, Stuart's advance down the west of England was untroubled compared with Hamilton's march three years earlier, but back in Scotland Stirling fell to English forces and Cromwell turned southwards to pursue Charles's army, leaving Monck in Scotland to destroy the military presence of the Party.

Charles had with him at most 12,000 men, including some 2,000 new levies, when he arrived at Worcester, the first major city in the country to welcome him. Cromwell was close behind him, and with reserve forces picked up on the way south, he led an army of some 28,000. On 29 August he swung west from Warwick and began to approach Worcester. The crossings on the Teme and Severn were seized and pontoon bridges were constructed over the next few days to supplement them. On 3 September, a year after Dunbar, the battle for England began. The Duke of Hamilton tried in vain to hold back the approach of Lambert at Powick. As the massive forces assembled by Cromwell pressed in on the city, there was really only one dangerous moment for the English. When the left wing crossed the Severn at Powick and advanced across the meadows to the east of the city, it drifted away from the right wing on the east bank of the river. Charles took advantage of this to launch a counter-attack from the east, or Sudbury gate of Worcester. Charles drove back the forces ahead of him, although he was soon overwhelmed by superior numbers when Cromwell led his own regiment back over the Severn, forcing the Royalists to withdraw into the city again. As Lambert approached the city, Charles's escape route to Wales was threatened.

Plate 14 Thomas Woodward, *The Battle of Worcester*, reproduced by courtesy of Worcester City Museum and Art Gallery.

The net tightened, and as sections of the Royalist army began to surrender, Charles had to be hustled out of the town under cover of a desperate charge by the Royalist horse down the High Street. It was the beginning of his dramatic escape to France.

In Scotland Monck captured the Committee of Estates on 28 August and on 1 September attacked Dundee with great savagery to persuade other towns to submit. By May 1652, the last three castles in the country had surrendered to the English. The country was annexed to England and its political institutions, so hard fought for twelve years earlier – the Committee of Estates, the Estates themselves and the General Assembly – were suppressed. From February 1652 Scotland had been governed by commissioners. Representatives of the burghs and shires were summoned and were presented with an 'offer that could not be refused'. If they did not accept the offer of union, they would be treated as a conquered nation. With great reluctance, the majority acquiesced.[11] For members of the nobility such as the Earl of Marr, union extended his personal financial disaster. When he added up the costs later, he claimed the wars of the 1640s had been a constant drain on his resources, and the disastrous campaigns of 1650–1 had proved so too. In the 1640s he had entertained Montrose on his way to Kilsyth, and the Covenanting army pursuing Montrose had caused 15,000 merks' worth (c. £1,875 sterling) of damage. For allowing Montrose to stay and for serving at Philliphaugh, where he lost 10,000 merks (c. £555-10s sterling) of goods and horses, Marr was fined 100,000 merks (c. £5,555-10s sterling). Unfortunately, the 1650s campaigns brought no relief. For a start, Marr should have received the rents of Stirling Castle, but although it was the linchpin of Leslie's defence, no rents were ever paid. Moreover, the garrison consumed coal from his mines and powder, and so did the English after it had fallen to them. The 1650s saw three of his houses held for 'manie years' by the English, his woods cut down and his property destroyed. His coal mines were rendered unprofitable because of the taxes charged on production. In all, Marr reckoned that the wars and the English occupation cost him 402,000 merks (£268,000 Scots, £22,333 sterling).[12]

IRELAND: THE LAST WAR

Fighting continued in Ireland after the war with Scotland had ended, but as with the last three castles in the northern kingdom, the war in Ireland was now a clearing operation aimed at removing pockets of Royalist resistance and safe havens on the west coast. Ormond had remained in Ireland for only a few months after Cromwell left, and when the marquis left Ireland he put Royalist affairs into Clanricarde's hands. While guerrilla operations by ex-Confederate army officers in groups known to the English as Tories continued outside Connaught, the main theatre of war switched to the last province for the remainder of the war after Limerick fell to a siege in November 1651.[13] Sligo and outlying garrisons surrendered in the spring of 1652, and the last garrison, Galway, with its governor Sir Thomas Preston, succumbed the following April.[14]

There was no Act of Union for Ireland; the country was simply absorbed *de facto* into the Commonwealth. Indeed, in many ways the governors of England 'showed every disposition to forget about it'.[15] The country was run by a committee, the Committee of the Commonwealth for the Affairs of Ireland, which ensured that taxation strategies had been put in place throughout the country. Surviving copies of the committee's treasury papers are held in the manuscripts department of the National Library of Ireland in Dublin. The schedules for Ulster – dated 4 October 1651, for £5,430 – and for Leinster – dated 5 November 1651, at £4,800 – give a good profile of the way in which the Commonwealth organized its levies. As in England and Wales, levies were authorized periodically by Parliament, and this one covered six months, each calculated to be twenty-eight days long, from 1 November. Each county was allotted a sum, and in Ulster only the barony of Farran in Louth was excluded. Tyrone, along with the barony of Trough from County Monaghan, paid the lowest sum, £100 per month; Antrim paid the highest at £1,500. In Leinster, East Meath (Meath) paid the highest sum, £1,500, in the province; in Queen's County (Laois) only the baronies of Bally Adam and Stradbally could be assessed at £100 apiece. The assessments were made on lands, tenements, hereditaments, rents, profits, goods and chattels. Any complaints were to be heard and acted upon and refusers sequestrated until fined sums not exceeding £40 or twenty-eight days in prison.[16] There were still problems even at this late stage in the war. An assessment levied on bread corn in the Leinster counties of Westmeath and Longford was hampered by the fact that the Commonwealth could not control the whole area. 'Besides 400 or 500 barrels which may be gotten out of County Longford, although ... could make no certain applotment as the greatest part is in rebel hands.[17] The tentacles of the

Commonwealth went further than this into the lives of the people in Ireland. Although it has been noted that Ireton has not been praised for his 'studious clemency' towards the Irish, it is also clear that some of his policies were reprehensible. On 11 May 1651 Ireton issued a proclamation forbidding intermarriage between the English and the Irish that echoed some of the provisions of the Statutes of Kilkenny of 1366. Officers were to be cashiered and men flogged if they fell in love with Irish women. Stereotypical views of the Irish were not allowed to be overturned by sentiment and close association. The leading rebels were still regarded in the same light as when the orders of the Privy Council put a price on them back in 1642. Only some of the names had changed: Lord Iveagh's or Lord Enniskillen's head would fetch the judicious murderer £200; Phelim O'Neill's head could still earn a killer £300, and so on. But death came in other ways, too. In Dublin, according to a report made in September 1650, some 1,100 people died of plague.[18]

Of the four nations, Ireland was on the verge of the most important social changes. When Ireton died in November 1651, he was succeeded temporarily by Edmund Ludlow. Lambert was then appointed to the lieutenancy, but when that office was abolished and replaced with a deputyship, Lambert declined the post. Instead, in August 1652 Ireton was eventually succeeded by Charles Fleetwood, who also married his widow, Cromwell's daughter Brigit. Fleetwood's deputyship marked the beginning of great social change, as has recently been noted:

> The English and French revolutions of the seventeenth and eighteenth centuries, frequently regarded as social movements, failed to transform to any degree the landed class of those countries. However, this was not the case in seventeenth-century Ireland where an immense transfer in the ownership of property occurred.[19]

This transfer is often known as the 'Cromwellian Land Settlement', but it is undoubtedly also true that the dramatic changes in culture and landownership were long-term processes which the period 1649–59 accelerated rather than initiated. The same may be said of parts of the Scottish Highlands too, where different immediate motivation, but similar post-war circumstances, caused landownership, and with it culture and religion, to be dramatically restructured under the Campbells. This process was part of the ongoing restructuring of Highland society referred to in chapter 1. Perhaps we should again look to the Highland/Ireland Gaelic nexus as a way to understand, or at least contextualize, the post-war settlements.

Although the post-war settlement is beyond the scope of this work, it is necessary here to give some outline of the process and its aims.[20] The Act for the Settlement of Ireland of 1652 was based upon the act of 1642, which established the adventurers, and the act of 1643, which allotted Irish land to soldiers who had served in Ireland. The act established ten categories of people in Ireland according to their part in the rebellion. The first five groups were exempt from pardon and could lose their property and their lives. These groups embraced not only people who had planned or assisted in the rebellion and those who had participated in murders and massacres, but also Jesuits, soldiers and people who did not surrender within twenty-eight days of the publication of the act. The next five categories included those who had held office in the Confederate army or the administration. They themselves would be banished and two-thirds of their estates confiscated, while the remaining third would be converted into land elsewhere and given to their wives and descendants. Confederate soldiers were allowed to convert one-third of their estates to land elsewhere if they surrendered within twenty-eight days. Additional groups listed people, even Protestants, who had not maintained good affection towards the Westminster Parliament.[21] 'Elsewhere' meant Connaught, or at least four counties of the province. A four-mile-wide boundary settled by English or Protestant ex-soldiers was created inside the provincial border and excluded from the settlement programme, but the construction of fortresses planned throughout the area was not completely carried out. County Sligo was supposed to be included in the settlement programme, but this plan was overturned by the persistence of soldiers who had served under Sir Charles Coote. Their continuing claims to have their arrears met by the provision of land parcels were successful, and in addition to Sligo, they received part of County Mayo, the barony of Tirawly. Coote himself, was given the provincial presidency for his contribution to the war effort (he had led the Protestant Connaught forces and eventually the Ulster-based Lagan army too).[22] One study of women in the war presents evidence that women, either as wives or landowners in their own right, went out to Connaught as part of the scheme. Like the men, they had to get certificates at Athlone before organizing their goods for the move. But the 480 unaccompanied women, sometimes in small kinship groups, received very small parcels of land by comparison with men.[23]

The experience of John Bellew, whose career has occasionally surfaced in this work, indicates the way in which land was parcelled up and exchanged. Bellew also serves as a good example of Irish resistance to the policy, for he refused to accept the terms he was offered. When we last left Bellew, he had been paroled after the battle of Rathmines. He went on to the fort at Terroghan, where he became the governor, and when he surrendered Terroghan, Bellew believed he saved his estates by doing so. Bellew was judged by the Commissions of Adjudication of Claims and Qualifications of the Irish to be in possession of lands worth £1,200 a year and £50 per year worth of fishing rights in the baronies of Ferrard and Ardee, County Louth. He was then put in the group whose estates were to be confiscated in return for lands in Connaught and was accordingly offered fishing rights worth in the region of £15 and lands worth £400 a year scattered the length and breadth of County Galway. Bellew refused to go to Connaught, however, despite the threat of death which hung over those refusing the terms of the Articles of Kilkenny. He remained in hiding for the next four years, trying to appeal against the judgement. At the Restoration, Bellew petitioned the king for the return of his lands. It seems that it took six years at least of obtaining certificates from the now Duke of Ormond for Bellew to achieve his own complete restoration.[24]

As a whole, the transplantation policy failed. Problems such as Coote's soldiers were at the heart of the failure of the programme. There were simply too many interest groups with claims to Irish lands for the Commonwealth to satisfy. Another problem was that so many Protestants who held estates already were able to qualify for confiscated lands. This meant that such men built up a small number of large estates instead of, as Cromwell had hoped, a large number of small estates. In west Ulster, a recent computer-based research project shows that 91 per cent of confiscated lands went to landowners, some of them Catholic, who had held estates before 1641.[25] For some Irish men and women the problems of the war continued in the transplantation to Connaught. About two hundred men were tried by the High Courts of Justice set up in Dublin. Sir Phelim O'Neill was condemned to death by the court in 1653 after being questioned closely on the origins of the commission he had claimed came from Charles I back in November 1641. The irony now was that the English wanted the assertion to be true. O'Neill, despite a possible promise of reprieve from Fleetwood, denied that his claim had been anything but a means to win political and material support for the rebellion. The Catholic religion was prohibited completely, and no covert toleration was to be allowed, although it was not until 6 January 1653 that this policy was announced. Priests had to surrender and leave the country or face execution, which many did. Creaghts too were suppressed. Transhumance was still considered uncivilized, and as a mark of the new civilization in Ireland, the migratory herders were to be dispersed to settled lands to prevent the 'inconvenience' of their living in a 'loose disorderly manner'. This order was made in late January 1653.[26] The concern for public order seen in Scotland and England was directed in Ireland not just towards the creaghts but also by the displaced and unemployed. One solution was transportation. In September 1653, Captain John Vernon and David Sellick of Bristol were to gather 250 'women of the Irish nation above 12 years of age and under forty-five, also 300 men above twelve and under fifty to be found in the country within 20 miles of Cork, Youghal, Kinsale, Waterford and Wexford to transport them into New England'.[27]

THE GOSPEL IN WALES

The fourth nation was only tangentially involved in the campaigns of 1649–53. Money and soldiers for the campaigns in Ireland, Scotland and England were raised in Wales, and concerted efforts were made to find any available. A paper entitled 'A Discovery of Concealed Money for the Commonwealth' drawn up by Thomas John ap Thomas shows the extent of the search throughout Carmarthenshire in detailed lists of personal debts, such as the unpaid composition money of Mr Henry Middleton of Llanarthny.[28] He had been a delinquent in the first civil war and had assisted Powell and Laugharne in the second. The list also included public debts. Middleton fitted both categories and demonstrated the post-war dependency of the government on former enemies. He had been a high constable in 1648 and had concealed £1,000 of monthly pay collected in the county. Others held money collected for other causes. John Davis of Llandeilo had raised a Royalist contribution totalling £360-5s-6d, and according to information received still had the money in his hands. He also had money raised for the British army in Ireland, possibly dating back to 1642, a sum totalling £800. Thomas Jones, an alderman of Carmarthen, was likewise supposed to have £400 which had been raised for the Royalists; and Rowland Gwyn of Cathramis still had £300 of contributions unaccounted for. There were older debts too. The final sum recorded showed that the inquisitors were digging deep. John Harris of Llanvenith was supposed to have £700 in ship money from 1637–9 in his hands in the early 1650s! Another paper suggests that the Carmarthenshire search was not singular. There was also a grand inquest of Haverfordwest. The incomplete draft of this inquiry unearthed John Wheeler, who appeared to have £111-11s-10d of tax in his hands, and John Davis, alderman, who had died holding £135 of monthly pay.[29]

More normal methods of exaction have left a few scattered records too. In May and June 1651 fifty footsoldiers destined for Ireland were raised in Flint, Anglesey, Merioneth and Radnorshire; and money was raised and paid to conduct other troops in Carmarthenshire and Cardiganshire to Milford Haven. The Cardiganshire militia troop under Lieutenant Richard Evans was seen to have a relish for the work, and an order was made for paying them £167 'as a gratuity and incouragement to the said troop for their forwardness in the public service'.[30] Haverfordwest was not so lucky. The monthly assessment of £45 was felt to be too great for the town to pay. From February 1649 the people of the town claimed that they were rated at the same level as larger towns such as Carmarthen, Cardigan, Swansea, Tenbigh and Pembroke. In a series of petitions the inhabitants claimed that the expenses of the wars still hung over their heads. They had built defences, then demolished them, supported several garrisons, looked after sick and wounded soldiers, and in 1649 had troops bound for Ireland billeted upon free quarter in the towns at a cost of £500.[31] The money being raised for Ireland, they claimed, had risen from £10 a month to £45 at the same time as the town became a staging post for Ireland. The petitions continued in 1652; one detailed petition demonstrated that the town had little in the way of public stock, having only twenty houses taken over from the pre-Reformation church, which yielded 'no profit but the rents and this goes to defray other charges'. Moreover, the public works, the two aqueducts, two bridges ('one a main bridge on the principal river of Milford'), two quays and two almshouses cost the town considerable sums. The town asked, rather optimistically, to be exempted from all future assessments while hoping, more realistically, for a reduction of the burden.

Perhaps the most important piece of legislation concerning Wales at this time was the Act for Better Propagating and Preaching of the Gospel in Wales. This act gave the state the power to seize church lands to finance large-scale evangelism and primary education. Further, a commission under the leadership of Colonel Thomas Harrison examined the credentials of the sitting incumbents and expelled those considered lacking. Some concessions were made to the knock-on effects of this change. One-fifth of the living of the expelled was set aside to support the wives and children of those dispossessed in this way. And they were legion. Some 278 men were thrown out, 196 of them from south Wales. This action influenced the recruiting of the 135 new preachers, sixty of whom were Welsh speakers, mostly concentrated in the south and on the borders. It has been suggested that despite the leaders' belief that the movement had an important influence on Welsh society, there were problems. Filling parishes was far more difficult than emptying them. English-speaking graduates were reluctant to venture far into the country, for instance. The scale of the problem reflected the difficulties experienced after the Reformation, when a large proportion of Welsh parishes remained empty.[32] In the 1650s, as in the reign of Elizabeth, itinerant ministers were employed to cover several parishes.

There was opposition to the act, too. Alexander Griffith, who had been ejected from Glasbury and Llanwnog in Radnorshire, attacked the commissioners as 'tinkers' and adventurers. He was not alone. Members of the old church – such as Huw Morys, Henry Vaughan and Rowland Watkyns – tried to exploit sympathy for the ejected ministers by contrasting them with members of the commission such as Phillip Jones. Jones, because of his recently acquired wealth, was accused of corruption, cupidity and maladministration.[33] Attacks on the social standing and honesty of the commissioners went hand in hand with attacks on the county committees and the area committees of sequestration set up in 1649. Sequestrators and excise men were hated figures, named 'boars of the forest' or likened to plague.[34] Jones made vast profits out of his position in the Glamorganshire administration, and he was a potent symbol of everything that former Royalists hated – a new man, and one who had profited from their own misfortune. He was not alone in facing the possibly groundless charges of racketeering, which flowed from a widely held view of the Commonwealth. This is also evidence that the Commonwealth never established itself in the hearts and minds of the Welsh.

THE MILLENNIUM

Although the religious enthusiasm for propagating the gospel in Wales may have been unique in its zeal, it was not alone. Similar attempts were made in the north of England and elsewhere in the four nations. For a number of people the civil wars and revolutions were more than a political and social event; they were a spiritual experience. Rather than simply forging a new Britain, these people were creating the kingdom of Christ within the four nations. When Gerrard Winstanley proposed the creation of Digger colonies, he may well have been aiming at a complete transformation of the nature of mankind, through the acceptance of digging by the land-owning class, as part of a millennial solution. Winstanley did use millennial language in his interpretation of the Fall. And the *Digger's Mirth* asserted that the common treasury would come about when the Beast, analogous in Winstanley's writings to the Norman yoke of government, gave up its crown. That digging played a part in this was made clear in *Fire in the Bush*, where Winstanley wrote: 'the Seed of life that lies under the clods of Earth, which in his time is now rising up to bruise the Serpents head, and to cast that imaginary murderer out of Creation'.[35]

In the past it has been argued that the revolutionary wars were wars of religion. This idea is not new; after all, one historian entitled his document collection *The Constitutional Documents of the Puritan Revolution*.[36] But since then years of Marxist reinterpretation have attempted to show that those acting in the name of religion were actually the driving forces of a capitalist society, and that religion merely provided them with the vocabulary of revolution. The assertion by modern historians that we should again take the religious language and attitudes at face value has been refreshing and challenging. Underlying this specific proposition is a crucial historical point, namely, that students of history must listen to the past rather than nod condescendingly, mentally turn to the protagonists and say 'Yes, but what you really meant was . . .'. This is not to refute the Marxist position altogether. Clearly the religious beliefs and fervour of men such as Pym and Cromwell did enable them to forge new political dynamics and, for Winstanley and Everard, new social dynamics too. But we must ask questions about their motivation. The idea that the wars were solely religious in nature is just as clearly problematic. Undoubtedly, Archibald Johnston and Samuel Rutherford saw the conflict as a religious one, and many other English and Welsh people saw their battle against King Charles's forces as a battle for the soul of the nation. In the case of others, like Cromwell himself, it was their successes that led them to see themselves as involved in God's war. Some of the king's opponents did not see it that way, however. To John Hutchinson, for example, religion was important, but not as important as freedom and liberty. For the Royalists, religion was important in a similar way, representing part of the monarchical powers being challenged by the revolution. Yet the motivation of the Royalist commanders has been demonstrated to be political, not religious.[37] We thus return to the essential problem concerning the notion of a war of religion: can it be deemed such if only some of its participants are fighting on religious issues? Probably not; but for some individuals it certainly was, and for the others, religion was at least one of a number of complex personal, social and political factors.

This brings us back to individuals and their underlying motivation. All sides were composed of people fighting for a variety of reasons, including political and religious ones, with enough common ground to bind them into a militant stance. In England and Wales, political and religious issues, separately or intermingled, probably dominated the two sides. In Ireland and Scotland, religion and politics combined with issues of race, culture and nationalism. There were other factors – self-defence, defence of property and attempts to regain property amongst them. There were the ambitious men, often referred to as second sons, or tinkers, who sought to create new opportunities for themselves out of the war. This phenomenon carried over into the non-combatant field too, where men and women sought to profit from the war, not necessarily to make money out of other people's misery but out of war-driven needs for weapons, ammunition, uniforms, beds and bedding, shoes, fodder and food. And across the four nations there were many more factors motivating those who fought, acted as suppliers, or sought to lie low.

But what of those who did see religion as crucial, those who worked in expectation of the coming of Christ? As the Scots stood on the border with England in 1639, Samuel Rutherford was convinced of the crusading nature of the war which was about to begin. Two years later, Hansard Knollys listened to the voice of the multitude with the conviction of a man expecting to hear of Christ's return. And as the wars were fought, some sought to make plain what had happened. Mary Carey described the war in the following terms when she petitioned Parliament in 1648:

It being the great design of God the Father to set up his Son our Lord Jesus Christ, as his King upon the holy hill of Zion, and (though the heathen rage, and the people imagine vain things, saying, come let us break their bonds asunder, and cast away their cords from us) to give him the heathen for his inheritance, and the uttermost parts of the earth for his possession. I say, this being God's design, he hath for the effecting of it, given all power and authority in heaven and in earth into his hand, and accordingly Jesus Christ hath undertaken to execute all God's decrees, which are mentioned in the Book of Revelation . . .

Revelation, 11:11
And after three days and a half, the Spirit of life from God entered them.

. . . For on the 23rd day of October, 1641, did not the beast begin the war in Ireland; and he continued overcoming the witnesses, the saints of Jesus Christ, in Ireland, and in England, until the 5th day of April 1645, and from the 23rd of October 1641, unto the 5th of April, 1645, there is just a thousand two hundred and sixty days; which according to the Scripture account . . . is three and a half years complete.

On the 5th day of April, 1645, the Parliament's Army, who had stood for the defence of the saints against the beast; and had been before that time exceedingly overcome, and were brought into a very low condition at that time being new modelled . . . having a great many precious saints in it . . . defeated all the enemies with whom they did encounter; . . .

Thus the 5th day of April, 1645, did the witnesses, the saints (of whom the beast thought to make a utter end) stand upon their feet having a Spirit of life from God put upon them.[38]

Carey was making an effort to galvanize Parliament into positive action to further the millennium. But for many of those working for the new millennium, 1649 marked the end of their hopes. Some had even fought for the king in 1648 as part of the conservative Presbyterian reaction to the triumph of the Independent army.[39] Disappointment was a major problem for many would-be saints over the next few years, both those awaiting an imminent second coming and those with more prosaic expectations of the millennium. A millennial belief lay at the heart of all Christian sects, but Christ's return was more imminent for some. The revolution, more specifically, the ultimate failure of Presbyterian attempts to create a centralized national church, had allowed many radical sects to flourish. They were not entirely new; there were networks of dissenting Protestants in England and Wales in the years before the war, just as there were networks of Catholics, though they can be described as 'a comparative rarity'.[40] These groups developed alongside the established church but rejected many of its principles, such as infant baptism, as well as its organizational structure. However, the war certainly encouraged the growth of these groups of Baptists, Anabaptists, and so on; and it did allow for the growth of new groups, some of which appeared in Thomas Edwards's *Gangraena* as well as in the illustrated version referred to in chapter 10. The General Baptists flourished in the 1640s, developing symbiotic political connections with the Levellers in London during 1647–8. The Levellers took much of their egalitarianism from the Baptists, according to one view.[41] As the Independents triumphed at the end of 1648, the Baptists eschewed the Levellers in 1649 in the search for the approval of the new regime. Baptists held that the strictures of Calvinism rejected so many that the ordinary people were left out of it; they therefore propagated instead a belief in general redemption, emphasizing human dignity. They had used the freedom of the press, instigated by the abolition of the Court of High Commission, to good effect. Lucy Hutchinson, for one, was influenced by Baptist pamphlets on infant baptism, which she read while pregnant, and went on to convert her husband to Baptist philosophy.[42] Moreover, the printed media allowed several sects to build support and sympathy in the army and in the City. By the 1650s regional associations of churches had begun to develop. For them the revolution was largely a success.

For some individuals the period offered the opportunity for a trail through the various sects. This theme is reflected in the title of Laurence Clarkson's book, *The Lost Sheep Found: Or The prodigal returned to his Father's house, after a journey through many Religious Countrys*, published in 1660.[43] Clarkson passed through many sects – Ranters, Seekers and Quakers amongst them – before taking over the group formed by and named after Ludovic Muggleton. Of all these groups, the one which has attracted the most recent controversy has been the Ranters, a nickname derived from their enthusiastic preaching. Debate has centred on whether or not the group existed at all as a collective or whether it was simply a label applied by outsiders to a series of individual religious pamphleteers. Whether or not they were a group, their religious professions suggest to some historians 'a reasonably consistent set of doctrines'. To others they were nothing less than a sect.[44] Women and men who were at the forefront of Ranter preaching and writing were essentially Antinomians, insisting that God's law was superior to all the laws of humankind. But unlike the Seekers, who sought God's will through prayer and patience, they went beyond the limits of most Antinomian groups in tackling the relationship of sin to God's law. Sin, Clarkson argued, was earthly and imaginary, created by mankind, not God. The logical extension of this view was that there could be no sin, and therefore no need for such institutions as marriage created to save mankind from sins of the flesh. The resulting apparently lax sexual morals opened the Ranters to attack from rival groups and conservative commentators, who saw them as sex-obsessed. Looking back later and criticizing the groups to which he had once belonged, Clarkson did not deny this charge:

> Now I being as they said, Captain of the rant, I had most of the principle women came [sic] to my Lodging for knowledge, which was then called the Head-quarters. Now in the height of this ranting, I was made still careful for moneys for my Wife, onely my body was given to other women.[45]

Moreover, the Ranters met in alehouses and taverns, one of which was run by the husband of Mary Middleton (Clarkson's mistress and one of the principal women he referred to), which again led to their being attacked as immoral. Another principal character, Abiezer Coppe, argued that there could be no blasphemy, and that what others thought was blasphemy was freedom from restraint. He was alleged once to have sworn from a pulpit for one hour at a stretch, and he was not alone.[46] Their argument, that if God were omnipotent evil or sin could not exist, unless it was part of God's plan, was hard to refute. But the very existence of a Ranter argument is questioned in one recent work on Ranters, which claims that the whole notion of the Ranters as a group is a false one created by two groups, their horrified seventeenth-century critics and twentieth-century radical historians. According to this study,

> views which the alleged Ranters did hold were widely divergent one from another. They did not seem to present anything like a coherent, cohesive or consistent body of ideas which could be usefully subsumed under one label

and moreover, in their writings 'the views expressed by the leading Ranters did not reflect the claims which historians made for them.'[47] As a result, the idea of the Ranters as a sect is rejected, along with any notion of their constituting an attack on Protestant ethics. These 'rejectionist' ideas have been subjected to a great deal of criticism;

the 'furore' has not yet died down, and the argument is still un-resolved by any new consensus. That contemporaries used the terms Ranter or a perceived Ranter philosopher as labels to tag enemies or as a measure to determine a personal position, like the religious radical Anna Trapnel, seems undeniable. Trapnel said once that she was glad to have escaped a 'ranting tenet' in the development of her own religious position, and so she must have had some notion of what Ranters as a group believed.[48] Nevertheless, the argument denying Ranters the status of a sect is powerful and challenging, leaving us to conclude that while they did exist and held a set of ideas recognizable to outsiders, on a more subtle level their ideas were a diffuse and possibly unresolved collection of beliefs.

It is less of a problem to categorize other groups. The Fifth Mon-archists, for example, were clearly definable. They involved mem-bers of the army leadership like Colonel Thomas Harrison and believed that the millennium was at hand, now that the four mon-archies or empires – Persian, Greek, Egyptian and Roman – had fallen. Their movement has recently been examined and their beliefs related to popular millenarianism. Their expectations of the Fall received a setback when the execution of Charles I was not followed by radical change. Indeed, the Commons proved to be a weak in-strument of change, partly because many of its members were in favour of further change, but also because until Charles Stuart was defeated and the Irish wars were at an end, other matters had to be dealt with before, or instead of, reform at home. Religious writers like Anna Trapnel believed that Parliament should be replaced by a theocratic government of the Saints, those who would rule with Christ.[49] When Cromwell drove the Commons from their chamber in 1653 and established a new Parliament of representatives chosen supposedly for their Godliness, disappointment was compounded. For although this assembly, which became known as Barbon's Par-liament after a leading London member, Praise-God Barbon, had twelve Fifth Monarchists sitting in it, it proved to be no more an agent of the millennium than the old House. Cromwell and the army clearly were not the agents of God's work, as once envisaged by Mary Carey. Returning to the text of the books of Revelation and Daniel, commentators found the references they required to describe what had happened. In one of Daniel's dreams, the apparition of the Goat with four horns represented the four divisions of Alexan-der's empire. When the four horns were observed closely, there appeared on the fourth horn a small growth, which was a small horn

representing Antiochus Epiphanes the usurper.[50] Cromwell was identified as being this small horn. As he sprang from one of the old
kingdoms, no reformation could be expected of him.

As for Cromwell himself, he was a millenarianist, like most others,
but he stood at a great distance from the people who saw this as a
short-term process. His political outlook was clearly influenced by
his religious views, although unlike other Independents, he had been
prepared to accept some form of Presbyterianism in the 1640s and
had drifted away from that moderate stance only slowly. The providence of God, demonstrated by the victories over the Royalists in
1646, the Welsh and the Scots in 1648, the Irish in 1649–50 and the
Scots again in 1650–1, convinced him of his role in God's work but
did not persuade him to espouse the views of any sect, although for
a while he was seen as being close to the Seekers.[51] Nevertheless, the
story of the years 1652–8, which fall outside the remit of this work,
is bound up with Cromwell's search for a godly magistracy in the
British republic.

REVOLUTION

So what had happened in the years 1638–51? Contemporaries
privileged enough to be able to leave a record were divided. For
the moderate Royalist MP turned statesman, Edward Hyde, Earl of
Clarendon, it was a rebellion caused by a discontented faction in
Parliament. The Royalist playwright, biographer and philosopher
Margaret Cavendish, Duchess of Newcastle, agreed, although she
was broader in her criticism of 'that rebellious and unhappy Parliament'.[52] The conservative Presbyterian Richard Baxter blamed the
war on both sides on '[t]he imprudence and violence of some members of the House, who went too high' and on the king's attempt to
overturn the political situation with military force.[53] Others, referred
to by Clarendon at the beginning of his work, detected longer-term
causes, something taken up by later historians. For those like Samuel
Rutherford and Archibald Johnston of Wariston, who related the
cause to religion, the roots of the problem lay with the incomplete
nature of the Reformation in the four nations after a century of
struggle. The early stages of this book were concerned to show that
there were underlying problems within the societies in the four
nations. Cultural, racial, religious, political and administrative problems at times caused immediate crises for the government, but could

not alone have led to the tremendous crisis of 1638–51. They are
the 'necessary causes' without which the events of 1638–51 could
not have occurred.[54] The character of Charles I and the nature of his
political and religious abilities and ambitions are crucial to the chain
of events. It is clear that the king's misguided attempt to be a ruthless centralizer in the four nations brought to a head many of the
underlying issues. Charles's main problem in this respect was that
he brought them all to a head at once. Had he not done so, he
might well have been able to bring the resources of three nations to
bear on the other one, as he had hoped to do in 1639. But if the
Welsh historians are to be fully believed, only Wales was relatively
stable in 1638. Ireland was restive under the rule of Wentworth,
whose government was steadily uniting disparate groups in opposition to it as well as enabling underlying discontent amongst the
Gaelic peoples to come to a head. England was riven by discontent
over many of Charles's reforms, not to the extent that existed in
Ireland and Scotland, but certainly in a way which was to weaken
the country's loyalty to the king. When Charles went to war with
Scotland to enforce policies already disapproved of in England, the
southern nation proved receptive to the Scots' revolutionary solutions to their problems with the errant ruler. Political revolution
therefore spread south and then west to Ireland. However, the cultural and religious perceptions of England and Scotland's political
elites stunted the revolution in Ireland and unleashed the rebellion
of 1641. It was the king's attempt to make use of the political instability caused by the Irish rebellion which dragged England and Wales
into war in 1642. His near success in 1643 and his pact with the
Confederates in Ireland then brought the Covenanters into the war
in 1644 out of a need to preserve their own revolution. The Irish
rebellion had exposed the fragility of the anti-Wentworth alliance
and the confused self-perceptions of the English and Irish Catholics,
which prevented the adoption of a hard line at Kilkenny. These
divisions, coupled with the fragmentation of the Gaelic elite over the
previous fifty years, led to problems of precedence in the armies of
the Confederation, which hampered the war effort. After the king
and moderate Covenanters were defeated in 1648, the English vic-
tors took revenge on the Irish nation for causing the war of 1642
and put a bloody end to the risings there. The Covenanters, too,
were defeated when their paranoia about the safety of the Kirk
forced them into an unholy alliance with Charles Stuart. In the
meantime the political revolution of 1648–9 in England and Wales

had built upon that of 1640–1 partly in order to consolidate it. But a deeper political and social revolution was defeated by the grandees and the Commonwealth Parliament, confining the revolution to one of ideas, which were to have a major influence on social and political thought throughout the next two hundred years.

But what of the people of England and Wales, 'not a half nor a quarter' of whom supported the revolution of 1648–9, according to Lady Fairfax? What did it all mean to those who composed no memoir and made no speeches in the House or on the scaffold justifying their stance? This work has presented excerpts from some of the narratives of the war which people were able to create through claims for losses. Any of the submissions sent to the Exchequer or to the Committee of Monies offer a narrative of the major events of one or other of the wars, centring upon the periodic crises provoked by the war – Webster's carts taken from Warwick in 1642, the Royalist attack on Salisbury in 1645 when William Phillips lost his hat, and so on. We have seen that John Fidkin of Hartlebury divided his narrative of the war into three important parts: a raid by Captain Hitchcock, the visitation of the Scots, and the siege of Hartlebury Castle. Marjorie Mitchell's war centred upon three major incidents: the descent of Lord Gordon in 1645, of Middleton in 1647 and of Leslie in 1649. In some places these personal narratives match the grand narrative of the war. They link with traditionally important dates – Edgehill, Montrose's campaign in Scotland, the Scots army's march into the west Midlands, and the Engagement – but they also provide a broader view of what the period meant to those involved. Small-scale sieges and individual acts of violence towards the people of the four nations make their narratives distinctive, pushing them beyond the limits of the grand narrative. Much work remains to be done in this area, and there is a great deal of material in the local record offices and the central repositories for students to use. All of it tells of the people's experience of civil war, despite gaps in the material highlighted in this work. Narrative frameworks can be created for those areas where material is patchy or non-existent. In Ireland, for example, the Ormond papers, Clanricarde's letters and the *Aphorismical Discovery* can be used to construct narrative frameworks for towns and people in the many regions where papers do not survive.

The conversion of the people's experiences into political positions can be seen in the petitions and declarations of the club movement or the women's petitions to Parliament. Politicization does not always mean radicalization, as it did within the New Model Army. While the stance of the club petitions may not have been original and may have owed a great deal to the moderate petitions of 1642, the method of their creation was new, and the narratives of the people burdened with taxes help us understand why they came to be created. According to one historian, neither the peasant classes, composed of those who had signed petitions, stood in defiance of armies and created their own narratives, nor even the farmers and industrialists, who profited from the war, or those who drafted petitions, won power in the revolution. Power instead was won by the army grandees and brought little benefit to the country at large. In counties of England like Hampshire, 'institutions were ruthlessly taken over by national political groups in the wake of revolution'.[55] In Devon, the voice of the people as expressed through traditional institutions was ignored by the county government, who neglected most of the complaints about the burdens of war except when it suited them. On the other hand, the people of Somerset were able to absorb the costs of war, and to benefit from the period, because of their fixed rents. In Warwickshire, it has been suggested, the gentry became more obsessed with their 'separateness' from the lower social orders and more wary of them and their political pretensions in the wake of war. This trend is echoed in other areas, notably those that experienced agrarian disorder in the revolution. It is probably the case, though, that as far as economic issues go, the results of the English revolution were 'distinctly ambiguous'.[56]

Scotland did not win as a result of the revolution either. After 1649 its own independence, and the political elites that emerged victorious against Charles I, were crushed by its more powerful southern neighbour, and 'little account was taken of Scottish views' in the British republic. The Presbyterian church, a major factor in the development of the first British revolution, failed to influence the development of a godly church in its neighbour state; and in response to the second English revolution it divided against itself. Scotland's resources were severely damaged by the series of wars it fought in Britain and Ireland, and the Scots could not compete with the relative abundance of resources in England.[57]

It has been suggested that Wales lost out too, its traditional elite being displaced by newcomers. Moreover, the republic which developed from the revolution was a 'monster without a head'.[58] Ireland, as we have seen, may have come out worse, its resources in some areas drained, and as many as 41 per cent of its people dead or gone from its shores. But the wars there should not be viewed as a complete disaster. As usual in war, some people profited, and the extent of destruction did allow for economic restructuring, which led to prosperity in the latter years of the century. But some people would not see that later prosperity, while destruction of the local and personal economies ensured only poverty and deprivation for many. Moreover, by the end of the 1650s the country was, even if the Cromwellian settlement was incomplete, firmly in the grip of the Protestant ascendancy, and any vestige of power had been stripped from most of the Catholic majority.[59]

And so at the end, what can we say of those ordinary folk like Thomas Richardson, a man accused of stealing a ewe, and his attitude to national affairs?

> we cannot assume that he had no views upon them. As with so many people like him, who are mere names in county and parish records, his place in the political pattern may simply be lost.[60]

The wars had to some extent united the people of the four nations in suffering and expense. However, the burden was not shared evenly, and we cannot talk of a common experience or of a 'British and Irish experience' in anything but the vaguest terms. We can look at their losses; the war invaded the fields, the yards and the kitchens of the people. It took the linen off their beds and the mirrors off their walls. It also killed many of them. Even if some estimates are on the high side, they give us a scale upon which to work. In England (and Wales), it has been calculated that 190,000 people, or 3.7 per cent of the population died; in Scotland there were 60,000 deaths, 6 per cent of the population. The estimate for Ireland, 618,000, or 41 per cent of the pre-war population, is far less satisfactory and needs major revision. Nevertheless, suffering was undeniably on an immense scale, even if we need to treat these estimates with healthy scepticism.[61] And what of those who survived? We can tell something of their experience through their narratives, but these reveal little of their political and social outlook, unless tied closely to their petitions. It was their war and their revolution as much as that of the grandees; it was they who pushed forward radicalism in the army, and radicalism and conservatism in the country at large. They forced themselves on the leaders, and made them lead. We do not know all of their names, but we can start finding them out, seeking out their 'unvisited' historical tombs. The great benefit of the period of these wars and revolutions in Britain and Ireland to the men and women of the four nations was that it enabled them to link their own personal sufferings and successes to the national political scene. In this way the revolution was empowering, and even if the power it conferred on men and women was to remain suppressed or dormant at times, it would not go away, for things once done could not be undone. The national civil wars had involved, and to some extent made use of, regional and cultural conflicts between 1639 and 1651, and this reality emphasizes the lack of a British identity at the grassroots level. The people of the four nations were not yet Britons, although the processes of internal colonization given a nudge by the civil wars may have helped to make Britons of their heirs. Their experience of the wars and the costs of those wars gave them a political perspective which ensured that the process of building the internal empire would not be done without taking them into account. If we cannot yet talk of a class consciousness in the people of the four nations during the seventeenth century, because of their experience of war and revolution, we certainly can talk of a political consciousness.

Notes

INTRODUCTION

1 Kearney, H., *The British Isles: A History of Four Nations*, Cambridge, 1993.

2 Hutchinson, L., *Memoirs of the Life of Colonel Hutchinson*, London, 1806; Gardiner, S.R., *History of the Great Civil War*, 4 vols, London, 1893, reprinted 1987, 1991; these editions are used throughout. Wedgwood, C.V., *The King's War*, London, 1958; the Penguin editions (1983) are used throughout.

3 Clarendon, Earl of (ed. W. Dunn Mackay), *The History of the Rebellion and Civil Wars in England*, Oxford, 1888. The edition reissued in 1992 is the one used throughout; Ashburnham, J., *A Narrative by John Ashburnham of His Attendance on King Charles the First*, 2 vols, London, 1830; Birch, J. (ed. J. and T.W. Webb), *Military Memoirs of Colonel John Birch*, London, 1873; Hutchinson, *Memoirs*; Cavendish, Margaret, Duchess of Newcastle, *The Life of William Cavendish, Duke of Newcastle, and Margaret His Wife*, London, 1667 (the undated London edition, edited by Sir Charles Firth, is used throughout); Whitelock, B., *Memorials of the English Affairs during the Reign of King Charles I*, 4 vols, Oxford, 1853; Jansson, M., ed., *Two Diaries of the Long Parliament*, Stroud, 1984; Ellis, H., ed., 'Letters of Sergeant Nehemiah Warton', *Archaeologia*, Vol. XXV, 1853; Adair, J., *By the Sword Divided*, London, 1983; Carlton, C., *Going to the Wars: The Experience of the British Civil Wars, 1638–1651*, London, 1992; Seaver, P., *Wallington's World: A Puritan Artisan in Seventeenth Century London*, Stanford, CA, 1985; Evelyn, J. (ed. John Bowle), *The Diary of John Evelyn*, Oxford, 1983, pp. 39–40; Clifford, Lady Anne (ed. D.J.H. Clifford), *The Diaries of Lady Anne Clifford*, Stroud, 1990, pp. 94–7.

4 Nottinghamshire Archive Office, PR2130, p. 12.

5 Colley, L., *Britons Forging the Nation 1707–1837*, New Haven, 1992, p. 3.

1 BRITAIN AND IRELAND IN 1638

1 Clarendon, Earl of (ed. W. Dunn Mackay), *The History of the Rebellion and Civil Wars in England*, Oxford, 1888, reissued 1992, Vol. 1, p. 85.

2 Johnston of Wariston, A. (ed. G.H. Paul, D.H. Fleming and J.D. Ogilvie), *Diary of Sir Archibald Johnston of Wariston*, Scottish History Society, LXI, Edinburgh, 1911, pp. 265–6.

3 Knollys, H., *A Glimpse of Sion's Glory*, London, 1641, in S. Prall (ed.), *The Puritan Revolution: A Documentary History*, London, 1968.

4 Samuel, R. and Thompson, P., eds, *The Myths We Live By*, London, 1990, pp. 6–7.

5 See Donald, P., *An Uncouncelled King: Charles I and the Scottish Troubles, 1637–41*, Cambridge, 1990, passim.

6 Lee, M., *The Road to Revolution: Scotland under Charles I, 1625–1637*, Chicago, 1985, pp. 209–11.

7 For a full examination of regions see Thirsk, J., ed., *The Agricultural History of England*, Cambridge, 1967, Vol. 4. For a brief summary of conditions in the south-west, see Underdown, D., *Revel, Riot and Rebellion: Popular Politics and Culture in England, 1603–60*, Oxford, 1985, ch. 4. For Scotland see: Smout, T.C., *The History of the Scottish People*, London, 1973, pp. 111–25; Whyte, I., *Agriculture and Society in Seventeenth Century Scotland*, Edinburgh, 1979; and Dogheson, R.A., *Land and Society in Early Scotland*, Oxford, 1981.

8 Hughes, A., *Politics, Society and Civil War in Warwickshire, 1620–1660*, Cambridge, 1987: Everritt, A., *The Community of Kent and the Great Rebellion*, Leicester, 1973; Wroughton, J., *A Community at War: The Civil War in Bath and North Somerset*, Bath, 1992; O'Dowd, M., *Power, Politics and Land: Early Modern Sligo, 1568–1688*, Belfast, 1991.

9 For women at war see: O'Dowd, M., 'Women and war in Ireland in the 1640s', in M. MacCurtain and M. O'Dowd, eds, *Women in Early Modern Ireland*, Edinburgh, 1991; Fraser, Antonia, *The Weaker Vessell*, London, 1984.

10 For women as deputy husbands, see Thatcher-Ulrich, L., *Good Wives*, New York, 1982, ch. 2. For women in the Scottish economy, see Houston, R.A., 'Women in the economy and society of Scotland, 1500–1800', in D.R.A. Houston and I. Whyte, eds, *Scottish Society, 1500–1800*, Cambridge, 1989. For women in English society, see Clarke, A. (ed. A.L. Erickson), *Women's Work in the Seventeenth Century*, London, 1992; Erickson, A.L. *Women and Property in Early Modern England*, London, 1993. For a discussion of women, society, economic and political roles, see Thompson, R., *Women in Stuart England and America*, London, 1974; Amussen, S., *An Ordered Society*, Oxford, 1988.

11 Hobby, E., *Virtue of Necessity: English Women's Writing, 1649–88*, London, 1988; Higgins, P. 'The reactions of women in the civil war', in B. Manning, ed., *Politics, Religion and the English Civil War*, London, 1973; and Crawford, P., 'Women's published writings 1600–1700', in M. Prior, ed., *Women in English Society*, London, 1985; Graham, E., Hinds, H., Hobby, E. and Wilcox, H., eds, *Her Own Life:*

Autobiographical Writings by Seventeenth-century English Women, London, 1989.

12 Whyte, *Agriculture and Society in Seventeenth Century Scotland*, p. 17.

13 Smout, *History of the Scottish People*, p. 99.

14 Devine, T.M., 'Social responses to agrarian "improvement": the Highland and Lowland clearances in Scotland', in I.D. Whyte and R.A. Houston, eds, *Agriculture and Society*, Edinburgh, 1979, pp. 149–51.

15 Mitchison, R., 'North and South: the development of the gulf in Poor Law practice', in Whyte and Houston, *Agriculture and Society*, p. 201.

16 Stevenson, D., 'The century of the Three Kingdoms', in J. Wormald, ed., *Scotland Revisited*, London, 1991, p. 107.

17 For a detailed analysis of the cultural issues and colonization see Withers, C.J., *Gaelic Scotland: The Transformation of a Cultural Region*, London, 1988, passim, and pp. 4–12 in particular.

18 Wormald, J., *Court, Kirk and Community*, London, 1981, p. 119.

19 For an examination of this see Wormald, *Court, Kirk and Community*, ch. 8, and Smout, *History of the Scottish People*, pp. 57–66.

20 Corish, P., *The Catholic Community in the Seventeenth and Eighteenth Centuries*, Dublin, 1981, ch. 2.

21 Clanricarde, Earl of (ed. J. Lowe), *Letter-Book of the Earl of Clanricarde, 1643–47*, Dublin, 1983, p. xvii; O'Dowd, *Power, Politics and Land*, pp. 106–7.

22 Gillespie, R., *The Transformation of the Irish Economy, 1550–1700*, Dublin, 1991, p. 32.

23 O'Riordan, M., 'The native Ulster *mentalité* as revealed in Gaelic sources, 1600–1650', in B. Mac Cuarta, ed., *Ulster 1641: Aspects of the Rising*, Belfast, 1993, pp. 61–91.

24 Historical Manuscripts Commission, *Calendar of Manuscripts of the Marquis of Ormonde*, New Series, Vol. 2, London, 1903, pp. 350–2.

25 Edwards, R.D., *An Atlas of Irish History*, second edition, London, 1991, p. 15.

26 Ellis, S.G., *Tudor Ireland: Crown, Community and the Conflict of Cultures 1470–1603*, London, 1994, pp. 168–9.

27 See Sommerville, J.P., *Politics and Ideology in England, 1603–1640*, London, 1986, pp. 27–34.

28 See Wrightson, K. *English Society*, London, 1984, for a readable general account of society; Lockyer, R., *The Early Stuarts*, London, 1989; Holbrooke, R., *The English Family*, London, 1984, and Durston, C., *The Family in the English Revolution*, Oxford, 1989, for the nature of the English family. For a specific example of a family during the civil war, see Slater, M., *Family Life in the Seventeenth Century*, London, 1984, which looks at the Verney family.

29 For an examination of the seventeenth-century context of local government, see Fletcher, A., *Reform in the Provinces*, New Haven, 1985.

30   For an introduction to the origins and duties of the office, see Gladwin, I., *The Sheriff*, London, 1974.

31   Clifford, Lady Anne (ed. D.J.H. Clifford), *The Diaries of Lady Anne Clifford*, Stroud, 1990, passim.

32   Professor Mark Fissel's book on the Anglo-Scottish wars, *The Bishops' Wars: Charles I's Campaigns against Scotland, 1638–1640*, Cambridge, 1994, contains a thorough and modern interpretation of the functioning of county militia and the lieutenancy.

33   Fletcher, A. and Stevenson, J., eds, *Order and Disorder in Early Modern England*, Cambridge, 1985, p. 16.

34   Cavendish, Margaret, Duchess of Newcastle, *Epistle to the Two Most Famous Universities. Philosophical and Physical Opinions*, 1663 edition.

35   The most authoritative study of constables is Kent, J., *The English Village Constable, 1580–1642: A Social and Administrative Study*, Oxford, 1986. For churchwardens see Cox, J.C., *Churchwardens' Accounts: From the Fourteenth Century to the Close of the Seventeenth Century*, London, 1913, passim; for women in office see p. 7. For comments of women churchwardens see Erickson, *Women and Property in Early Modern England*; Amussen, *An Ordered Society*, p. 135. For a good example of conflicts in perceptions of orders see Wrightson, K., 'Two concepts of order: justices, constables and jurymen in seventeenth century England', in J. Brewer and J. Styles, eds, *An Ungovernable People: The English and their Law in the Seventeenth and Eighteenth Centuries*; London, 1983. For Jane Kitchen see below and Bennett, M., ed., *A Nottinghamshire Village in War and Peace: The Accounts of the Constables of Upton, 1640–1666*, Nottingham, 1995, and Historical Association, *Short Guides to Records, No. 26: Constables' Accounts*, London, 1993.

36   Rees, W., *An Historical Atlas of Wales from Early to Modern Times*, London, 1951, p. 51.

37   Williams, G., *Renewal and Reformation: Wales c.1415–1642*, Oxford, 1993, pp. 273–5.

38   Williams, P., 'The attack on the Council of the Marches, 1603–1642', *Transactions of the Cymmradorion Society*, 1961, pp. 1–2.

39   Ibid., pp. 16–18.

40   Lee, *Road to Revolution*, pp. 4–5.

41   Donald, *An Uncouncelled King*, p. 17.

42   Ibid., p. 27.

43   Morrill, J.S., *The Nature of the English Revolution*, London, 1993, pp. 92–3.

2   THE SCOTTISH REBELLION

1   From the Supplication and Complaint, in Fleming, D.H., ed., 'Scotland's Supplication and Complaint against the Book of Common Prayer

(Otherwise Laud's Liturgy), the Book of Cannons and the Prelates, 18 October 1637', *Proceedings of the Society of Antiquaries of Scotland,* Vol. LX, 1925–6, p. 372.

2   Stevenson, D., *The Scottish Revolution, 1637–1644,* Newton Abbot, 1973, p. 53; Lee, M., *The Road to Revolution: Scotland under Charles I, 1625–1637,* Chicago, 1985, p. 154.

3   Russell, C., *The Fall of the British Monarchies, 1637–42,* Oxford, 1991, pp. 47–8.

4   Ibid., pp. 49–50.

5   Fleming, 'Scotland's Supplication and Complaint against the Book of Common Prayer', pp. 371–3.

6   Donald, P., *An Uncouncelled King: Charles I and the Scottish Troubles, 1637–41,* Cambridge, 1990, pp. 52–3.

7   Russell, *Fall of the British Monarchies,* p. 51.

8   Stevenson, *The Scottish Revolution,* p. 82.

9   Morrill, J.S., 'The Scottish National Covenant of 1638 in its British context', in *The Nature of the English Revolution',* London, 1993, pp. 104–5.

10   Ibid., p. 105; Donald, *An Uncouncelled King,* p. 77.

11   Mitchison, R., *Lordship to Patronage: Scotland, 1603–1745,* second edition, Edinburgh, 1990, p. 42. Stevenson, D., *The Covenanters: The National Covenant and Scotland,* Edinburgh, 1988, p. 32.

12   MacInnes, A.I., *Charles I and the Making of the Covenanting Movement, 1625–1641,* Edinburgh, 1991, p. 173.

13   Ibid., p. 1.

14   Taylor, L.B., ed., *Aberdeen Council Letters,* Oxford, 1950, Vol. 2, pp. 88–9.

15   MacInnes, *Charles I and the Making of the Covenanting Movement,* pp. 166–8.

16   Ibid., p. 184.

17   Ibid., p. 185; Taylor, *Aberdeen Council Letters,* pp. xv–xvi.

18   MacInnes, *Charles I and the Making of the Covenanting Movement,* pp. 185–6.

19   Donaldson, G., *Scotland: James V–James VII,* Edinburgh, 1990, pp. 320–1. MacInnes, *Charles I and the Making of the Covenanting Movement,* p. 187.

20   Donaldson, *Scotland,* p. 321.

21   Fissel, M.C., *The Bishops' Wars: Charles I's Campaigns against Scotland, 1638–1640,* Cambridge, 1994, pp. 3–4, 10.

22   Perceval-Maxwell, M., *The Outbreak of the Irish Rebellion of 1641,* Dublin, 1994, pp. 26, 43.

23   Gillespie, R., 'Destabilising Ulster, 1641–2', in B. Mac Cuarta, ed., *Ulster 1641: Aspects of the Rising,* Belfast, 1993, p. 111.

24   *Calendar of State Papers Relating to Ireland in the Reign of Charles I, 1633–47,* London, 1901, pp. 222–3.

25 Stevenson, D., *Highland Warrior: Alasdair MacColla and the Civil Wars*, Edinburgh, 1994, pp. 64–5; Ohlmeyer, J., *Civil War and Restoration in the Three Stuart Kingdoms: The Career of Randal MacDonnell, Marquis of Antrim, 1609–1683*, Cambridge, 1993.

26 Fissel, *The Bishops' Wars*, p. 9.

27 Sharpe, K., *The Personal Rule of Charles I*, New Haven, 1992, p. 940.

28 CSPD, 1635–6, p. 92; CSPD, 1637, p. 532.

29 CSPD, 1639, pp. 134, 151, 241.

30 CSPD, 1639, pp. 134, 224, 475.

31 Cornwall County Record Office, P19/9/19.

32 Morrill, J.S., *The Revolt of the Provinces: Conservatives and Radicals in the English Civil War*, London, 1976, pp. 28–30.

33 See Fissel, *The Bishops' Wars*, pp. 200–7, for a discussion of social origins of the trained band army assembled in 1639.

34 Ibid., p. 6.

35 CSPD, 1638–9, pp. 286, 290, 444; CSPD, 1639, p. 129; Fissel, *The Bishops' Wars*, p. 199.

36 Cornwall County Record Office, P19/9/19.

37 Norfolk County Record Office, PD254/112, ff. 1–2.

38 Bond, S.M., ed., *The Chamber Order Book of Worcester, 1602–1650*, Worcester, 1974, pp. 322, 329.

39 MacInnes, *Charles I and the Making of the Covenanting Movement*, p. 190, p. 208n.

40 A merk, or mark, was 13s/4d. One pound Scots was worth 1/12th of one pound sterling.

41 CSPD, 1638–9, pp. 154–5.

42 CSPD, 1639, p. 103.

43 CSPD, 1638–9, p. 176.

44 Ibid., pp. 85–6.

45 Reid, S., *The Campaigns of Montrose*, Edinburgh, 1990, ch. 1.

46 Fissel, *The Bishops' Wars*, pp. 26–9.

47 Ibid., p. 33.

48 John Scally of the National Library of Scotland, who is currently working on the role of Hamilton in the period 1638–9, notes that Hamilton was more than just a servant of the king's wishes and that he was attempting to mediate between the king and the Covenanters. It is Scally's view that Hamilton advised the king to accept the legality of the Covenant to prevent further radicalization. This is part of the substance of his paper, 'The career of James, 3rd Marquis and 1st Duke of Hamilton', at the conference Celtic Dimensions of the British Civil Wars, held at Strathclyde University on 5 April 1995.

49 Wedgwood, C.V., *The King's Peace, 1637–1641*, Harmondsworth, 1983, p. 276.

50 MacTavish, D.C., ed., *Minutes of the Synod of Argyll, 1639–1651*, Edinburgh, 1943, pp. xiii, 7.

51 Ibid., p. 278.
52 Stevenson, *The Scottish Revolution*, pp. 166–8; Wedgwood, *The King's Peace*, pp. 294–5; MacInnes, *Charles I and the Making of the Covenanting Movement*, p. 194.
53 Wedgwood, *The King's Peace*, pp. 296–9; MacInnes, *Charles I and the Making of the Covenanting Movement*, p. 194.

3 PARLIAMENTS IN OPPOSITION

1 Cavendish, Margaret, Duchess of Newcastle (ed. C.H. Firth), *The Life of William Cavendish, Duke of Newcastle, and Margaret His Wife*, London, nd, pp. 7–8.
2 Kearney, H.F., *Strafford in Ireland 1633–1641: A Study in Absolutism*, Cambridge, 1989, p. 72; Wedgwood, C.V., *Thomas Wentworth, First Earl of Strafford, 1593–1641: A Revaluation*, London, 1961, pp. 272–3.
3 For an analysis of this Parliament see Kearney, *Strafford in Ireland*, pp. 43–6, 53–4.
4 Ibid., pp. 55, 60.
5 Russell, C., *The Fall of the British Monarchies, 1637–42*, Oxford, 1991, pp. 92–3.
6 Cope, E., *Politics without Parliaments*, London, 1987, p. 185.
7 Russell, *Fall of the British Monarchies*, p. 94.
8 Ibid., pp. 94–5; Kishlansky, M., *Parliamentary Selection*, Cambridge, 1987, pp. 13–18.
9 Cust, R., 'Politics and the electorate in the 1620s', in R. Cust and A. Hughes, eds, *Conflict in Early Stuart England*, London, 1989, pp. 158–9.
10 Ibid., pp. 152, 154; Gruenfelder, J.K., 'The electoral influence of the Earls of Huntingdon, 1603–1640', *Transactions of the Leicestershire Archaeological and Historical Society*, Vol. L, 1974–5, p. 24.
11 Perceval-Maxwell, M., *The Outbreak of the Irish Rebellion of 1641*, Dublin, 1994, p. 70.
12 Ibid., p. 76.
13 Cope, E.S. and Coates, W.H., eds, *Proceedings of the Short Parliament of 1640*, London, 1977, pp. 53–4.
14 Russell, *Fall of the British Monarchies*, p. 103.
15 Cope and Coates, *Proceedings of the Short Parliament*, pp. 134–40.
16 Ibid., pp. 70, 178.
17 Clarendon, Earl of (ed. W. Dunn Mackay), *The History of the Rebellion and Civil Wars in England*, Oxford, 1992, p. 183.
18 CSPD, 1640, pp. 105, 269, 657.
19 Nottinghamshire Archive Office, QSM1/11, ff. 204–61.
20 Stocks, H.E., ed., *Records of the Borough of Leicester, 1603–1689*, Cambridge, 1923, p. 292.

21 Fissel, M.C., *The Bishops' Wars: Charles I's Campaigns against Scotland, 1638–1640*, Cambridge, 1994, pp. 51–2.
22 Ibid., pp. 264–6, 270.
23 Ibid., pp. 278–82.
24 Ibid., pp. 272–3, 277; CSPD, 1640, p. 450.
25 CSPD, 1640, pp. 477–8.
26 CSPD, 1639–40, p. 172.
27 Fissel, *The Bishops' Wars*, p. 286; Russell, *Fall of the British Monarchies*, p. 142.
28 Morrill, J.S., *The Revolt of the Provinces: Conservatives and Radicals in the English Civil War*, London, 1976, p. 34.
29 Cope, *Politics without Parliaments*, p. 213.
30 Morrill, J. and Walter, J., 'Order and disorder in the English Revolution', in A. Fletcher and J. Stevenson, eds, *Order and Disorder in Early Modern England*, Cambridge, 1985, p. 140.
31 Dodd, A.H., 'Wales and the second bishops' war', *Bulletin of the Board of Celtic Studies*, Vol. XII, 1948, pp. 93–4.
32 CSPD, 1640, p. 377.
33 MacInnes, A.I., *Charles I and the Making of the Covenanting Movement, 1625–1641*, Edinburgh, 1991, pp. 195–6. These are the beginnings of what Dr John Young has seen as the development of a Scottish 'House of Commons tradition', with power and influence being increasingly exercised by the representative of the shires: 'The Scottish parliament 1639–61: a political and constitutional analysis', 3 vols, unpublished Ph.D. thesis, Glasgow University, 1993. This is to be the basis of a forthcoming book.
34 Scottish Record Office, GD406/1/1236 and 1237. The letter to Hamilton is dated 28 February 1640, that to the king, 1 April 1640.
35 Wood, M., ed., *Extracts from the Records of the Burgh of Edinburgh 1626–1641*, 2 vols, Edinburgh, 1936, pp. 236, 238.
36 Nicholson, J., ed., *Minute Book kept by the War Committee of the Covenanters in the Stewartry of Kirkcudbright, 1640–1*, Kirkcudbright, 1855, p. 6.
37 Ibid., pp. 9–11, 24–6, 30, 36.
38 Ibid., pp. 26–7; Taylor, L.B., ed., *Aberdeen Council Letters*, Vol. 2, Oxford, 1950, p. 169.
39 Scottish Record Office, GD406/1/1237.
40 Stuart, J., ed., *Extracts from the Council Register of the Burgh of Aberdeen, 1643–1747*, Edinburgh, 1871–2, pp. 214–18.
41 Fissel, *The Bishops' Wars*, pp. 39–53, passim.
42 Dodd, 'Wales and the second bishops' war', p. 92.
43 Hertfordshire County Record Office, D/P12/9/1, f. 1.
44 Russell, *Fall of the British Monarchies*, p. 143.
45 Ibid., p. 145.

46 Ibid., p. 149.
47 Gardiner, S.R., ed., *The Constitutional Documents of the Puritan Revolution*, Oxford, 1979, pp. 134–6.
48 Perceval-Maxwell, *Outbreak of the Irish Rebellion*, p. 77.
49 Ibid., p. 78.
50 Russell, *Fall of the British Monarchies*, p. 155.
51 Ibid., pp. 161–4.
52 Brunton, D. and Pennington, D.H., *Members of the Long Parliament*, Cambridge, Mass., 1954, p. 1.
53 Morrill, *Revolt of the Provinces*, pp. 30, 148–52.
54 Russell, *Fall of the British Monarchies*, p. 207.
55 Ibid., pp. 229–31.
56 Hughes, A., *The Causes of the English Civil War*, London, 1991, p. 166.
57 Ibid., p. 230.
58 Jenkins, G.H., *Protestant Dissenters in Wales*, Cardiff, 1992, p. 13.
59 Delbanco, A., *The Puritan Ordeal*, Cambridge, Mass., 1989, pp. 101–12; Bremer, F.J., 'To live exemplary lives: Puritans and Puritan communities as lofty lights', *The Seventeenth Century*, Vol. VII, No. 1, Spring, 1992.
60 Russell, *Fall of the British Monarchies*, p. 169.
61 Gardiner, *Constitutional Documents*, pp. 138–9.
62 Wedgwood, *Thomas Wentworth*, p. 319.
63 Perceval-Maxwell, M., 'Ulster 1641 in the context of political developments in the three kingdoms', in B. Mac Cuarta, ed., *Ulster 1641: Aspects of the Rising*, Belfast, 1993, p. 100.
64 Russell, *Fall of the British Monarchies*, p. 284.
65 Wedgwood, *Thomas Wentworth*, p. 341.
66 Ibid., pp. 350–1.
67 Gardiner, *Constitutional Documents*, pp. 144–55, 158–9.
68 Russell, *Fall of the British Monarchies*, ch. 6.
69 Smout, T.C., *A History of the Scottish People*, London, 1973, p. 60.
70 Russell, *Fall of the British Monarchies*, pp. 292–3.

4 REBELLION IN IRELAND

1 'Remonstrance of the Catholics of Ireland', in Gilbert, J.T., ed., *A Contemporary History of Affairs in Ireland from 1641 to 1652*, 3 vols, Dublin, 1879–80, Vol. 1, p. 360.
2 Calendar of State Papers, Ireland (CSPI), 1633–47, London, 1901, pp. 333–4.
3 Kearney, H.F., *Strafford in Ireland 1633–1641: A Study in Absolutism*, Cambridge, 1989, p. 210.

4 Gillespie, R., *The Transformation of the Irish Economy, 1550–1700*, Dublin, 1991, pp. 38–9.

5 Perceval-Maxwell, M., 'Ulster 1641 in the context of political developments in the three kingdoms', in B. Mac Cuarta, ed., *Ulster 1641: Aspects of the Rising*, Belfast, 1993, p. 103.

6 Kearney, *Strafford in Ireland*, p. 213; Perceval-Maxwell, 'Ulster 1641', p. 104.

7 Perceval-Maxwell, 'Ulster 1641', pp. 104–5.

8 Clarke, A., 'The breakdown of authority, 1640–1641', in T.W. Moody, F.X. Martin and F.J. Byrne, eds, *A New History of Ireland*, Oxford, 1991, Vol. 3, p. 287.

9 Russell, C., 'The Scottish party in English Parliaments, 1640–2, OR the myth of the English Revolution', *Historical Research*, Vol. 66, No. 159, 1993, passim.

10 Gardiner, S.R., ed., *The Constitutional Documents of the Puritan Revolution*, Oxford, 1979, pp. 163–6.

11 Stevenson, D., *The Scottish Revolution, 1637–1644*, Newton Abbot, 1973, and *The Covenanters: The National Covenant and Scotland*, Edinburgh, 1988, pp. 49–50, 223; Russell, C., *The Fall of the British Monarchies, 1637–42*, Oxford, 1991, p. 303.

12 Russell, *Fall of the British Monarchies*, pp. 309–11; Stevenson, *The Scottish Revolution*, p. 207; Donaldson, G., *Scotland: James V–James VII*, Edinburgh, 1990, p. 328.

13 MacInnes, A.I., *Charles I and the Making of the Covenanting Movement, 1625–1641*, Edinburgh, 1991, p. 201.

14 Donaldson, *Scotland*, p. 329; Stevenson, *The Covenanters*, p. 50; Russell, *Fall of the British Monarchies*, pp. 319–21.

15 Russell, *Fall of the British Monarchies*, pp. 322–9; Donaldson, *Scotland*, pp. 328–9.

16 Gillespie, R., 'Destabilising Ulster, 1641–2', in Mac Cuarta, *Ulster 1641*, p. 110.

17 Ibid., pp. 108–9; National Archives, Ireland (NAI), M1121/1/1, Transcripts of the Bellew of Louth Family Papers, passim.

18 Gillespie, 'Destabilising Ulster', p. 110.

19 Ibid., p. 112; Stevenson, D., *Highland Warrior: Alasdair MacColla and the Civil Wars*, Edinburgh, 1994, p. 74.

20 Casaway, J.I., *Owen Roe O'Neill and the Struggle for Catholic Ireland*, Philadelphia, 1984, pp. 49–50; Stevenson, *Highland Warrior*, p. 74; Ohlmeyer, J., *Civil War and Restoration in Three Stuart Kingdoms. The Career of Randal MacDonnell, Marquis of Antrim, 1609–1683*, Cambridge, 1993, pp. 96–9.

21 Russell, *Fall of the British Monarchies*, pp. 394–5; Perceval-Maxwell, *The Outbreak of the Irish Rebellion of 1641*, Dublin, 1994, pp. 192–9.

22 Perceval-Maxwell, *Outbreak of the Irish Rebellion*, p. 200.

23 Casaway, *Owen Roe O'Neill*, pp. 46–9.
24 Corish, P., 'The rising of 1641 and the Catholic confederacy', in Moody et al., *A New History of Ireland*, pp. 291–3.
25 Perceval-Maxwell, *Outbreak of the Irish Rebellion*, pp. 216–17.
26 These accounts are now housed in the Library of Trinity College, Dublin.
27 NAI, M1121/1/1, ff. CLIIII, CLV.
28 NAI, M1121/1/2, ff. 17, XXVII, 18, XXVIII.
29 Gilbert, *A Contemporary History of Affairs in Ireland*, Vol. 2, p. 385.
30 Ibid., p. 389.
31 CSPI, 1633–47, p. 540.
32 NAI, M1121/1/2, ff. 105, LXXXXVIIb, f. 111, LXXXXVIII.
33 Ibid., f. 108, LXXXXVIIe.
34 O'Dowd, M., 'Women and war in Ireland in the 1640's', in M. Mac-Curtain and M. O'Dowd, eds, *Women in Early Modern Ireland*, Edinburgh, 1991, pp. 95–7.
35 Gillespie, R., 'Mayo and the rising of 1641', *Cathair Na Mart*, Vol. 5, 1985.
36 Ibid., p. 40.
37 Gilbert, *A Contemporary History of Affairs in Ireland*, Vol. 1, pp. 360–1.
38 Ibid., pp. 393–5.
39 Edwards, R.D., *An Atlas of Irish History*, London, 1991, pp. 207–16.
40 NAI, M2450, Treasury Orderbook of the Lord Justices and Council, 1642, Vol. 1, f. 129.
41 Historical Manuscripts Commission, *Calendar of Manuscripts of the Marquis of Ormonde*, New Series, London, 1902–3, Vol. 2, p. 173.
42 NAI, M2450, Vol. 2, f. 465.
43 Perceval-Maxwell, *Outbreak of the Irish Rebellion*, p. 262.
44 Cressy, D., *Bonfires and Bells*, London, 1989, p. 77; Whitelock, B., *Memorials of English Affairs from the Beginning of the Reign of Charles I to the Restoration of Charles II*, Oxford, 1853, Vol. 1, p. 145.
45 Ibid., p. 277.
46 Ibid., p. 279.
47 See Gardiner, *Constitutional Documents*, pp. 202–32.
48 Clarendon, Earl of (ed. W. Dunn Mackay), *The History of the Rebellion and Civil Wars in England*, Oxford, 1992, Vol. 1, pp. 417–18.
49 Seaver, P., *Wallington's World: A Puritan Artisan in Seventeenth Century London*, Stanford, 1985, pp. 166–7.
50 Ibid., pp. 164–5.
51 Clarendon, *History of the Rebellion*, pp. 419–20.
52 Manning, B., *The English People and the English Revolution, 1640–1649*, London, 1976, pp. 84–92.
53 See Gardiner, *Constitutional Documents*, pp. 233–6 for the text.
54 Manning, *The English People*, p. 86.

55 Wedgwood, C.V., *The King's War*, Harmondsworth, 1983, p. 53; Manning, *The English People*, p. 90.
56 See Manning, *The English People*, pp. 89–92.
57 Ibid., p. 101.
58 Russell, *Fall of the British Monarchies*, p. 447.
59 Crawford, P., *Denzil, First Lord Holles*, London, 1979, p. 21; Holles had said to Finch: 'If we be a Parliament, and assembled here by the King's commandment, and trusted by those that sent us hither, you are our servant: and our servants ought to obey us'; Whitelock, *Memorials*, Vol. 1, p. 153.
60 Wedgwood, *The King's War*, pp. 60–2.
61 Whitelock, *Memorials*, p. 154.
62 Wilson, J., ed., *Buckinghamshire Contributions for Ireland 1642 and Richard Greville's Military Accounts, 1642–1645*, Buckingham, 1983; Public Record Office, Webb, C., Surrey, 'Contributors for Protestant Refugees from Ireland 1642', unpublished transcript, 1983. The collection as a whole is SP28/191–204.

5   THE AGONY OF CHOOSING SIDES

1 A letter from Henry Oxinden of Deane to Henry Oxinden of Barham, 27 January 1642, cited in Morrill, J.S., *The Revolt of the Provinces: Conservatives and Radicals in the English Civil War*, London, 1976, pp. 138–9.
2 Prall, S., ed., *The Puritan Revolution: A Documentary History*, London, 1968, pp. 86–96.
3 Morrill, *Revolt of the Provinces*, p. 34.
4 Williams, G., *Renewal and Reformation: Wales, c.1415–1642*, Oxford, 1993, p. 486; Dodd, A.H., 'Anglesey in the civil war', *Transactions of the Anglesey Antiquarian Society*, 1952, pp. 6–7.
5 Sharp, B., *In Contempt of All Authority*, Berkeley, 1980, p. 224 and passim; Lindley, K., *Fenland Riots and the English Revolution*, London, 1982, pp. 112–38 and passim.
6 The material for this analysis comes from post-doctoral work undertaken in the Department of History at Loughborough University with funding provided by the British Academy, 1986–8. Initial findings were presented as a paper at the Seventeenth-century Studies Conference, Durham University, July 1987.
7 Morrill, *Revolt of the Provinces*, p. 36.
8 Fletcher, A., *The Outbreak of the English Civil War*, London, 1985, pp. 229–30.
9 Ibid., p. 244.
10 Ibid., p. 233.

11 Wedgwood, C.V., *The King's War*, Harmondsworth, 1983, pp. 91–3; Corish, P.J., 'The rising of 1641 and the Catholic confederacy, 1641–5', in T.W. Moody, F.X. Martin and F.J. Byrne, eds, *A New History of Ireland*, Oxford, 1976, p. 296.

12 Wedgwood, *The King's War*, p. 97.

13 Ibid., p. 111; Corish, 'The rising of 1641', p. 303.

14 Corish, 'The rising of 1641', p. 297.

15 O hAnnrachain, T., 'Rebels and confederates: the stance of the Irish clergy in the 1640s', paper at the Celtic Dimensions of the British Civil Wars conference, University of Strathclyde, 5 April 1995.

16 Ibid., pp. 299–304; Historical Manuscripts Commission (HMC), *Calendar of Manuscripts of the Marquis of Ormonde*, New Series, London, 1902–3, Vol. 2, pp. 246–7.

17 Wedgwood, *The King's War*, p. 97.

18 Fletcher, *Outbreak of the English Civil War*, p. 246.

19 Wedgwood, *The King's War*, pp. 87–90.

20 Gardiner, S.R., ed., *The Constitutional Documents of the Puritan Revolution*, Oxford, 1979, pp. 248–9.

21 Morrill, *Revolt of the Provinces*, p. 40; Clarendon, Earl of (ed. W. Dunn Mackay), *The History of the Rebellion and the Civil Wars in England*, Oxford, 1992, Vol. 2, p. 204.

22 Morrill, *Revolt of the Provinces*, p. 40; Fletcher, *Outbreak of the English Civil War*, p. 323; Fissel, M.C., *The Bishops' Wars: Charles I's Campaigns against Scotland*, Cambridge, 1994, pp. 133–4.

23 Gardiner, *Constitutional Documents*, p. 260.

24 British Library, Additional MSS 34217 Instructions to the Northamptonshire Commissioners.

25 Clarendon, *History of the Rebellion*, Vol. 2, pp. 196–7.

26 Ibid., p. 186. For the lists of commissioners of array see the Dugdale Transcripts of the Commissioners for Several Counties, Northamptonshire County Record Office, Finch-Hatton MSS 133, passim.

27 Bennett, M., 'The king's gambit: Charles I and Nottingham in the summer of 1642', *Transactions of the Thoroton Society of Nottinghamshire*, Vol. XCVI, 1992, p. 139.

28 Fletcher, *Outbreak of the English Civil War*, ch. 11 passim. See also the maps on pp. 349 and 357.

29 Eales, J., *Puritans and Roundheads: The Harleys of Brampton Bryan and the Outbreak of the English Civil War*, Cambridge, 1990, pp. 130–5.

30 Ibid., pp. 146–7.

31 Bennett, M., 'Between Scylla and Charybdis: the creation of rival administrations at the beginning of the English civil war', *The Local Historian*, Vol. 22, No. 4, November, 1992, passim and particularly pp. 192–4.

32 Ibid., p. 192.

33 Gardiner, *Constitutional Documents*, pp. 249–54.
34 Kenyon, J.P., *The Civil Wars of England*, London, 1989, p. 31.
35 Adamson, J.S.A., 'The baronial context of the English civil war', *Transactions of the Royal Historical Society*, 1990, pp. 96–101.
36 Newman, P.R., *The Old Service: Royalist Regimental Colonels and the Civil War, 1642–46*, Manchester, 1993, p. 21.
37 Bennett, M., 'The Royalist war effort in the north Midlands, 1642–6', unpublished Ph.D. thesis, Loughborough University, 1986, ch. 4.
38 Morrill, *Revolt of the Provinces*, pp. 136, 141.
39 Eales, *Puritans and Roundheads*, p. 147; Seaver, P., *Wallington's World: A Puritan Artisan in Seventeenth Century London*, Stanford, 1985, p. 157; Hutchinson, L., *Memoirs of the Life of Colonel John Hutchinson*, London, 1806, p. 78.
40 Hutchinson, *Memoirs*, p. 95.
41 Russell, C., *The Fall of the British Monarchies, 1637–42*, Oxford, 1991, p. 519.
42 Hughes, A., *Politics, Society and Civil War in Warwickshire*, Cambridge, 1987, p. 140.
43 Nottingham County Library, *My Lord Newark's Speech to the Trained Bands of Nottinghamshire at Newark*, London, 1642.
44 Holmes, C., *Seventeenth Century Lincolnshire*, Lincoln, 1980, p. 147; Malcolm, J.L., *Caesar's Due: Loyalty and King Charles, 1642–1646*, London, 1983, p. 235.
45 Holmes, *Seventeenth Century Lincolnshire*, pp. 123–30, 153–5, and 'Drainers and fenmen', in A. Fletcher and J. Stevenson, eds, *Order and Disorder in Early Modern England*, Cambridge, 1985, pp. 166–95; Lindley, *Fenland Riots*, passim.
46 See Payne, J., *The Keeper of the Magazine Identifyd*, Hereford, 1995.
47 Bennett, 'The Royalist war effort', p. 29.
48 Hutchinson, *Memoirs*, p. 86.
49 Malcolm, *Caesar's Due*, p. 36.
50 Hughes, *Politics, Society and Civil War*, pp. 143–5.
51 Hutton, R.E., *The Royalist War Effort*, London, 1982, p. 22.
52 Fletcher, *Outbreak of the English Civil War*, pp. 326–8.
53 Hutton, *The Royalist War Effort*, pp. 22 ff.; Bennett, 'The Royalist war effort', pp. 177–8, 'Between Scylla and Charybdis', p. 194.
54 Malcolm, *Caesar's Due*, pp. 43–5, and her article, 'A king in search of soldiers: Charles I in 1642', *Historical Journal*, Vol. XXI, No. 2, 1978; and Wanklyn, M. and Young, P., 'A king in search of soldiers: Charles I in 1642, a rejoinder', *Historical Journal*, Vol. XXIV, No. 1, 1981.
55 Nottinghamshire Archive Office, PR1710, Upton Constables' Accounts, 1640–1666, f. 11.
56 Quoted in Adair, J., *By the Sword Divided*, London, 1983, p. 43.
57 Gardiner, S.R., *History of the Great Civil War*, 4 vols, Adlestrop, 1991,

Vol. 1, p. 23; Public Record Office, SP28/174. This Exchequer return is misfiled in the materials for Worcestershire.

58 Young, P., *Edgehill, 1642: The Campaign and the Battle*, Kineton, 1967, is probably still the best secondary source for the battle. See also Wedgwood, *The King's War*, pp. 134–40; Kenyon, *The Civil Wars*, pp. 56–7.

59 Kenyon, *The Civil Wars*, p. 59.

60 Gardiner, *History*, Vol. 1, pp. 57–63.

61 HMC, *Ormonde*, Vol. 1, pp. 65–7.

62 Gillespie, R., *The Transformation of the Irish Economy, 1550–1700*, Dublin, 1991, pp. 15–16.

63 National Archives, Ireland (NAI), M2450, Treasury Orderbook of the Lord Justices and Council, Vol. 1, ff. 271–333.

64 Gillespie, *Transformation*, pp. 28–9; Perceval-Maxwell, M., *The Outbreak of the Irish Rebellion of 1641*, Dublin, 1994, p. 31.

65 NAI, M2450, Vol. 1, f. 208.

66 Ibid., Vol. 2, f. 135.

67 Ibid., Vol. 2, ff. 103, 243.

68 Ibid., Vol. 2, ff. 259, 271.

69 HMC, *Ormonde*, Vol. 2, pp. 106–7.

70 NAI, M2450, Vol. 2, f. 299.

71 Caulfield, R., ed., *The Council Book of the Corporation of Youghal*, Guildford, 1878, pp. 216–17, 218–19, 223–4, 225.

72 Richardson, R.C., ed., *Town and Countryside in the English Revolution*, Manchester, 1992.

73 Hobson, M.G. and Salter, H.E., eds, *Oxford Council Acts, 1626–1665*, Oxford, 1933, p. 111.

74 Bond, S.M., ed., *The Chamber Order Book of Worcester, 1602–1650*, Worcester, 1974, pp. 357, 360–1.

75 City of York Archives, B36, City of York House Book, Vol. 36, f. 79r.

76 Baker, W.T.B., ed., *Records of the Borough of Nottingham, 1625–1702*, Nottingham, 1900, Vol. 5, pp. 206–7.

77 Stocks, H.E., ed., *Records of the Borough of Leicester, 1603–1688*, Cambridge, 1923, pp. 317–21.

78 Hughes, A., 'Coventry and the English Revolution', in Richardson, *Town and Countryside*, p. 83.

6 THE WAR DEVELOPS

1 Sergeant Henry Foster describing the first battle of Newbury, cited in Adair, J., *By the Sword Divided*, London, 1983, p. 107.

2 Underdown, D., *Revel, Riot and Rebellion: Popular Politics and Culture in England, 1603–60*, Oxford, 1985, p. 146; Hutton, R.E., *The Royalist War Effort*, London, 1982, pp. 33–4.

3   Kenyon, J.P., *The Civil Wars of England*, London, 1989, p. 62.
4   Jenkins, G., *The Foundations of Modern Wales*, Oxford, 1993, p. 6.
5   Hutton, *The Royalist War Effort*, pp. 34–5.
6   Ibid., pp. 27, 30, 32.
7   Clwyd County Record Office, D/DM/223/139, Letter of Charles I to the Sheriff of Flint.
8   Public Record Office (PRO), SP28/190 Exchequer Papers, Associated Counties Misc.; Wilson, J., ed., *Buckinghamshire Contributions for Ireland 1642 and Richard Greville's Military Accounts, 1642–1645*, Buckingham, 1983, p. 109.
9   Gardiner, S.R., ed., *History of the Great Civil War*, 4 vols, Adlestrop, 1991, pp. 67–71, 84–5.
10 Kenyon, *The Civil Wars*, p. 69.
11 Cavendish, Margaret, Duchess of Newcastle (ed. C.H. Firth), *The Life of William Cavendish, Duke of Newcastle, and Margaret His Wife*, London, nd, p. 13.
12 Ibid., pp. 33, 71.
13 Tucker, N., *North Wales in the Civil War*, Wrexham, 1992, pp. 33–4.
14 Much of this section is based on early work: Bennett, M., 'The Royalist war effort in the north Midlands, 1642–6', unpublished Ph.D. thesis, Loughborough University, 1986, ch. 5. See also Stone, B., *Derbyshire in the Civil War*, Cromford, 1992, pp. 22–35; Hutton, *The Royalist War Effort*, pp. 43–8.
15 Hutton, *The Royalist War Effort*, pp. 54–5.
16 Ibid., pp. 56–7.
17 Kenyon, *The Civil Wars*, p. 67.
18 Gardiner, *History*, p. 33.
19 Fletcher, A., *The Outbreak of the English Civil War*, London, 1985, p. 382; Bennett, 'The Royalist war effort', p. 181.
20 Hutton, *The Royalist War Effort*, pp. 39, 44.
21 Bennett, 'The Royalist war effort', pp. 180–1.
22 Gardiner, *History*, pp. 74–5, 79–81.
23 Bennett, 'The Royalist war effort', ch. 2, passim and in particular p. 49; the counties are Nottinghamshire, Derbyshire, Leicestershire, Rutland and Staffordshire.
24 Clwyd County Record Office, Misc. MSS 254.
25 Bodleian Library, MS Dugdale 19, ff. 2r, 4, 5, 5r, 6.
26 Ibid., ff. 8–21.
27 Morrill, J.S., *The Revolt of the Provinces: Conservatives and Radicals in the English Civil War*, London, 1976, pp. 55–7, remains the most concise overall analysis of the committees and the related structures. See also Everritt, A., *The Community of Kent and the Great Rebellion 1640–1660*, Leicester, 1973; Pennington, D. and Roots, I., eds, *The Committee at Stafford, 1643–5*, Manchester, 1957; Bennett, 'The Royalist war effort',

ch. 3; and Hughes, A., *Politics, Society and Civil War in Warwickshire*, Cambridge, 1987, ch. 5 for individual county studies; Holmes, C., *The Eastern Association in the English Civil War*, Cambridge, 1974, remains the only full study of a regional association.

28   Morrill, *Revolt of the Provinces*, p. 57.
29   Beats, L., 'The East Midland Association, 1642–44,' *Midland History*, Vol. 4, 1978, pp. 160–75.
30   Canny, N., *From Reformation to Restoration: Ireland, 1534–1660*, Dublin, 1987, p. 208.
31   Corish, P., *The Catholic Community in the Seventeenth and Eighteenth Centuries*, Dublin, 1981, pp. 46–7.
32   Casaway, J.I., *Owen Roe O'Neill and the Struggle for Catholic Ireland*, Philadelphia, 1984, p. 97.
33   Corish, *The Catholic Community*, p. 43.
34   Casaway, *Owen Roe O'Neill*, pp. 89–90; Canny, *From Reformation to Restoration*, p. 213.
35   Historical Manuscripts Commission, *Calendar of Manuscripts of the Marquis of Ormonde*, New Series, London, 1902–3, Vol. 2, p. 245.
36   Casaway, *Owen Roe O'Neill*, pp. 87–9.
37   Clanricarde, Earl of (ed. J. Lowe), *Letter-Book of the Earl of Clanricarde, 1643–47*, Dublin, 1983, p. 1.
38   Stevenson, *Highland Warrior*, pp. 96–7.
39   Ibid., p. 98.
40   Gardiner, *History*, Vol. 2, pp. 125–6.
41   Ibid., p. 127.
42   Ashton, R., *The English Civil War: Conservatism and Revolution*, London, 1978, p. 200.
43   Kenyon, *The Civil Wars*, p. 91.
44   Aylmer, G.E., *Rebellion or Revolution: England from Civil War to Restoration*, Oxford, 1986, p. 56.
45   See Wedgwood, C.V., *The King's War*, Harmondsworth, 1983, p. 227.
46   For the student wishing to study this aspect of parliamentary politics, there is a wealth of material. Aylmer, *Rebellion or Revolution*, deals with the issues with almost breathtaking clarity. J.H. Hexter's *The Reign of King Pym*, Cambridge, Mass., 1941, is immensely important. A more recent critique is Manning, B., 'Parliament, "party" and "community" in the English civil war', *Historical Studies*, Vol. 14, 1983; to look at the development of these positions regarding the politics of the New Model Army, see also Kishlansky, M., *The Rise of the New Model Army*, Cambridge, 1979, and 'Ideology and politics in the parliamentary armies, 1645–9', in J.S. Morrill, ed., *Reactions to the English Civil War*, London, 1982; and Gentles, I., *The New Model Army in England, Ireland and Scotland, 1645–1653*, Oxford, 1992.
47   Kenyon, *The Civil Wars*, p. 68.

48 Ibid., p. 70.
49 Ibid., p. 71; Wroughton, J., *A Community at War: The Civil War in Bath and North Somerset*, Bath, 1992, pp. 103–11.
50 Ingram, M.E., *The Manor of Bridlington*, Bridlington, 1977, pp. 51–7; Bridlington, The Bayle, Constables' Papers; Ashcroft, M.Y., ed., *Scarborough Records, 1641–60*, Northallerton, 1991, pp. 23.
51 One in Lincolnshire, Rutland and East Anglia for Lord Widdrington, and the other of the north Midlands for Henry Hastings.
52 Kenyon, *The Civil Wars*, p. 90, for example, is one.
53 See Gardiner, *History*, Vol. 2, pp. 194–7; and for a more recent valuable critique, Wanklyn, M., 'Royalist strategy in the south of England, 1642–44', *Southern History*, 1982; Kenyon, *The Civil Wars*, also tackles the issue on p. 80. Bennett, 'The Royalist war effort', pp. 195–8, demonstrates the Royalists' strength in this region at the end of the year. Peter Newman argued at a conference at Birmingham University in 1986 for the September deadline for Royalist initiative; I think there are grounds for allowing a leeway of two or three months more, before Waller's new army proved itself and before Leven crossed the Tweed.
54 Atkin, M. and Laughlin, W., *Gloucester and the Civil War*, Stroud, 1992.
55 Ibid., p. 71, citing John Corbet's *The Historical Relation of the Military Government of Gloucester*, 1645.

7   THE COSTS OF WAR

1 Nottinghamshire Archive Office, PR1710, f. 34, notes in the Upton account book at the end of Jane Kitchen's tenure as constable.
2 Bennett, M., ed., *A Nottinghamshire Village in War and Peace: The Accounts of the Constables of Upton, 1640–1666*, Nottingham, 1995, passim. Kent, J., *The English Village Constable, 1580–1642: A Social and Administrative Study*, Oxford, 1986; Price, F.D., ed., *The Wigginton Constables' Book*, London, 1971; Fox, L., ed., *Coventry Constables' Presentments*, Oxford, 1986; and Wrightson, K., 'Two concepts of order: justices, constables and jurymen in seventeenth century England', in J. Brewer, and J. Styles, eds, *An Ungovernable People: The English and their Law in the Seventeenth and Eighteenth Centuries*, London, 1983.
3 Wrightson, 'Two concepts of order'; Kent, J., ' "Folk justice" and royal justice in Early Modern seventeenth century England: a charivari in the Midlands', *Midland History*, Vol. VIII, 1983.
4 Leicestershire County Record Office, DE720/30, Branston Constables' Accounts, 1611–1676, 62v.
5 Thomas-Sandford, C., *Sussex in the Great Civil War and Interregnum*, London, 1910; Goodwin, G.N., *The Civil War in Hampshire, 1642–45*, London and Southampton, 1904; Coate, M., *Cornwall in the Great*

Civil War, Truro, 1933; Wood, A.C., *Nottinghamshire in the Civil War*, Oxford, 1937.

6 Cliffe, J.T., *The Yorkshire Gentry from the Reformation to the English Civil War*, London, 1969; Everritt, A., *The Community of Kent and the Great Rebellion, 1640–1660*, Leicester, 1973; Holmes, C., *The Eastern Association in the English Civil War*, Cambridge, 1974; Underdown, D., *Somerset in the Civil War and Interregnum*, Newton Abbott, 1973, *Revel, Riot and Rebellion: Popular Politics and Culture in England, 1603–60*, Oxford, 1985, *Fire from Heaven: Life in an English Town in the Seventeenth Century*, London, 1992; Wroughton, J., *A Community at War: The Civil War in Bath and North Somerset*, Bath, 1992.

7 Hughes, A., *Politics, Society and Civil War in Warwickshire, 1620–1660*, Cambridge, 1987; Tennant, P., *Edgehill and Beyond: The People's War in the South Midlands, 1641–45*, Stroud, 1992; Sherwood, R.E., *Civil Strife in the Midlands*, Chichester, 1974 (this was republished as *The Civil War in the Midlands*, Stroud, 1992).

8 Guttery, D.R., *The Great Civil War in Midland Parishes: The People Pay*, Birmingham, 1950.

9 Porter, S., 'The fire-raid in the English civil war', *War and Society*, Vol. 2, No. 2, September 1984, p. 37.

10 Porter, S., *Destruction in the English Civil Wars*, Stroud, 1994, p. 31.

11 Anderson, M.S., *War and Society in Europe of the Old Regime, 1618–1789*, Leicester, 1988, pp. 53–4, 144.

12 Bennett, M., 'Contribution and assessment: financial exactions in the English civil war, 1642–46', *War and Society*, Vol. 5, No. 1, 1986; Carlton, C., *Going to the Wars: The Experience of the British Civil Wars, 1638–1651*, London, 1992, p. 398, n. 73.

13 Hughes, *Politics, Society and Civil War*, p. 270.

14 Everritt, *The Community of Kent*, p. 219; Hughes, *Politics, Society and Civil War*, p. 263.

15 Holmes, *The Eastern Association*, p. 137.

16 Wroughton, *A Community at War*, p. 162.

17 Kenyon, J.P., *Stuart England*, Harmondsworth, 1985, p. 159; Hutton, R.E., *The Royalist War Effort*, London, 1982.

18 Roy, I., 'The Royalist army in the first civil war', D.Phil., Oxford University, 1963; Morrill, J.S., *Revolt of the Provinces: Conservatives and Radicals in the English Civil War*, London, 1976, pp. 53–4.

19 Hutton, *The Royalist War Effort*, p. 86.

20 Bodleian Library, MS Dugdale 19.

21 Bennett, M., 'The Royalist war effort in the north Midlands, 1642–6', unpublished Ph.D. thesis, Loughborough University, 1986, pp. 217–20.

22 Ibid., pp. 193, 195.

23 Ibid., p. 198.

24 Morrill, *Revolt of the Provinces*, pp. 54–5; Bennett, 'The Royalist war effort', p. 87.
25 Hughes, *Politics, Society and Civil War*, pp. 239–45.
26 Ibid., pp. 57–8.
27 Huntingdonshire County Record Office, 2735/9/1, Great Staughton Parish Constables' Accounts, 1643–1712.
28 Ibid., ff. 123r, 124.
29 Bedfordshire County Record Office, TW 1006; Bridlington Town Chest, The Bayle, Bridlington, Constables' Papers.
30 This section is derived from Bennett, 'The Royalist war effort'.
31 Ibid., pp. 199, 219.
32 Ibid., p. 195.
33 Ibid., p. 61; Roberts, A., 'The depredations of the civil war in south west Leicestershire', *The Leicestershire Historian,* Vol. 3, No. 4, 1985–6, p. 8.
34 Staunton Hall Family Papers 34 Warrant to Col. Staunton to levy sums on towns. Thanks to Mrs Elizabeth Staunton for granting me access to the family archives at the Hall.
35 Bennett, 'The Royalist war effort', p. 68, using Leicestershire County Record Office, DE1605/56, p. 72; Nottinghamshire Archive Office, PR1531, np.
36 Staunton Hall Family Papers 34. There is a copy of this in Historical Manuscripts Commission, *Report on Manuscripts in Various Collections*, London, 1914, Vol. VII, pp. 373–4, but it contains some errors of transcription.
37 Staunton Hall Family Papers 34/16 The Account Book of Lt. Gervase Hewet. Thanks to Rev. Stuart Jennings of Nottingham Trent University for his help with transcription; Bennett, *A Nottinghamshire Village*, passim.
38 Staffordshire Record Office, D3712/4/1, Mavesyn Ridware Parish Book, np, double-page entry for 1645 totals.
39 Stocks, H.E., ed., *Records of the Borough of Leicester, 1603–1688*, Cambridge, 1923; Baker, W.T.B., ed., *Records of the Borough of Nottingham, 1625–1702*, Nottingham, 1900.
40 William Salt Library, Salt MSS 48/49, Minute Book of the County Committee at Stafford, pp. 1, 23; this has been published as Pennington, D. and Roots, I., eds, *The Committee at Stafford, 1643–5*, Manchester, 1957.
41 Staunton Hall Family Papers 34/16.
42 Lichfield Cathedral Library, MS Lich. 24, ff. 78–80.
43 Public Record Office (PRO), SP28/189 Exchequer Papers, Yorkshire and Wales.
44 Bridlington, The Bayle, Constables' Accounts, 1633–1653; Ingram, M.E., *The Manor of Bridlington*, Bridlington, 1977, pp. 51–7.

45 Ashcroft, M.Y., ed., *Scarborough Records, 1641–1660*, Northallerton, 1991, pp. 30–1, 269–78.
46 PRO, SP28/189.
47 West Yorkshire Archive Service: Leeds District Archives, TN/PO/2b/ I, II, III, IV.
48 PRO, SP28/189.
49 Newman, P.R., *The Battle of Marston Moor*, Chichester, 1981, p. 17.
50 Ibid. Victoria County Histories, *A History of Yorkshire: North Riding*, London, 1968, Vol. 2, pp. 137–8, 214–16.
51 West Yorkshire Archive Service: Leeds District Archives, Vyner MS 5757, C. 48/15.
52 West Yorkshire Archive Service: Leeds District Archives, TN/PO/2b/ I, II, III, IV.
53 PRO, SP28/189.
54 West Yorkshire Archive Service: Leeds District Archives, TN/PO/2b/ I, II, III, IV.
55 Durham County Record Office, D/Sa/E585.6 Salvin Estate Papers.
56 PRO, SP28/153 Exchequer Papers, Derbyshire to Essex; Wroughton, *A Community at War*.
57 Victoria County Histories, *A History of Yorkshire: East Riding*, London, 1979, Vol. 3, pp. 129, 132.
58 PRO, SP28/189.
59 Hutton, *The Royalist War Effort*, pp. 36, 57.
60 Gloucestershire County Record Office, D621 E2.
61 Gloucestershire County Record Office, D640 L6 Parliamentary Tax Levies in Hartpury.
62 Hereford and Worcestershire County Record Office (St Helen's, Worcester) BA 10/54/2, Bundle B, Assessments.
63 In all of the rating lists, there were no discernible incidences of joint ownership of land between husband and wife. Margaret Spufford's *Contrasting Communities*, Cambridge, 1974, gives examples of this form of ownership, and so there could well be a greater proportion of land in women's hands than these examples show.
64 PRO, SP28/187 Exchequer Papers, Westmoreland to Worcestershire.
65 Gwent County Record Office, Misc. MSS 648, Letter-Book of Richard Herbert, D.L., np.
66 National Library of Wales, LL/MB/11 Results and Orders of His Majesty's Commissioners of Array, 1643–44; Raymond, S.A., 'Glamorgan Arraymen, 1642–5', *Morgannwg*, Vol. 24, 1980, p. 16.
67 National Library of Wales (NLW), MS 17091E Letters and Papers Addressed to Walter Powell of Llantilio; MS 17088A The Diary of Walter Powell of Llantilio, 1603–54; Gwent County Record Office, Misc. MSS 648.
68 PRO, SP28/251 County Committee Papers.

69 Dore, R.N., 'Sir Thomas Myddleton's attempted conquest of Powys, 1644–5', *Montgomeryshire Collections*, Vol. 57, 1961.
70 Dodd, A.H., 'Anglesey in the civil war', *Transactions of the Anglesey Antiquarian Society*, 1952, p. 15.
71 Bennett, M., 'The Royalist war effort', p. 134.
72 NLW, MS 17091E, f. 6.
73 Ibid. The instructions were issued on 11 December, and the money was to be at Llantilio by the 22nd.
74 Ibid., f. 18.
75 Ibid., ff. 8, 10, 11, 18, 40, 43.
76 Gwent County Record Office, Misc. MSS 648.
77 NLW, MS 17091E, ff. 46, 47, 48.
78 Dore, 'Sir Thomas Myddleton's attempted conquest', p. 103.
79 Stevenson, D., 'The financing of the cause of the Covenanters, 1638–51', *Scottish Historical Review*, Vol. 51, No. 152, October 1972; Hazlett, H., 'The financing of the British armies in Ireland: 1641–9', *Irish Historical Studies*, Vol. 1, 1938, and 'A history of the military forces operating in Ireland, 1641–49', 2 vols, unpublished Ph.D. thesis, University of Belfast, 1938; Stevenson, D., *Highland Warrior: Alasdair MacColla and the Civil Wars*, Edinburgh, 1994.
80 Stevenson, 'Financing of the cause of the Covenanters', p. 100.
81 Scottish Record Office (SRO), PA8/2 Charges of Loan and Taxt; Stevenson, 'Financing of the cause of the Covenanters', p. 101.
82 Ibid., pp. 102–3.
83 Ibid., pp. 100–3.
84 Ibid., p. 108.
85 SRO, PA7/6 Supplementary Papers regarding loan and taxt, Doc. 162.
86 Ibid., ff. 320–1.
87 Wood, M., *Extracts from the Records of the Burgh of Edinburgh, 1626–1641*, 2 vols, Edinburgh, 1936, pp. 44, 64; Marwick, J.D., ed., *Extracts of the Records of the Burgh of Glasgow, 1630–1663*, Glasgow, 1881, pp. 68, 89, 94.
88 Stuart, J., ed., *Extracts from the Council Register of the Burgh of Aberdeen, 1643–1747*, 2 vols, Edinburgh, 1871–2, p. 12.
89 Ibid., p. 91.
90 Hazlett, 'A history of the military forces operating in Ireland'; Gillespie, R., 'The Irish economy at war', in J. Ohlmeyer, ed., *Ireland From Independence to Occupation, 1641–1660*, Cambridge, 1995.
91 PRO, SP63/263, 53 Excise and Other Levies (Ireland) and SP64 264, 31 Account Book of the Court of Revenue of the Catholic Confederacy, 1644–47.
92 O'Dowd, M., *Power, Politics and Land: Early Modern Sligo, 1568–1688*, Belfast, 1991, p. 127.
93 The first was in 1711 at the Council Office and the second was in

the civil war of 1922, when the Dublin Public Record Office was shelled by the Free State forces trying to dislodge Republicans at the Four Courts. The only three books to have survived 1711 were destroyed in the flames. Two of these were books of arrears and assessments covering 1645–9. The third book contained material from the Kilkenny justice system; Wood, H., ed., *A Guide to the Records Deposited in the Public Record Office of Ireland*, Dublin, 1919, p. 199.

94 Ibid., p. 168; Wood is citing Gilbert, J.T., ed., *A Contemporary History of Affairs in Ireland from 1641 to 1652*, Dublin, 1879, Vol. 1, p. 78. It is a hostile description, similar in tone to the letter sent by the Lord Justices to Charles I in September 1643.

95 SP63/263, 53 and SP64/264, 31, passim; and Gillespie, 'The Irish economy at war', p. 167.

96 Caulfield, R., ed., *The Council Book of the Corporation of Youghal*, Guildford, 1878, p. 227.

97 Gillespie, 'The Irish economy at war', p. 164.

98 Hogan, J., ed., *Letters and Papers Relating to the Irish Rebellion*, Dublin, 1930, p. 184.

99 Ibid., p. 13.

100 Casaway, J.I., *Owen Roe O'Neill and the Struggle for Catholic Ireland*, Philadelphia, 1984, p. 64.

101 Hogan, *Letters and Papers*, p. 99.

102 Graham, J.M., 'Rural society in Connaught', in N. Stephens and R.E. Glasscock, eds, *Irish Geographical Studies*, Belfast, 1970, p. 197.

103 Ibid.

104 Casaway, *Owen Roe O'Neill*, pp. 87, 104, 119.

105 Caulfield, *Council Book*, pp. 225–6.

106 Ibid., pp. 227–8, 545.

107 Representative Church Body Library, Dublin, Vestry Book, St John's Parish, pp. 163–88, 208–15, 230–7, 245–7, 260–4.

108 For a brief discussion of women and property in Ireland see O'Dowd, *Power, Politics and Land*, pp. 73–4, and Nichols, K., 'Women and property in sixteenth century Ireland', in M. McCurtain and M. O'Dowd, eds, *Women in Early Modern Ireland*, Edinburgh, 1991.

109 Nottinghamshire Archive Office, DD39/5 Toton Rentals, 1626–45.

110 Hereford and Worcestershire County Record Office, Last Will and Testament of Humphrey Billinges. Thanks for this reference to Mark Gittings of the Leicestershire Family History Society. Leicestershire County Record Office, PR/1/4/33, PR/1/45/8; Nottinghamshire Archive Office, PRMW 13/2. Thanks to Douglas Clinton of the Leicestershire WEA for these references. I'd also like to thank the Nottinghamshire County Archivist, Adrian Henstock, for providing me with the background information to the Dand story.

111 Edward Besly's work is essential: *English Civil War Coin Hoards*,

London, 1987, pp. 59–61, 67–8; Barclay, C. and Besly, E., *A Little Barrel of Ducatoons: The Civil War Coinage of Yorkshire*, York, 1994; see also Seaby, W.A., 'Coin hoards of the rebellion period (1641–9) from Ulster', *British Numismatic Journal*, Vol. 29, 1959, pp. 408.

8 VICTORY AND DEFEAT

1 Helen Boteler to her father Sir William Boteler an Committeeman for Bedfordshire, *c*1645. On the back of the letter Sir William had totted up part of the county's levies for the 'Scotch Army'. Bedfordshire County Record Office, TW953 Papers of the late Charles Trevor-Wingfield.
2 West Yorkshire Archive Service: Leeds District Archives, TN/PO/Zb/I.
3 Gardiner, S.R., *History of the Great Civil War*, Adlestrop, 1991, Vol. 1, p. 259.
4 Ibid., p. 300.
5 Bennett, M., 'The Royalist war effort in the north Midlands, 1642–6', unpublished Ph.D. thesis, Loughborough University, 1986, p. 220; Hutton, R.E., *The Royalist War Effort*, London, 1982, p. 101; Kenyon, J.P., *The Civil Wars of England*, London, 1989, p. 95.
6 Holmes, C., *The Eastern Association in the English Civil War*, Cambridge, 1974, pp. 237–8; Bennett, 'The Royalist war effort', pp. 139, 141.
7 Kenyon, *The Civil Wars*, pp. 124–5.
8 Hutton, *The Royalist War Effort*, pp. 122–3.
9 Dore, R.N. and Lowe, J., 'The battle of Nantwich, 25 January 1644', *Transactions of the Lancashire and Cheshire Historical Society*, 1961.
10 Hutton, *The Royalist War Effort*, pp. 126–7.
11 Newman, P.R., *The Battle of Marston Moor*, Chichester, 1981, pp. 14–15.
12 Ibid., p. 19.
13 Ibid., p. 24, and 'The defeat of John Belasyse: civil war in Yorkshire, January–April 1644', *Yorkshire Archaeological Journal*, Vol. CII, 1980; Bennett, 'The Royalist War effort', p. 222.
14 Kenyon, *The Civil Wars*, p. 94.
15 Ibid., p. 98.
16 Wenham, P., *The Great and Close Siege of York, 1644*, Kineton, 1970 (republished as *The Siege of York*, 1994). See pp. 17–21.
17 Ibid., p. 22.
18 City of York Archives, B36 City of York House Book, Vol. 36, f. 101.
19 Ibid., p. 42, citing Simeon Ashe's letter to a friend.
20 For the defences in general see Royal Commission on Historical Monuments, *Report on York*, Vol. 2, London, 1972; for the attack on the Manor see Wenham, *The Great and Close Siege*, ch. 5.

21 See Newman, *Battle of Marston Moor*, pp. 40–3.

22 Newman, P., *Marston Moor: The Sources and the Battle*, York, 1978; Young, P., *Marston Moor, 1644: The Campaign and the Battle*, Kineton, 1970, is useful for the inclusion of so many reprinted primary sources.

23 Cavendish, Margaret, Duchess of Newcastle (ed. C.H. Firth), *The Life of William Cavendish, Duke of Newcastle, and Margaret His Wife*, London, nd, pp. 79, 81, 83.

24 City of York Archives, B36, f. 102; Wenham, *The Great and Close Siege*, pp. 90–5; Scott, D., 'Politics and government in York, 1640–1662', in R.C. Richardson, ed., *Town and Countryside in the English Revolution*, Manchester, 1992, p. 50.

25 Newman, *Battle of Marston Moor*, pp. 138–9.

26 Spence, R.T., *Skipton Castle in the Great Civil War*, Skipton, 1991, p. 66.

27 Ashcroft, M.Y., ed., *Scarborough Records*, Northallerton, 1991, Vol. 2, p. 40.

28 Baumber, M., *General at Sea*, London, 1989.

29 Kenyon, *The Civil Wars*, p. 112.

30 Gardiner, *History*, Vol. 2, p. 11.

31 Ibid.; Kenyon, *The Civil Wars*, p. 112.

32 Gardiner, *History*, Vol. 2, p. 12; Newman, *Battle of Marston Moor*, pp. 98–101, 121; Cavendish, *Life*, p. 40.

33 Kenyon, *The Civil Wars*, p. 113.

34 Kenyon, *The Civil Wars*, p. 121, refers to this conversation.

35 Gentles, I., *The New Model Army in England, Ireland and Scotland, 1645–1653*, Oxford, 1992; see pp. 3–10.

36 Adamson, J.S.A., 'The baronial context of the English civil war', *Transactions of the Royal Historical Society*, 1990, pp. 113–15.

37 Wiltshire County Record Office, G23/1/40, f. 52.

38 Ibid., ff. 5, 7, 37, 43, 111.

39 Underdown, D., *Revel, Riot and Rebellion: Popular Politics and Culture in England, 1603–60*, Oxford, 1985, p. 155.

40 Morrill, J.S., *The Revolt of the Provinces: Conservatives and Radicals in the English Civil War*, London, 1976, p. 112.

41 Lynch, G.J., 'The risings of the clubmen in the English civil war', unpublished M.A. thesis, Manchester University, 1973; Morrill, *Revolt of the Provinces*, pp. 98–111; Hutton, *The Royalist War Effort*, pp. 159–65 and 'The Worcestershire clubmen in the English civil war', *Midland History*, Vol. V, 1979–80; Gladwish, P., 'The Herefordshire clubmen: a reassessment', *Midland History*, Vol. X, 1985; Osborne, S., 'The war, the people, and the absence of clubmen in the Midlands, 1642–46', *Midland History*, Vol. XIX, 1994.

42 Hutton, 'The Worcestershire clubmen', p. 42: Lynch, 'The risings of the Clubmen', pp. 63–4.

43 Morrill, *Revolt of the Provinces*, p. 114.

44 Sherwood, R.E., *Civil Strife in the Midlands*, Chichester, 1974, p. 175.

45 Gladwish, 'The Herefordshire clubmen', pp, 65–6.
46 Lindley, K., *Fenland Riots and the English Revolution*, London, 1982, p. 60.
47 This is just one of many cases in the Star Chamber records for the reign of James VI and I; it is not likely to be an exception, STAC 8/219/23.
48 Sharp, B., *In Contempt of All Authority*, Berkeley, 1980, pp. 127–9, 134–41.
49 Osborne, 'The war, the people', passim,
50 Hutton, *The Royalist War Effort*, pp. 148, 156.
51 Derbyshire County Record Office, D258M/34/10, ff. 3–5.
52 Gentles, *The New Model Army*, pp. 28–9; Ashley, M., *The Battle of Naseby and the Fall of King Charles I*, Stroud, 1992, p. 50.
53 Gentles, *The New Model Army*, p. 31.
54 Bedfordshire County Record Office, TW959.
55 Gentles, *The New Model Army*, pp. 54–5; Ashley, *The Battle of Naseby*, pp. 58–61.
56 Bennett, 'The Royalist war effort', pp. 238–43.
57 The best accounts are Woolrych, A., *Battles of the English Civil War*, London, 1961; Ashley, *The Battle of Naseby*; Denton, B., *Naseby Fight*, Leigh-on-Sea, 1988 (perhaps the best of all); Young, P., *Naseby 1645: The Campaign and the Battle*, London, 1985, is flawed but the primary sources are very useful.
58 *A True Relation of the Victory Obtained over the King's Forces . . .*, cited in Young, *Naseby 1645*, p. 373.
59 Bennett, 'The Royalist war effort', p. 243. See William Salt Library, MSS 550, letters of Loughborough to Prince Rupert, July 1645 and 30 July 1645 for Loughborough's reasons for surrender.
60 Gentles, *The New Model Army*, p. 66.
61 Baxter, R. (ed. N.H. Keeble), *The Autobiography of Richard Baxter*, London, 1985, p. 42; Gentles, *The New Model Army*, pp. 68–9.

9 WAR IN THE CELTIC NATIONS, 1644–7

1 Part of Ian Lom MacDonald's poem on the battle of Inverlochy, cited in Stevenson, D., *Highland Warrior: Alasdair MacColla and the Civil Wars*, Edinburgh, 1994, p. 158.
2 Tucker, N., *North Wales in the Civil War*, Wrexham, 1992 (originally published 1958), pp. 84–7.
3 Hutton, R.E., *The Royalist War Effort*, London, 1982, p. 183.
4 Ibid., p. 184; Jenkins, G., *The Foundations of Modern Wales*, Oxford, 1993, p. 17.
5 Hutton, *The Royalist War Effort*, pp. 184–5.
6 Ibid., p. 189.

7   Ibid., p. 185; Jenkins, *Foundations*, p. 14.
8   Rees, F., 'Breconshire during the civil war', *Brycheiniog*, Vol. 8, 1962, p. 3.
9   Bennett, M., 'The Royalist war effort in the north Midlands, 1642–6', unpublished Ph.D. thesis, Loughborough University, 1986, p. 245.
10 Wedgwood, C.V., *The King's War*, Harmondsworth, 1983, pp. 482–3.
11 Hutton, *The Royalist War Effort*, pp. 186–7; Jenkins, *Foundations*, p. 18.
12 Ibid.
13 Hutton, *The Royalist War Effort*, p. 151.
14 See Stevenson, *Highland Warrior* for the best introduction to this area.
15 Ibid., pp. 121–2.
16 Ibid., p. 124.
17 Wood, M., ed., *Extracts from the Records of the Burgh of Edinburgh, 1626–1641*, Edinburgh, 1938, p. 52.
18 Reid, S., *The Campaigns of Montrose*, Edinburgh, 1990, pp. 53–4; Lenihan, P., 'Celtic warfare revisited: the Irish Confederates at war', paper presented to the Celtic Dimensions to the British Civil Wars conference, Strathclyde University, 5 April 1995.
19 Stevenson, *Highland Warrior*, pp. 128–9.
20 Stuart, J., ed., *Extracts from the Council Register of the Burgh of Aberdeen, 1643–1747*, Edinburgh, 1871–2, p. 28.
21 Ibid., pp. x, 28–9.
22 Stevenson, *Highland Warrior*, pp. 135–7; Withers, C.J., *Gaelic Scotland: The Transformation of a Cultural Region*, London, 1988, p. 73.
23 Stuart, *Extracts*, p. 32.
24 Stevenson, *Highland Warrior*, pp. 140–1.
25 Reid, *Campaigns of Montrose*, pp. 84–9.
26 Stevenson, *Highland Warrior*, p. 157.
27 Ibid., p. 158.
28 Ibid., p. 160. See also Stevenson's references for sources for an examination of this important aspect of the wars.
29 Stuart, *Extracts*, pp. 48–9.
30 Scottish Record Office (SRO), PA7/6, No. 162.
31 For the traditional view see Gardiner, S.R., *History of the Great Civil War*, Adlestrop, 1987, Vol. 2, pp. 222–7; Seymour, W., *Battles in Britain*, London, 1975, pp. 131–2; and Bennett, M., *Travellers' Guide to the Battlefields of the English Civil War*, Exeter, 1990, pp. 132–4, see fns 32 and 33 for alternative perspectives.
32 Reid, *Campaigns of Montrose*, p. 112.
33 For Stevenson's convincing account see *Highland Warrior*, pp. 172–85.
34 See Reid's account, *Campaigns of Montrose*, pp. 124–33, which overturns that set out by Stevenson and others.
35 Stevenson, *Highland Warrior*, pp. 198–200.
36 Reid, *Campaigns of Montrose*, pp. 134–41, 143–50.
37 Stevenson, *Highland Warrior*, p. 202.

38 Marwick, J.D., ed., *Extracts of the Records of the Burgh of Glasgow, 1630–1662*, Glasgow, 1881, pp. 74–5.

39 Reid, *Campaigns of Montrose*, pp. 156–61.

40 Stevenson, *Highland Warrior*, pp. 219–21.

41 Ibid., pp. 223, 225.

42 Ibid., p. 226.

43 Ibid., but also see MacTavish, D.C., ed., *Minutes of the Synod of Argyll, 1639–1651*, Edinburgh, 1943, passim, also pp. 99, 106.

44 SRO, PA7/6, No. 162, ff. 319, 329.

45 See McKerral. A., *Kintyre in the Seventeenth Century*, Edinburgh, 1948, pp. 76–7, 80–1, for a good account of the condition of the region and for an examination of Argyll's colonization in the wake of the war.

46 O'Dowd, M., *Power, Politics and Land: Early Modern Sligo, 1568–1688*, Belfast, 1991, p. 126.

47 Ohlmeyer, J., *Civil War and Restoration in the Three Stuart Kingdoms. The Career of Randal MacDonnell, Marquis of Antrim, 1609–1683*, Cambridge, 1993, pp. 137–8.

48 Ibid., p. 141.

49 Ibid., p. 147.

50 Caulfield, R., ed., *The Council Book of the Corporation of Youghal*, Guildford, 1878, pp. 223–7, 250, 264–6.

51 For an analysis of the campaign, see Casaway, J.I., *Owen Roe O'Neill and the Struggle for Catholic Ireland*, Philadelphia, 1984, pp. 103–12, and Wheeler, S., 'Four armies in Ireland', in J. Ohlmeyer, ed., *Ireland From Independence to Occupation, 1641–1660*, Cambridge, 1995, pp. 51–2.

52 Corish, P., 'Ormond, Rinuccini and the Confederates, 1645–9', in T.W. Moody, F.X. Martin and F.J. Byrne, eds, *A New History of Ireland*, Oxford, 1976, p. 318.

53 O'Dowd, *Power, Politics and Land*, pp. 128–9.

54 Wheeler, 'Four armies', pp. 54–5.

55 The poem is cited anonymously in Gilbert, J.T., ed., *A Contemporary History of Affairs in Ireland from 1641 to 1652*, Dublin, 1879–80, Vol. 1, p. 116.

56 Casaway, *Owen Roe O'Neill*, pp. 130–8; Wheeler, 'Four armies', p. 55.

57 Clanricarde, Earl of (ed. J. Lowe), *Letter-Book of the Earl of Clanricarde, 1643–47*, Dublin, 1983, pp. 343–4.

58 Corish, 'Ormond', p. 322.

10 THE RADICAL AND CONSERVATIVE IMPETUS

1 The first line is from Psalm 118 and included as part of Calamy, E., *The Souldiers Pocket Bible*, London, 1643, p. 15. The second quote is from Cranford, J. (printer), *The Souldiers Catechisme Composed for the*

Parliaments Army, 1644, London, nd, pp. 23–4; it is the tenth response to the question 'What are the chiefe Arguments and considerations to make a souldier couragious in the parliament's service?'

2   Fox, L., *A Country Grammar School*, Oxford, 1967, p. 43. See also Tennant, P., *Edgehill and Beyond: The People's War in the South Midlands, 1641–45*, Stroud, 1992, pp. 135–60.

3   The most useful accounts of this period are to be found in Ashton, R., *Counter-Revolution: The Second Civil War and its Origins*, New Haven, 1994; Hughes, A., *Politics, Society and Civil War in Warwickshire, 1620–1660*, Cambridge, 1987; Everritt, A., *The Community of Kent and the Great Rebellion, 1640–1660*, Leicester, 1973; Roberts, S.K., *Recovery and Restoration in an English County: Devon Local Administration*, Exeter, 1985; Coleby, A.M., *Central Government and the Localities: Hampshire, 1649–1689*, Cambridge, 1987.

4   Broughton, S., 'The constables' accounts of Great Staughton', Huntingdonshire County Record Office, 1989, p. 1; Victoria County Histories, *A History of Huntingdonshire*, London, 1932 (reprinted 1974), Vol. 2, p. 354.

5   Ibid., pp. 358–62.

6   Huntingdonshire County Record Office, 2735/9/1 Great Staughton Parish Constables' Book.

7   Ibid., pp. 1–2.

8   Ibid., ff. 124–1. The pages are in reverse order.

9   Ibid., f. 123r.

10   Ibid., f. 123; Wedgwood, C.V., *The King's War*, Harmondsworth, 1983, pp. 482–3.

11   Ashton, *Counter-Revolution*, p. 44.

12   Ibid., p. 51.

13   Braddick, M.J., 'Popular politics and public policy: the excise riot at Smithfield in February 1647 and its aftermath', *Historical Journal*, Vol. 34, No. 3, 1991, pp. 597, 612–13.

14   Morrill, J.S., *The Revolt of the Provinces: Conservatives and Radicals in the English Civil War*, London, 1976, p. 125.

15   Gardiner, S.R., ed., *The Constitutional Documents of the Puritan Revolution*, Oxford, 1979, pp. 297–304.

16   Gentles, I., *The New Model Army in England, Ireland and Scotland, 1645–1653*, Oxford, 1992, pp. 133–4.

17   Ibid., p. 132.

18   Kishlansky, M., *The Rise of the New Model Army*, Cambridge, 1979, 'Ideology and politics in the Parliamentarian armies, 1645–9', in J.S. Morrill, ed., *Reactions to the English Civil War*, London, 1982, and *Parliamentary Selection*, Cambridge, 1987; Adamson, J.S.A., 'The baronial context of the English civil war', *Transactions of the Royal Historical Society*, 1990, passim.

19   Gentles, *The New Model Army*, pp. 118–19.

20   Calamy, *The Souldiers Pocket Bible.*
21   Cranford (printer), *The Souldiers Catechisme.*
22   Howard Shaw, for example, in *The Levellers,* London, 1968, says of them: 'Four men were mainly responsible for directing Leveller fortunes'.
23   Gregg, P., *Freeborn John: A Biography of John Lilburne,* London, 1986, (first published 1961), pp. 137–43.
24   *A Catalogue of the several Sects and opinions in England and Other Nations: With a brief rehearsall of their false and dangerous tenents,* R.A., London, 1647.
25   Shaw, *The Levellers,* p. 43.
26   Gentles, *The New Model Army,* p. 148.
27   Ibid., p. 149.
28   Ibid., p. 151.
29   Ibid., pp. 152–3.
30   Brailsford, H.N., *The Levellers and the English Revolution,* Nottingham, 1983 (first published 1961), p. 170.
31   Ibid., p. 171; Gentles, *The New Model Army,* p. 158.
32   Ibid., p. 162; Kenyon, J.P., *The Civil Wars of England,* London, 1989, pp. 170–1.
33   Ibid., p. 166; Gentles, *The New Model Army,* p. 158.
34   Brailsford, *The Levellers,* pp. 197, 206.
35   Kenyon, *The Civil Wars,* p. 167.
36   Gardiner, *Constitutional Documents,* pp. 316–27.
37   Kenyon, *The Civil Wars,* p. 170.
38   Ibid., p. 172; Aylmer, G.E., ed., *The Levellers in the English Revolution,* London, 1975, p. 29.
30   Macpherson, C.B., *The Political Theory of Possessive Individualism,* Oxford, 1962.
40   Ibid., pp. 107–54.
41   Ashton, R., *The English Civil War: Conservatism and Revolution,* London, 1978, p. 309.
42   Sanderson, J., *But the People's Creatures: The Philosophical Basis of the English Civil War,* Manchester, 1989, p. 116.
43   Manning, B., *The English People and the English Revolution, 1640–1649,* Harmondsworth, 1978, pp. 332–3.
44   Shaw, *The Levellers,* p. 34.
45   See Woodhouse, A.H., ed., *Puritanism and Liberty,* London, 1966, for the Clarke MSS version of the Putney debates; for this quotation see p. 53.
46   Aylmer, G.E., *Rebellion or Revolution: England from Civil War to Restoration,* Oxford, 1986, p. 90.
47   Gentles, *The New Model Army,* pp. 225–6.

11   ENGAGEMENT TO EXECUTION

1   Scottish Record Office (SRO), PA7/6, No. 155 Account of the sufferings of Dolphinton.
2   Stevenson, D., *Revolution and Counter-Revolution in Scotland, 1644–1651*, London, 1977, p. 55.
3   Ibid., p. 59.
4   Ashton, R., *Counter-Revolution: The Second Civil War and its Origins*, New Haven, 1994, pp. 14–15; Stevenson, *Revolution*, pp. 62–3.
5   Ibid., p. 94.
6   Ashton, *Counter-Revolution*, p. 36.
7   Stevenson, *Revolution*, p. 95, citing the Journal of the House of Lords.
8   Gardiner, S.R., *History of the Great Civil War*, Adlestrop, 1991, Vol. 4, pp. 50–2.
9   Ibid., pp. 100–1.
10   Ibid., p. 104.
11   Wood, M., ed., *Extracts from the Records of the Burgh of Edinburgh, 1626–1641*, Edinburgh, 1938, pp. 147–8, 150, 151–2.
12   Ibid., p. 152.
13   Marwick, J.D., ed., *Extracts of the Records of the Burgh of Glasgow, 1630–1662*, Glasgow, 1881, p. 132.
14   Ibid., pp. 133–4.
15   Ibid., pp. 142–3.
16   SRO, PA7/6, No. 155.
17   See Ashton, *Counter-Revolution*, pp. 97, 103, 109–10, 341–6 for the latest work to date on the rising and its context.
18   Jenkins, G., *The Foundations of Modern Wales*, Oxford, 1993, p. 20.
19   Gardiner, *History*, p. 84.
20   Jenkins, *Foundations*, p. 21.
21   Gardiner, *History*, p. 112.
22   Ashton, *Counter-Revolution*, p. 459.
23   Cited in Nichols, J., *The History and Antiquities of the County of Leicestershire*, London, 1804, Vol. 3, part 2, appendix, p. 39.
24   Bennett, M., 'The Royalist war effort in the north Midlands, 1642–6', unpublished Ph.D. thesis, Loughborough, 1986, pp. 91–3.
25   Hughes, A., *Politics, Society and Civil War in Warwickshire, 1620–1660*, Cambridge, 1987; see ch. 2 and p. 272.
26   Everritt, A., *The Community of Kent and the Great Rebellion, 1640–1660*, Leicester, 1973, p. 143.
27   Wroughton, J., *A Community at War: The Civil War in Bath and North Somerset*, Bath, 1992, pp. 168–71.
28   Roberts, S.K., *Recovery and Restoration in an English County: Devon Local Administration*, Exeter, 1985, p. 16.
29   Ibid., pp. 10–12.

30 For a strong contextual basis for study of Christmas during the period, see Hutton, R., *The Rise and Fall of Merry England*, Oxford, 1994, pp. 207–10.

31 Ketton-Cremer, R.W., *Norfolk in the Civil War*, Hamden, CT, 1970, pp. 334–49.

32 See Everritt, *The Community of Kent*, pp. 233–4 for an account of the rebellion of the Kent Royalists.

33 Hutton, *Rise and Fall*, pp. 210–11.

34 Morrill, J.S., 'The church in England, 1642–9'. Dr Morrill first published the essay in his book, *Reactions to the English Civil War*, London, 1982; it has since been reprinted in his collection of essays, *The Nature of the English Revolution*, London, 1993.

35 Hutton, *Rise and Fall*, pp. 213–14.

36 Capp, B., *Cromwell's Navy*, Oxford, 1992, p. 17. Ch. 1 of this work is the most recent, and perhaps the best account of the navy in 1648.

37 Ibid., pp. 29–32.

38 Historical Manuscripts Commission, *Fourteenth Report*, London, 1895, pp. 281–90, is a copy of a 'Diary or account of Siege of Colchester, Anno 1648'.

39 Ibid., pp. 288–9.

40 Capp, *Cromwell's Navy*, p. 35.

41 Kenyon, J.P., *The Civil Wars of England*, London, 1989, p. 189.

42 Adams, S., 'Charles I and the making of the radical south-west of Scotland', paper presented to the Celtic Dimensions to the British Civil Wars conference, 5 April 1995, Strathclyde University.

43 The best account of the revolt probably remains Norman Tucker's in *North Wales in the Civil War*, Wrexham, 1992, ch. 13.

44 Ibid. Contains a transcript of Mytton's own report of the battle.

45 See Dodd, A.H., 'Anglesey in the civil war', *Transactions of the Anglesey Antiquarian Society*, 1952.

46 SRO, PA7/6, No. 156.

47 Wheeler, S., 'Four armies in Ireland', in J. Ohlmeyer, ed., *Ireland From Independence to Occupation, 1641–1660*, Cambridge, 1995, pp. 58–9.

48 Corish, P., 'Ormond, Rinuccini and the Confederates', in T.W. Moody, F.X. Martin and F.J. Byrne, eds, *A New History of Ireland*, Oxford, 1976, p. 328.

49 Wheeler, 'Four armies', p. 59.

50 Corish, 'Ormond', p. 330.

51 Casaway, J.I., *Owen Roe O'Neill and the Struggle for Catholic Ireland*, Philadelphia, 1984, pp. 210–16.

52 Ibid., pp. 221–6.

53 Gardiner, *History*, p. 163.

54 Ibid., pp. 224–5.

55 National Archives, Ireland, M1121/1/2, Transcripts of the Bellew of Louth Family Papers, LXXXXVIII, 105–6, 111–12.

56 Casaway, *Owen Roe O'Neill*, pp. 231–3.
57 Ibid., p. 234.
58 Ibid., pp. 246–8.
59 For a discussion of blood-guilt in the context of the period see Baskerville, S., *Not Peace But a Sword: The Political Theology of the English Revolution*, London, 1993, pp. 85–95.
60 Gardiner, *History*, p. 235.
61 Brailsford, H.N., *The Levellers and the English Revolution*, Nottingham, 1983, pp. 266–7.
62 For the most authoritative account of the purge see Underdown, D., *Pride's Purge*, Oxford, 1971.
63 Aylmer, G.E., ed., *The Levellers in the English Revolution*, London, 1975, p. 41.
64 Wedgwood, C.V., *The Trial of Charles I*, Harmondsworth, 1983, pp. 128, 154–5.
65 Ibid., p. 132.

12 THE PEOPLE'S REACTION

1 The annotation in a churchwardens' account book from Kirkby Malzeard, Yorkshire; North Yorkshire County Record Office, PR/KMZ/2/2.
2 Hutton, R.E., *The British Republic*, London, 1990, p. 4.
3 Manning, B., *1649: The Crisis of the English Revolution*, London, 1992, pp. 14–19, 24. Manning also analyses the input of the army, arguing that it was politicized before 1647, as Gentles suggested in *The New Model Army in England, Ireland and Scotland, 1645–1653*, Oxford, 1992. The effect of Manning's argument is to support the idea that 1648–9 was an extension of an earlier train of events, i.e. a revolution.
4 Ashton, R., *The English Civil War: Conservatism and Revolution, 1603–49*, London, 1978, pp. 317–52.
5 See Adamson, J.S.A., 'Oliver Cromwell and the Long Parliament', in J.S. Morrill, ed., *Oliver Cromwell and the English Revolution*, London, 1990, passim and pp. 82–3 in particular.
6 Hutton, *The British Republic*, p. 6.
7 Ibid.
8 Aylmer, G.E., ed., *The Levellers in the English Revolution*, London, 1975, pp. 142–3.
9 Gentles, *The New Model Army*, pp. 319–21.
10 Manning, *1649*, pp. 190–2.
11 Ibid., p. 157.
12 Brailsford, H.N., *The Levellers and the English Revolution*, Nottingham, 1983, p. 119.
13 Manning, *1649*, p. 157 summarizes this argument.
14 See Higgins, P., 'The reactions of women, with special reference to women petitioners', in B. Manning, ed., *Politics, Religion and the English*

Civil War, London, 1973 for a recent discussion, and McArthur, E.A., 'Women petitioners and the Long Parliament', *English Historical Review*, Vol. XXIV, 1909 for an older view. To place this in the context of the world of women's writing see Hobby, E., *Virtue of Necessity: English Women's Writing, 1649–88*, London, 1988, pp. 16–18.

15   Hobby, *Virtue of Necessity*, p. 17; Manning, *1649*, p. 163.

16   Brailsford, *The Levellers*, pp. 528–35.

17   Gentles, *The New Model Army*, pp. 331–3.

18   Ibid., pp. 518–19.

19   Lindley, K., *Fenland Riots and the English Revolution*, London, 1982, ch. 6 passim, p. 196 in particular. Morrill, J.S. and Walter, J.D., 'Order and disorder in the English revolution', in A. Fletcher and J. Stevenson, eds, *Order and Disorder in Early Modern England*, London, 1985, p. 161.

20   Holmes, C., 'Drainers and fenmen', in Fletcher and Stevenson, *Order and Disorder*, pp. 167–8.

21   Manning, *1649*, p. 160.

22   Woodhouse, A.C., ed., *Puritanism and Liberty*, London, 1966, p. 379.

23   Manning, *1649*, pp. 123–4.

24   This excerpt is from Brailsford, *The Levellers*, p. 656, but it is still sung in folk clubs, with verses added to reflect current social issues. New verses were added during the miners' strike of 1984–5, and in 1985 the socialist singer/songwriter Billy Bragg recorded a version.

25   Bradley, I., 'Gerrard Winstanley, England's pioneer Green', *History Today*, Vol. 39, August, 1989, p. 14.

26   Hill, C., *The World Turned Upside Down*, Harmondsworth, 1975, ch. 7 passim, p. 135 in particular.

27   Morrill and Walter, 'Order and disorder', p. 160.

28   Historical Manuscripts Commission, *Calendar of Manuscripts of the Marquis of Ormonde*, New Series, London, 1902–3, Vol. 1, pp. 128–32.

29   Casaway, J.I., *Owen Roe O'Neill and the Struggle for Catholic Ireland*, Philadelphia, 1984, p. 250.

30   O'Dowd, M., *Power, Politics and Land: Early Modern Sligo, 1568–1688*, Belfast, 1991, pp. 128–9.

31   Casaway, *Owen Roe O'Neill*, pp. 251–2.

32   National Archives, Ireland, M1121/1/1, Transcripts of the Bellew of Louth Family Papers, LXXXXVII, f. 106.

33   Ibid., pp. 253–5.

34   Gardiner, S.R., *History of the Commonwealth and Protectorate, 1649–1656*, Adlestrop, 1988, pp. 115–25.

35   Hutton, *The British Republic*, pp. 47–8.

36   Cromwell, O. (ed. T. Carlyle), *Oliver Cromwell's Letters and Speeches*, 3rd edition, London, nd, p. 298; Gardiner, *History of the Commonwealth*, p. 124.

37   Cromwell, *Letters and Speeches*, p. 311.

38   Caulfield, R., ed., *The Council Book of the Corporation of Youghal*, Guildford, 1878, p. 558.

39 *Calendar of State Papers Relating to Ireland in the Reign of Charles I, 1647–60*, London, 1903, pp. 370–3.

40 Smout, T.C., *A History of the Scottish People*, London, 1973, pp. 107, 144. See also chapters 7 and 9 above.

41 Marwick, J.D., ed., *Extracts of the Records of the Burgh of Glasgow, 1630–1662*, Glasgow, 1881, p. 182.

42 Wood, M., ed., *Extracts from the Records of the Burgh of Edinburgh, 1626–1641*, Edinburgh, 1938, pp. 232–3.

43 Stuart, J., ed., *Extracts from the Council Register of the Burgh of Aberdeen, 1643–1747*, Edinburgh, 1871–2, p. 94.

44 Ibid., p. 113; Wood, *Extracts*, p. 195.

45 Beier, A., *Masterless Men*, London, 1985, puts this in context.

46 For the village context see Bennett, M., ed., *A Nottinghamshire Village in War and Peace: The Accounts of the Constables of Upton, 1640–1666*, Nottingham, 1995. The proportion of village income increases to 5 per cent if the monthly pay is removed from the community budget.

47 I must thank Adrian Henstock, County Archivist at Nottinghamshire Archive Office, for this suggestion, which he made while I was working on the Upton constables' accounts referred to in note 46.

48 Hertfordshire County Record Office, D/P110/5/1 Thundridge Constables' Accounts, 1622–1675.

49 Huntingdonshire County Record Office, 2735/9/1 Great Staughton Parish Constables' Book.

50 As the spread of travellers is fairly even, and as the proportion of them passing through by September 1652 is only 60 per cent of the previous year's total, it may be evidence of a decline of about 20 per cent.

51 Underdown, D., *Fire From Heaven: Life in an English Town in the Seventeenth Century*, London, 1992, pp. 220–3.

52 Bond, S.M., ed., *The Chamber Order Book of Worcester, 1602–1650*, Worcester, 1974, pp. 451, 453, 456, 458.

53 North Yorkshire County Record Office, PR/TH/3/1/1 Thirsk Churchwardens' Accounts, 1630–1683.

54 North Yorkshire County Record Office, PR/MAS/3/1/1 Masham Parish Churchwardens' Accounts, 1542–1677.

55 North Yorkshire County Record Office, PR/OUL/2/1 Little Ouseburn Churchwardens' Accounts.

56 North Yorkshire County Record Office, PR/KMZ/2/2, Kirkby Malzeard Churchwardens' Accounts, 1576–1655, pp. 63–4, 67–8, 70–2.

13 A CROWNING MERCY

1 Oliver Cromwell's letter to the Speaker on the day after the battle of Worcester, 1651. Cromwell, O. (ed. T. Carlyle), *Oliver Cromwell's Letters and Speeches*, London, nd, p. 459.

2 Marwick, J.D., ed., *Extracts of the Records of the Burgh of Glasgow, 1630–1662*, Glasgow, 1881, pp. 158–9.

3 Reid, S., *The Campaigns of Montrose*, Edinburgh, 1990, pp. 177–8.
4 Argyll and Montrose now lie in St Giles Cathedral almost opposite each other across the nave. For some reason, the Covenant is displayed next to Montrose's tomb. Both are really upstaged by Jenny Geddes's modern memorial.
5 Hutton, R.E., *The British Republic*, London, 1990, p. 49.
6 Ibid., p. 51.
7 Cambridgeshire County Record Office, P53/12/1.
8 West Yorkshire Archive Service: Leeds District Archives, Vyner MSS 5982 C/30/A/6 pp. 1–3, 23.
9 Scottish Record Office, GD124/10/388, GD124/17/208 (Marr and Kellie Muniments).
10 Brown, K.M., *Kingdom or Province: Scotland and the Regal Union*, London, 1992, p. 135.
11 Stevenson, D., 'Cromwell, Scotland and Ireland', in J.S. Morrill, ed., *Oliver Cromwell and the English Revolution*, London, 1990, p. 165.
12 Scottish Record Office, GD124/17/15 Losses of the Earl of Marr.
13 It was estimated that there were as many as 50,000 Irish soldiers still in arms, many of them being Tories in action against the English in 1651; Berresford-Ellis, P., *Hell or Connaught! The Cromwellian Colonisation of Ireland, 1652–1660*, Belfast, 1988, p. 35.
14 Wheeler, S., 'Four armies in Ireland', in J. Ohlmeyer, ed., *Ireland From Independence to Occupation, 1641–1660*, Cambridge, 1995, passim and pp. 64–5 in particular; O'Dowd, M., *Power, Politics and Land: Early Modern Sligo, 1568–1688*, Belfast, 1991, p. 130.
15 Hutton, *The British Republic*, p. 49.
16 National Library, Ireland, MS 11, 959 Transcripts of Commonwealth Records, ff. 17–18, 26.
17 Ibid., f. 29.
18 National Library, Ireland, MS 856–7 Transcripts of Documents by J.T. Gilbert.
19 McKenny, K., 'The seventeenth-century land settlement in Ireland: towards a statistical interpretation', in Ohlmeyer, *Ireland*, p. 181.
20 For full discussions see McKenny, 'Seventeenth-century land settlement'; Berresford-Ellis, *Hell or Connaught!*, which is an exciting and readable account; and O'Dowd, *Power, Politics and Land*, which sets this into the context of Connaught, and County Sligo in particular, in ch. 8.
21 Berresford-Ellis, *Hell or Connaught!*, pp. 50–1.
22 O'Dowd, *Power, Politics and Land*, pp. 131–3.
23 O'Dowd, 'Women and war in Ireland in the 1640s', in M. MacCurtain and M. O'Dowd, eds, *Women in Early Modern Ireland*, Edinburgh, 1991, pp. 105–8.
24 National Archives, Ireland, M1121/1/2 Transcripts of the Bellew of

Louth Family Papers, LXXXXV, ff. 89–99, LXXXXVI, ff. 101–4, LXXXXVIII, ff. 111–14.

25 O'Dowd, 'Women and war in Ireland', p. 133; McKenny, 'Seventeenth-century land settlement', pp. 199–201.

26 Berresford-Ellis, *Hell or Connaught!*, pp. 59–60.

27 National Archives, Ireland, M4974 Caulfield Papers, np.

28 Public Record Office (PRO), SP28/251 County Committee Papers.

29 PRO, SP28/189 Exchequer Papers, Yorkshire and Wales.

30 Ibid.; these papers do not seem to be more precisely catalogued.

31 Charles, B.G., ed., *Calendar of the Records of the Borough of Haverfordwest, 1539–1660*, Cardiff, 1967, pp. 90, 94, 97.

32 Jenkins, G.H., *Protestant Dissenters in Wales*, Cardiff, 1992, pp. 17–20.

33 Ibid., pp. 20–1.

34 Jenkins, G.H., *The Foundations of Modern Wales*, Oxford, 1993, p. 37.

35 Kenyon, T., *Utopian Communism and Political Thought in Early Modern England*, London, 1989, pp. 187–9.

36 For John Morrill's argument see Part One of *The Nature of the English Revolution*, London, 1993.

37 Newman, P.R., *The Old Service: Royalist Regimental Colonels and the Civil War, 1642–46*, Manchester, 1993. See the Introduction, passim, and pp. 3, 11 in particular; also refer to chapter 5 above.

38 Otten, C., ed., *English Women's Voices, 1500–1700*, Miami, 1992, pp. 100–4.

39 Morrill, J.S., 'The impact of Puritanism', in J.S. Morrill, ed., *The Impact of the English Civil War*, London, 1991, p. 66.

40 McGregor, J.F. and Reay, B., eds, *Radical Religion in the English Revolution*, Oxford, 1986, p. 12. Their book is an excellent and accessible collection of essays.

41 McGregor, J.F., 'The Baptists: fount of all heresy', in McGregor and Reay, *Radical Religion*, p. 52.

42 Hutchinson, L., *Memoirs of the Life of Colonel John Hutchinson*, London, 1806, pp. 269–71.

43 A reprint of this was published by the Rota at Exeter University in 1974.

44 McGregor, J.F., 'Seekers and Ranters', in McGregor and Reay, *Radical Religion*, p. 129; Morton, A.L., *The World of the Ranters: Religious Radicalism in the English Revolution*, London, 1970.

45 Clarkson, *The Lost Sheep Found*, p. 26.

46 Hill, C., *The World Turned Upside Down*, Harmondsworth, 1975, pp. 201–2.

47 See Davis, J.C., *Fear, Myth and History: The Ranters and the Historians*, Cambridge, 1986. For a succinct description of Davis's argument and the controversy which followed the publication of his book, see Davis's article, 'Fear, myth and furore: Reappraising the Ranters', *Past and*

Present, No. 129, November, 1990. The quotations are from the journal article, p. 81.

48   Hill, *The World,* p. 207.

49   For the contextualization of women religious writers, see Hobby, E., *Virtue of Necessity: English Women's Writing, 1649–88,* London, 1988, ch. 1.

50   See Daniel VII and VIII.

51   Davis, J.C., 'Cromwell's religion', in Morrill, *Oliver Cromwell and the English Revolution,* provides an enlivening examination of the issue. For Cromwell and the Seekers, see McGregor, J.F., 'Seekers and Ranters', in McGregor and Reay, *Radical Religion,* pp. 127–8.

52   Cavendish, Margaret, Duchess of Newcastle (ed. C.H. Firth), *The Life of William Cavendish, Duke of Newcastle, and Margaret His Wife,* London, nd, pp. 7–8.

53   Baxter, R. (ed. N.H. Keeble), *The Autobiography of Richard Baxter,* London, 1985, p. 29.

54   Aylmer, G.E., *Rebellion or Revolution: England from Civil War to Restoration,* Oxford, 1991, pp. 101–2.

55   Manning, B., *The English People and the English Revolution, 1640–1649,* Harmondsworth, 1978, p. 340; Coleby, A.M., *Central Government and the Localities: Hampshire, 1649–1689,* Cambridge, 1987, p. 14.

56   Hughes, A., *Politics, Society and Civil War in Warwickshire, 1620–1660,* Cambridge, 1987, pp. 342–3; Roberts, S.K., *Recovery and Restoration in an English County: Devon Local Administration,* Exeter, 1985, p. 20; Wroughton, J., *A Community at War: The Civil War in Bath and North Somerset,* Bath, 1992, p. 162; Underdown, D., *Revel, Riot and Rebellion: Popular Politics and Culture in England, 1603–60,* Oxford, 1985, pp. 281, 285; Sharpe, B., 'Rural discontents and the English revolution', in R.C. Richardson, ed., *Town and Countryside in the English Revolution,* Manchester, 1992, p. 269.

57   Brown, *Kingdom or Province,* pp. 137–8; Mitchison, R., *Lordship to Patronage: Scotland, 1603–1745,* Edinburgh, 1990, pp. 62–5.

58   Jenkins, *Foundations,* pp. 40–2.

59   Carlton, C., *Going to the Wars: The Experience of the British Civil Wars, 1638–1651,* London, 1992, p. 214; Gillespie, R., 'The Irish economy at war', in Ohlmeyer, *Ireland,* pp. 179–81.

60   Hutton, *The British Republic,* p. 3.

61   Carlton, *Going to the Wars,* pp. 202–14.

Bibliography

PRIMARY MANUSCRIPT SOURCES ARRANGED BY
RECORD OFFICE

BEDFORDSHIRE COUNTY RECORD OFFICE

TW895–1014 Papers of the late Charles Trevor-Wingfield

BODLEIAN LIBRARY

MS Dugdale 19, A register of Docquets of all Letters Patent and other Documents . . . from 23 January 1643 to 11 June 1646

BRIDLINGTON, THE BAYLE (PAPERS BELONGING TO THE LORDS FEOFFEE)

Constables' Accounts, 1633–1653
Billeting Lists 1–8
Cesses and Levies
Receipts, 1643–8
Receipts, 1644

BRITISH LIBRARY

Additional MSS 5752, ff. 388–9, 399–402, Letters of Thomas Leveson
Additional MSS 6688 Derbyshire Collections
Additional MSS 6689 Derbyshire Collections
Additional MSS 34217 Instructions to the Northamptonshire Commissioners
Additional MSS 18980–2, ff. 89–91, 147, 159, 160, Letters of Prince Rupert to Lord Loughborough
Additional MSS 29548, ff. 7–9, Commissions addressed to Sir Christopher Hatton

Additional MSS 46553 Lexington Papers
Harleian MSS 986 Notebook of Richard Symonds
Stowe MSS 155, f. 7, letter of Thomas Leveson to constables of Burton and Tothill

CAMBRIDGESHIRE COUNTY RECORD OFFICE

P46/1/1 Comberstone Parish Register
P53/12/1 Croydon cum Clopton Accounts, 1651–1818
P145/5/1 Stretchworth Churchwardens' Accounts
R58/5/3 Maynard Collection, Vol. 3

CHESHIRE COUNTY RECORD OFFICE

DFI 192 Church Lawton Constables' Accounts (transcript of Harleian MS 1943)
P109/13 Church Lawton Constables' Lists

CLWYD COUNTY RECORD OFFICE

D/DM/223/139 Letter of Charles I to the Sheriff of Flint
D/GW/2145 Civil War Notices
D/GW/B/1020 Letters of Civil War News
D/HE/462–78 Papers and Letters of Evan Edwards
D/HE/874–5 Edwards Papers
Misc. MSS 254 Letter from Charles I to the High Sheriff of Monmouthshire, 21 December 1642

CORNWALL COUNTY RECORD OFFICE

P19/9/1–25 St Breock Constables' Accounts

DERBYSHIRE COUNTY RECORD OFFICE

D803 M29 Copybook of Sir George Gresley
D258M/34/10 Gell Manuscripts

DEVONSHIRE COUNTY RECORD OFFICE

3248A/10/56–7 Okehampton Constables' Disbursements, 1642–44

DURHAM COUNTY RECORD OFFICE

D/Sa/E585.6 Salvin Estate Papers
EP DU SO 118 Durham St Oswald Parish Register
EP/Ga SM4/1 Gateshead St Mary's Minutebook, 1626–1678

GLOUCESTERSHIRE COUNTY RECORD OFFICE

D621 E2 Accounts of Sir Nicholas Raynton of Maugersbury
D640/L6–7 Parliamentary Tax Levies in Hartpury
P338/CO/1/1 Tortworth Tythingmen's Accounts
P338/CO/1/2 Tortworth Constables' Accounts
P343/VE/2/1 Twyning Parish Book

GWENT COUNTY RECORD OFFICE

Misc. MSS 253–8 Letters of Charles I to Sheriffs of Monmouth
Misc. MSS 648 Letter-Book of Richard Herbert D.L.

HEREFORD AND WORCESTERSHIRE COUNTY RECORD OFFICE, ST HELEN'S, WORCESTER

850 Salwarpe BA 10/54/2 Bundles B, D, E and F
Last Will and Testament of Humphrey Billinges

HERTFORDSHIRE COUNTY RECORD OFFICE

D/P12/9/1 Baldock Assessments for Constables' Rates
D/P17/12/1 Bengeo Churchwardens', Overseers', Constables' and Surveyors' Formal Accounts, 1646–early 18th century
D/P26/10/1 Bushey Rate Book, 1632–49
D/P71/5/2 Little Munden Constables' Rate Assessments
D/P89/12/1 Sacombe Parish Officers' Accounts, 1613–1733
D/P110/5/1 Thundridge Constables' Accounts, 1622–1675
Off. Acc. Cheshunt Constables' Accounts, 1631–92

HUNTINGDONSHIRE COUNTY RECORD OFFICE

2661/5/1 Buckden Parish Book, 1627–1714
2735/9/1 Great Staughton Parish Constables' Book

LANCASHIRE COUNTY RECORD OFFICE

PR2597/1 Latham Constables' Order for Collection of Money, 1650
QDV II Returns in Blackburn Hundred of Papist Delinquents

LEICESTERSHIRE COUNTY RECORD OFFICE

DE625/60 Waltham on the Wolds Constables' Accounts, 1608–1706
DE670/14 Edmondthorpe Constables' Accounts
DE720/30 Branston Constables' Accounts, 1611–1676
DE730 Barker MSS
DE1605/56 Stathern Constables' Accounts
DE1965/41 Belton Constables' and Churchwardens' and Overseers' Accounts, 1601–1739
DE2461/135 Preston (Rutland) Receipts
PR/1/4/33 Will and Inventory of George Goodman
PR/1/45/8 Will of Joseph Willmore Gt, of Ashby-de-la-Zouch

LICHFIELD CATHEDRAL LIBRARY

MS Lich. 24, A True and Perfect Account of the Expenses of Col. Richard Bagot

LICHFIELD JOINT RECORD OFFICE

D30 LIII B Contributions to the Garrison in the Close

LINCOLNSHIRE ARCHIVE OFFICE

Addlethorpe and Ingoldmells Constables' Accounts, 1637–84
ANC XII/A/5 Commission for the maintenance of a regiment to Lord Willoughby
ANC XII/A/6 Commission to Lord Willoughby for a regiment of horse
ANC XII/14 Commission of Array
South Kyme Constables' Accounts, 1639–85

NATIONAL ARCHIVES, IRELAND

M981/1/14 Esmonde Papers relating to the Siege of Duncannon
M1121/1/1–2 Transcripts of the Bellew of Louth Family Papers

M2450 Treasury Orderbook of the Lord Justices and Council, 2 Vols, 1642
M4974 Caulfield Papers

NATIONAL LIBRARY, IRELAND

MS 345, Plunkett MSS, A Treatise of Account of the War and Rebellion in Ireland
MS 758 Copies of Documents Relating to Government, Finance and Administration, 1650–6
MSS 856–7 Transcripts of Documents by J.T. Gilbert
MS 11,959 Transcripts of Commonwealth Records Formerly in the Public Record Office of Ireland

NATIONAL LIBRARY OF WALES

LL/MB/11 Results and Orders of His Majesty's Commissioners of Array, 1643–44
LL/MB/17 Results and Orders of His Majesty's Commission of Array, 1643–44 (Glamorganshire)
MSS 17088A The Diary of Walter Powell of Llantilio, 1603–54
MSS 17091E Letters and Papers Addressed to Walter Powell of Llantilio
Plymouth Deeds: 1368–9, Petition of people of Flint and John Byron's reply

NORFOLK COUNTY RECORD OFFICE

PD100/258 Diss Constables' Accounts, 1635–49
PD144/70 Fersfield Constables' Accounts, 1606–1706
PD219/126 East Harling Constables' Accounts, 1617–1692
PD254/112 Carleton Rode Constables' Accounts, 1621–72
PD437/83 Hardwick Constables' Accounts, 1598–1720

NORTH YORKSHIRE COUNTY RECORD OFFICE

Readers here are expected to use the microfilm versions of documents, hence the Mic. numbers.
PR/KMZ/2/2 (Mic. 1204) Kirkby Malzeard Churchwardens' Accounts, 1576–1655
PR/MAS/3/1/1 (Mic. 995) Masham Parish Churchwardens' Accounts, 1542–1677

PR/OUL/2/1 (Mic. 1462./0341) Little Ouseburn Churchwardens' Accounts
PR/TH/3/1/1 (Mic. 1611) Thirsk Churchwardens' Accounts, 1630–1683
PR/TW/3/1 (Mic. 1161) Thornton Watless General Register, 1574–1722
Scarborough Borough Records, Mic. 1320/906, /918, /1083, /1085, /1144, /1208

NORTHAMPTONSHIRE COUNTY RECORD OFFICE

Finch-Hatton MSS 133

NOTTINGHAM COUNTY LIBRARY, ANGEL ROW, NOTTINGHAM

Various printed pamphlets, including:
My Lord Newark's Speech to the Trained Bands of Nottinghamshire at Newark, London, 1642

NOTTINGHAMSHIRE ARCHIVE OFFICE

DD39/5 Toton Rentals, 1626–45
DD4P 55/49 Billeting Charges in Devon
DD294/1 Petition of the Vale of Belvoir
PR1531 Coddington Constables' Accounts, 1641–1769
PR1710 Upton Constables' Accounts, 1640–1666
PR2130 Edwinstowe Constables' Accounts
PR5767 Thorpe Constables' Accounts
PRMW13/2 Accounts of William Dand
QSM1/11

OXFORDSHIRE COUNTY RECORD OFFICE

MS DD Par Wheatley b5, Overseers' Accounts, 1638–61
MS DD Par Spelsbury d5, Churchwardens' and Overseers' of the Poor Accounts, 1525–1707

PUBLIC RECORD OFFICE (CHANCERY LANE)

SP28/152 Exchequer Papers, Cambridge to Cumberland
SP28/153 Exchequer Papers, Derbyshire to Essex
SP28/161 Exchequer Papers, Lancashire to Lincolnshire
SP28/174 Exchequer Papers, Northumberland to Shropshire

SP28/187 Exchequer Papers, Westmoreland to Worcestershire
SP28/189 Exchequer Papers, Yorkshire and Wales
SP28/190 Exchequer Papers, Associated Counties Misc.
SP28/194 Contributions for Distressed Protestants from Ireland, 1642
SP28/251 County Committee Papers
SP63/263, 53 Excise and Other Levies (Ireland)
SP64/264, 31 Account Book of the Court of Revenue of the Catholic
  Confederacy, 1644–47

STAR CHAMBER PAPERS: JAMES VI AND I

STAC 8/219/23

REPRESENTATIVE CHURCH BODY LIBRARY, DUBLIN

Vestry Book, St John's Parish, Dublin (Transcripts)

WILLIAM SALT LIBRARY, STAFFORD

Salt MSS 48/49 Minute Book of the County Committee at Stafford
Salt MSS 479–564 Civil War Letters

SCOTTISH RECORD OFFICE

B9/12/8 Burntisland Council Minutes

Marr and Kellie Muniments

GD124/10/388 Levies on the Shires
GD124/17/9 Receipts and Other Financial Documents
GD124/17/12 Rents and Debts, 1650
GD124/17/15 Losses of the Earl of Marr
GD124/17/208 Receipt of Lord Erskine, 1650

Henderson of Fordell Muniments

GD172/1500 Receipt of John Fletcher
GD172/1509 Receipt of John Dickenson

Hamilton Muniments

GD406/1/1236 and 1237, 2156 Letters

Parliamentary Papers

PA7/6 Supplementary Papers regarding Loan and Taxt
PA8/2 Charges of Loan and Taxt
PA11/1 Committee of Estates
PA11/3 Committee of Estates
PA11/4 Committee of Estates, Register, March 1645–March 1646
PA11/5 Parliamentary Papers
PA16/3/2/5 The Account of Sir Alexander Hepburne, August 1643–March 1645

STAFFORDSHIRE RECORD OFFICE

D3451/2/2 Pattingham Parish Book
D3539/2/1 Biddulph Parish Book
D3712/4/1 Mavesyn Ridware Parish Book

STAUNTON HALL

Family Papers 34/16 The Account Book of Lt. Gervase Hewet

SUFFOLK RECORD OFFICE (BURY ST EDMUNDS)

Warrants to the Constables of Chelworth

WEST YORKSHIRE ARCHIVE SERVICE:
LEEDS DISTRICT ARCHIVES

Calverley 82 Memorandum and Account Book of Overseers, 1633–1724
TN/PO/2B/I–IV Civil War Assessments and Disbursements for the Armies for Whorlton
Vyner MSS 5755, 5757, 5813 Various Warrants and Assessments for Fountains Abbey Estate
Vyner MSS 5982 C/30/A/6 Account book of household expenses of George Norton of Worton

WILTSHIRE COUNTY RECORD OFFICE

GD/1/40 Notes of Goods and Chattels taken by force from Salisbury Citizens

G23/1/40 Notes of goods and chattels taken by force from Salisbury citizens' households by Royalist soldiers
413/502 Rate for Maintenance of Fairfax's Army

CITY OF YORK ARCHIVES

B36 City of York House Book

PRINTED PRIMARY SOURCES

Ashburnham, J., *A Narrative by John Ashburnham of His Attendance on King Charles the First*, 2 vols (Payne and Foss, London, 1830).
Ashcroft, M.Y., ed., *Scarborough Records, 1600–1640* (North Yorkshire Record Office, Northallerton, 1991).
—— ed., *Scarborough Records, 1641–1660* (North Yorkshire Record Office, Northallerton, 1991).
Baker, W.T.B., ed., *Records of the Borough of Nottingham, 1625–1702* (Nottingham Corporation, Nottingham, 1900).
Baxter, R. (ed. N.H. Keeble), *The Autobiography of Richard Baxter* (Dent, London, 1974, 1985).
Bennett, M., ed., *A Nottinghamshire Village in War and Peace: The Accounts of the Constables of Upton, 1640–1666* (Thoroton Society, Nottingham, 1995).
Birch, J. (ed. J. and T.W. Webb), *Military Memoirs of Colonel John Birch* (Camden Society, London, 1873).
Bond, S.M., ed., *The Chamber Order Book of Worcester, 1602–1650* (Worcestershire Historical Society, Worcester, 1974).
Bonsey, C. and Jenkins, J.G., eds, *Ship Money Papers and Richard Greville's Note-book* (Buckinghamshire Record Society, Buckingham, 1965).
Calamy, E., *The Souldiers Pocket Bible* (London, 1643).
Calendar of State Papers: Domestic, Charles I (Kraus Reprint, Liechtenstein, 1967).
Calendar of State Papers Relating to Ireland in the Reign of Charles I, 1633–47 (HMSO, London, 1901).
Calendar of State Papers Relating to Ireland in the Reign of Charles I, 1647–60 (HMSO, London, 1903).
Calendar of Wynn of Gwydir Papers, 1515–1690 (National Library of Wales, Aberystwyth, 1926).
A Catalogue of the several Sects and opinions in England and Other Nations: With a brief rehearsall of their false and dangerous tenents (R.A., London, 1647).
Caulfield, R., ed., *The Council Book of the Corporation of Youghal* (Guildford, 1878).
Cavendish, Margaret, Duchess of Newcastle (ed. C.H. Firth), *The Life of William Cavendish, Duke of Newcastle, and Margaret His Wife* (Routledge, London, nd).

——, *Epistle to the Two Most Famous Universities. Philosophical and Physical Opinions* (1663).

Charles, B.G., ed., *Calendar of the Records of the Borough of Haverfordwest, 1539–1660* (University of Wales Press, Cardiff, 1967).

Clanricarde, Earl of (ed. J. Lowe), *Letter-Book of the Earl of Clanricarde, 1643–47* (Irish Manuscripts Commission, Dublin, 1983).

Clarendon, Earl of (ed. W. Dunn Mackay), *The History of the Rebellion and Civil Wars in England* (Clarendon Press, Oxford, 1888, 1992).

Clarkson, Laurence, *The Lost Sheep Found: Or The prodigal returned to his Father's house, after a journey through many Religious Countrys* (reprint published by the Rota, Exeter University, 1974; first published 1660).

Clifford, Lady Anne (ed. D.J.H. Clifford), *The Diaries of Lady Anne Clifford* (Alan Sutton, Stroud, 1990).

Cope, E.S. and Coates, W.H., eds, *Proceedings of the Short Parliament of 1640* (Royal Historical Society, London, 1977).

Cranford, J. (printer), *The Souldiers Catechisme Composed for the Parliaments Army, 1644* (Cresset Press, London, nd).

Cromwell, O. (ed. I. Roots), *Speeches of Oliver Cromwell* (Dent, London, 1989).

—— (ed. T. Carlyle), *Oliver Cromwell's Letters and Speeches* (3rd edition, Ward Lock and Co., London, nd).

Dickenson, W.C. and Donaldson, G., eds, *A Source Book of Scottish History, 1567–1707*, Vol. 3 (Nelson, Edinburgh, 1954, 1961).

Erickson, J., ed., *The Journal of the House of Commons, 1547–1900* (Readex Microprint, New York, 1964).

Everitt-Green, M., ed., *Calendar of the Committee for Compounding* (Kraus Reprint, Liechtenstein, 1967).

——, ed., *Calendar of the Committee for the Advance of Money* (Kraus Reprint, Liechtenstein, 1967).

Firth, C.H., ed., 'Journal of Prince Rupert's Marches' (*English Historical Review*, Vol. XIII, 1899).

Firth, C.H. and Rait, R.S., eds, *Acts and Ordinances of the Interregnum* (HMSO, London, 1911).

Fleming, D.H., ed., 'Scotland's Supplication and Complaint against the Book of Common Prayer (Otherwise Laud's Liturgy), the Book of Cannons and the Prelates, 18 October 1637', (*Proceedings of the Society of Antiquaries of Scotland*, Vol. LX, 1923).

Fox, L., ed., *Coventry Constables' Presentments* (Oxford University Press, for the Dugdale Society, Oxford, 1986).

Gardiner, S.R., ed., *The Constitutional Documents of the Puritan Revolution* (Clarendon Press, Oxford, 1979; first published 1889).

Gibson, J.S.W. and Brinkworth, E.R.C., eds, *Banbury Corporation Records, Tudor and Stuart* (Banbury Historical Society, Banbury, 1977).

Gilbert, J.T., ed., *A Contemporary History of Affairs in Ireland from 1641 to 1652*, 3 vols (Irish Archaeological and Celtic Society, Dublin, 1879–80).

Graham, E., Hinds, H., Hobby, E. and Wilcox, H., eds, *Her Own Life: Autobiographical Writings by Seventeenth-century English Women* (Routledge, London, 1989).

Historical Association, *Short Guides to Records, No. 26: Constables' Accounts* (Historical Association, London, 1993).

Historical Manuscripts Commission, *Thirteenth Report* (HMSO, London, 1891).

——, *Fourteenth Report* (HMSO, London, 1895).

——, *Report on Manuscripts in Various Collections*, Vol. 7 (HMSO, London, 1914).

——, *Report on the Manuscripts of the Marquis of Ormond* (HMSO, London, 1899).

——, *Calendar of Manuscripts of the Marquis of Ormonde*, 2 vols, New Series (HMSO, London, 1902–3).

——, *Report on the Papers of Reginald Rawdon Hastings* (HMSO, London, 1930).

——, *Report on the Records of the Borough of Exeter* (HMSO, London, 1916).

Hobson, M.G. and Salter, H.E., eds, *Oxford Council Acts, 1626–1665* (Oxford University Press, Oxford, 1933).

Hogan, J., ed., *Letters and Papers Relating to the Irish Rebellion* (Stationery Office, Dublin, 1930).

Howells, B.E., ed., *A Calendar of Letters Relating to North Wales, 1533–c.1700* (University of Wales Press, Cardiff, 1967).

Hutchinson, L., *Memoirs of the Life of Colonel John Hutchinson* (Longman, Orme, Rees and Brown, London, 1806).

Jansson, M., ed., *Two Diaries of the Long Parliament* (Alan Sutton, Stroud, 1984).

Johnson, D.A. and Vaisey, D.G., eds, *Staffordshire and the Great Rebellion* (Staffordshire County Council, Stafford, 1964).

Johnston of Wariston, A. (ed. G.H. Paul, D.H. Fleming and J.D. Ogilvie), *Diary of Sir Archibald Johnston of Wariston*, 3 vols (Scottish History Society, Edinburgh, 1911, 1919, 1940).

Lockyer, R., *The Trial of Charles I* (Folio Society, London, 1959).

Kenyon, J.P., ed., *The Stuart Constitution* (Cambridge University Press, Cambridge, 1966; second edition, 1986).

Luke, Sir Samuel (ed. I.G. Phillips), *Journal of Sir Samuel Luke*, 3 vols (Oxfordshire Record Society, Oxford, 1950–3).

MacTavish, D.C., ed., *Minutes of the Synod of Argyll, 1639–1651* (Edinburgh University Press, Edinburgh, 1943).

Marwick, J.D., ed., *Extracts of the Records of the Burgh of Glasgow, 1630–1662* (Scottish Burgh Record Society, Glasgow, 1881).

Morley, H., ed., *Character Writings of the Seventeenth Century* (Routledge, London, 1891).

Nicholson, J., ed., *Minute Book kept by the War Committee of the Covenanters in the Stewartry of Kircudbright 1640–1* (Nicholson, Kirkcudbright, 1855).

Otten, C., ed., *English Women's Voices, 1500–1700* (Florida University International Press, Miami, 1992).

Pennington, D. and Roots, I., eds, *The Committee at Stafford, 1643–5* (Staffordshire Historical Collections, Manchester, 1957).

Prall, S., ed., *The Puritan Revolution: A Documentary History* (Routledge and Kegan Paul, London, 1968).

Price, F.D., ed., *The Wigginton Constables' Book* (Phillimore, London, 1971).

Roy, I., ed., *The Royalist Ordinance Papers* (Oxfordshire Record Society, Oxford, 1964).

Royal Commission on Historical Monuments, *Report on York* (HMSO, London, 1972).

Rushworth, J., *Historical Collections*, 7 vols (London, 1657–1701).

Stevenson, D., *The Government of Scotland under the Covenanters, 1637–1651* (Scottish History Society, Edinburgh, 1982).

Stocks, H.E., ed., *Records of the Borough of Leicester, 1603–1688* (Cambridge University Press, Cambridge, 1923).

Stuart, J., ed., *Extracts from the Council Register of the Burgh of Aberdeen, 1643–1747*, 2 vols (Scottish Burgh Record Society, Edinburgh, 1871–2).

—— , ed., *Minutes of the Committee for the Loan Monies and Taxations of the Shire of Aberdeen*, Vol. III (Spalding Club Miscellany, Edinburgh, 1846).

Symonds, R. (ed. C.E. Long), *Diary of the Marches of the Royal Army* (Camden Society, London, 1859).

Taylor, L.B., ed., *Aberdeen Council Letters*, Vol. 2 (Oxford University Press, Oxford, 1950).

Terry, C.S., ed., *Papers Relating to the Army of the Solemn League and Covenant, 1643–7*, 2 vols (Edinburgh University Press, Edinburgh, 1917).

Verney, F.P., ed., *Memoirs of the Verney Family during the Civil War* (Tabard Press, London, 1970).

Whitelock, B., *Memorials of English Affairs from the Beginning of the Reign of Charles I to the Restoration of Charles II* (Oxford University Press, Oxford, 1853).

Wilson, J., ed., *Buckinghamshire Contributions for Ireland 1642 and Richard Greville's Military Accounts, 1642–1645* (Buckinghamshire Record Society, Buckingham, 1983).

Wood, H., ed., *A Guide to the Records Deposited in the Public Record Office of Ireland* (HMSO, Dublin, 1919).

Wood, M., ed., *Extracts from the Records of the Burgh of Edinburgh 1626–1641*, 2 vols (Oliver and Boyd, Edinburgh, 1936, 1938).

SECONDARY SOURCES

BOOKS

Adair, J., *By the Sword Divided* (Century Press, London, 1983).

—— , *Cheriton, 1644: The Campaign and the Battle* (Roundwood Press, Kineton, 1973).

Amussen, S., *An Ordered Society* (Blackwell, Oxford, 1988).

Anderson, M.S., *War and Society in Europe of the Old Regime, 1618–1789* (Leicester University Press, Leicester, 1988).

Ashley, M., *The Battle of Naseby and the Fall of King Charles I* (Alan Sutton, Stroud, 1992).

Ashton, R., *The English Civil War: Conservatism and Revolution, 1603–49* (Weidenfeld and Nicolson, London, 1978).

——, *Counter-Revolution: The Second Civil War and its Origins* (Yale University Press, New Haven, 1994).

Atkin, M. and Laughlin, W., *Gloucester and the Civil War* (Alan Sutton, Stroud, 1992).

Aylmer, G.E., *Rebellion or Revolution: England from Civil War to Restoration* (Oxford University Press, Oxford, 1991).

——, *The Interregnum: The Quest for a Settlement* (Macmillan, London, 1972).

——, ed., *The Levellers in the English Revolution* (Thames and Hudson, London, 1975).

Barclay, C. and Besly, E., *A Little Barrel of Ducatoons: The Civil War Coinage of Yorkshire* (Yorkshire Museum, York, 1994).

Baskerville, S., *Not Peace But a Sword: The Political Theology of the English Revolution* (Routledge, London, 1993).

Baumber, M., *General at Sea* (John Murray, London, 1989).

Beier, A., *Masterless Men* (Methuen, London, 1985).

Bennett, M., *Lord Loughborough, Ashby de la Zouch and the English Civil War* (Ashby Museum, Ashby-de-la-Zouch, 1984).

——, *The English Civil War* (Longman, London, 1995).

——, *Travellers' Guide to the Battlefields of the English Civil War* (Webb and Bower, Exeter, 1990).

Berresford-Ellis, P., *Hell or Connaught! The Cromwellian Colonisation of Ireland, 1652–1660* (Hamish Hamilton, London, 1975; Blackstaff Press, Belfast, 1991).

Besly, E., *Coins and Medals of the English Civil War* (Seaby, London, 1990).

——, *English Civil War Coin Hoards* (British Museum, London, 1987).

Birkenhead, Earl of, *Strafford* (Hutchinson, London, 1938).

Blackmore, D., *Arms and Armour of the English Civil War* (Royal Armouries, London, 1990).

Blackwood, B.G., *The Lancashire Gentry and the Great Rebellion, 1640–1660* (Chetham Society, Manchester, 1978).

Bone, Q., *Henrietta Maria, Queen of the Cavaliers* (University of Illinois Press, Urbana, Ill., 1972).

Boon, G.C., *Cardiganshire Silver and the Aberystwyth Mint in Peace and War* (National Museum of Wales, Cardiff, 1981).

Brailsford, H.N., *The Levellers and the English Revolution* (Spokesman University Paperback, Nottingham, 1983; first published 1961).

Brewer, J. and Styles, J., eds, *An Ungovernable People: The English and their*

Law in the Seventeenth and Eighteenth Centuries (Hutchinson, London, 1983).

Brighton, J.T., *Royalists and Roundheads in Derbyshire* (Bakewell and District Historical Society, Bakewell, 1981).

Brown, K.M., *Kingdom or Province: Scotland and the Regal Union* (Macmillan, London, 1992).

Brunton, D. and Pennington, D.H., *Members of the Long Parliament* (Harvard University Press, Cambridge, Mass., 1954).

Canny, N., *From Reformation to Restoration: Ireland, 1534–1660* (Helicon, Dublin, 1987).

Capp, B., *Cromwell's Navy* (Clarendon Press, Oxford, 1992).

Carlton, C., *Going to the Wars: The Experience of the British Civil Wars, 1638–1651* (Routledge, London, 1992).

Casaway, J.I., *Owen Roe O'Neill and the Struggle for Catholic Ireland* (University of Pennsylvania Press, Philadelphia, 1984).

Clarke, A. (ed. A.L. Erickson), *Women's Work in the Seventeenth Century* (Routledge, London, 1992).

Cliffe, J.T., *The Puritan Gentry* (Routledge and Kegan Paul, London, 1984).

——, *The Yorkshire Gentry from the Reformation to the English Civil War* (Athlone Press, London, 1969).

Coate, M., *Cornwall in the Great Civil War* (Bradford Barton, Truro, 1963; reprint of 1933 edition).

Colley, L., *Britons Forging the Nation 1707–1837* (Pimlico, New Haven, 1992).

Collinson, P., *The Birthpangs of Protestant England* (Macmillan, London, 1988).

Coleby, A.M., *Central Government and the Localities: Hampshire, 1649–1689* (Cambridge University Press, Cambridge, 1987).

Cope, E., *Politics without Parliaments* (Allen and Unwin, London, 1987).

Corish, P., *The Catholic Community in the Seventeenth and Eighteenth Centuries* (Helicon, Dublin, 1981).

Cox, J.C., *Churchwardens' Accounts: From the Fourteenth Century to the Close of the Seventeenth Century* (Methuen, London, 1913).

Crawford, P., *Denzil, First Lord Holles* (Royal Historical Society, London, 1979).

Cressy, D., *Bonfires and Bells* (Weidenfeld and Nicolson, London, 1989).

Cronne, H.A., Moody, T.W. and Quinn, D.B., eds, *Essays in British and Irish History in Honour of James Eadie Todd* (Frederick Muller, London, 1949).

Cust, R. and Hughes, A., eds, *Conflict in Early Stuart England* (Longman, London, 1989).

Davis, J.C., *Fear, Myth and History: The Ranters and the Historians* (Cambridge University Press, Cambridge, 1986).

Delbanco, A., *The Puritan Ordeal* (Harvard University Press, Cambridge, Mass., 1989).

Denton, B., *Naseby Fight* (Partizan Press, Leigh-on-Sea, 1988).

Dogheson, R.A., *Land and Society in Early Scotland* (Oxford University Press, Oxford, 1981).

Donaldson, G., *Scotland: James V–James VII* (Mercat Press, Edinburgh, 1990; originally published 1965).

Donald, P., *An Uncouncelled King: Charles I and the Scottish Troubles, 1637–41* (Cambridge University Press, Cambridge, 1990).

Durston, C., *The Family in the English Revolution* (Blackwell, Oxford, 1989).

Eales, J., *Puritans and Roundheads: The Harleys of Brampton Bryan and the Outbreak of the English Civil War* (Cambridge University Press, Cambridge, 1990).

Edwards, R.D., *An Atlas of Irish History* (Routledge, London, 1973; second edition 1991).

Eley, G. and Hunt, W., eds, *Reviving the English Revolution: Reflections and Elaborations on the Work of Christopher Hill* (Verso, London, 1988).

Ellis, S.G., *Tudor Ireland: Crown, Community and the Conflict of Cultures 1470–1603* (Longman, London, 1994).

Erickson, A.L., *Women and Property in Early Modern England* (Routledge, London, 1993).

Everritt, A., *The Community of Kent and the Great Rebellion, 1640–1660* (Leicester University Press, Leicester, 1973).

—— , *The Local Community and the Great Rebellion* (Historical Association, London, 1969).

Firth, C.H., *Cromwell's Army* (Greenhill, London, 1992; first published 1902).

Fissel, M.C., *The Bishops' Wars: Charles I's Campaigns against Scotland, 1638–1640* (Cambridge University Press, Cambridge, 1994).

Fletcher, A., *Reform in the Provinces* (Yale University Press, New Haven, 1985).

—— , *The Outbreak of the English Civil War* (Arnold, London, 1985).

—— and Stevenson, J., eds, *Order and Disorder in Early Modern England* (Cambridge University Press, Cambridge, 1985).

Fraser, A., *The Weaker Vessell* (Methuen, London, 1984).

Friedman, J., *Miracles and the Pulp Press during the English Revolution* (University College London Press, London, 1993).

Gardiner, S.R., *History of the Great Civil War*, 4 vols (Windrush Press, Adlestrop, 1987 and 1991; originally published 1893).

—— , *History of the Commonwealth and Protectorate, 1649–1656* (Windrush Press, Adlestrop, 1988; originally published 1903).

Garner, A.A., *Boston and the Great Civil War* (Richard Key, Boston, 1972).

Gentles, I., *The New Model Army in England, Ireland and Scotland, 1645–1653* (Blackwell, Oxford, 1992).

Gillespie, R., *The Transformation of the Irish Economy, 1550–1700* (Economic and Social History Society of Ireland, Dublin, 1991).

Gladwin, I., *The Sheriff* (Gollancz, London, 1974).

Goodwin, G.N., *The Civil War in Hampshire, 1642–45* (London and Southampton, 1904).

Gregg, P., *Freeborn John: A Biography of John Lilburne* (Harrap, London, 1961; republished 1986).

Guttery, D.R., *The Great Civil War in Midland Parishes: The People Pay* (Cornish Bros, Birmingham, 1950).

Hardacre, P., *The Royalists during the Puritan Revolution* (Martinus Nijhoff, The Hague, 1956).

Harrington, P., *Archaeology of the English Civil War* (Shire, Princes Risborough, 1992).

Hexter, J.H., *The Reign of King Pym* (Harvard University Press, Cambridge, Mass., 1941).

Hibbard, C., *Charles I and the Popish Plot* (University of North Carolina, Chapel Hill, 1983).

Hill, C., *God's Englishman: Oliver Cromwell and the English Revolution* (Penguin, Harmondsworth, 1979; originally published 1970).

——, *Puritanism and Revolution* (Peregrine, Harmondsworth, 1986; originally published 1958).

——, *The English Bible and the Seventeenth Century Revolution* (Allen Lane, London, 1993).

——, *The English Revolution* (Lawrence and Wishart, London, 1979; originally published 1940).

——, *The World Turned Upside Down* (Penguin, Harmondsworth, 1975; originally published 1972).

Hobby, E., *Virtue of Necessity: English Women's Writing, 1649–88* (Virago, London, 1988).

Holbrooke, R., *The English Family* (Longman, London, 1984).

Holmes, C., *Seventeenth Century Lincolnshire* (History of Lincoln Committee, Lincoln, 1980).

——, *The Eastern Association in the English Civil War* (Cambridge University Press, Cambridge, 1974).

Houston, R.A. and Whyte, I.D., eds, *Scottish Society, 1500–1800* (Cambridge University Press, Cambridge, 1989).

Hughes, A., *Politics, Society and Civil War in Warwickshire, 1620–1660* (Cambridge University Press, Cambridge, 1987).

——, *The Causes of the English Civil War* (Macmillan, London, 1991).

Hutton, R.E., *The British Republic* (Macmillan, London, 1990).

——, *The Rise and Fall of Merry England* (Oxford University Press, Oxford, 1994).

——, *The Royalist War Effort* (Longman, London, 1982).

Ingram, M.E., *The Manor of Bridlington* (The Lords Feoffees, Bridlington, 1977).

Jenkins, G.H., *Protestant Dissenters in Wales* (University of Wales Press, Cardiff, 1992).

—, *The Foundations of Modern Wales* (Oxford University Press, Oxford, 1987, 1993).

Jones, C., Newitt, M. and Roberts, S., *Politics and People in Revolutionary England: Essays in Honour of Ivan Roots* (Blackwell, Oxford, 1986).

Kearney, H.F., *Strafford in Ireland 1633–1641: A Study in Absolutism* (Cambridge University Press, Cambridge, 1989; originally published 1959).

—, *The British Isles: A History of Four Nations* (Cambridge University Press, Cambridge, 1993).

Kent, J., *The English Village Constable, 1580–1642: A Social and Administrative Study* (Oxford University Press, Oxford, 1986).

Kenyon, J.P., *The Civil Wars of England* (Weidenfeld and Nicolson, London, 1989).

—, *Stuart England* (Penguin, Harmondsworth, 1985).

Kenyon, T., *Utopian Communism and Political Thought in Early Modern England* (Pinter, London, 1989).

Ketton-Cremer, R.W., *Norfolk in the Civil War* (Archon, Hamden, Conn., 1970).

Kishlansky, M., *Parliamentary Selection* (Cambridge University Press, Cambridge, 1987).

—, *The Rise of the New Model Army* (Cambridge University Press, Cambridge, 1979).

Lee, M., *The Road to Revolution: Scotland under Charles I, 1625–1637* (University of Illinois Press, Chicago, 1985).

Lindley, K., *Fenland Riots and the English Revolution* (Heinemann, London, 1982).

Liu, T., *Puritan London: A Study of Religion and Society in the City Parishes* (University of Delaware Press, Newark, 1986).

Lloyd, H.A., *Gentry of South West Wales, 1540–1640* (University of Wales Press, Cardiff, 1968).

Lockyer, R., *The Early Stuarts* (Longman, London, 1989).

Mac Cuarta, B., ed., *Ulster 1641: Aspects of the Rising* (Institute of Irish Studies, Belfast, 1993).

MacCurtain, M. and O'Dowd, M., eds, *Women in Early Modern Ireland* (Edinburgh University Press, Edinburgh, 1991).

McGregor, J.F. and Reay, B., eds, *Radical Religion in the English Revolution* (Oxford University Press, Oxford, 1986).

MacInnes, A.I., *Charles I and the Making of the Covenanting Movement, 1625–1641* (John Donald, Edinburgh, 1991).

McKerral, A., *Kintyre in the Seventeenth Century* (Oliver and Boyd, Edinburgh, 1948).

Macpherson, C.B., *The Political Theory of Possessive Individualism* (Clarendon Press, Oxford, 1962).

Malcolm, J.L., *Caesar's Due: Loyalty and King Charles, 1642–1646* (Royal Historical Society, London, 1983).

Manning, B., ed., *Politics, Religion and The English Civil War* (Edward Arnold, London, 1973).

——, *1649: The Crisis of the English Revolution* (Bookmarks, London, 1992).

——, *The English People and the English Revolution, 1640–1649* (Penguin, Harmondsworth, 1978).

Manning, R.B., *Village Protest: Social Protest and Popular Disturbances in England, 1509–1640* (Oxford University Press, Oxford, 1988).

Mitchison, R., *Lordship to Patronage: Scotland, 1603–1745* (Edinburgh University Press, 1983; second edition 1990).

Moody, T.W., Martin, F.X. and Byrne, F.J., eds, *A New History of Ireland*, Vol. 3 (Oxford University Press, Oxford, 1976, 1991).

Morrill, J.S., ed., *Oliver Cromwell and the English Revolution* (Longman, London, 1990).

——, ed., *The Impact of the English Civil War* (Collins and Brown, London, 1991).

——, ed., *Reactions to the English Civil War* (Macmillan, London, 1982).

——, *The Nature of the English Revolution* (Longman, London, 1993).

——, *The Revolt of the Provinces: Conservatives and Radicals in the English Civil War* (Longman, London, 1976, 1980).

——, *Revolution and Restoration: England in the 1650s* (Collins and Brown, London, 1992).

Morton, A.L., *The World of the Ranters: Religious Radicalism in the English Revolution* (Lawrence and Wishart, London, 1970).

Newman, P., *Marston Moor: The Sources and the Battle* (Borthwick Institute, York, 1978).

Newman, P.R., *The Old Service: Royalist Regimental Colonels and the Civil War, 1642–46* (Manchester University Press, Manchester, 1993).

——, *The Battle of Marston Moor* (Anthony Bird, Chichester, 1981).

——, *Royalist Officers in England and Wales, 1642–60* (Garland Press, New York, 1981).

Nichols, J., *The History and Antiquities of the County of Leicestershire* (John Nichols, London, 1804).

O'Dowd, M., *Power, Politics and Land: Early Modern Sligo, 1568–1688* (Institute of Irish Studies, Belfast, 1991).

Ohlmeyer, J., *Civil War and Restoration in the Three Stuart Kingdoms. The Career of Randal MacDonnell, Marquis of Antrim, 1609–1683* (Cambridge University Press, Cambridge, 1993).

——, ed., *Ireland From Independence to Occupation, 1641–1660* (Cambridge University Press, Cambridge, 1995).

Payne, J., *The Keeper of the Magazine Identifyd* (Severinus Press, Hereford, 1995).

Perceval-Maxwell, M., *The Outbreak of the Irish Rebellion of 1641* (Gill and Macmillan, Dublin, 1994).

Porter, S., *Destruction in the English Civil Wars* (Alan Sutton, Stroud, 1994).

Quintrell, B., *Charles I* (Longman, London, 1993).

Reeve, J., *Charles I and the Road to Personal Rule* (Cambridge University Press, Cambridge, 1989).

Rees, W., *An Historical Atlas of Wales From Early to Modern Times* (Faber and Faber, London, 1951).

Reid, S., *The Campaigns of Montrose* (Mercat Press, Edinburgh, 1990).

Richardson, R.C., *The Debate on the English Revolution Revisited* (Routledge, London, 1988).

—— , ed., *Town and Countryside in the English Revolution* (Manchester University Press, Manchester, 1992).

Roberts, S.K., *Recovery and Restoration in an English County: Devon Local Administration* (University of Exeter, Exeter, 1985).

Russell, C., *The Causes of the English Civil War* (Oxford University Press, Oxford, 1990).

—— , *The Fall of the British Monarchies, 1637–42* (Oxford University Press, Oxford, 1991).

—— , ed., *The Origins of the English Civil War* (Methuen, London, 1973, 1984).

Samuel, R. and Thompson, P., eds, *The Myths We Live By* (Routledge, London, 1990).

Sanderson, J., *But the People's Creatures: The Philosophical Basis of the English Civil War* (Manchester University Press, Manchester, 1989).

Seaver, P., *Wallington's World: A Puritan Artisan in Seventeenth Century London* (Stanford University Press, Stanford, 1985).

Seymour, W., *Battles in Britain* (Sidgwick and Jackson, London, 1975).

Sharp, B., *In Contempt of All Authority* (University of California Press, Berkeley, 1980).

Sharpe, K., *The Personal Rule of Charles I* (Yale University Press, New Haven, 1992).

Shaw, H., *The Levellers* (Longman, London, 1968).

Sherwood, R.E., *The Civil War in the Midlands* (Alan Sutton, Stroud, 1992; first published as *Civil Strife in the Midlands*, Phillimore, Chichester, 1974).

Slater, M., *Family Life in the Seventeenth Century* (Routledge and Kegan Paul, London, 1984).

Smout, T.C., *The History of the Scottish People* (Fontana, London, 1973).

Sommerville, J.P., *Politics and Ideology in England, 1603–1640* (Longman, London, 1986).

Spence, R.T., *Skipton Castle in the Great Civil War* (Skipton Castle, Skipton, 1991).

Spufford, M., *Contrasting Communities* (Cambridge University Press, Cambridge, 1974).

Stephens, N. and Glasscock, R.E., eds, *Irish Geographical Studies* (Queens University, Belfast, 1970).

Stevenson, D., *Highland Warrior: Alasdair MacColla and the Civil Wars* (Saltire Society, Edinburgh, 1994; originally published 1980).

——, *The Covenanters: The National Covenant and Scotland* (Saltire Society, Edinburgh, 1988).

——, *Revolution and Counter-Revolution in Scotland, 1644–1651* (Royal Historical Society, London, 1977).

——, *The Scottish Revolution, 1637–1644* (David and Charles, Newton Abbot, 1973).

Stone, B., *Derbyshire in the Civil War* (Scarthin Books, Cromford, 1992).

Stone, L., *The Causes of the English Revolution* (Routledge and Kegan Paul, London, 1977).

——, *The Crisis of the Aristocracy* (Clarendon Press, Oxford, 1965).

Tennant, P., *Edgehill and Beyond: The People's War in the South Midlands, 1641–45* (Alan Sutton, Stroud, 1992).

Thatcher-Ulrich, L., *Good Wives* (Alfred A. Knopf, New York, 1982).

Thirsk, J., ed., *The Agricultural History of England* (Cambridge University Press, Cambridge, 1967).

Thomas-Sandford, C., *Sussex in the Great Civil War and Interregnum* (Chiswick Press, London, 1910).

Thompson, R., *Women in Stuart England and America* (Routledge, London, 1974).

Toynebee, M., *Strangers in Oxford: A Sidelight on the Civil War* (Phillimore, Chichester, 1973).

Trease, G., *Portrait of a Cavalier: William Cavendish, First Duke of Newcastle* (Macmillan, London, 1979).

Tucker, N., *North Wales in the Civil War* (Bridge Books, Wrexham, 1992).

Underdown, D., *Fire From Heaven: Life in an English Town in the Seventeenth Century* (Harper Collins, London, 1992).

——, *Pride's Purge* (Clarendon Press, Oxford, 1971).

——, *Revel, Riot and Rebellion: Popular Politics and Culture in England, 1603–60* (Clarendon Press, Oxford, 1985).

——, *Somerset in the Civil War and Interregnum* (David and Charles, Newton Abbot, 1973).

Victoria County Histories, *History of the County of Bedford*, Vols 1 and 2 (Institute of Historical Research, London, 1904 and 1908).

——, *Hertfordshire*, Vols 1–4 (Institute of Historical Research, London, 1971; originally published 1902, 1908, 1912, 1914).

——, *A History of Huntingdonshire*, Vol. 2 (Institute of Historical Research, London, 1974; originally published 1932).

——, *A History of Cambridgeshire and the Isle of Ely*, Vols 6 and 8 (Institute of Historical Research, London, 1978, 1982).

——, *A History of Worcestershire*, Vol. 4 (Institute of Historical Research, London, 1971; originally published 1924).

——, *A History of Yorkshire*, Vol. 3 (Institute of Historical Research, London, 1974; originally published 1913).

——, *A History of Yorkshire: East Riding*, Vols 2, 3 and 4 (Institute of Historical Research, London, 1974, 1976, 1979).

——, *A History of Yorkshire: North Riding*, Vol. 2 (Institute of Historical Research, London, 1968; originally published 1923).

Warner, T., *Newark: Civil War and Siegeworks* (Nottinghamshire County Council, Nottingham, 1992).

Wedgwood, C.V., *Thomas Wentworth, First Earl of Strafford, 1593–1641: A Revaluation* (Jonathan Cape, London, 1961).

——, *The King's Peace, 1637–1641* (Penguin, Harmondsworth, 1983; originally published 1955).

——, *The King's War* (Penguin, Harmondsworth, 1983; originally published 1958).

——, *The Trial of Charles I* (Penguin, Harmondsworth, 1983; originally published 1964).

Wenham, P., *The Great and Close Siege of York, 1644* (Roundway Press, Kineton, 1970; republished as *The Siege of York*, Jonson, York, 1994).

Whyte, I., *Agriculture and Society in Seventeenth Century Scotland* (John Donald, Edinburgh, 1979).

—— and Houston, R.A., eds, *Agriculture and Society* (John Donald, Edinburgh, 1979).

Williams, G., *Renewal and Reformation: Wales, c. 1415–1642* (Oxford University Press, Oxford, 1993).

Withers, C.J., *Gaelic Scotland: The Transformation of A Cultural Region* Routledge, London, 1988).

Wood, A.C., *Nottinghamshire in Civil War* (S.R. Reprint, Wakefield, 1971; originally published 1937).

Woodhouse, A.H., ed., *Puritanism and Liberty* (Dent and Sons, London, 1966).

Woods, T.P., *Prelude to Civil War* (Russell Publishing, Salisbury, 1980).

Woolrych, A., *Battles of the English Civil War* (Pan, London, 1961).

Wormald, J., ed., *Scotland Revisited* (Collins and Brown, London, 1991).

——, *Court, Kirk and Community* (Edward Arnold, London, 1981).

Wrightson, K., *English Society* (Hutchinson, London, 1984).

Wroughton, J., *A Community at War: The Civil War in Bath and North Somerset* (Lansdown Press, Bath, 1992).

Young, P., *Edgehill, 1642: The Campaign and the Battle* (Roundway Press, Kineton, 1967).

——, *Marston Moor, 1644: The Campaign and the Battle* (Roundway Press, Kineton, 1970).

——, *Naseby 1645: The Campaign and the Battle* (Century, London, 1985).

——, ed., *Newark upon Trent: The Civil War Siegeworks* (HMSO, London, 1964).

JOURNAL ARTICLES

Adamson, J.S.A., 'The baronial context of the English civil war', *Transactions of the Royal Historical Society*, 1990.

Barnard, T.C., 'Crises of identity among Irish Protestants, 1641–85', *Past and Present*, No. 127, May, 1990.

Baskerville, S., 'Blood guilt in the English Revolution', *The Seventeenth Century*, Vol. VIII, No. 2, autumn, 1993.

Beats, L., 'The East Midland Association, 1642–44', *Midland History*, Vol. 4, 1978.

Bennett, M., 'Between Scylla and Charybdis: the creation of rival administrations at the beginning of the English civil war', *The Local Historian*, Vol. 22, No. 4, November, 1992.

——, 'Contribution and assessment: financial exactions in the English civil war, 1642–46', *War and Society*, Vol. 5, No. 1, 1986.

——, 'The king's gambit: Charles I and Nottingham in the summer of 1642', *Transactions of the Thoroton Society of Nottinghamshire*, Vol. XCVI, 1992.

——, 'Leicestershire's Royalist officers and their war-effort in the county, 1642–46', *Transactions of the Leicestershire Archaeological and Historical Society*, Vol. LIX, 1984–5.

Bernard, G.W., 'The Church of England, c1529–c1642', *History*, Vol. 75, No. 224, June, 1990.

Braddick, M.J., 'Popular politics and public policy: the excise riot at Smithfield in February 1647 and its aftermath', *Historical Journal*, Vol. 34, No. 3, 1991.

Bradley, I., 'Gerrard Winstanley, England's pioneer Green', *History Today*, Vol. 39, August, 1989.

Bremer, F.J., 'To live exemplary lives: Puritans and Puritan communities as lofty lights', *The Seventeenth Century*, Vol. VII, No. 1, Spring, 1992.

Canny, N., 'Protestants, planters and apartheid', *Irish Historical Studies*, Vol. XXV, No. 98, November, 1986.

——, 'The ideology of English colonisation from Ireland to America', *William and Mary Quarterly*, Vol. 30, 1973.

Cotton, A.B., 'Cromwell and the self-denying ordinance', *History*, Vol. LXII, 1977.

Davis, J.C., 'Fear, myth and furore: reappraising the Ranters', *Past and Present*, No. 129, November, 1990.

Dodd, A.H., 'Anglesey in the civil war', *Transactions of the Anglesey Antiquarian Society*, 1952.

——, 'Civil war in East Denbighshire', *Transactions of the Denbighshire Historical Society*, Vol. 3, 1954.

——, 'Wales and the second bishops' war', *Bulletin of the Board of Celtic Studies*, Vol. XII, 1948.

Dore, R.N., 'Sir Thomas Myddleton's attempted conquest of Powys, 1644–5', *Montgomeryshire Collections*, Vol. 57, 1961.

—— and Lowe, J., 'The battle of Nantwich, 25 January 1644', *Transactions of the Lancashire and Cheshire Historical Society*, 1961.

Durston, C., 'Signs and wonders and the English civil war', *History Today*, Vol. 37, October, 1987.

Eames, A., 'Seapower and Caernarvonshire 1642–60', *Transactions of Caernarfonshire Historical Society*, Vol. 16, 1955.

Ensberg, J., 'Royalist finances during the English civil war', *Scandinavian Economic History Review*, Vol. 14, Pt 2, 1966.

Fleming, D., 'Faction and civil war in Leicestershire', *Transactions of the Leicestershire Archaeological and Historical Society*, Vol. LVII, 1981–2.

Gillespie, R., 'Mayo and the rising of 1641', *Cathair Na Mart*, Vol. 5, 1985.

Gladwish, P., 'The Herefordshire clubmen: a reassessment', *Midland History*, Vol. X, 1985.

Gratton, M., 'The military career of Richard, Lord Molyneux, *c*.1623–54', *Transactions of the Lancashire and Cheshire Historical Society*, Vol. 134, 1984.

Gruenfelder, J.K., 'The electoral influence of the Earls of Huntingdon, 1603–1640', *Transactions of the Leicestershire Archaeological and Historical Society*, Vol. L, 1974–5.

Hazlett, H., 'The financing of the British armies in Ireland: 1641–9', *Irish Historical Studies*, Vol. 1, 1938.

Hughes, A., 'Warwickshire on the eve of civil war: a county community?' *Midland History*, Vol. VII, 1982.

——, 'The king, the Parliament and the localities during the English civil war', *Journal of British Studies*, Vol. 24, April, 1985.

Hutton, R.E., 'The failure of the Lancashire Cavaliers', *Transactions of the Lancashire and Cheshire Historical Society*, Vol. 129, 1980.

——, 'The structure of the Royalist party', *Historical Journal*, Vol. 23, No. 3, 1981.

——, 'The Worcestershire clubmen in the English civil war', *Midland History*, Vol. V, 1979–80.

Jones, J.G., 'Aspects of local government in pre-Restoration Caernarfonshire', *Transactions of the Caernarfonshire Historical Society*, Vol. 33, 1972.

——, 'Caernarfonshire administration: activities of the justices of the peace', *Welsh Historical Review*, Vol. V, 1970.

Kaplan, L., 'Steps to war: Scots and Parliament, 1642–3', *Journal of British Studies*, Vol. IX, 1970.

Kent, J., '"Folk justice" and royal justice in Early Modern seventeenth century England: a charivari in the Midlands', *Midland History*, Vol. VIII, 1983.

Laurence, A., 'Women's work and the English civil war', *History Today*, Vol. 42, 1992.

McArthur, E.A., 'Women petitioners and the Long Parliament', *English Historical Review*, Vol. XXIV, 1909.

MacEiteagain, D., 'Unmasking Eoghan Ruadh O'Neill', *History Ireland*, Vol. 2, No. 3, 1994.

Mack, P., 'Women as prophets during the English civil war', *Feminist Studies*, Vol. 8, No. 1, 1982.

Makey, W.H., 'Elder of Stow Liberton, Canongate and St Cuthbert's in the mid-seventeenth century', *Records of the Scottish Church History Society*, Vol. XVII, 1969.

Malcolm, J.L., 'A king in search of soldiers: Charles I in 1642', *Historical Journal*, Vol. 21, No. 2, 1978.

Manning, B., 'Parliament, "party" and "community" in the English civil war', *Historical Studies*, Vol. 14, 1983.

Newman, P.R., 'Catholic Royalists of northern England', *Northern History*, Vol. XV, 1979.

——, 'Catholic Royalist activists in the north, 1642–6', *Recusant History*, Vol. 14, Pt 1, 1977.

——, 'The defeat of John Belasyse: civil war in Yorkshire, January–April 1644', *Yorkshire Archaeological Journal*, Vol. CII, 1980.

——, 'The Royalist officer corps as a reflection of the social structure', *Historical Journal*, Vol. 26, Pt 4, 1983.

O'Riordan, C., 'Thomas Ellison, the Hixon estate and the civil war', *Durham County Local History Society Bulletin*, No. 39, December, 1987.

Ohlmeyer, J., 'The Marquis of Antrim: a Stuart turn-kilt?', *History Today*, Vol. 43, 1993.

Osbourne, S., 'The war, the people, and the absence of clubmen in the Midlands, 1642–46', *Midland History*, Vol. XIX, 1994.

Porter, S., 'The fire-raid in the English civil war', *War and Society*, Vol. 2, No. 2, September, 1984.

Raymond, S.A., 'Glamorgan Arraymen, 1642–5', *Morgannwg*, Vol. 24, 1980.

Rees, F., 'Breconshire during the civil war', *Brycheiniog*, Vol. 8, 1962.

Roberts, A., 'The depredations of the civil war in south west Leicestershire', *The Leicestershire Historian*, Vol. 3, No. 4, 1985–6.

Roy, I., 'England turned Germany? The aftermath of the civil war in its European context', *Transactions of the Royal Historical Society*, 5th Series, Vol. 28, 1978.

Russell, C., 'The British background to the Irish rebellion of 1641', *Historical Research*, Vol. 61, No. 145, 1988.

——, 'The Scottish party in English Parliaments, 1640–2, OR the myth of the English Revolution', *Historical Research*, Vol. 66, No. 159, 1993.

——, 'Why did Charles I fight the civil war?', *History Today*, Vol. 34, 1984.

Seaby, W.A., 'Coin hoards of the rebellion period (1641–9) from Ulster', *British Numismatic Journal*, Vol. 29, 1959.

Seddon, P., 'The Nottinghamshire elections for the Short Parliament of

1640', *Transactions of the Thoroton Society of Nottinghamshire*, Vol. LXXXIV, 1976.

Stephenson, R.B.K. and Porteous, J., 'Two Scottish seventeenth century coin hoards', *British Numismatical Journal*, Vol. 42, 1972.

Stevenson, D., 'The financing of the cause of the Covenanters, 1638–51', *Scottish Historical Review*, Vol. 51, No. 152, October, 1972.

Tucker, N., 'Rupert's letters to Anglesey and other civil war correspondence', *Transactions of the Anglesey Antiquarian Society*, 1958.

Wanklyn, M., 'Royalist strategy in the south of England, 1642–44', *Southern History*, 1982.

—— and Young, P., 'A king in search of soldiers: Charles I in 1642, a rejoinder', *Historical Journal*, Vol. 24, No. 1, 1981.

Williams, P., 'The attack on the Council of the Marches, 1603–1642', *Transactions of the Cymmrddorion Society*, 1961.

UNPUBLISHED THESES

Bennett, M., 'The Royalist war effort in the north Midlands, 1642–6', Ph.D., Loughborough University, 1986.

Hazlett, H., 'A history of the military forces operating in Ireland, 1641–49', 2 vols, Ph.D., University of Belfast, 1938.

Lynch, G.J., 'The risings of the clubmen in the English civil war', M.A., Manchester University, 1973.

Newman, P.R., 'The Royalist army in northern England, 1642–46', 2 vols, D.Phil., York University, 1978.

Roy, I., 'The Royalist army in the first civil war', D.Phil., Oxford, 1963.

Wheeler, J., 'English army finance and logistics, 1642–60', Ph.D., University of California, 1980.

Wanklyn, M., 'The king's army in the west, 1642–46', M.A., Manchester University, 1966.

Young, J., 'The Scottish Parliament 1639–61: a political and constitutional analysis', 3 vols, Glasgow University, 1993.

Index

Note: page numbers in *italic* refer to an illustration.

'This is an excellent introduction to the period that will be stimulating to scholars as well as accessible to students. It integrates original primary research into a persuasive and up-to-date synthesis. It is also the first overview of its kind to take full account of the "archipelagic" dimension of the Civil Wars.'

Dr David L. Smith, Selwyn College, Cambridge

'For those interested in understanding the "war of the four nations," which engulfed and eventually devastated mid-seventeenth century Britain, this is the place to start.'

Professor Thomas E. Cogswell, University of Kentucky

For the Evisons, Bennetts, Thurlows, Picks, Tylers and the Garstins:

> for the growing good of the world is partly dependent upon unhistoric acts; and that things are not so ill with you and me as they might have been, is half owing to the number who live faithfully a hidden life, and rest in unvisited tombs.
>
> George Eliot, *Middlemarch*